J.J.P. Oud and the International Style

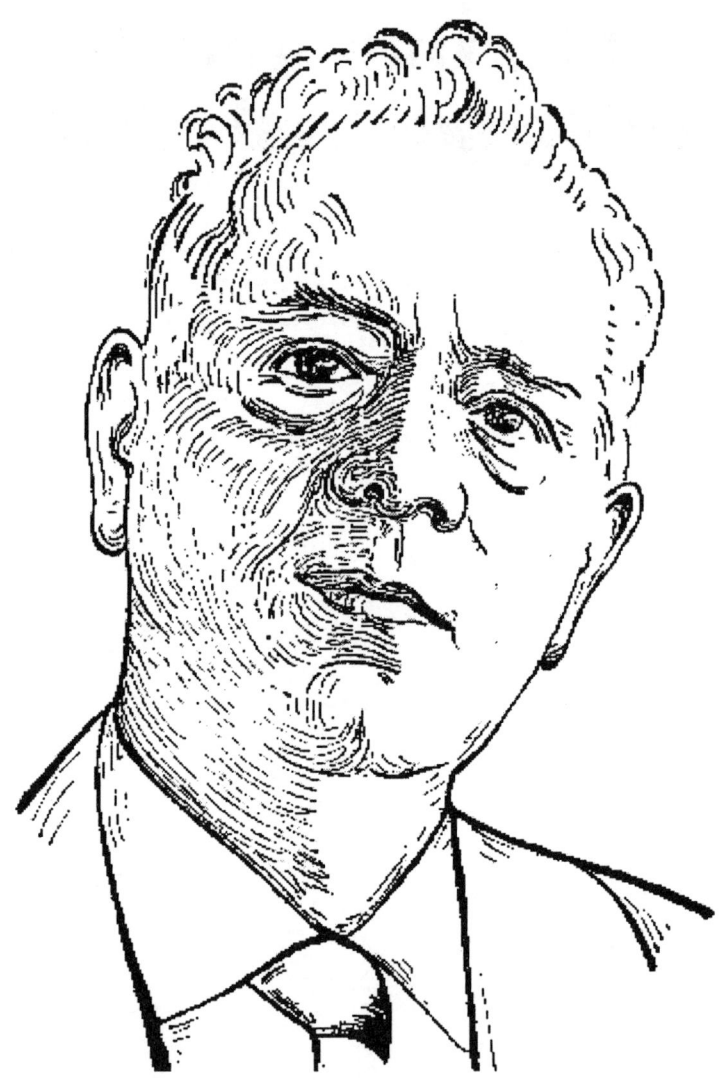

Jacobus Johannes Pieter Oud (1890–1963). Based on a sketch by Leo Petro, entitled "One of the Greatest, Architect J.J.P. Oud" and made at Maison Louise, Cave d'Art, Gravenstraat 1a, The Hague. By permission of the *Nederlands Architectuurinstituut*. Archive/collection Oud.

J.J.P. Oud and the International Style

A Bio-Bibliography

Donald Langmead

Bio-Bibliographies in Art and Architecture, Number 5
Russell T. Clement, *Series Adviser*

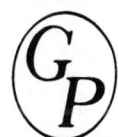

GREENWOOD PRESS
Westport, Connecticut • London

This book is for my granddaughter EBONY FAITH SULTAN.

Library of Congress Cataloging-in-Publication Data
Langmead, Donald.
  J.J.P. Oud and the international style : a bio-bibliography / Donald Langmead.
    p. cm.—(Bio-bibliographies in art and architecture, ISSN 1055–6826 ; no. 5)
  Includes bibliographical references and index.
  ISBN 0–313–30100–X (alk. paper)
  1. Oud, J.J.P. (Jacobus Johannes Pieter), 1890–1963—Bibliography. 2. International style (Architecture)—Bibliography. 3. Oud, J.J.P. (Jacobus Johannes Pieter), 1890–1963—Library.
  I. Title. II. Series.
  Z8648.43L36   1999
  [NA1153.O8]
  720.92—dc21   98–41648

British Library Cataloguing in Publication Data is available.

Copyright © 1999 by Donald Langmead

All rights reserved. No portion of this book may be reproduced, by any process or technique, without the express written consent of the publisher.

Library of Congress Catalog Card Number: 98–41648
ISBN: 0–313–30100–X
ISSN: 1055–6826

First published in 1999

Greenwood Press, 88 Post Road West, Westport, CT 06881
An imprint of Greenwood Publishing Group, Inc.

Printed in the United States of America

The paper used in this book complies with the
Permanent Paper Standard issued by the National
Information Standards Organization (Z39.48–1984).

10 9 8 7 6 5 4 3 2 1

Contents

Preface	vii
Abbreviations	xi
The Rise and Fall of a Hero	1
Annotated Bibliography	
1910-1919	29
1920-1929	35
1930-1939	57
1940-1949	75
1950-1959	85
1960-1969	109
1970-1979	129
1980-1989	145
1990-1998	175
Guide to Archives	193
List of Works	203
J.J.P. Oud's Library	213
Index of Personal Names	251

Photo essay follows page 28

Preface

My earlier study, *Dutch Modernism: Architectural Resources in the English Language*, stimulated my curiosity about the architect Jacobus Johannes Pieter Oud, who overnight plummeted from virtual apostleship to vile apostasy in the religion of Modern Architecture. It was puzzling that, in the face of his early near-apotheosis, what I had seen of his work in the so-called "International Style", whether in images or in the life (so to speak), was far from prepossessing. Bland, some would say. So what had made him great—"one of the greatest," as one obituary-writer put it?

I read of the adulation in which he had been held on both sides of the Atlantic at the end of the 1920s, yet could recollect no reference to him, one way or the other, by either lecturers or peers from my own student days, late in the 1950s. Admittedly, the pursuit of that apparent anomaly is hardly a reason to compile a bibliography, but the interest it stirred was compelling. A wide and determined literature search established, for me at least, that Oud the Internationalist was the (not altogether unwilling) creation of others. And although competent, he was not a particularly *great* architect. But that is to anticipate the essay.

Structure
The book is in five parts. An essay about the impact of (mostly) foreign critical journalism upon Oud's world fame introduces an annotated bibliography of the international literature, 1911 to date, a guide to the major archival source and an indication of other minor archival collections, a chronological list of works and projects, and a list of the titles in Oud's art and architecture library.

Bibliography
This bibliography does not claim to be exhaustive. However, it is the result of a careful search and it attempts to evaluate most entries in the hope that future researchers will be saved from pursuing unfruitful leads.

The substructure was assembled by reference to major English-language architectural bibliographies such as the *Avery Index*, the *Art Index*, the *RIBA Periodicals Index*, as well as successive editions of the Dutch *Repertorium betreffende Nederlandsche Monumenten van Geschiedenis en Kunst*. Of great value was the excellent bibliographical card system in the Architecture Library at Delft *Technische Universiteit*, which I understand was one of Giovanni Fanelli's sources for the list of publications in *Moderne Architectuur in Nederland 1900-1940*. That library has recently developed ABSIS, a complex and extremely useful electronic bibliographical database covering recent volumes of all the journals in its large multilingual collection. Unfortunately, ABSIS is not yet on line, but is accessible from the library of the *Nederlands Architectuurinstituut* (NAi) and at Delft.

Other published bibliographies were consulted. Early among them was W. Jos. de Gruyter, et al., *J.J.P. Oud, Architect*, the well-illustrated catalog of an exhibition at the Boijmans-van Beuningen Museum, Rotterdam, February-March 1951, whose excellently detailed bibliography seems to be the basis for some later ones, including Henk Engel et al., *Architectuur van J.J.P. Oud*, Rotterdam, 1981 and Umberto Barbieri, *J.J.P. Oud*, Rotterdam, 1987. That in Hans Oud, *J.J.P. Oud Architekt 1890-1963: feiten en herinnerigen gerangschikt*, Den Haag, 1984 was of particular use. The only English language attempt is Sara Richardson, *J.J.P. Oud: A Bibliography*, Monticello, [1989] in which a short, derivative essay prefaces a partial (and partially accurate) bibliography.

Most of the newspaper references were discovered by searching the Oud archive at the NAi. Many items are pasted in thematic albums; because they are mostly clippings—some of Oud's own, some from clipping services—page numbers are often omitted. Others are loose, or carelessly stuffed into envelopes and manila folders. As this book goes to press, the Oud archive is being reorganized by Martien de Vletter.

Entries in the bibliography are chronologically arranged, first by decades. Within those, each year is divided into two sections: books and monographs, and journals. Each section is set out alphabetically by the surname of the author; anonymous items are located at the end of the section, arranged alphabetically by title of book or journal. There is a continuous numbering sequence from 001 to the end, cross referenced to the list of works and the index.

The format of each entry is normally as follows: author (if known); title of book or article; bibliographical information; language and translation of title; annotation, outlining textual content and approach, nature and sometimes quality of illustrations. Because bibliographical information between sources is inconsistent and to avoid clutter, I have adopted the rule that the amount of information for each entry should be the minimum required to locate the item.

The amount of material, when one considers the carefully nurtured press coverage that Oud received, mostly within Holland, is daunting. Space would not permit one to enter each item separately. Therefore some more or less arbitrary choices have been made when selecting one item from among many on a particular theme. National newspapers have been given precedence over provincial ones, articles with a by-line over anonymous ones. Reviews of exhibitions have been included with the entry describing the catalog. News items concerning such things as completions, or renovations or demolitions of buildings have been grouped together; when an item is reprinted elsewhere, that has been noted. Translations have not been provided of the titles of minor and secondary items, or those where the meaning is obvious.

Guide to Archives

The archives of J.J.P. Oud (especially his correspondence) are widely dispersed. However, by far the largest amount of material is housed at the NAi, Rotterdam. Other collections, mostly fragmentary assemblings of drawings, blueprints and photographs are held by the Canadian Centre for Architecture, Montreal, Quebec; the library of the Royal Institute of British Architects, London; The Hague *Gemeentemuseum*; the *Letterkundig Museum*, also in The Hague and the *Fondation Custodia, Institut Néerlandais*, Paris. The general organization of the NAi Oud archive is described in the present work.

List of Works

The chronological list has been compiled from three principal sources: Hans Oud, *J.J.P. Oud Architekt 1890-1963*; Barbieri, *J.J.P. Oud*; and Fanelli, *Moderne Architectuur in Nederland*, 1978 (which is not as complete or as detailed as the others and omits many earlier works). Other variations are noted. Built and unbuilt designs are indicated by a change of font.

J.J.P. Oud's Library

Oud was an avid book collector. That is borne out by the variety of the titles recorded by Colenbrander. While about half the nearly 3,000 volumes in his personal library are about art, architecture and design—including around 500 works on architecture—there is a wealth of highly diverse fiction and nonfiction. The partial list in this section, covering only architecture, art and related fields, is by general topic area, alphabetically by authors within languages. Publications are classified in the language in which they were published, not by the nationality of the author.

Acknowledgements

This book would not have been written without the willing help of many people. The University of South Australia provided encouragement and assistance, both in kind and financially through its supported researcher scheme and other mechanisms, funding two visits to The Netherlands to carry out research, and providing the time to analyze the material when back in Adelaide. Thanks to many colleagues at the University: Peter Cox and Sam Noonan, formerly of Audio-visual Services; Christine Kearney, Secretary of the School of Architecture and Design; Glenys Letcher, Built Environment Librarian, and the inter-library loans staff of the University Library.

In 1996 I was awarded a generous exchange fellowship by the *Koninklijke Nederlands Academie voor Wetenschappen*, through the aegis of the Australian Academy for the Humanities, to support the final stages of my investigation in Holland in mid-1997. Drs. Mariet Willinge of the *Nederlands Architectuurinsti-*

tuut in Rotterdam put me into contact with the *Instituut voor Kunst en Architectuur Geschiedenis* of the University of Groningen, who acted as hosts. I am indebted to Professor Ed Taverne, director of that institute, for the welcome, and especially to Dr Cornelis Wagenaar, himself an intrepid Oud scholar, for managing the fund and for advice and support in many ways while I was in Rotterdam. Dr Wagenaar also read the final draft of the essay "The rise and fall of a hero"; his constructive criticism and suggested changes have been most welcome.

I am privileged to have established an excellent working relationship with Mariet Willinge and the *Collectie* staff at the *Nederlands Architectuurinstituut*, Rotterdam. Surnames would be too formal in expressing gratitude to our friends in the Library, Cristel, Fien and Alfred who helped my wife and me with our research during two visits, each of several weeks. They went beyond the call of duty, even when the collection was officially closed to the public. By lessening our load they increased their own and were always cheerful doing it.

Special appreciation is due to Ir. C.G.T. (Chris) Smeenk, Information Specialist of the *Faculteit der Bouwkund Bibliotheek* (Architecture Library), *Delft Technische Universiteit* who over many years has continued to provide much help, constructive criticism and advice, as well as friendship. Thanks, too, for the willing help of the librarians, Mrs Cissy Claassen and Mrs Henny van der Leest.

I had occasion to investigate (on a rather more formal basis) other collections in The Netherlands, from whom we received courteous and efficient attention: the *Rijksbureau voor Kunsthistorische Documentation* (State Office for the Documentation of Art History), and the *Koninklijke Bibliotheek* (National Library), both in The Hague.

Niels and Elisabeth Prak of Rotterdam kindly lent us their pleasant house for several weeks in 1997. Our good friends Gerry and Edmond Schroots of Nieuwerkerk a/d IJssel also lent us their house in 1996 and again in 1997, besides going out of their way to show us (as always) hospitality. A special thanks to Olaf, who surrendered his room for us. Thanks, too, to Cees and Dirrie Ravesteijn, who are likewise hospitable and insist on providing a welcome break from work whenever we are in Holland.

As always, my deepest appreciation goes to my wife who, besides denying herself the pleasure of our grandchildren's company for months at a time, continues to efficiently manage everything else in the life of a preoccupied academic. On, between and after our visits to Holland she searched, photocopied, collated, labeled, translated, indexed—and all with saintly patience. Coby, how can I thank you?

Donald Langmead
Paradise, South Australia
August 1998

Abbreviations

AA	Architectural Association (London)
AIA	American Institute of Architects
ANZ	Australia and New Zealand
L'Architettura	*L'Architettura: Cronache e Storia*
avbd	avondblad (evening edition)
Builder	*The Builder*
BNA	Bond Nederlands Architecten
Bouw	*Bouw. Centraal Weekblad voor het Bouwwezen.*
Bouwbedrijf	*Het Bouwbedrijf*
Casabella	variously *La Casa Bella* (1928-32), *Casabella* (1933-37), *Casabella Costruzioni* (1938-39), *Costruzioni Casabella* (1940-43, 1946) and *Continuata* (1954-64)
CIAM	Congrès Internationaux d'Architecture Moderne
Cimaise	*Cimaise: Art et Architecture Actuels/ Present Day Art and Architecture*
Delft TH	Delft Technische Hogeschool (later Technische Universiteit)
Forum	*Forum. Maandschrift voor Letteren en Kunst*
Graphic	*The Graphic*
Groene Amsterdammer	*De Groene Amsterdammer* aka *Nieuwe Amsterdammer*
Ingenieur	*De Ingenieur*
Journal RAI Canada	*Journal, Royal Architectural Institute of Canada*
KNOB	Koninklijke Nederlandse Oudheidkundige Bond
Lotus	*Lotus International*
Maasbode	*De Maasbode*
MIT	Massachusetts Institute of Technology

Abbreviations xii

NAi	*Nederlands Architectuurinstituut* (Netherlands Architecture Institute)
n.l.	no location (of publications)
n.p.	no pagination (of publications)
NRC Handelsblad	formerly *Nieuwe Rotterdamsche Courant, Nieuwe Rotterdamse Courant*
odbd	ochtendblad (morning edition)
Parool	*Het Parool*
Pencil Points	later *Progressive Architecture* (after 1944)
PTT	Netherlands Post, Telegraph and Telephone service
RIBA	Royal Institute of British Architects
Studio	*The Studio,* later *Studio International*
Telegraaf	*De Telegraaf*
UK	United Kingdom
US, USA	United States of America
Vaderland	*Het Vaderland*
V.A.N.K.	Vereeniging voor Ambachts- en Nijverheidkunst
Vrije Volk	*Het Vrije Volk*
Volkskrant	*De Volkskrant*

J.J.P. Oud and the International Style

The Rise and Fall of a Hero

Around 1930, European and American art critics and historians created a Mount Rushmore of modern architecture. On its face were the towering figures of Le Corbusier, Walter Gropius, Ludwig Mies van der Rohe—and the Dutch architect J.J.P. Oud. Although the names of the first three are still household words (at least in households where architecture is spoken of) Oud remained there for little more than fifteen years. The mechanics of fame are complex and the tool of architectural writing that carved him in that loftiest place of Modernism also—and much more quickly—obliterated his image.

Oud's removal is analogous with processes described in George Orwell's novel *1984*. The anti-hero Winston Smith worked for the Ministry of Truth, revising, even destroying, historical evidence that did not serve the ends of the Party. In real life, after Stalinist agents assassinated Leon Trotsky in Mexico in August 1940, the Soviet "ministry of truth" expunged him from the official history of Bolshevism, even to retouching photographs. It was nothing new: the same kind of thing had been applied in dynastic Egypt. International Modernism was a totalitarian architecture, so we should not be surprised that its protagonists protected their dogmas in similar ways. Oud was removed from their pantheon when he manifested what they regarded as aberrant behavior.

The very volume of the literature by and about him, set out in the following bibliography, should convince the reader that Oud is indeed an important figure in twentieth century architecture. Yet, in an almost desultory career spanning fifty-seven years he undertook only ninety or so projects, less than half of which were realized. Of just five outside The Netherlands, only one was built.

This essay is not a biography. That has been written by someone much closer to Oud.[1] Neither is it an appraisal of his architecture. Rather, it examines the relationship between the place afforded him in the international literature of architecture and his ephemeral fame. But it must sketch his professional career.

2   Oud and the International Style

Jacobus Johannes Pieter Oud was the second of three sons, born on 9 February 1890 to middle-class parents living in Koemarkt, Purmerend, North Holland.[2] With typical Calvinistic practicality, his name was soon shortened to "Ko."[3] After elementary schooling in his home town, at the age of thirteen he was sent to the Quellinus School of Decorative Arts in Amsterdam, about 15 kilometers (10 miles) away. He remained there until some time in 1906, studying drawing and painting.[4] His domineering father, a pragmatic businessman, had objected to the boy becoming a painter.[5] Denied his first choice of career, Ko pursued—albeit not too energetically—an architectural education.[6]

The years 1906 and 1907 were momentous for the youth. In 1906 he produced his first built design, a conventionally planned townhouse in Purmerend for a relative, A. Hertog-Oud. He also met the already famous architect Hendrik Petrus Berlage, through the latter's daughter Corrie, a fellow-student at the Quellinus School. Late in the following year he became supervisor/draftsman in the Amsterdam architectural office of Joseph Th. J. Cuypers and Jan Stuijt, when they were undertaking mostly domestic commissions as well as the town halls of Bloemendaal and Heemstede. Through the Heemstede project, Ko met his future wife (although she was then only twelve years old), J.M.A. (Annie) Dinaux.[7] They would become engaged in 1911 and marry in 1918.

After only six months with Cuypers and Stuijt, largely confined to the office because (as a Protestant) he was unacceptable in on-site dealings with some Roman Catholic clients, Oud left in May 1908. He then enrolled at the *Rijksnormaalschool voor Tekenonderwijs* in Amsterdam, mainly because he was frustrated by gaps in his theoretical knowledge and in 1910 received a diploma in structural and mechanical engineering draftsmanship. The more formal and esthetic aspects of this disjointed education were complemented by attending lectures in various disciplines at Delft *Technische Hogeschool* for most of 1910 and 1911. Like others who have undergone a similar experience, Oud later deprecated the value of formal training, an attitude that quickly evaporated when he was awarded an honorary doctorate from Delft in 1955.[8]

Possibly on Berlage's advice, early in 1912 Ko went to work in the Munich office of Theodor Fischer. Among the projects in the German's practice were low-income housing for Munich's western extensions and development plans for several towns. More significant as a pedagogue than as a practitioner, Fischer was then lecturing at the Munich Polytechnic, and Oud attended his classes.

Lessons learnt in Germany were salutary. After only three months with Fischer, Ko returned home, impressed with the work of Alfred Mesel and Joseph Olbrich and determined to produce an architecture that exploited new construction and materials. He set up a sole practice in Purmerend. A handful of realized commissions included houses, premises for the *Vooruit* Laborers' Association, also in Purmerend, a residence for his brother Gerrit in Aalsmeer and the Schinkel Cinema, Purmerend. This early work hybridized of a number of influences: Stuijt, Berlage, Hermann Muthesius (and through him the English Arts and Crafts) as well as regional characteristics.[9]

Ko Oud's architectural horizons were about to be widened. In 1911 he met

Willem Marinus Dudok, who was then an officer in the Royal Engineers, living beside the Herengracht in Purmerend. Dudok's landlord had told him: "You must take a look at a couple of numbers further up the street. A young chap lives there who spends all his time drawing little houses for his pleasure."[10]

Seeking more prestigious commissions, Oud moved to Leiden in 1913. Little came of the relocation: some public building projects, never built, and a few house designs, only one of which—an English-looking country residence at Blaricum for Mrs van Essen-Vinckers, in 1915—was realized. In Leiden Oud renewed his acquaintance with Dudok, who in February 1913 had been appointed as its Engineer and Deputy Director of the Public Works Department. In December 1914 the two architects collaborated on a housing development, Woonwijk Leiderdorp, completed in 1916. The 24 two-story row cottages for workers were architecturally unremarkable, resembling much of the Hilversum public housing that Dudok designed after 1916. But they in no way signaled the houses that Oud later built in Rotterdam or Stuttgart, and that won him international recognition.

Ko was seeking an architecture based on the needs and possibilities of his own time, satisfying "general economic feasibility, universal social attainability, in general of social-esthetic necessity, and compactness, austere, exact, simple and regular in form."[11] While Leiderdorp was being built he became involved with Theo van Doesburg (born Christiaan Emil Marie Küpper).

Küpper had studied drama at Cateau Esser's School of Dramatic Arts in Amsterdam and tried his hand at writing poetry and prose. After about 1899 he taught himself to paint and draw and in 1902, when he was nineteen, he embarked upon a free-lance artistic and literary career. His earliest paintings—conservative, "muddy, Rembrandtesque"—date from 1904. In 1912 he began publishing art critiques, mostly in a magazine read by Theosophists, Freemasons and other mystical groups. Its title *Eenheid [Unity]*, enshrined an important idea within Küpper's own emerging philosophy. But until he was thirty he occupied "only a marginal position in the Dutch art world."[12] He first encountered the artistic avant-garde during military service in 1915, when he met the poet Anthony Kok and the philosopher Evert Rinsema. Around then, he changed his name to that of his stepfather, Theodorus Doesburg. Back in civilian life in 1916 he met Oud.

In turn, Oud introduced van Doesburg to another young architect, Jan Wils, whom he had met about four years earlier through Berlage, then Wils' employer. The three soon became involved with the architect Bart van der Leck and the expatriate Hungarian painter Vilmos Huszár . In May 1916, with Oud as president and van Doesburg as vice-secretary, the Leiden art club *De Sphinx* was founded.[13]

Very soon the Leiden enclave established, together with the philosopher Anthony Kok, and the painter Piet Mondrian, the avant-garde artists' group known by the exclusivist name, De Stijl (The Style). Over the next ten years others would join: fiery architect Robert van 't Hoff and Belgian sculptor Georges Vantongerloo (both in 1917); furniture designer Gerrit Thomas Rietveld (1918); architect Cor van Eesteren and German industrial designer Werner Graeff (both in 1922); painter Cesar Domela Nieuwenhuis (1924) and German designer Friedrich Vordemberge-Gildewart (1925). Late arrivals balanced early departures.

4   Oud and the International Style

From the start the group was at best loose knit, at worst unraveling through conflicts between van Doesburg and another—any other—member. Its fabric inevitably came apart as members withdrew one by one, unwilling and unable to work with the dogmatic van Doesburg. Van der Leck lasted only until 1918; Wils and van 't Hoff until 1919; Oud and Vantongerloo left in 1921; the perserverant Mondrian in 1925. Others endured longer professional links with van Doesburg. But the group never achieved unity of purpose; there were no meetings and membership seems to have lain solely in contributing to its journal *De Stijl*.

The publication was van Doesburg's most significant contribution to twentieth century art, appearing under his garrisoned editorship from October 1917 until his death in 1931 (his sometime collaborators produced a posthumous memorial issue in 1932). To create an illusion of international cooperation he invented contributors, himself writing under the pseudonyms of the "poet" I. K. Bonset (from 1920) and the "Italian philosopher" Aldo Camini (from 1921).

In terms of architecture, De Stijl, seeking a unity in the arts and between art and society, flirted with Constructivism, developed theories of Neoplasticism and what Oud called Cubism. For all that, its intellectualized theories seldom generated architectural realities that could accurately or honestly be described as De Stijl architecture. The few realized projects were nevertheless spectacular: Gerrit Rietveld's Schröder house, Utrecht, designed with his client Truus Schröder in 1924, clearly expressed ideas developed within De Stijl, has become an icon of European modernism. Van Doesburg's Café Aubette, Strasbourg (1926-27 with Jean and Sophie Arp) carried "painting into architecture, theory into practice." And of course, Oud's director's hut at the Oud-Mathenesse housing development of 1923 and the facade of the Café De Unie, Rotterdam of 1925 both embodied principles of color and composition developed within De Stijl. All these "heroic relics" have been restored or rebuilt at great cost. That in itself is testimony to their importance in the history of modern art.

De Stijl was just one of many small artistic, not to say architectural, groups that blossomed in Holland after the Great War. Others included the expressionistic Amsterdam School, growing out of the long established *Architectura et Amicitia* group and given impetus after 1918 by the publication of *Wendingen*, and the Rotterdam modernist *Opbouw*. Widely divergent ideas and architectural products developed beside mutual disrespect but there was also a binding force.

Perhaps because it offered relief from the multifarious problems born of capitalism, the combined philosophy, mysticism and religion of Theosophy held wide appeal in the industrializing world from the turn of the century. As its ideas permeated Dutch art otherwise irreconcilable groups eagerly embraced it. Many De Stijl members were Calvinist-turned-Theosophist, espousing an holistic worldview "in which the geometric is the essence of the real"—a universal unity, including art and culture, and the socio-political issues of life. That response exposes socialism and internationalism as linking factors at the time of De Stijl's birth. The so-called Delft School provided a a balancing voice after about 1923. Roman Catholic, nationalistic, anti-socialist and artistically conservative, it has (somewhat inaccurately) been painted the villain in many Modernist histories, especially after 1950. Yet its "leader", Professor Jan Marinus Granpré Molière, was one of the key figures in the modernization of Dutch architecture and a significant contributor to the rise of modern urbanism.

Through De Stijl, the Dutch provided much theoretical and some practical input to the Modern Movement. Not least, as already hinted, the group formed an early major conduit for Frank Lloyd Wright's "penetration of Europe" by introducing and commenting upon his work to a wide audience. And, as correctly observed by Alfred Barr of the New York Museum of Modern Art, De Stijl also dominated German architecture and art in the mid-1920s.[14]

Oud contributed to the group in several ways: he embraced the notion of collaboration between the artist and the architect; he wrote for *De Stijl*; and importantly, he provided for Dutch architects valuable insights into the pervasive ideas of Wright, then incipient in The Netherlands.

In July 1916 he began collaborating with van Doesburg.[15] For what ended up, through no fault of Oud's, as a conservative house for W. De Geus, mayor of Broek in Waterland, van Doesburg designed a leadlight panel for the rear door, bearing the municipal coat-of-arms—hardly an artistic breakthrough.[16]

There followed in 1917 the conversion of a beachfront house at Katwijk aan Zee to villa *Allegonda*, in collaboration with van Doesburg and the painter Menso Kamerlingh Onnes. Oud transformed the neoclassical villa *Sigrid* into an asymmetrical play of cubistic masses approached through half-enclosed colonnaded porches and an open terrace. The attempts to establish "flow" between interior and exterior, and the pragmatic detail of built-in closets perhaps reflect Ko's emerging interest in Wright. Although wanting more control of the scheme, van Doesburg produced only a leadlight window in the stairwell; Menso's son, Harm Hendrick, designed other decorative details.

Later in the year Oud, van Doesburg and Harm Kamerlingh Onnes collaborated on *De Vonk*, a vacation house for young working class girls at the coastal resort of Noordwijkerhout. Here Oud produced a highly conservative two-story building with symmetrical gabled wings joined by a central service/circulation core, all in dark red brick, crowned with terracotta tiled roofs. Its sober external appearance was relieved (but not much) by van Doesburg's ceramic tile spandrel panels above and beside the main entrance—part of the Dutch domestic tradition—and floor tiling in a system of yellow for the circulation spaces on both floors.[17] Kamerlingh Onnes designed the stairwell window.

Ko's professional relationship with van Doesburg was becoming strained because of the painter's wish to dominate. Oud was not alone in that. Almost contemporary with *De Vonk* was the De Lange town house at Alkmaar by Jan Wils. Van Doesburg designed leadlight windows and carved balusters to the main stair. Externally, Wils limited a proposed color scheme to the joinery frames, despite van Doesburg's wish to "contradict" architectonic forms with large brightly-colored geometric patterns. Oud rejected a similar request to "destroy" the architectural spaces inside *De Vonk*.[18]

But they collaborated just once more in 1919, when Oud was Rotterdam's chief housing architect, on the Spangen housing developments. Van Doesburg again provided—and not without dissension—the color schemes.[19] Only the first was realized and arguments over the second provided a wedge to split the realtionship between two highly complex, artistic personalities. It is stressed that, important as these attempts to integrate art and architecture may have been, the painter's part had little to do with space.

To write for *De Stijl* was to belong to De Stijl. Oud produced a total of seven pieces for the journal: three each in 1918 and 1919 and one in 1920. His first essay, "The monumental in townscape," dated Leiden, 9 July 1917 was a staccato polemical essay in the journal's inaugural edition, pleading for integration of the arts, universal esthetic agreement, and (prophetically) the standardization of mass housing.[20] "Art and machine," of six months later, demonstrates that he was awakening to the inevitability and potential of a machine-based culture and a machine esthetic,[21] a process confirmed by subsequent pieces.

The ideas were developed in his "Architectural exposition of Frank Lloyd Wright's Robie house" in the following issue—a very important critique that exposes Oud's understanding of the pragmatic and formal sources of Wright's domestic architecture, perhaps before anyone else in Europe.[22] Berlage had introduced Ko to the works of Wright around 1912 at the latest, as he attested:

> As a young architect I saw [Wright's] work for the first time one evening at Berlage's house, when he—after his American tour—showed us small pictures of it. I was delighted: it was a revelation to me, and Berlage, usually reserved, spoke with greatest awe about the extraordinary means of light penetration and development of space, and so on.[23]

Oud's other important De Stijl piece was "Architecture and standardization of mass building," written in February-March 1918.[24] He was then about to confront Rotterdam's enormous social housing problem. A year later he followed with an "architectural exposition" whose first section, "Mass building and street architecture," revisited the issues, using his 1918 design for workers' flats as an example. "Reinforced concrete and architecture" lauded the material's potential, but Holland had not then developed the necessary technology to exploit it.[25]

Oud's other shorter pieces in *De Stijl*—a polemic entitled "Orientation",[26] a book review;[27] and a rather belated eulogy of the Futurists—[28] while *hinting* at the way in which his own philosophy was developing, are nevertheless not such strong indicators as the articles outlined above.

Architectural journalism was not new to Oud. His first polemical efforts appeared in parochial newspapers or student magazines. At that early stage, even when writing about others, he found room for self-promotion. But by 1912 he was contributing minor pieces to a few national architectural and building industry journals. A year later his domestic architecture was first published outside The Netherlands. After 1914 he became a regular contributor to *Bouwkundig Weekblad,* providing descriptions of his own work, reviews and (most importantly) essays defending modernism and the new developments in painting and the imminent confluence of the arts. Oud's son Hans wrote that his father was a "complicated human being whose real motives were often hidden behind feigned motives."[29] It is suggested that even in his early writings, when his ideas were perhaps half formed, he trimmed his philosophical sails to suit the wind; the more pragmatic issues of architecture—construction, system building, economy, detailing—were probably a different matter.

During his association with De Stijl, Oud did not limit his literary work to its journal, or his intellectual efforts to its boundaries. Indeed, his most important writings of 1920, extending his theme of standardized housing and mass construction, appeared in *Bouwkundig Weekblad*.[30] In February 1921 he declared his views in "On future architecture and its architectonic possibilities," a seminal lecture to *Opbouw*, a group of progressive Rotterdam architects committed to safeguarding the profession. Voicing frustration at the persistence of historical formalism, and clearly enthralled by progress and the potential of the machine, Oud expected imminent changes. He condemned ornament as the "universal panacea for architectural impotence"—words which would return to haunt him—and predicted an imminent architecture whose "constructive functionalism attains to beauty." The publication of the lecture throughout much of Europe before 1928 did much to establish Oud's reputation among modernist architects, who were also entertaining the notion of a new objectivity.

Anyway, the fact that Oud had given the *Opbouw* lecture and "independently" expressed his views enraged van Doesburg and Mondrian. While the former's anger was over what he construed as "an act of disloyalty", Mondrian was annoyed because Oud, although speaking of Cubism and Futurism, had omitted Neoplasticism. While ignored in the script of the lecture, Mondrian's and van Doesburg's work had in fact been illustrated by lanternslides. The text was published a few months later in *Bouwkundig Weekblad*, to be almost immediately reprinted in Germany and Czechoslovakia, and very soon in Belgium.[31] Oud did not write for *De Stijl* after 1920. Much later, he documented his brief experiences within the group, not (one suspects) without bias.[32]

Oud's interchanges with two other architects, Robert van 't Hoff and Jan Wils, while they were all associated with De Stijl are important to his own perceptions of the work of Wright. Van 't Hoff practiced architecture very briefly. An idealistic, disciplined and businesslike young man who espoused socially responsible building, he was the only Dutch architect to have *personal* contact with Wright before 1931. His houses at Huis ter Heide near Utrecht, both designed in 1914, were Europe's first built copies of Wright's work. The concrete Villa Henny cloned the American's cubic esthetic and the Verloop house mimicked the prairie houses. More significantly, when van 't Hoff returned from visiting Wright in 1914 he carried illustrated documents about the Chicagoan's architecture. They would have interested his colleagues; the Midway Gardens and early designs of the American System-built projects, unpublished in Europe, complemented material earlier encountered in publications and lectures.

Van 't Hoff met van Doesburg around 1916. There is little doubt that the Villa Henny attracted the painter. In eighteen months with De Stijl, van 't Hoff built only a houseboat. In 1918 he joined the Communist Party and briefly turned to designing mass housing as an expression of his political convictions. None was built. He quit De Stijl in October 1919 because van Doesburg would not fully support the communist cause. Although he said and wrote little about it, van 't Hoff was a valuable resource in bringing Wright's post-1910 work to the attention of Europe. Another De Stijl architect, Jan Wils, took up the task of propaganda.

Architectural historian Ezio Godoli describes Wils' secondary role in Dutch modernism (he was first "a professional of quality") as "shelling out formal instances from Wright to . . . the neoplastic architecture program."[33] But Wils was never parsimonious; nor was his sharing limited to the confines of Neoplasticism. In 1912 Berlage had advised European architects to look at Wright's work; Wils showed his Dutch peers exactly what they would find. His exegesis was not really effective beyond The Netherlands but his influence *within* Holland was unparalleled, through journals beyond De Stijl's narrow audience: *Levende Kunst, Elseviers Geïllustreerd Maandschrift,* and *Wendingen.*[34]

Wils contributed twice to *De Stijl* withdrawing in 1919 because van Doesburg was "playing the little dictator."[35] His pieces about Wright were neither concise nor incisive[36] but his substantial "De nieuwe bouwkunst. Bij het werk van Frank Lloyd Wright," for the art magazine *Levende Kunst* anticipated De Stijl's *Manifesto V* and van Doesburg's "Towards a Plastic Architecture" of 1924.[37]

Wils found in Wright's writings the rejection of any historical esthetic for a new form simplified by function, mass, space, and material. Wright's emphasis upon economy of means and his idea about identifying space by extended planes would also be repeated in De Stijl's catechism, as would the notion about integrated decoration and form, and the spatial achievement of what van Doesburg termed "monumentality." De Stijl's criteria for plastic architecture did not come *only* from Wright, or *only* through Wils. But Wils expounded his insights just as the group's philosophy was forming and Van Doesburg and Oud later transmitted them to much of Europe.

Even if one speculates such details as the built-in closets in all Oud's private houses after about 1912, little of his work before about 1918 showed an obvious affinity for Wright.[38] Some writers therefore suggest that he learnt of the American only after meeting Wils and van 't Hoff.[39] It has been demonstrated that that was not so. Yet there can be no question that Oud's association with Wils since about 1912 and especially van 't Hoff after 1917 greatly enhanced his understanding of Wright's work. Most of the information he received was in the form of images. Although van 't Hoff doubtless possessed articles by and about Wright amongst his "foreign publications" he seems not to have made them public.[40]

Within De Stijl the confluence of ideas about architectural space was not between any of the architects and van Doesburg but between the architects themselves. Berlage had stressed Wright's consummate control of space. That was emphasized in Wils' analysis and perhaps he, van 't Hoff and Oud discussed it. Wils examined the evidence more carefully than van 't Hoff; Oud's response was a little slower to come and more pragmatic when it did: he was interested in Wright's technique and technology and less in philosophy and esthetic response.

In 1918 Oud designed "a double workers' house in reinforced concrete." Echoing van 't Hoff, he claimed that the material would liberate architecture from limits imposed by brick construction, but did not explain how. He added that concrete would "achieve a purer planar definition of the building, more monumentality [i.e., De Stijl plasticity] and better synthesis," whatever that meant. He also explained the thermal advantages of cavity walls.[41] The thickset building could have been a parody of an illustration from Wasmuth's *Ausgeführte Bauten und Entwürfe von Frank Lloyd Wright,* of 1910. Yet Oud had been careful with the geometry of the plans and elevations, and his effort won van Doesburg's praise.

The houses were not built, even as prototypes. Oud, possibly encouraged by the publication of the Villa Henny,[42] continued to experiment with the design of concrete dwellings, a matter he may have discussed with van 't Hoff. The Dutch building industry developed a commercially workable concrete technology after 1920. Oud was apparently anxious to achieve the smooth walls that concrete could give—evidenced by much of his subsequent domestic design—but he had to be content with appearance. The workers' houses in Hoek van Holland, sometimes touted as concrete construction, were stuccoed brick like Erich Mendelsohn's Einstein Tower at Potsdam, probably for the same practical reasons. In every apparent way Oud's houses throughout the 1920s were dissociated from De Stijl and from Wright.

However, he produced two designs, never built, that *were* visually related to Wright's architecture. Oud's father was the client. The distillery warehouse of 1915-16 and still house and offices of 1919 (both at Purmerend) have been described and analyzed *ad infinitum.* Each was replete with Wrightian elements, although they are more readily observable in the warehouse, redolent also of the office wing of the Deutz Motor Company's model factory at the 1914 Cologne *Deutscher Werkbund* exhibition, designed by Gropius and Adolf Meyer. Oud may have been interested in the *Werkbund* through Theodor Fischer, who had been a founding member in 1907. The buildings for the Cologne exhibition were published soon after completion.[43] And Oud admitted that he was familiar with them.[44] Wright was the obvious source of Gropius' building and Oud's warehouse.

In plan at least, the Purmerend designs were determined by the geometry of the square, in common with the earlier works of Wils and van 't Hoff and all of Wright's designs before 1910. That may have been coincidental since neither Wright nor the Hollanders held the franchise on that geometry. It had persisted in Dutch architectural theory since the Renaissance.[45] Mathematically formal systems had enjoyed widespread acceptance in The Netherlands through the beginning of the twentieth century, promulgated in the theoretical writings of such *Architectura* architects as H.J.M. Walenkamp and J.L.M. Lauweriks.[46]

Oud demonstrated a special interest in Wright's plans. In a critique of the Robie house published in *De Stijl* in 1918,[47] he wrote of functional planning, plan-generated plastic form, integrated details, and the exploitation of modern materials and technology (about which he was partly mistaken) to capture the spirit of the age. Ironically, he condemned "picturesque" houses designed solely for esthetic reasons while criticizing the building on just those grounds.

Significantly, he found Wright's plans to be a "source of esthetic pleasure for the practiced critic", that their "composition [was] evident and clearly, neatly arranged" while the "proportions and compartition of the spaces in themselves and in relation to each other" were "finely tuned." Oud spoke of the *functionality* of the plans as a separate issue, while his praise of the composition was explicitly stated to be on esthetic grounds. Such comment is meaningless without reference to a paradigm, some accepted formal system. The language Oud used suggests that, perhaps helped by his colleagues, he had identified the geometry applied to the Robie house. They were trained by architects who used such formal systems to design in the belief that good composition conformed to a universal, harmonious canon. When studying any architect's work, it would have been natural to first try to discover the foundation of a "finely tuned" approach to proportion and division of space.

Oud did not meet Wright until 1951 and then almost by accident. But he understood Wright's architecture and that might have been why H.Th.Wijdeveld asked him to write for the now-famous *Wrightnummers* of *Wendingen* in 1925. Frequently republished and translated, "The influence of Frank Lloyd Wright on the architecture of Europe" was widely read in Europe and elsewhere over the next decade.[48] Oud believed that Wright towered "above the surrounding world" and that his work was "flawless." Yet, echoing Berlage's warning of four years earlier,[49] he commented that because of the "pernicious" effects of mimicry, Wright's influence in Europe was not "happy . . . in all respects." And he warned against ascribing the emergence of the plasticity of modern architecture to Wright alone, "for at the time when the adoration of Wright's work by his colleagues on this side of the Atlantic had reached its culminating point, European architecture itself was in a state of ferment, and cubism was born."

Oud's "cubism" was not equatable with the French artistic movement of around 1910. He used the word to describe De Stijl's neoplastic philosophy that he said was critical in the development of modern architecture. While recognizing that Wright wanted an architecture

> based on the needs and possibilities of our own time, satisfying its requirements of general economic feasibility, universal social attainableness, in general of social-esthetic necessity, and resulting in compactness, austerity, and exactness of form, in simplicity and regularity

Oud charged that the American had "continually escaped" from that architecture "on the wings of his great visionary faculty", leaving it to be tried in more actual consistency in neoplasticism. Nothing in Oud's 1925 essay showed how Wright's ideas were forced through De Stijl's ideological filters, or that Oud himself applied them to society.

In 1926 he boasted to Gustav Platz that he knew "something about this 'cubistic dynamic', because the first attempts" were his own! "If you were to look for earlier examples," he said, "you would find none. Architectural cubism goes back to Mondrian, not Wright: I brought the ideas of Mondrian into architecture."[50]

Oud's friend W. Jos. de Gruyter wrote in 1931 that Wright's impact upon the Dutch architect was fleeting and "judged by the results . . . of little value" to him.

The contrast between the two architects was marked:

> The cubistic weight of Wright's characteristic design, elevated by an almost spontaneous, impressive gesture, in his own work becomes magnificent massing, with no thought of deliberately picturesque games played with horizontals and verticals. Oud is not a bit guilty of picturesqueness, but he conformed to the other side of this cubistic heaviness, designing with an obvious, almost ascetic methodology; the rather sluggish, heavy results feel lifeless.[51]

The point was illustrated with two of Oud's unrealized designs earlier published in *De Stijl*: standard workers' dwellings[52] and the semidetached concrete houses already discussed. Their "unconstrained design" was unimaginable without Wright's input. De Gruyter believed that Wright had already affected the "so-called" neoplastic painting of Mondrian and others; thus, whatever they had taught Oud was also of Wright, only secondhand!

The Dutch architectural historian Niels Prak remarks that students of architecture believe that "the road to fame for the 'great makers' [of architecture]" follows this direction:

> Their talent is recognized by the architectural community, they receive favorable reviews, win prizes and finally are granted honorary doctorates. This is true, but not the whole story. Many famous architects have put in as much work on building a reputation as has, say, a football star.
>
> It does not mean that the fame is undeserved. Solid achievement is required for critical acclaim in the highly competitive world of international architecture. Every practicing architect knows that only a few are going to "make it" because . . . from a crowd of contenders there is but little room at the top. On stage the fairy tale of the slowly recognized talent and the gradual winning over of the world architectural community is carefully maintained, but behind the scenes much intrigue and manipulation goes on.[53]

Oud may have promoted Wright in Europe, and in significant ways. But it seems that he was rather more intent on promoting himself. Anyway, late in 1922 Wright, away across the Atlantic, claimed that he knew of only two Dutch architects: Berlage and Oud.[54]

Van Doesburg and Oud, largely through their own energy and self-publicity became significant figures in Europe during the 1920s, through publications and lectures. Their influence was reciprocated by the visits to Holland of such foreigners as Ludwig Mies van der Rohe, Mendelsohn and El Lissitzky. But the exposition of Wright's work in *De Stijl*, all in Dutch, had little impact outside Holland. The Dutch have been obliged by geography, polity and economics to be multilingual. Their larger neighbors have not. While the journal eventually gained an international voice (or the illusion of one through van Doesburg's legerdemain) it first had a limited audience. That is not to say that others outside Holland were unaware of it, as literary reviews in any number of journals demonstrate. And if foreign architects could not read the words, they could at least look at the plethora of images, for what they were worth. So *De Stijl* was the source of drawings of Oud's unrealized designs and the ones that eventually caught the imagination of his international contemporaries were the *strandboulevard* houses he proposed for Scheveningen in 1917 and the standardized workers' row houses of 1918.[55]

Apart from an article reprinted in Germany about the house for his brother Gerrit, Oud's designs were not seen outside The Netherlands until 1921.[56] Then Adolf Behne wrote a general article in Bruno Taut's short-lived journal *Frühlicht*,[57] which illustrated both the projects at Purmerend. In the next ten years there were nearly 140 publications of Oud's work in the international architectural press: in Europe, Austria, Belgium, Czechoslovakia, England, Finland, France, Germany (which accounted for half the number), Hungary, Italy, Poland, Spain and Switzerland; and in the United States of America after 1926. The number of publications peaked around 1927-28.

If one is seeking Oud's first conscious effort to establish his reputation in Europe, it could well have been through soliciting the wide publication of "Over de toekomstige bouwkunst en hare architectonische mogelijkheden," after 1922.[58] Since 1918 he had been chief housing architect for Rotterdam and his public housing projects for the growing city, of primary interest to many European countries reconstructing after World War I, was beginning to attract international attention. The realized projects of the period included Blocks I and V (1918) and Blocks VIII and IX (1919-20), Spangen; Tusschendijken (1920-23)[59] and emergency housing, Oud-Mathenesse (the *Witte Dorp*), (1922-23).

During the war, Germany had been shut off from architectural developments in neutral Holland, so Oud's visits across the border after 1918 were important in re-establishing contacts or making new ones, with such key architectural figures as Behne, Gropius, Bruno Taut, Walter Curt Behrendt, Ludwig Hilberseimer and the painter Laszlo Moholy-Nagy. It was through the latter that Ko was invited in 1921 to participate with Gropius, Adolf Meyer, Hilberseimer and others, in a closed competition to design a house in the exclusive Grünewald district of Berlin for the industrialist Dr H. Kallenbach. Oud won. Perhaps because of differences with the potential contractor and certainly because of imminent meteoric inflation in Germany the project was abandoned. This success nevertheless established Oud in the western European arena as an architect of quality.[60]

Through the early 1920s Oud extended his visits to other parts of Europe. His work was exhibited at the Weimar Bauhaus Art and Technics exhibition in 1923 and he lectured there in August.[61] Indeed, he was becoming quite the international speaker, addressing gatherings of architects in Berlin, Magdeburg and, of course, Weimar in 1923, and to the Zurich Association of Architects and Engineers in February 1924, and the Stavba Architectural Association, Prague, in November 1924. The titles of the lectures suggest that the content would have been fairly constant.[62] He also lectured in Amsterdam and Rotterdam.

It is difficult to see what attracted European colleagues to him, especially the protagonists of the incipient new objectivity. It seems unlikely that it was his built work. Of twenty-five realized projects before 1924, only the cubistic villa *Allegonda* departed from the strong Dutch vernacular tradition that permeated his domestic designs. The major housing complexes in Rotterdam—Tusschendijken and Spangen—were hardly artistically innovative, though they won attention as social housing projects. And apart from the colorful, cubistic (dare one dub it De Stijlish?) director's shed at Oud-Mathenesse, there was little out of the ordinary in the *Witte Dorp* of 1922-23. Perhaps it *was* the images of unrealized designs.

One would expect the "foreign" architectural press to have been the means of his early propagation into Europe. But before 1924 he was published only eight times outside The Netherlands, mostly in Germany. Hans Oud's claim that his father "made an international reputation with the municipal housing at Spangen and Tuss[ch]endijken"[63] should be qualified: that happened mostly after 1925, before which Tusschendijken was not published beyond Holland, and Spangen only three times, and then only as a fragment of more general articles.[64] A survey of the European literature demonstrates that foreign interest in Oud peaked in the years 1925-28, mainly in Germany and France. Neither was his reputation based on those two schemes alone. After 1932, Europe's waning attention passed to his more "international"-looking housing at Kiefhoek, Hoek van Holland and the Weissenhofsiedlung.

A series of publications made 1925 a key year. Oud's essay "Yes and no: confessions of an architect" appeared in *Europa Almanach*, to be reprinted in *Wasmuths Monatshefte fur Baukunst* shortly after, with large photographs and drawings of the Tusschendijken, Spangen and Oud Mathenesse housing projects.[65] In spring 1925 the opulent Paris journal *L'Architecture Vivante* published a section entitled "Town planning in Holland" drawing attention to the same schemes, all copiously illustrated with site plans, architectural drawings and photographs.[66] Perhaps the most significant publication, widely accessible because it was mostly pictures, was the inaugural *Bauhausbuch*, Walter Gropius' *Internationale Architektur*, which added the incomplete Hoek van Holland houses to images of Oud's Rotterdam housing.[67] Oud reviewed it and the companion volumes for his Dutch colleagues.[68] He had maintained contact with Bauhaus people when they moved from Weimar to Dessau in 1924, as well as with other architects' and artists' groups in Germany, Austria and Czechoslovakia.

Number ten in the *Bauhausbücher* series was *Holländische Architektur*, an anthology of some of Oud's writings, published in Munich, 1926. Besides his essays "Confession," "The future architecture and its architectonic possibilities," "The influence of Frank Lloyd Wright in Europe," and "The development of modern architecture in Holland," there were nearly sixty images of a wide range of work, mostly his own. An enlarged edition of 1929 added a foreword, two more essays—"Yes and no: confessions of an architect" and "Whither the New Building? Art and standardization"—an afterword, and several images.[69]

Also in 1926, plans were launched for an exhibition entitled "The Dwelling", a cooperative venture between Stuttgart's local government and the *Deutscher Werkbund*.[70] Ko's propaganda had paid off. He was invited by Mies van der Rohe to participate in the Weissenhofsiedlung, a model suburban housing project where prototype houses would be built to the designs of Europe's fifteen purported leading architects. Other contributors included Mies van der Rohe, Gropius, Victor Bourgeois, Hans Poelzig, Max Taut, Le Corbusier; the only other Hollander involved was Mart Stam.

Hans Oud attributes the prestigious invitation to the Rotterdam housing projects and the lectures his father had given in Germany.[71] It is reiterated that very little of Oud's housing design before 1926 belonged to the "new" architecture: exceptions were the Hoek van Holland and Kiefhoek developments. Only the former had been published—once—before 1926.[72] Although the *Witte Dorp* director's site office and the facade of the Café De Unie were anything but traditional, they were distinctively De Stijl expressions and hardly belonged to the anonymous cubic box architecture then spreading through western Europe. Oud's unsuccessful competition entries for the Rotterdam Stock Exchange and the Hotel Stiassni, Brno, Czechoslovakia fit the bill, so to speak, but neither was published before 1927.

It is therefore suggested that the chance to build at Stuttgart was won through Oud's personal communication, perhaps with photographs but certainly with persuasive words, of his "modern" architecture, during his visits to Germany in the early 1920s. Further, it becomes evident that the Stuttgart project, completed in 1927, drew attention to Oud's earlier work, not the other way around. Such a conclusion is logical, since the Weissenhofsiedlung was such a showpiece of European modern architecture and the eyes of the world were upon it. Anyway, it was only after 1927 that Oud was noticed further afield—in Poland, Spain, Finland, Hungary and especially Italy—and in English and American journals.

Oud's first great champion in the English-speaking world was the precocious twenty-five year old American art historian and critic Henry-Russell Hitchcock Jr. His essay "The architectural work of J.J.P. Oud" appeared in the New York journal, *The Arts*, early in 1928.[73] Oud was then, as noted, little known beyond Holland, France and Germany. Hitchcock presented him, rather inaccurately, as reacting against the Amsterdam School's "eclectic romanticism and expressionistic picturesqueness." The American's modernist bias can be seen in his discussion of the Tusschendijken, Hoek van Holland and Oud-Mathenesse projects. The piece provoked a response from Oud, albeit only in a letter to a Rotterdam newspaper.[74] In May 1928 Hitchcock wrote a two-installment article for the New York based *Architectural Record* that developed the ideas in his earlier essay, categorizing Oud with what he called the "new pioneers," in contrast to the "new traditionalists." According to Hitchcock, Oud stood beside Le Corbusier and Gropius as a prophet of the "new manner," his work "at its best and latest . . . quite on a par" with theirs.[75] That promoted him from the top *fifteen* architects to the top *three*. All this was quite a revelation to English-speaking audiences.

It had a particularly powerful effect upon Philip Cortelyou Johnson, a recent arts graduate of Harvard University. In an afterword to his *Writings* (1979), Johnson claimed that his conversion to Modernism and his desire to become a modern architect took place as he read Hitchcock's *The Arts* essay on Oud.[76] Johnson completed architectural studies at Harvard in 1943 and remained a single-minded advocate of Modernism until a decided lapse in 1978 (when he, like his former idol Oud) turned to ornamentation. Hitchcock and Johnson, individually and together, established Oud's reputation outside Europe. That would be achieved by 1932 and reach its climax in the New York Museum of

Modern Art's first architectural exhibition, *The International Style: Architecture since 1922*, reviewing ten years of modern architecture. There is some substance in the claim, made by the anonymous author of Oud's obituary in *Architectural Review* that others—for example Gropius and Hitchcock—were more responsible for his success than Oud himself was.[77] It is not all the truth; others were involved, too, and Oud was not beyond persistent self-promotion.

But first things first. In January 1928 Hitchcock wrote to Oud from Paris, seeking information for a monograph that he shortly hoped to publish. Probably because of his declining health, Oud took several months to reply.[78] It seems that delays were attenuated because the "monograph" finally appeared in Paris in 1931 as the slim volume II of *Les Cahiers d'Architecture Contemporaine*, a bland six-page biography followed by 44 pages of plans and photographs of projects and realized buildings.[79]

Oud's anxiety about establishing an international name for himself, manifested by an abundant international correspondence, widening travels for lectures and exhibitions in Europe, and his activities on national and foreign committees, when added to his continuing work for the Rotterdam municipality, put a strain on his emotional health, which had shown signs of weakness as early as 1911 or 1912. Many of his plans were disappointed, many invitations declined after about 1929. It is ironic that his efforts for self-promotion began to bear fruit just as he suffered a breakdown, which effectively stopped his career for about ten years, and forever changed his destiny. As Hans Oud comments

> The culminating point of Oud's creative production, historically speaking, lies in the 1920s. After then he was in a psychically [*sic*] bad condition for a number of years; dismissal and unemployment followed. In this utterly unfavorable period lies the beginning of a new phase of life: the "mid-life crisis". This, together with the economic crisis and the war years, was evidently fatal for the further development of Oud's potential. There followed no period of great creative achievement.[80]

But care should be taken when reading Hans Oud's biography of his father. Critical reception of the book was cautious: apart from blander notices, there were pointed reviews, including one in the national newspaper *NRC-Handelsblad*, entitled, "A son takes revenge," and another, "Hans Oud and the rows with his father" in the *Volkskrant*. Indeed, the book is less than complimentary, less than objective. Oud's eclipse after about 1930 was part of a wider phenomenon, the demise of progressive architecture in Europe, and of course especially Germany, induced when Nazism came to power in 1933.

Philip Johnson was keen to promote Oud's architecture where he could. And he soon had the opportunity. In 1930 he became, at the age of twenty-four, the first director of the Department of Architecture and Design at New York's Museum of Modern Art. He had just returned from an extended tour of Europe, where he traveled for some of the time with Hitchcock. Still dazzled by Oud, in 1930 Johnson wrote him from Berlin that he found the Germans' ignorance of the Hollander's work—a telling insight for the student of Oud—"abysmal." Johnson promised to obviate that fault, at least for the American public, in a book propagandizing modern architecture more clearly than Hitchcock had done in 1929 in *Modern Architecture, Romanticism and Integration.*

His letter makes it clear that the book in question was *The International Style: Architecture since 1922*, to be published in conjunction with the Museum of Modern Art's first architectural exhibition:

> Of course the criticism will be purely esthetic much to the distress of our German *sachlich* friends who think of nothing but sociology. We want to discuss new materials, brick again and tile etc.; then colors, and street planning. But principally the esthetic foundation of the style. The German critics are too apt to claim that the style has other than esthetic foundations, whereas the point of the book will be to show just what this esthetic foundation is and how it came about. This is perhaps too ambitious, but I think Hitchcock is very intelligent and we can make quite a stab at the problem.[81]

It may be inferred that at some time (possibly in 1928) Oud and Johnson had talked about architectural intent in the Hollander's public housing schemes, and that Oud had confided that he was indeed more interested in the esthetic than in the sociological aspects of architecture.

Such a view was proffered in 1978 by the Dutch architectural historian Ben Rebel, who, after examining the images created by Oud's publicists and himself, concluded that while he had "great merit" in the esthetic sphere he was not a "socially-concerned builder of housing."[82] Oud had confirmed this in 1951:

> At the beginning I was working on laborers' dwellings and my aim was to find a good and agreeable form for them; a form—so to speak—as exact and as clear as the form of a good car, a good steamer, a good electrical tool. In other words, I was searching for a good "common" form. And we have attained much in this respect.[83]

And that fit exactly what Oud had recognized and admired in Wright's architecture a quarter of a century earlier.[84]

Arrangements for the New York exhibition proceeded apace. In 1931 Johnson produced a pamphlet, *Built to Live In*, heralding the show; Oud's Hoek van Holland houses were illustrated.[85] Johnson's respect for Oud went beyond mere words when in 1931 he commissioned the architect to design a house for Johnson's parents in Pinehurst, North Carolina. Financial stringency in the Great Depression meant that the project had to be shelved. Early in July 1931 Johnson asked Oud for the model of the house, adding the bait, "After all consider that I am propagating really only you and Mies and if I have [the house model] to propagate with it, it will help your cause and my campaign no end."[86] Oud was ill, sometimes in hospital, sometimes in recuperation but hardly ever at his Rotterdam office throughout July and August. His responses were tardy, but the Pinehurst model was ready for inclusion in Hitchcock and Johnson's show.

When the Museum of Modern Art exhibition was mounted in the following February and March, Oud was the Dutch architect accorded special attention in the catalog essay published in *Modern Architecture*.[87] Hitchcock later recalled

> The director, Alfred Barr, asked Philip Johnson and me to organize this event. . . . The work of Le Corbusier, Oud, Gropius, Mies van der Rohe, and, by contrast, that of Wright occupied the principal place in the exhibition. But there was also work by other Americans, notably Hood, Howe and Lescaze and Neutra, and some forty architects all told, representing building of the day in fifteen countries. Concurrently with the exhibition we prepared *The International Style: Architecture since 1922*.[88]

This was "the book" to which Johnson had referred in 1930. Reviewing a decade of modern architecture, it first addressed the *idea* of style, before concluding that there was indeed an International Style—Barr capitalized the word "style" in his preface but the authors did not—recognizable by several essential elements: space enclosed, regularity, and rejection of ornament. Oud's De Stijl associations were discussed and the effect of Dutch Neoplasticism on Gropius noted. The Kiefhoek, Hoek van Holland and Stuttgart houses were illustrated, although all the photographs in the book, some provided by the architects, others taken by the authors are poorly reproduced.[89]

Manfredo Tafuri and Francesco Dal Co perceptively comment that "the didactic intent of the book was obvious from [Barr's] introduction," going on to point out that in their desire to "isolate certain general principles from contemporary architectural production, the authors" generated

> an oversimplified and limited analysis which predicated a nonexistent unity, and worse, understandable. . . . Many of the principles that Hitchcock and Johnson isolated were. . . products of a determined struggle against reducing all avant-garde experimentation to a "style."[90]

That compulsion naturally led to an inflexibility of view that could only result in brittleness. Later, when Oud stepped outside the guidelines set by the young Americans, he fell from grace. But we anticipate.

By 1932 Oud's apotheosis—implemented by Hitchcock and Johnson—was complete. *International Architecture* added the finishing touches to his head carved beside those of Gropius, Mies van der Rohe and Le Corbusier upon Modernism's Mount Rushmore. Johnson told Oud in a letter of November 1933: "In a general canvas of architectural schools we find that your name is the best known of all the modern architects and the only one to which no exception could be taken as would be the case of Mies or Le Corbusier."[91]

That may have provided something of a palliative for the depression that had enshrouded Oud for several years, and from which he was just beginning to emerge. Since 1928 there had been few realized commissions: a church for the Restored Apostolic Community at Kiefhoek (1928-29), a study interior for M.J.I. de Jonge van Ellemeet, Rotterdam (1930); and chair designs—mostly in tubular steel—for the furniture manufacturers Metz & Co (beginning in 1931). As well as the Johnson house, there were two other domestic designs; none was built. For the Rotterdam municipality Oud made plans for a housing development at Blijdorp, also discontinued. Between 1928 and 1930 Ko stayed with his family at Kijkduin near The Hague, resisting regular approaches from his colleagues to maintain contact; "of creative work no word was spoken."[92] His state of mind may be gauged from the large number of books on psychiatry that he acquired: nearly twenty by Freud and several more by Jung indicate more than a passing interest.

When he emerged from the deepest phase of his illness in 1933 Oud resigned his local government post to re-enter private practice from his own house in Hillegersberg near Rotterdam. He continued to pace himself, writing little and declining invitations to travel and to lecture. His practice was less than frenetic: despite several projects, until 1937 only one small commission was actually realized: renovations to the library of D. Hannema's Rotterdam house.

It is not surprising that he faded from the international literature as the decade passed. Architectural periodicals, like all periodicals, are seekers of novelty and voracious consumers of information. Because Oud had produced little since Kiefhoek and the Weissenhofsiedlung row houses—certainly icons of modernism but no longer newsworthy—interest dissolved abroad and (despite attempts to promote himself through his own writings) at home.

Two commissions were to change his fortunes and the architectural world's perception both of his work and his role in modernism. The first, received in 1937, was for the tourist class lounge and smoking room, and first class swimming pool of the S.S. *Nieuw Amsterdam*, prestigious flagship of the Holland-America Line. The second came in 1938 through winning a closed competition for a new headquarters building for the *Bataafsche Import Maatschappij* (later Shell Nederland) in The Hague. Oud's design was chosen over those of A.J.Kropholler, Dirk Roosenburg and Gijsbert Friedhoff. The Shell Building has been discussed in a thorough monograph that explores the commission, design, and construction, evaluates the building and examines public, and national and international professional response.[93] That response is important to the present essay.

The *wehrmacht* subjugated tiny Holland after a few days of *blitzkrieg* in May 1940. Throughout the ensuing Nazi occupation, when communication with the allied nations was obviously severed, architectural events in The Netherlands were obscured. The number of nationalistic-from-exile publications increased towards the end of the war, and after the June 1945 liberation links, particularly those with the English-speaking world, were quickly re-forged. Foreign journals caught up with hitherto unseen Dutch buildings completed in the war years, such as the Shell Building. And that was quite a surprise.

Oud was soon contacted by a perplexed Philip Johnson, who wrote, "Since I saw you I have become an architect and built a few things" and added,

> Giedion says that you built traditional buildings including one for the Shell Oil people that was quite conservative. I have seen only an interior purported to be by you on the *Nieuw Amsterdam*. But it did not look like your work. Tell me what you are doing.[94]

Until the end of the year there followed a flurry of letters between the two architects, and also between Oud and Douglas Haskell, editor of *Architectural Record*, who was seeking to publish something about Holland's postwar reconstruction, and the Shell Building, for which Oud would be paid.[95]

When the photographs of the Shell Building reached him, Haskell was taken aback, and wrote to Oud

> This was a rather surprising building to the editors and it would have been unnatural for us to present it without, so to speak, a question mark. You had not yourself in your notes gone into the question of the esthetic treatment which seemed to involve a widespread departure. . . . If there were a chance to talk I would want to challenge sharply what you are doing.[96]

Spoken as though he had a right to challenge Oud! Johnson's response, although more polite, was similar: "Your plans arrived, and I was very interested to study them, but as you can guess, I was again disappointed by the wealth of (to me) irrelevant details and the general axial formality of the scheme." And he remarked with some insight, "I'm afraid I'm getting old-fashioned—just stuck in the twenties."[97]

Haskell published the Shell Building under the snide title "Mr Oud embroiders a theme."[98] The building was reviewed in an inconclusive discussion of the apparent change in Oud's direction, which also criticized him for "decorating." To make its point the journal also illustrated the Hoek van Holland houses and the Rotterdam stock exchange. The *Record* piece observed

> Some twenty-five years ago, the young J.J.P. Oud was one among a small number of great leaders who shared a fresh insight. They found architecture too cluttered with fairy tales, Latin, and obscure reference, to make coherent sense. So they swept the boards clear of all embroidery and determined to tell the story of their own day, and tell it in terms only of clear, factual, direct and current speech.

before accusing that in the Shell building Oud had "[resorted] to embroidery."

> The plan [is] hard to distinguish from straight academic. Its major forms seem to be not enascent from the problem but are recognizable as repertory out of the architect's notebook. The very insistent, heavy, separate, imposed pattern of "decoration" seems visually related not to a keen process of expanding apperception but . . . to the pleasant reminiscences of peasant art.

The response is what one might expect from a religious acolyte—and that's not too outlandish an analogy—betrayed by a guru, who having shown others "the steep and thorny way to heaven" lapses himself from the truth. That is the problem with every dogmatic construct in human experience, whether in politics, religion or architecture: it leaves no room to move, no room to grow, no room to learn. By the late 1940s quite a few European modernists had immigrated to the United States, and many of them had taken up influential teaching posts.

Most American architects had adopted European modernism—most, but not all. In October 1947 Frank Lloyd Wright drafted a letter—the paragraphs cited here were never sent—to H.Th.Wijdeveld, complaining, "This country is overfilled with left wing modernists" and listed "Gropius, Corbu, Mies, Mendelsohn, Breuer and others" who were "still there with the negation I made in 1906 and the

Oud and the International Style

emphasis of the horizontal I practiced in 1910," still subscribing to a "cliched superficial esthetic." Confusing the politics at issue, Wright observed

> The breach between myself and these men has widened. They think, speak and work in two dimensions while idealizing the third and vice versa. I feel that I am as far beyond them now as I was in 1910 and their apostasy has only served to betray the cause of organic architecture in the nature of materials which I believe to be the architecture of Democracy.
>
> The thing they do is to me distinctly Nazi. And they cannot so see it at all. ... The Universities are loaded with these imports and while I suppose it is all better than the country might have had without them, it is all a miscarriage of the deeper thing I desired and in which I believed and for which I hoped.
>
> Yes, modern architecture, so called, is way back there in 1910 so far as its actual body now goes as the latest thing in education."[99]

The general enthusiasm of the post-war generation of American architects for the stereotypical "glass boxes on stilts" of Internationalism was founded upon the assurance first given by Hitchcock and Johnson that Oud and the others had discovered architectural Truth and were to be admired and followed. That Oud should now recant must have offended them deeply. Perhaps Johnson spoke for his colleagues when he confessed

> I do not know what to say. Maybe I ought to wait until I can see you and we can talk over the whole thing together. Frankly, to me the building looks like a return to Dutch tradition rather than the next step in international architecture. ... No one but a Dutchman would have built it just that way. That is fine but why call it international?[100]

Or perhaps he was dismayed because he had lost face.

Other journals questioned the Shell Building, although more gently. The Dutch architect Johannes van den Broek, exploring "streams in the new Dutch architecture" claimed that Oud's natural tendency broke through modernist stringency to decorate the building.[101] A countryman Jan Piet Kloos classified it as an example of the New Empiricism, whatever that meant.[102] But the American critic Lewis Mumford saw it as evidence that Oud, "on approaching maturity, promptly reached back for certain elements [he] had dropped in [his] first one-sided absorption in expressing technical processes."[103] The accuracy of that observation is debatable, but discussion is beyond the ambit of this essay. Bruno Zevi, then editor of *L'Architettura*, did not "write off" Oud because of the Shell Building; nevertheless, he believed Oud was wrong to think he could design outside of "a cultural context."[104] In all the furore—the Shell Building had certainly inspired architectural debate—through the late 1940s only the *RIBA Journal* remained as passive as the British can be, offering description, *sans* critical comment.[105]

Of course, Oud was affronted by what he called the *Record*'s "terrible accusations." Responding to the editors, he pointed out that there are "degrees in the usual things of our existence", and he believed the same to be true of architecture. Observing that "domestic building in our society has a different function from that of an office building, a town-hall or a church," he continued, "It seems to me at present quite all right that the new domestic architecture should be the basis of a new architecture; that it should already be a new architecture itself, I deny emphatically." He explained

> new architecture is what I strove for in my Shell building. It may be that it has more traditional ballast in it than former work of mine. I don't know. But it would not be the first time in my efforts that I went back a bit to make myself fit for going on further along the way I seek to explore.[106]

Fourteen years after he designed the Shell Building—his "favorite child"— and five years after the skirmish with his American critics, Oud declared

> The Shell building is an effort to strive again after architecture as a matter of the soul. As a consequence you will find in it resources that through the ages have proved to be good bearers of psychological feeling: of forms that have some underlying substance for universal apprehension. They concern geometry, symmetry, harmony, proportion. Also now and then—hierarchy. Further: questions like those of modules, ornament and so on are faced. Different styles are based on such objective esthetic frameworks, and time has shown that with them just as much variety in outward appearance is possible as with the human skeleton which has been the basis for millions of shapes of men and women. I may explain that with the Shell building I tried to avoid a lot of mistakes such as I made in former works which were praised now and then by my colleagues from over the Ocean.[107]

But the critical die was cast. Many influential architectural writers turned their backs on Oud, others turned against him. Instances are many and only a couple must suffice here. The American Talbot Hamlin, who had in the 1940 edition of his *Architecture through the Ages* praised Oud for his "precise elegance and . . . imaginative use of the simplest forms" chastised him in the revised edition of 1953 for decorating the Shell Building. A few years later Nikolaus Pevsner, the prolific and authoritative British architectural historian slyly and rudely dismissed the building as "Beton-Rococo."[108]

Gradually, as the years passed, less and less appeared about Oud in the international architectural press. His later projects received little or no attention outside The Netherlands. But they included important cultural icons such as the National Military Monument *Grebbeberg* (1948) and the National Monument in Amsterdam (1949, with sculptor John Rädecker), as well as large commissions like the *Vrijzinnig Christelijk* high school in The Hague (1949-56), the rehabilitation center for children with poliomyelitis at Arnhem (1952-60), an office building for *De Utrecht* Life Insurance Co in Rotterdam (1954-61), his magnum opus, the *Nederlands Congresgebouw* (executed under the supervision of Hans Oud) in The Hague (1956-69) and Almelo town hall, designed in 1962 and built after Ko's death. Well into the 1970s, when foreigners wrote of Oud, it was as an historical figure of early modernism, the first to "reveal the temper, . . . preoccupations and preferred architectural forms of the budding International Style"[109] who apparently had built nothing after about 1930.

And what of Hitchcock, Oud's chief transatlantic champion? As the decades passed, Hitchcock had gathered credibility and moral authority. When he forsook Oud, everyone did. He completely ignored the Hollander in an essay of 1951, "The International Style twenty years after,"[110] a choice that had significant ramifications. By 1958, when Hitchcock published *Architecture, Nineteenth and Twentieth Centuries,* his first fervent admiration for Oud had clearly diminished, although he still grouped him with the "second generation" of moderns, including Le Corbusier and Gropius. A few years later, he wistfully remarked in a foreword to a reprint of *The International Style* that "hindsight suggests that Holland might have been better—or also—represented by Rietveld than by Oud, who withdrew from production in 1930 for some years because of illness."[111] That was all. That was enough.

The question may be asked, Was Oud really in the vanguard of International modernism? And that begs a further question: Was there ever such a style as predicated by Barr, Hitchcock and Johnson? That is a highly complex issue and (thankfully) beyond our present scope.

As to Oud, an objective overview of his quite sparse oeuvre indicates that, if he was a seeker after truth he looked in several places for it: the Dutch vernacular; the work of Berlage and that of Wright; and (while in the international spotlight) in the ascetically sterile and ephemeral forms of western European "objective" architecture, only to find it at last, as one might expect of such an individualist, in being true to himself:

> We architects have to be full to the brim of idealism. Rigorous against our enemies; rigorous against our friends. If we wish to save architecture from the leveling trends of the moment, from the killing influence of a functionalism that has elevated itself from a means to an end, we shall have to exert ourselves for it much more than we do now. An architect without architectural ideals is not an architect: he is a builder. The most important thing we want at present is architecture. We shall need all our energy for it![112]

NOTES

1. Hans Oud, *J.J.P. Oud Architekt 1890-1963: feiten en herinnerigen gerangschikt,* The Hague, Nijgh en van Ditmar, 1984 is the published version of Oud's son's doctoral thesis. The book was received with reservation in Holland. See especially van Rooy, "Een zoon neemt revanche [a son takes revenge]", *NRC-Handelsblad,* 4 May 1984, p CS 7; Kloos, "Hans Oud en de ruzies van z'n vader", *Volkskrant,* 8 June 1984 and van der Geer, "Oud jr schreeft onthullend boek over [writes a revealing book about] Oud sr", *Rotterdamse Nieuwsblad,* 18 May 1984. For biographical detail see also Hans Esser, "J.J.P. Oud," in Carel Blotkamp (ed.), *De Stijl: the formative years,* Cambridge, Mass, MIT Press, 1986; Carsten-Peter Warncke, *The Ideal as Art. De Stijl, 1917-1931.* Cologne, Taschen, 1991.
2. The eldest brother Pieter Jacobus (1886-1968) built a career in politics at both the municipal level as *burgermeester* of Rotterdam and at the national level. The youngest, Gerrit Kassen (b. 1984) eventually became a banker.
3. Oud's estate is registered as J.J.P. (Ko) Oud with *Stichting Beeldrecht,* Amstelveen.

4. Oud summarized his education in a letter to Henry-Russell Hitchcock, June 1928. Oud archive, NAi.
5. The argument of Roland Günther, "Balance. De Stijl and the tradition of Dutch urban culture," *Daidalos*, 15 March 1985, pp 83-93 is based on the assertion that Oud was a frustrated painter.
6. Hans Oud, *J.J.P. Oud*, p 213.
7. ———, "Watchful widow," *Holland Herald*, vol 1, 1966, no 2, pp 20-21.
8. Johannes Hendrik van den Broek, "J.J.P. Oud; eredoctor in de technische wetenschappen." *Forum*, vol 10, 1955, pp 210-12.
9. Hans Oud, *J.J.P. Oud*, p 213. See also Umberto Barbieri, *J.J.P. Oud*, Rotterdam, Uitgeverij 010, 1987, pp 14-21, 26-27.
10. Maria Rethmeier-Dudok to J.J. de Wolf, 22 August 1974. Dudok archive, NAi.
11. J.J.P. Oud, "The influence of Frank Lloyd Wright on the architecture of Europe", *Wendingen*, vol 7, 1925, p 88.
12. Blotkamp, *De Stijl*, p 5.
13. "Gezelschap: De Sphinx," *Nieuwe Rotterdamsche Courant*, 22 January 1917, , p 1. Dutch: The review of the group's first exhibition in Leiden, 18-31 January 1917 mentions the painters, notably Harm Kamerlingh Onnes and Oud's "tasteful" drawings. See *Leidsch Dagblad*, 22 January 1917, p 1 and *Eenheid*, 3 February 1917, p 2.
14. Alfred H. Barr, *Cubism and Abstract Art*, New York, Museum of Modern Art, 1936. The catalog was reprinted 1964, 1974.
15. For insights into the relationship from van Doesburg's point of view see van Doesburg, "Grondbegrippen der nieuwe beeldende kunst, 1915-1918," *Tijdschrift voor Wijsgebeerte*, vol 13, 1919, pp 169-88, which deals with Oud's cubism and reprints his correspondence with van Doesburg. Facsimile, *Grondbegrippen der Nieuwe Beeldende Kunst*, Nijmegen, Sun, 1983, ed Cees Boekraad et al., includes a discussion of the collaboration. Carel Blotkamp, *Mondriaan in Detail*, Utrecht/Antwerp, Veen, 1987 contains a sub-section on the relationships between van Doesburg and Oud.
16. Oud made his first design for the house in July 1916. While the general layout was retained, the client (disappointingly) seems to have chosen a much more conservative style. For a comparison of the two versions see Umberto Barbieri, *J.J.P. Oud*, Rotterdam, 1987, pp 22-23.
17. There are rarely published color images of the floor designs for *De Vonk* in Evert van Straaten, *Theo van Doesburg, Painter and Architect*, The Hague, SDU Uitgeverij, 1988.
18. Hans Oud, *J.J.P. Oud*, pp 41-42. See also Donald Langmead and Donald Leslie Johnson, *Architectural Excursions: Frank Lloyd Wright, Holland and Europe*, Westport CT, Greenwood Press, 1999, chapter 4.
19. Hans Oud, *J.J.P. Oud*, pp 68-70. See also van Straaten, *Theo van Doesburg, Painter and Architect*, The Hague, 1988; Henk Engel, "Van huis tot woning," *Plan*, 1981, no 9, pp 34-39; Sergio Polano, "De nieuwe kleurbeelding in architectuur. Beschouwing over De Stijl" in Jan de Heer, (ed.), *Kleur en Architectuur*, Uitgeverij 101, 1986.
20. J.J.P. Oud, "Het monumentale stadsbeeld." *De Stijl*, vol 1, 1917, no 1, pp 10-11. Parts were reprinted *ibid*, vol 5, 1922, pp 207-08. Also published in Wiekart (ed.), *Ter Wille van een Levende Bouwkunst*, The Hague, Nijgh en van Ditmar, 1962. For Italian and English translations see respectively Polano, "Notes on Oud . . .", *Lotus*, no 16, 1977 and Jaffé (ed.), *De Stijl*, London, Thames and Hudson, 1970.
21. J.J.P. Oud, "Kunst en machine [Art and machine]," *De Stijl*, vol 1, 1918, no 3, pp 25-27. Reprinted in Wiekart (ed.), *Ter Wille van een Levende Bouwkunst*, 1962. For

Italian and English translations see respectively Polano, "Notes on Oud . . .", *Lotus*, no 16, 1977 and Jaffé (ed.), *De Stijl*, London, 1970, pp 96-98. Cf. Oud, "Kunst, Handwerk und Maschine." *Thuringer Allgemeine Zeitung*, vol 75, 1924, no 190, p 6.

22. J.J.P. Oud, "Architectonische beschouwing bij bijlage VIII, woonhuis van Fred C. Robie door F.L.Wright." *De Stijl*, vol 1, 1918, no 4, pp 38-41. For not altogether accurate Italian and English translations see respectively Polano, "Notes on Oud . . .", *Lotus,* no 16, 1977 and Beckett et al., *The Original Drawings of J.J.P. Oud, 1890-1963*, London, Architectural Press, 1963.
23. J.J.P. Oud, [Obituary for Frank Lloyd Wright], *Groene Amsterdammer* (18 April 1959), 9.
24. J.J.P. Oud, "Bouwkunst en normalisatie bij den massabouw." *De Stijl,* vol 1, 1918, no 7, pp 77-79. For Italian and English translations see respectively Polano, "Notes on Oud . . .", *Lotus,* no 16, 1977; Timothy Benton et al., *Form and Function: a Sourcebook for the History of Architecture*, London, Crosby, Lockwood, Staples, 1975.
25. J.J.P. Oud, "Architectonische beschouwingen." *De Stijl*, vol 2, 1919, no 7, pp 79-84. A number of experimental concrete houses were built after about 1910, and Wright seems to have been the source of later ones, possibly through Wasmuth's Charles Robert Ashbee and Wright. *Frank Lloyd Wright Chicago*, Berlin, Wasmuth, 1911.
26. J.J.P. Oud, "Orientatie." *De Stijl*, vol 3, 1919, no 2, p 13.
27. J.J.P. Oud, "Boekbespreking. Dr. Otto Grautauff, *Formzertrümmerung und Formaufbau in der bildenden Kunst* ." *De Stijl*, vol 2, 1919, no 10, pp 113-14.
28. J.J.P. Oud, "Architectonische beschouwing bij bijlage III." *De Stijl*, vol 3, 1920, no 3, p 25.
29. Hans Oud, *J.J.P. Oud*, p 215.
30. J.J.P. Oud, "Het bouwen van woningen in (gewapend) beton," *Bouwkundig Weekblad*, vol 41, 1920, pp 89-94; 131-36; "Gemeentelijke volkswoningen, polder 'Spangen' te Rotterdam," *ibid*, vol 41, 1920, pp 219-22.
31. J.J.P. Oud, "Over de toekomstige bouwkunst en hare architectonische mogelijkheden." *Bouwkundig Weekblad*, vol 42, 1921, pp 147-60.
32. J.J.P. Oud, *Mein Weg in 'De Stijl'*, The Hague/Rotterdam, Nijgh en van Ditmar, 1960.
33. Ezio Godoli, *Jan Wils, Frank Lloyd Wright e De Stijl*, Florence, Modulo,1980 as translated in Daniele Baroni, "Jan Wils," *Ottagono,* vol 22, 1987, March, p 51.
34. Jan Wils, "De nieuwe bouwkunst. Bij het werk van Frank Lloyd Wright," *Levende Kunst*, vol 1, 1918, pp 207-19; *idem*, "De nieuwe tijd. Eenige gedachten bij het werk van Frank Lloyd Wright," W*endingen*, vol 2, 1919, no 6, pp 14-17; *idem*, "Frank Lloyd Wright," *Elseviers Geïllustreerd Maandschrift*, vol 61, 1921, pp 216-27.
35. Jan Wils to H.Th.Wijdeveld, 20 December 1968. Wijdeveld archive, NAi.
36. Jan Wils, "De nieuwe bouwkunst," *De Stijl*, vol 1, 1918, January, pp 31-33; *idem*, "Schets voor een landhuis met holle beton-wanden," *ibid,* 1(June 1918), 96.
37. Theo van Doesburg, "Tot een beeldende architectuur," *De Stijl*, vol 6, no 6/7, 1924, pp 78-83.
38. For Oud's early work see Günther Stamm, "Het jeugdwerk van de architekt J.J.P. Oud 1906-1917," *Museumjournaal*, vol 22, 1977, pp 260-65.
39. The view taken by Reyner Banham, *Theory and Design in the First Machine Age*, London, Architectural Press, 1960, has been frequently reiterated by others.
40. Dutch literature on Wright before 1925 cites one version or another of Wright's "In the cause of architecture," first published in *Architectural Record*, 12 March 1908.
41. J.J.P. Oud, "Architectonische beschouwingen." *De Stijl*, vol 2, 1919, May, pp 79-84. Oud's ideas are applied to the design for a double workers' dwelling.

42. Several pieces by van 't Hoff and van Doesburg about the Villa Henny appeared in *De Stijl*, vol 2, 1919, pp 26-33.
43. See, for example, Jan Gratama, "Kroniek LIX: de Duitsche Werkbund en zijn beteekenis voor Nederland." *Bouwkundig Weekblad*, vol 34, 1914, pp 311-15; Willem Penaat, "De Duitsche Werkbund en een Hollandsche Driebond: Duitsche Werkbund." *ibid*, pp 339-41, 356-58, 364-65 (reprinted from *Het Orgaan van de Ned. Vereeniging voor Ambachts- en Nijverheidskunst*); H.L.Kalk, "Excursie 'Deutsche Werkbund' tentoonstelling." *Architectura*, vol 22, 1914, p 214; "De 'Deutsche Werkbund' tentoonstelling." *ibid*, pp 59-60, 261-62, 265-66, 273-74, 286-87, 298, 302-03, 315. Fritz Stahl, "Die architektur der Werkbund-austellung," *Wasmuths Monatsheft für Baukunst*, vol 1, 1914-15, pp 153-204.
44. J.J.P. Oud, "Architectonische beschouwing: B. Gewapend beton en bouwkunst," *De Stijl*, vol 2, 1919, May, p 79.
45. See, for example, W. Kuyper, *Dutch Classicist Architecture* Delft, University Press, 1980, chapters 14-18.
46. Suzanne Shulof Frank, "J.L.M.Lauweriks and the Dutch school of proportion," *A.A. Files*, 1984, September, pp 61-67. Cf. Nico.Tummers, "De Hagener Impuls," *Bouwkundig Weekblad*, vol 85, 1967, pp 412-64 and Manfred Bock, "Five *Architectura* architects," *Museumjournaal*, vol 5, 1976, pp 200-08; 216-19. There is an extended and fascinating comparison of proportional systems employed respectively by Wright, Sullivan, Berlage and Lauweriks in Anthony Alofsin, *Frank Lloyd Wright The Lost Years, 1910-1922. A study of influence*, Chicago, University of Chicago Press, 1993, chapter 1.
47. J.J.P. Oud, "Architectonische beschouwing bij bijlage VIII," *De Stijl*, 1(1918), 39. The English translation in Jane Beckett, et al..., *The Original Drawings of J.J.P. Oud 1890-1963*, (London, 1963), 27-29, does not convey Oud's differentiation of functional planning and formal systematic planning. My translation by Coby Langmead-Ravesteijn (held by the author) is more accurate.
48. J.J.P. Oud, "The influence of Frank Lloyd Wright on the architecture of Europe." *Wendingen*, vol 7, 1925, pp 85-91, reprinted in H.Th.Wijdeveld (ed.), *The Life-Work of the American Architect Frank Lloyd Wright*, Santpoort, C.A.Mees, 1925. See also Oud, *Holländische Architektur*, Munich, Langen, 1926; *idem.*, "De invloed van . . . Wright op de architectuur in Europa," *Architectura*, vol 30, 1926, pp 85-89; *idem.*, "Wplyw Franka Wright'a na architekture europejska," *Architektura i Budownictwo* (Warsaw), vol 9, 1933, no 6, pp 188-89.
49. H.P.Berlage, 1921. "Frank Lloyd Wright," *Wendingen*, vol 4, 1921, no 11. An English translation appeared in *ibid*, 7, vol 7, 1925, no 6, reprinted in Wijdeveld, *The Life-Work of the American Architect Frank Lloyd Wright*, Santpoort, 1925.
50. Oud to Platz, 8 July 1926. Oud archive, NAi.
51. W. Jos. de Gruyter, "Moderne Nederlandsche Bouwkunst en J.J.P. Oud," *Elseviers Geïllustreerd Maandschrift*, vol 82, 1931, August, p 174.
52. J.J.P. Oud, "Architectonische beschouwingen," *De Stijl*, vol 2, 1919, no 7, pp 79-84.
53. Neils Prak, foreword to Langmead and Johnson, *Architectural Excursions: Frank Lloyd Wright, Holland and Europe*, Westport, 1998.
54. Wright to Berlage, 30 November 1922, Berlage archive, NAi; Wright to Oud, 30 November 1922. Oud archive.
55. Both projects are included in Adolf Behne, "Holländische Baukunst in der Gegenwart," *Wasmuths Monatshefte für Baukunst*, vol 1, 1922, no 1-2, pp 20-21 and the standardized workers' housing in Mart Stam, "Holland und die Baukunst unserer Zeit," *Schweizerische Bauzeitung*, vol 82, 1923, pp 225-29.

56. See *Nordische Baukunst*, November 1914, p 36 translated "Woonhuis te Aalsmeer," published in *Klei*, vol 5, 1913, 1 November, pp 321-23. The German journal reproduced the photographs but not the drawings.
57. Adolf Behne, "Architekten," *Frühlicht*, 1921, no 2, winter.
58. J.J.P. Oud, "Over de toekomstige bouwkunst en hare architectonische mogelijkheden." *Bouwkundig Weekblad*, vol 42, 1921, pp 147-60. See also *Frühlicht*, no 4, 1922, pp 113-18 (German); *Stavba*, 1922, no 10, pp 177-192 (Czechoslovakian); *La Cité*, 1923, no 5, pp 73-85 (French); *Baukunst*, May 1925, pp 98-101; and "Architecture and the future", *Studio*, 1928, pp 401-06 (English).
59. The Spangen developments were discussed and illustrated in Ernst Stockmeyer, "Monumentale Miethaus-Architektur [apartment-houses] in Holland," *Schweizerische Bauzeitung*, vol 80, 1922, pp 257-59. See also Ludwig Hilbersheimer, "J.J.P. Ouds Wohnungsbauten," *Das Kunstblatt*, 1923, pp 289-93.
60. J.J.P. Oud, "Ontwerp voor een woonhuis in Berlijn." *Bouwkundig Weekblad*, vol 43, 1922, p 341.
61. Adolf Behne, "De 'Bauhaus'-tentoonstelling te Weimar." *Klei*, vol 15, 1923, pp 245-53 mentions Oud's "admirable" lecture about the development of modern architecture in Holland. See Taverne, "De architect en de huisvrouw", *NRC-Handelsblad*, 13 May 1983; de Wit, *ibid*, 13 May 1983.
62. See P. Meyer, "Die Entwicklung der Moderne Baukunst in Holland; Vergangenheit, Gegenwart, Zukunft," *Schweizerische Bauzeitung*, vol 83, 1924, pp 134-37 and cf. J.J.P. Oud, "L'evolution de l'architecture moderne aux Pays-Bas", *Stavba*, vol 3, 1924, p 96. For the full text see Oud, *Holländische Architektur*, 1926. The same talk had been given in Berlin, 21 January 1923; at the Weimar Bauhaus, 17 August 1923; and in Rotterdam, 16 October 1923.
63. Hans Oud, *J.J.P. Oud*, p 213.
64. Adolf Behne, "Holländische Baukunst in der Gegenwart," *Wasmuths Monatshefte für Baukunst*, 1922, vol 1, no 1-2, pp 1-33; Ernst Stockmeyer, "Monumentale Miethaus-Architektur in Holland," *Schweizerische Bauzeitung*, vol 80, 1922, pp 257-59; and Karel Teige, "De Stijl a Hollandská moderna," *Stavba*, vol 3, 1924, no 2, pp 33-41.
65. J.J.P. Oud, "Ja und Nein. Bekenntnisse eines Architekten." *Europa Almanach*, Potsdam, 1925, pp 18-20. Cf. *Wasmuths Monatshefte fur Baukunst*, vol 9, 1925, pp 140-47.
66. Jean Badovici, "Entretiens sur l'architecture vivante." *L'Architecture Vivante*, 1925, spring/summer, pp 10-14, plates 1-15.
67. Walter Gropius, *Internationale Architektur*, Munich, 1925. Passau, 1927.
68. J.J.P. Oud, "De Bauhaus Bucher," *Bouwkundig Weekblad*, vol 46, 1925, p 587. reviews Gropius, *Internationale Architektur*; Moholy-Nagy, *Malerei, Photographie, Film* and van Doesburg, *Grundbegriffe der Neuen Gestaltenden Kunst*.
69. J.J.P. Oud, *Holländische Architektur*, Munich, 1926. The book was in German; essay titles have here been translated into English.
70. Burgee, J. (ed.), *Bau und Wohnung. Die Bauten der Weissenhofsiedlung in Stuttgart errichtet in 1927 nach Vorschlagen des Deutschen Werkbundes in Auftrag der Stadt Stuttgart und in Rahmen der Werkbund Austellung 'Die Wohnung'*, Stuttgart, 1927.
71. Hans Oud, *J.J.P. Oud*, p 99.
72. Adolf Behne, "Zwei Holländische Architekten." *Bauwelt*, 1926, 20 May, no 20, p 13.
73. Henry-Russell Hitchcock, Jr., "The architectural work of J.J.P. Oud." *The Arts*, vol 13, 1928, pp 97-103. See also Paolo Scrivano, "J.J.P. Oud and Dutch architecture in the writings of Henry-Russell Hitchcock." *Zodiac*, no 18, 1997-98, pp 90-103.

74. J.J.P. Oud, "Tijdschriften," *Nieuwe Rotterdamsche Courant*, 6 June 1928.
75. Henry-Russell Hitchcock, Jr., "Modern architecture: II. The new pioneers," *Architectural Record*, vol 63, 1928, May, pp 453-60.
76. Philip Johnson, *Writings*, New York, 1979, afterword. In 1955 Johnson's story was different; see John Peter, *The Oral History of Modern Architecture*, 1994, Abrams, p 225.
77. ——, "J.J.P. Oud: 1890-1963," *Architectural Review*, vol 134, 1963, p 310.
78. Hitchcock to Oud, 16 January 1928, Oud archive. See also Hitchcock to Oud, 30 May 1926 and Oud to Hitchcock, June 1926.
79. Henry-Russell Hitchcock, Jr., *J.J.P. Oud*, Paris, Cahiers d'Art, ca. 1931.
80. Hans Oud, *J.J.P. Oud*, pp 214-215.
81. Johnson to Oud, n.d. [1930?], Oud archive. Hitchcock's foreword to the 1966 edition of *International Architecture*, p vii, says that the New York exhibition was planned in 1931; this letter suggests otherwise.
82. Ben Rebel, "Volkswoningbouw van J.J.P. Oud." *Nederlands Kunsthistorisch Jaarboek*, vol 28, 1977, pp 127-68. See also "Oud als sociale woningbouwer," in Hans Oud, *J.J.P. Oud*, pp 115-124.
83. "Speech delivered by Mr J.J.P. Oud to members of the International Association of Art Critics during their visit to the Shell Netherland [*sic*] Building at The Hague on the 9 July 1951," p 1. Mimeographed document, Oud archive.
84. J.J.P. Oud, "The influence of Frank Lloyd Wright on the architecture of Europe." *Wendingen*, vol 7, 1925, p 88.
85. Philip Johnson, *Built to Live In*, New York, Museum of Modern Art, 1931.
86. Johnson to Oud, 8 July 1931. Oud archive.
87. Alfred Barr, Henry-Russell Hitchcock Jr., Philip Johnson and Lewis Mumford, *Modern Architecture*, New York, Museum of Modern Art, 1932.
88. Henry-Russell Hitchcock Jr., Foreword to *International Architecture*, New York, Museum of Modern Art, 1966, p vii.
89. Henry-Russell Hitchcock, Jr. and Philip Johnson, *The International Style: Architecture since 1922*, New York, Museum of Modern Art, 1932. Reprinted 1966, 1995.
90. Manfredo Tafuri and Francesco Dal Co, *Modern Architecture*, London, Faber/Electa, 1986, pp 210-11.
91. Johnson to Oud, 23 November 1933. Oud archive.
92. Hans Oud, *J.J.P. Oud*, p 113.
93. Ed R.M. Taverne and Dolf Broekhuizen, *Oud's Shell Building: design and reception*, Rotterdam, NAi, 1995.
94. Johnson to Oud, 5 September 1945. Oud archive.
95. Douglas Haskell [*Architectural Record*] to Oud, 28 September 1945; Oud to Haskell, 17 October 1945; Oud to Johnson, 23 October 1945; *Oud to Haskell [Architectural Record]*, 30 October 1945. Oud archive.
96. Haskell to Oud, 13 December 1946. Oud archive.
97. Johnson to Oud, 16 December 1946. Oud archive.
98. ——, "Mr Oud embroiders a theme," *Architectural Record*, vol 100, 1946, December, pp 80-84. See "Oud in de Amerikaanse pers," *Forum*, vol 2, 1947, pp 71-73, following editorial comment. See also "Periodical report," *Architectural Record*, November 1952, pp 348-50.
99. Wright to Wijdeveld, 21 October 1947 (draft), Wright Archives, Scottsdale, Arizona.
100. Johnson to Oud, 25 November 1945. Oud archive.
101. J.H. van den Broek,"Stroomingen en tendenties in de nieuwe Nederlandsche architectuur," *Bouw*, vol 1, 1946, pp 4-11.

Oud and the International Style

102. Jan Piet Kloos, "The Dutch melting pot," *Architectural Review*, vol 103, 1948, no 646, p 137-56.
103. Lewis Mumford, "Monumentalism, symbolism and style," *Architectural Review*, vol 105, 1949, April, pp 173-80.
104. Bruno Zevi, "Jacobus Johannes Pieter Oud è morto," *L'Architettura*, vol 9, 1963, July, pp 146-47.
105. ———, "Head office, Shell Company. . ." *RIBA Journal*, vol 53, 1946, pp 162-66. English. A brief history of the building precedes a general description of its construction. No criticism is offered.
106. "Mr Oud replies. . ." *Architectural Record*, vol 101, March 1947, p 18, as cited in by Oud in a speech to the International Association of Art Critics, 9 July 1951. See following note.
107. "Speech delivered by . . . Oud to members of the International Association of Art Critics . . . 9 July 1951," p 4.
108. Nikolaus Pevsner, "Modern architecture and the historian or the return of historicism" *RIBA Journal*, vol 68, 1961, April, pp 230-40.
109. Reyner Banham, *Age of the Masters*, London, Architectural Press, 1975, p 34. Originally published as *Guide to Modern Architecture*, London, Architectural Press, 1962.
110. Henry-Russell Hitchcock Jr., "The International Style twenty years after," *Architectural Record*, August 1951.
111. Hitchcock, [Foreword] to Hitchcock and Johnson, *The International Style: Architecture since 1922*, New York, 1966, pp x-xi.
112. "Speech delivered by . . . Oud to members of the International Association of Art Critics . . . 9 July 1951," p 4.

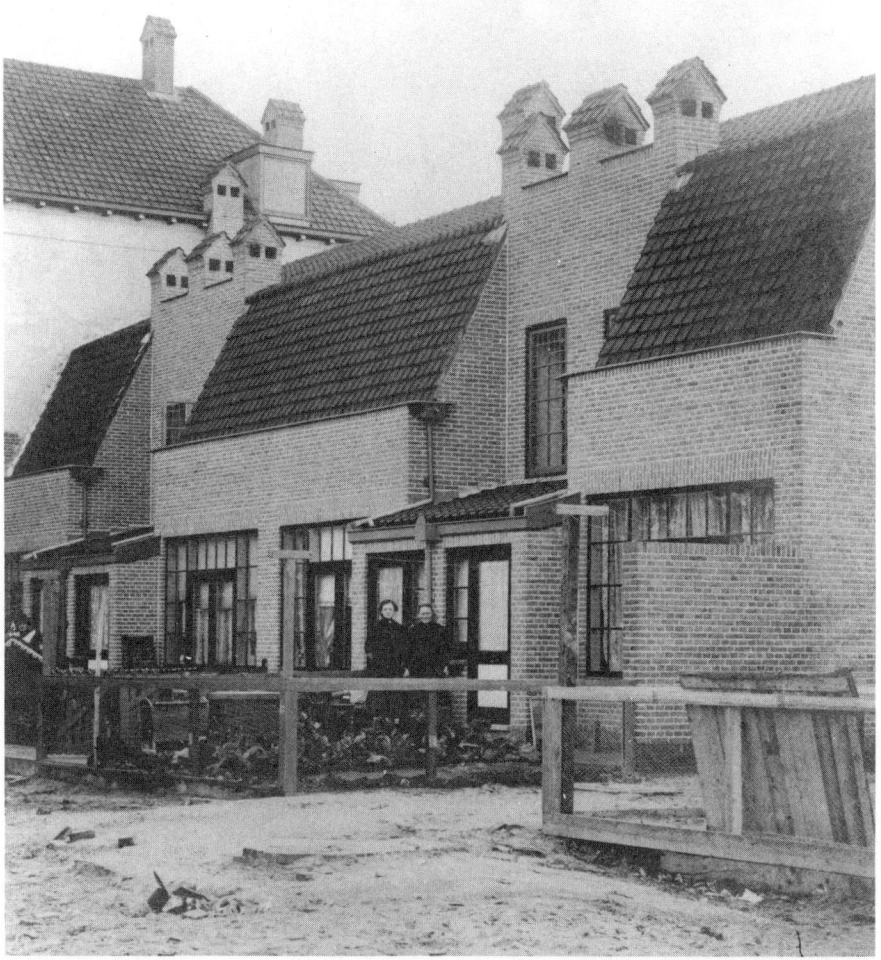

Plate 1. Premises for "Vooruit" Working Mens' Association, Wilhelminalaan 10, Purtmerend, The Netherlands. 1912. Jacobus Johannes Pieter Oud, Architect. View of rear of workers' houses, showing the tiny gardens. The treatment of the fronts of the houses was much more monolithic, hardly distinguishable in scale from the building (in the background of the photograph) that housed the Association's meeting hall and offices. © JJP Ko Oud 1912 Beeldrecht. Reproduced by Permission of VI$COPY LTD, Sydney 1998.

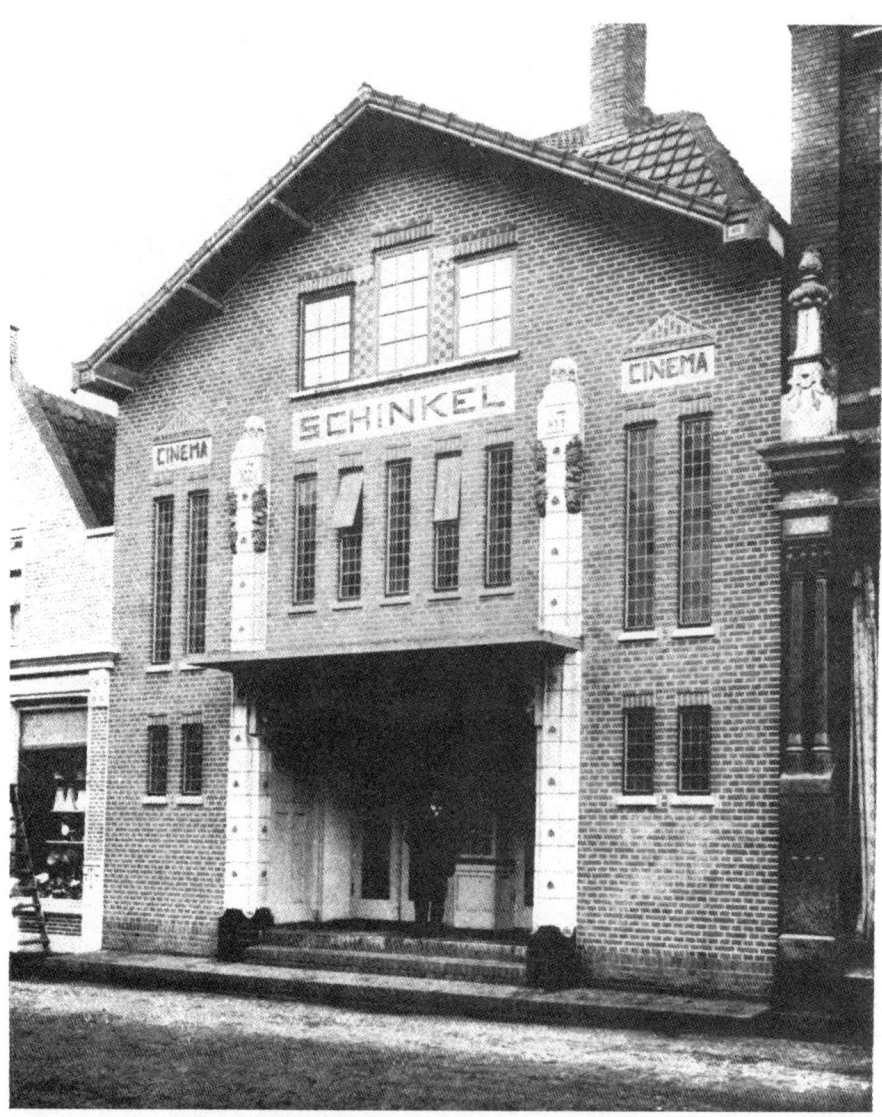

Plate 2. Schinkel cinema, Dubbele Buurt 16, Pumerend, The Netherlands. 1912. Jacobus Johannes Pieter Oud, Architect; Willem C. Brouwer, Ceramicist. The 220-seat cinema was integrated with a dwelling at the upper level back. The somber bricks of the facade must have been somewhat enlivened by Brouwer's glazed tile decoration in blue and gold. © JJP Ko Oud 1912 Beeldrecht. Reproduced by Permission of VI$COPY LTD, Sydney 1998.

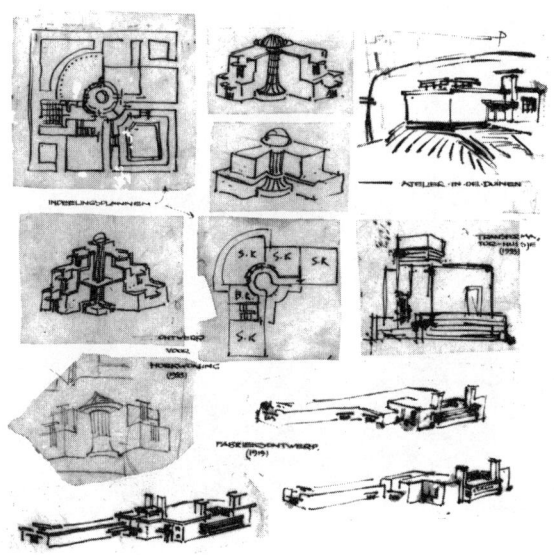

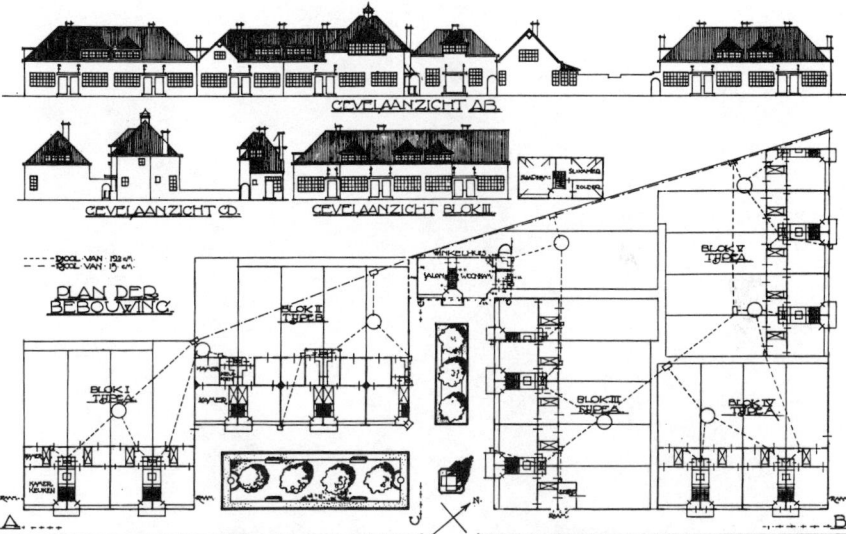

Plate 3 (top). Preliminary studies. Various dates. Jacobus Johannes Pieter Oud, Architect. Oud preferred to make conceptual sketches to be formalized by a drafter. The five drawings top left are "corner houses" (1923); top right is a studio at Katwijk aan Zee, for Theo van Doesburg (1919); below it is a transformer house (1923); across the bottom are his 1919 versions of a factory and bonded warehouse at Purmerend. None of the projects was realized. © JJP Ko Oud 1912 Beeldrecht. Reproduced by Permission of VI$COPY LTD, Sydney 1998.

Plate 4 (bottom). Workers' housing development, Leiderdorp, near Leiden, The Netherlands. 1914 (built 1915–16, demolished 1978). W. M. Dudok and Jacobus Johannes Pieter Oud, Architects. The 24 houses were architecturally conservative and socially ideal. © JJP Ko Oud 1912 Beeldrecht. Reproduced by Permission of VI$COPY LTD, Sydney 1998.

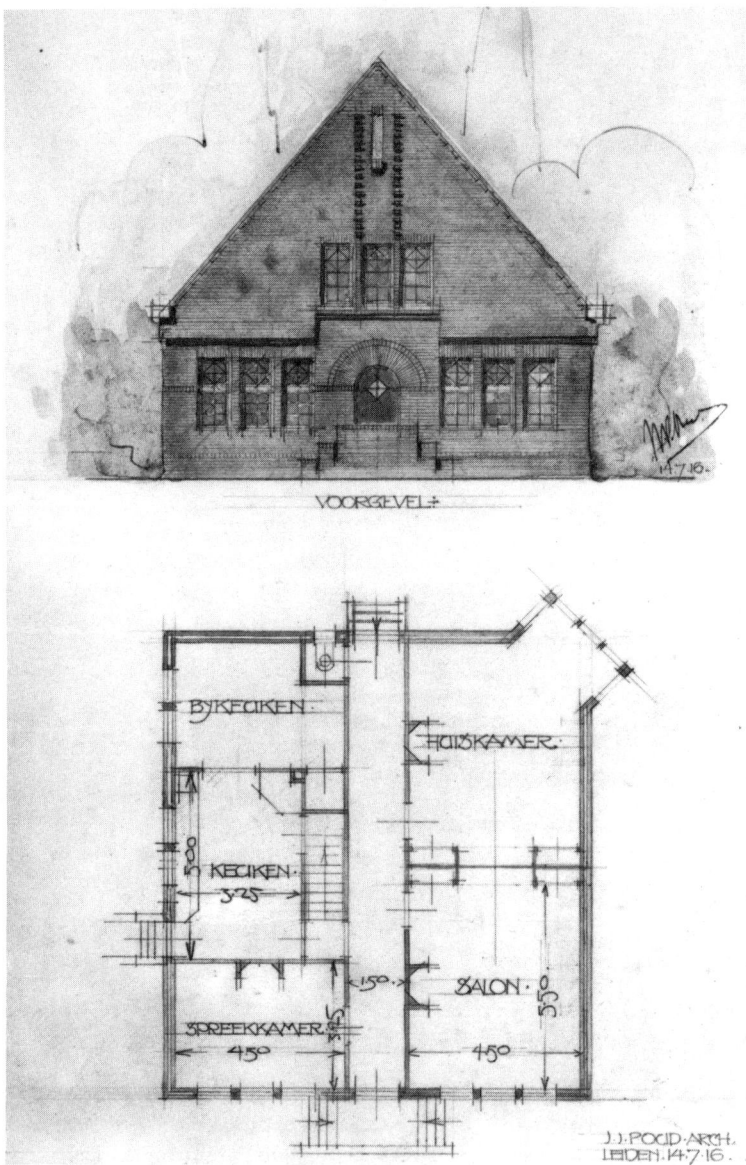

Plate 5. Proposed housed for W. de Geus, Broek in Waterland, The Netherlands. 1916. Jacobus Johannes Pieter Oud, Architect. Rendered pencil and watercolor drawing of first proposal. Top: principal elevation; bottom: ground floor plan. The house as built had much the same spatial organization. But (perhaps because of the client's conservatism) the vigor of the external form, redolent of many contemporary villas by Co Brandes and other architects in fashionable Wassenaar, was surrendered for a more traditional outcome. Theo van Doesburg designed a leadlight panel for the rear door. © JJP Ko Oud 1912 Beeldrecht. Reproduced by Permission of VI$COPY LTD, Sydney 1998.

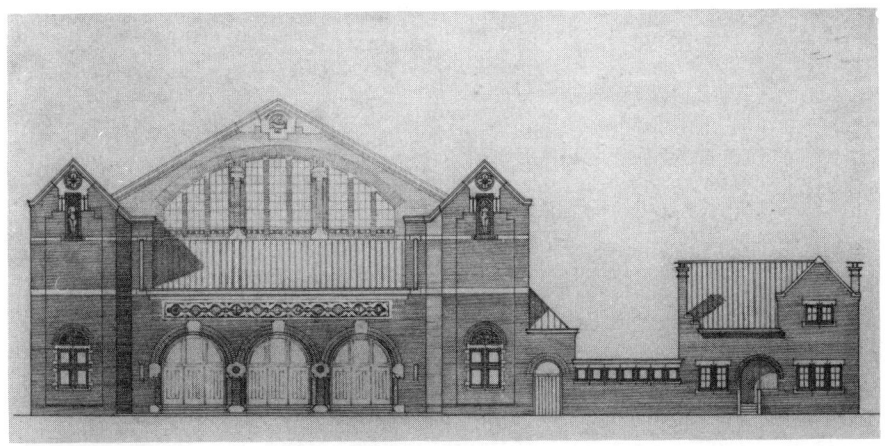

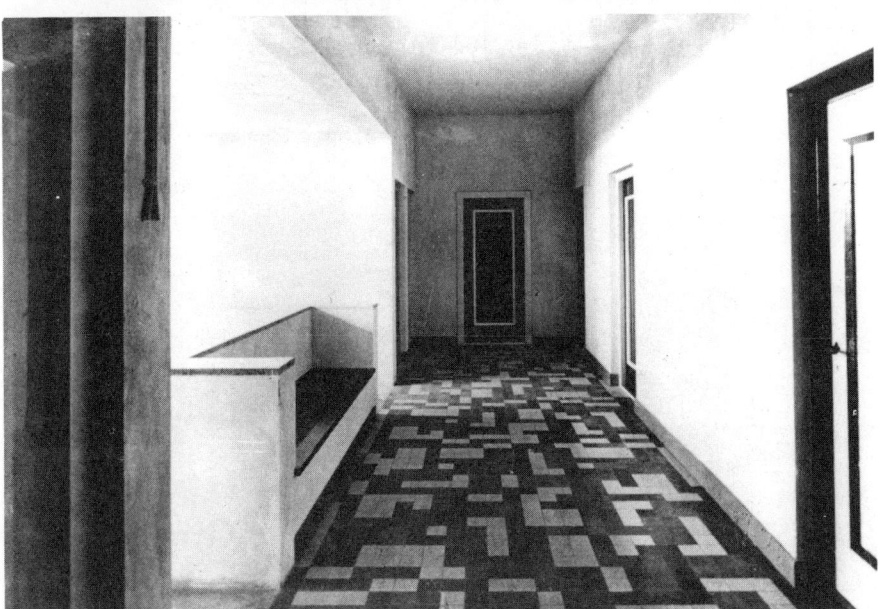

Plate 6 (top). Design for a public bath house, Blaricum, The Netherlands. 1915–16. Jacobus Johannes Pieter Oud, Architect. Drawing of principal elevaiton. The architectural competition entry clearly owes something to Berlage's Amsterdam Stock Exchange. Like two of Oud's contemporary designs—*De Vonk* holiday house and a nursing home in Hilversum—it demonstrates his current affinity for symmetry. © JJP Ko Oud 1912 Beeldrecht. Reproduced by Permission of VI$COPY LTD, Sydney 1998.

Plate 7 (bottom). De Vonk holiday house, Westeinde 94, Noordwijkerhout, The Netherlands. 1917. Jacobus Johannes Pieter Oud, Architect; Theo van Doesburg and H. H. Kamerlingh Onnes, Decorative Artists. First floor corridor. The color scheme and the tile layout (in browns, beiges and yellow) was designed by van Doesburg. © JJP Ko Oud 1912 Beeldrecht. Reproduced by Permission of VI$COPY LTD, Sydney 1998.

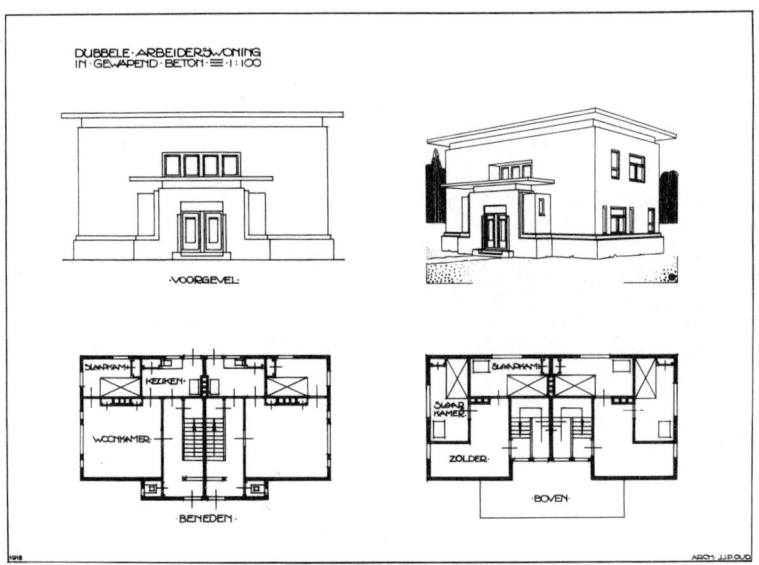

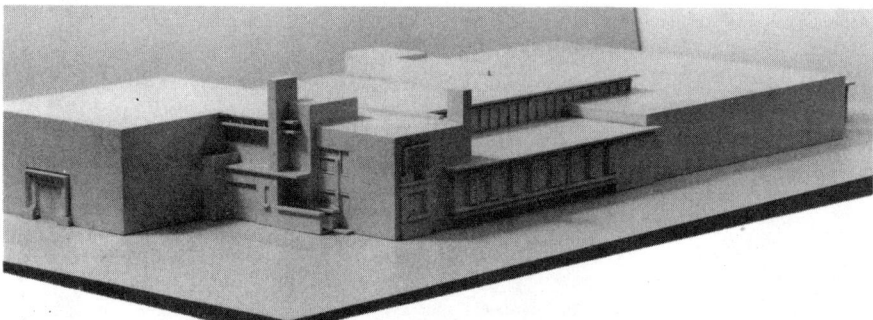

Plate 8 (top). Design for semi-detached reinforced concrete houses for workers. 1918. Jacobus Johannes Pieter Oud, Architect. Principal elevation, perspective and floor plans. The drawings were published in *De Stijl*, no. 7, 1919. The strong influence of Frank Lloyd Wright's cubic esthetic, seen in his buildings of a decade or two earlier, is unmistakable; indeed, the chunky little houses seem to parody the American's work. © JJP Ko Oud 1912 Beeldrecht. Reproduced by Permission of VI$COPY LTD, Sydney 1998.

Plate 9 (bottom). Design for a factory, offices and store. 1919. Jacobus Johannes Pieter Oud, Architect. Photograph of model. This unrealized proposal was paired with another for a distillery and bond store, both for the wine merchants Wed. G. Oud Pzn and Co. A first proposal of 1916 was more conservative: a deep prismatic building with a mansard roof and a symmetrical facade. The 1919 design hybridized De Stijl rectilinearity, cubist massing and not a few elements of Wrightian architecture, the latter perhaps partly through the filter of Gropius' and Meyer's Deutz Motor model factory at the 1914 *Deutsche Werkbund*. © JJP Ko Oud 1912 Beeldrecht. Reproduced by Permission of VI$COPY LTD, Sydney 1998.

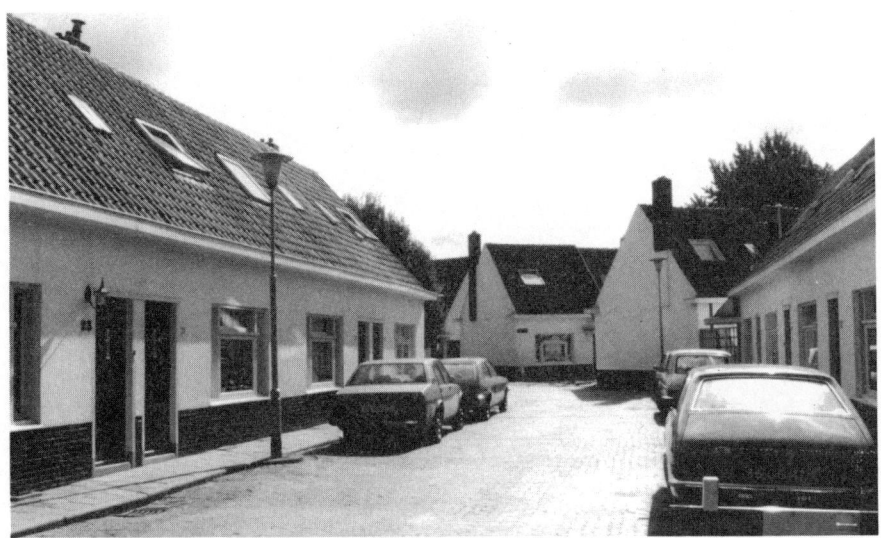

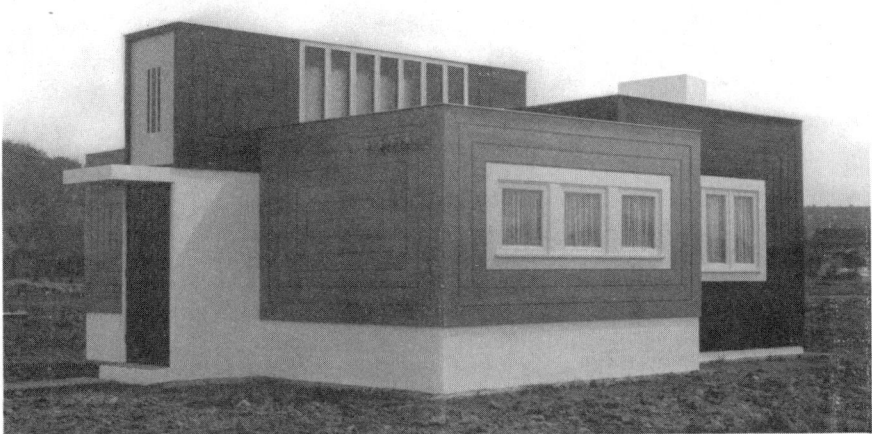

Plate 10 (top). The Witte Dorp, Oud-Mathenesse, The Netherlands. 1922–23. Jacobus Johannes Pieter Oud, Architect. Streetscape. Rotterdam municipality built the "white village" of 343 two-story dwellings as "semi-permanent" housing. The name was derived from the white stuccoed brick walls; the roofs were of terracotta tiles and joinery was painted in primary colors: doors were blue and windows were yellow. Oud's buildings were demolished in the face of public outcry in 1987. Photograph by Donald Langmead, 1987.

Plate 11 (bottom). Site Director's hut, Oud-Mathenesse, The Netherlands. 1923. Jacobus Johannes Pieter Oud, Architect. The little wooden building was the nerve center of the construction site and is one of Oud's two emphatic references to the ideas of De Stijl, in terms of both plasticity and color. Yet in such details as the external cladding one can see references to contemporary pattern and form used by architects of the Amsterdam School. It was rebuilt by a paint company in 1992 at a cost of 100,000 guilders; a year later it was moved to the reconstructed village. © JJP Ko Oud 1912 Beeldrecht. Reproduced by Permission of VI$COPY LTD, Sydney 1998.

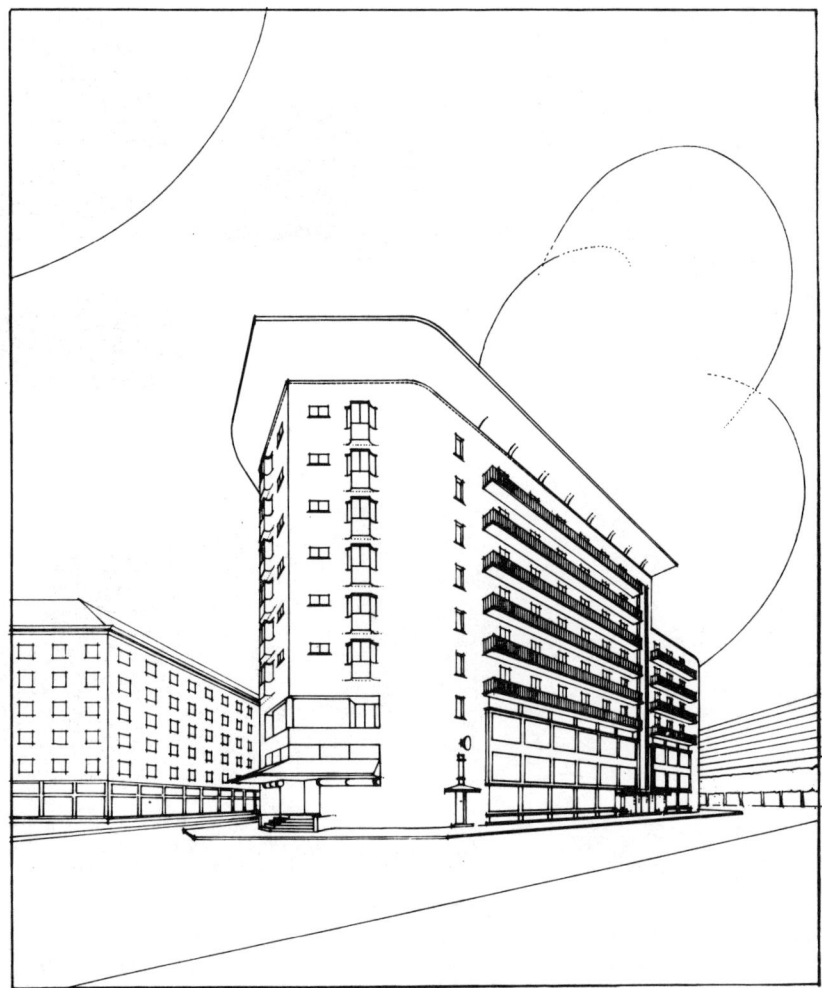

Plate 12. Design for Hotel Stiassni, Brno, Czechoslovakia. 1926. Jacobus Johannes Pieter Oud, Architect. Perspective line drawing. By 1926 Oud had established a reputation in Europe through his writings and lectures, and in April of that year he was commissioned to design a hotel for a difficult, irregular site. The plans were developed in some detail but the project did not proceed past this rather clumsy preliminary scheme. © JJP Ko Oud 1912 Beeldrecht. Reproduced by Permission of VI$COPY LTD, Sydney 1998.

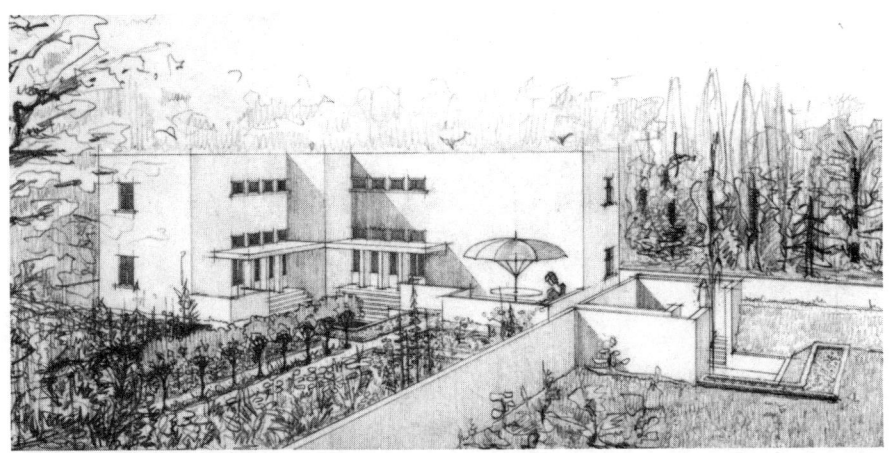

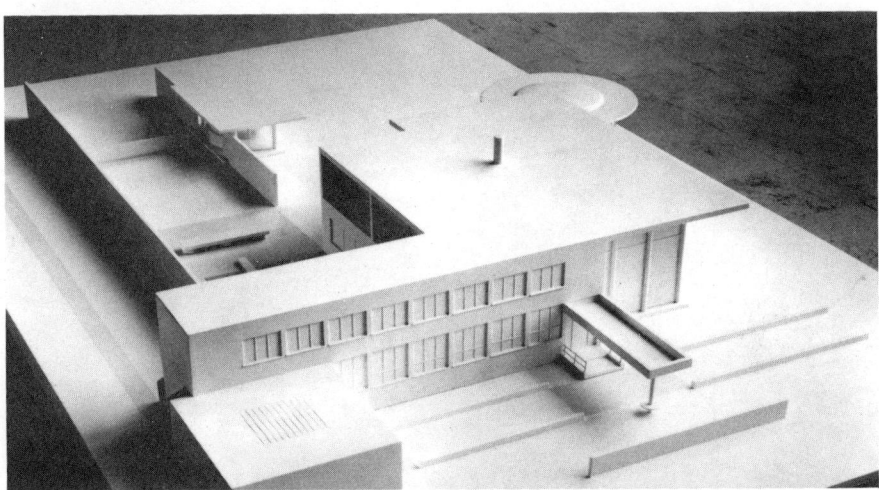

Plate 13 (top). Design for Kallenbach villa, Berlin-Grünewald, Germany. 1922. Jacobus Johannes Pieter Oud, Architect. Perspective drawing. In 1921 Oud successfully participated in a closed competition to design this industrialist's house in an exclusive residential area. The white cubes, the flat roof and the monumental corner entrances to the house from the well-defended garden are all evidence of the architect's search for style. © JJP Ko Oud 1912 Beeldrecht. Reproduced by Permission of VI$COPY LTD, Sydney 1998.

Plate 14 (bottom). Design for Johnson villa, Pinehurst, North Carolina, U.S.A. 1930–31. Jacobus Johannes Pieter Oud, Architect. Photograph of model. Philip Johnson claimed that he set out to become a modern architect after he saw Oud's work in a 1928 journal. Two years later he commissioned the Hollander to design a house in Pinehurst, North Carolina (never realized) for his parents. © JJP Ko Oud 1912 Beeldrecht. Reproduced by Permission of VI$COPY LTD, Sydney 1998.

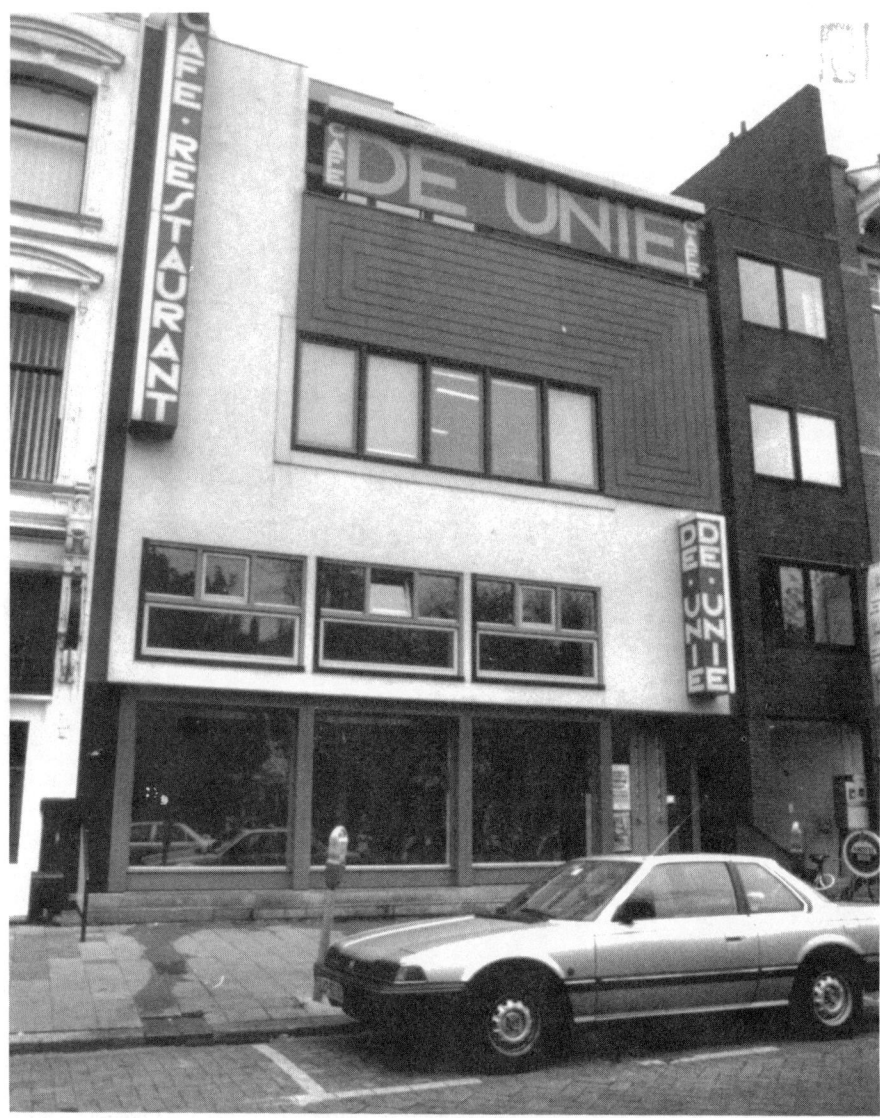

Plate 15. Café De Unie, Mauritsweg 35, Rotterdam, The Netherlands. Jacobus Johannes Pieter Oud, Architect. Reconstructed facade. The original building of 1924, destroyed in the bombing of May 1940, stood in Coolsingel-Calandplein. This replica was built in 1985–86. Together with the site director's hut at Oud-Mathenesse (Plate 11), the facade was an attempt to express De Stijl principles of composition and the use of strong primary colors. The two L-shaped elements are white and red; the upper floor windows are framed in yellow and black, the ground floor windows in blue; the signs are white on a blue ground. Photograph by Donald Langmead, 1990.

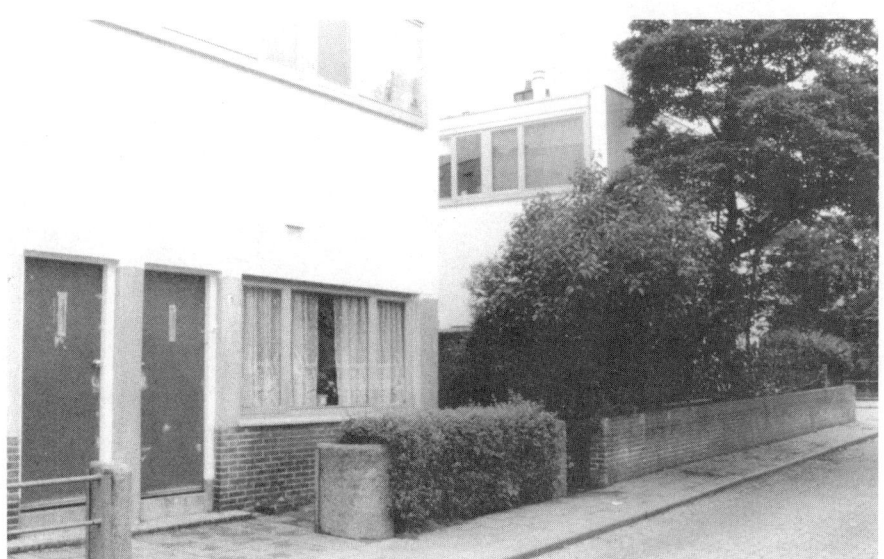

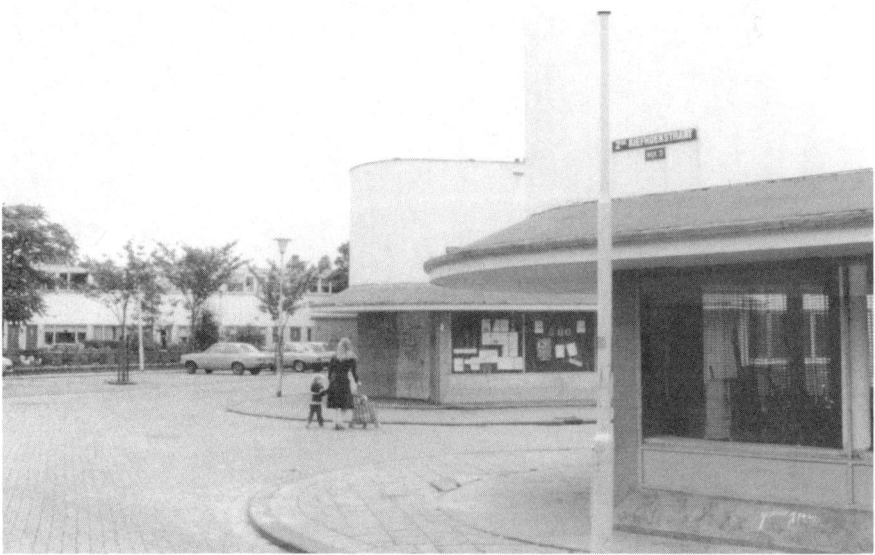

Plate 16 (top). Kiefhoek housing development, Rotterdam, The Netherlands. 1925–29. Jacobus Johannes Pieter Oud, Architect. Detail of house-fronts. The most widely published of all of Oud's designs, the public housing development consisted of 300 houses for workers, built very economically. In 1990–92 architect Wytze Patjin converted each pair of houses into a single dwelling, while generally maintaining their external appearance. Photograph by Donald Langmead, 1981.

Plate 17 (bottom). Kiefhoek housing development, Rotterdam, The Netherlands. 1925–29. Jacobus Johannes Pieter Oud, Architect. shop-houses. the symmetrically-disposed shops form a sort of arrowhead at the main entrance to the project. All have now been restored although the approach taken generated wide debate about the definitions of restoration, renovation, reconstruction and replication. Photogaph by Donald Langmead, 1981.

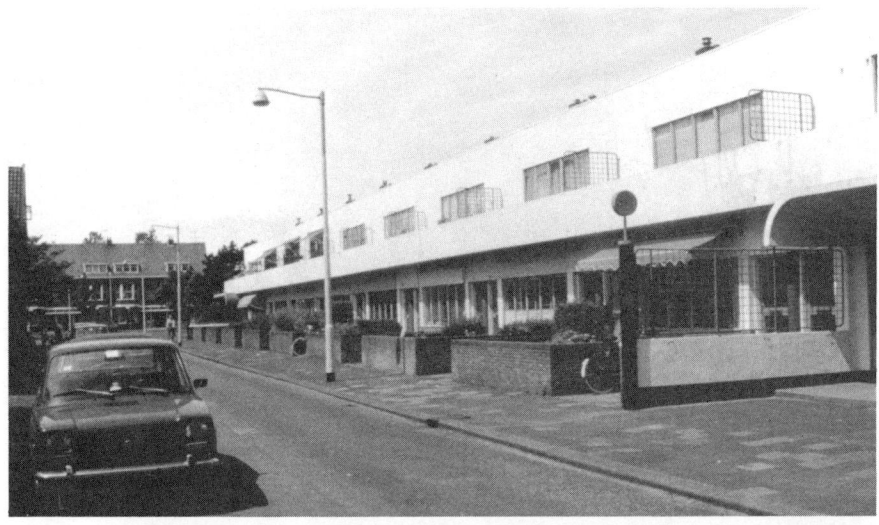

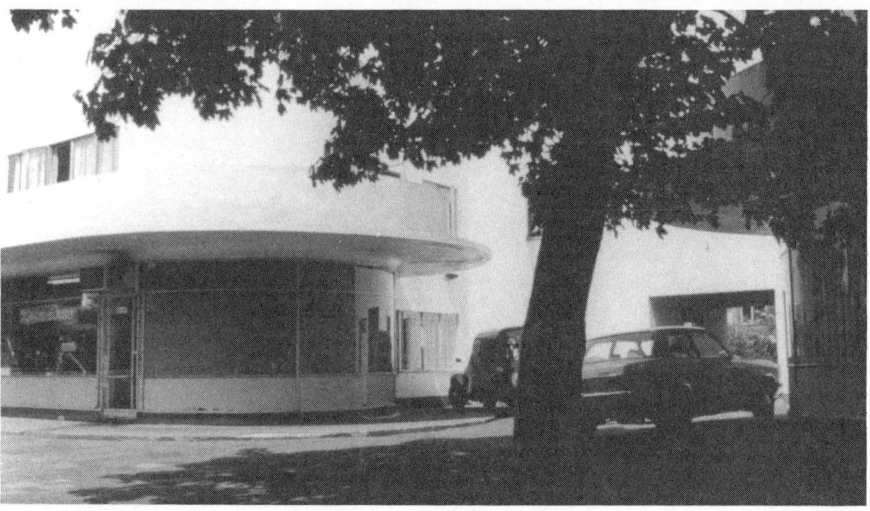

Plate 18 (top). Workers' row houses, 2e Scheepvaartstraat 91–113, Hoek van Holland, The Netherlands. 1924–27. Jacobus Johannes Pieter Oud, Architect. General view looking west. The relatively large houses are built of brick and stuccoed to obtain the smooth finish that characterizes Oud's internationally accepted housing schemes. The Hoek van Holland project was among the most widely published of his buildings. Photograph by Donald Langmead, 1981.

Plate 19 (bottom). Workers' row houses, 2e Scheepvaartstraat 91–113, Hoek van Holland, The Netherlands. 1924–27. Jacobus Johannes Pieter Oud, Architect. Central shops. The two rows of houses are terminated at either end by shops with curved windows—a familiar "New Objectivity" element that must have frustrated Oud's former De Stijl associates—and this pair frames a portal leading to a large public open space behind the houses. Photograph by Donald Langmead, 1981.

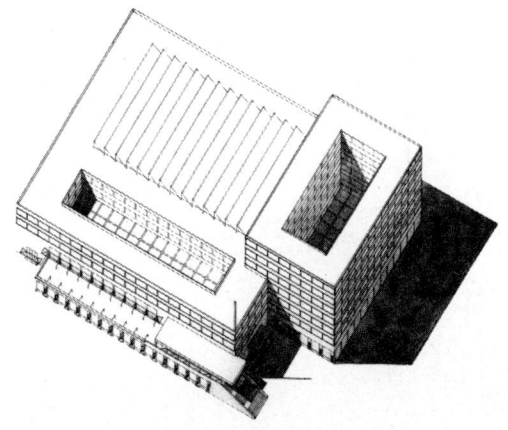

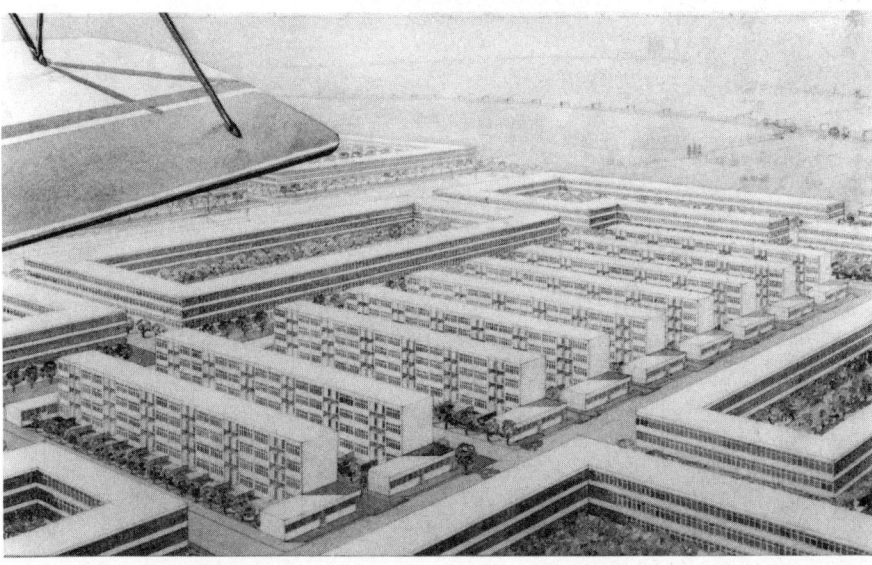

Plate 20 (top). Competition entry, Rotterdam Stock Exchange. 1926. Jacobus Johannes Pieter Oud, Architect. Isometric aerial view. Oud entered the closed competition as a private architect, under the pseudonym "Motto x." Despite his lack of success the austere design contributed to his acceptance among New Objectivists in The Netherlands and beyond. © JJP Ko Oud 1912 Beeldrecht. Reproduced by Permission of VI$COPY LTD, Sydney 1998.

Plate 21 (bottom). Design for Blijdorp housing development, Rotterdam. 1931. Jacobus Johannes Pieter Oud, Architect. Aerial perspective drawing. The characterless barracks-like medium rise buildings, happily never executed, were Oud's last work for the Rotterdam municipality before resigning in 1933. There was even a roof garden, in keeping with international trends. By permission of the Netherlands Architecture Institute. Archive/collection Oud. Reprophotography: RETINA.

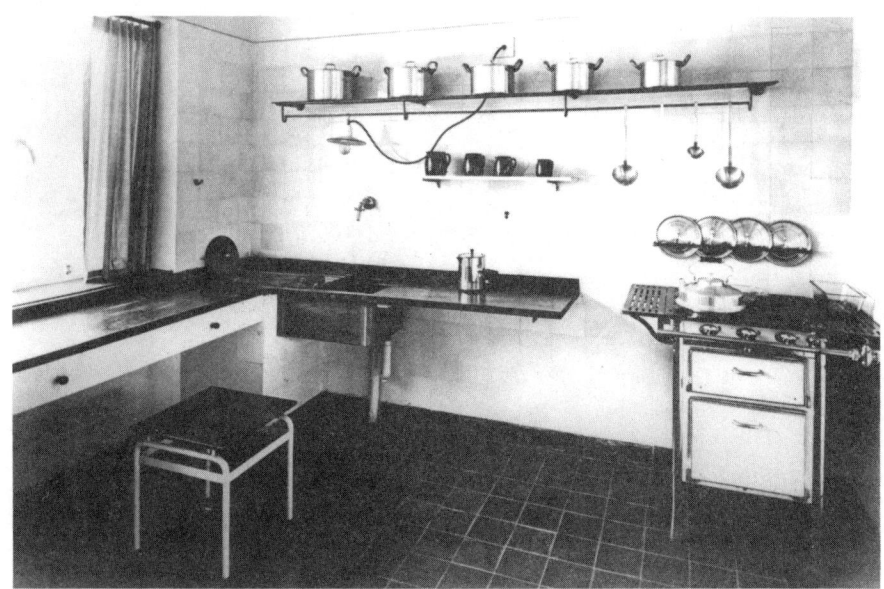

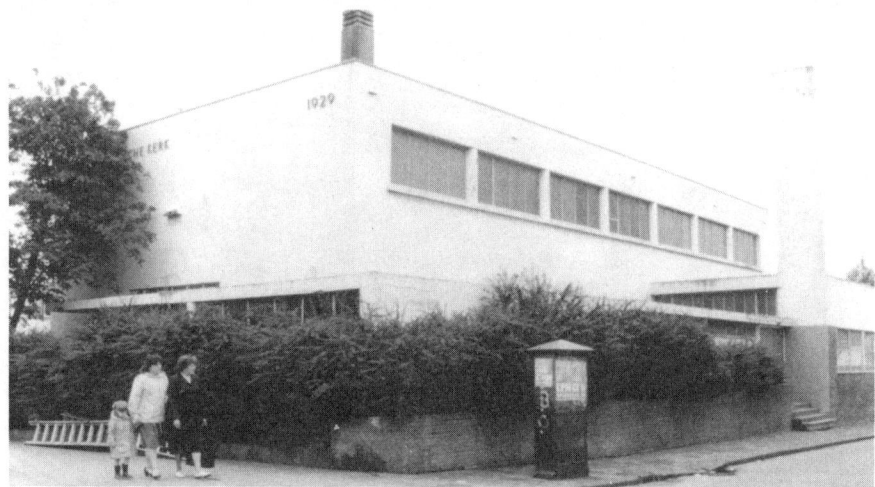

Plate 22 (top). Row houses, Weissenhofsiedlung, Stuttgart, Germany. 1927. Jacobus Johannes Pieter Oud, Architect. Interior of kitchen. In 1926 Oud was invited, among fifteen of Europe's leading architects, to participate in the construction of a model suburban housing estate for an exhibition entitled "The Dwelling," a cooperative venture of the Stuttgart municipality and the *Deutscher Werkbund*. This "rational" and influential kitchen in one of the five row houses he designed was then "state of the art." © JJP Ko Oud 1927 Beeldrecht. Reproduced by Permission of VI$COPY LTD, Sydney 1998.

Plate 23 (bottom). Church for the *Hersteld Apostolische Gemeente*, Eemstein 23, Kiefhoek, Rotterdam, The Netherlands. 1928–29. Jacobus Johannes Pieter Oud, Architect. The church was Oud's first public building in Rotterdam. The cubist forms, whitewashed stuccoed walls and accents of primary colors were all in the spirit of De Stijl. Photograph by Donald Langmead, 1981.

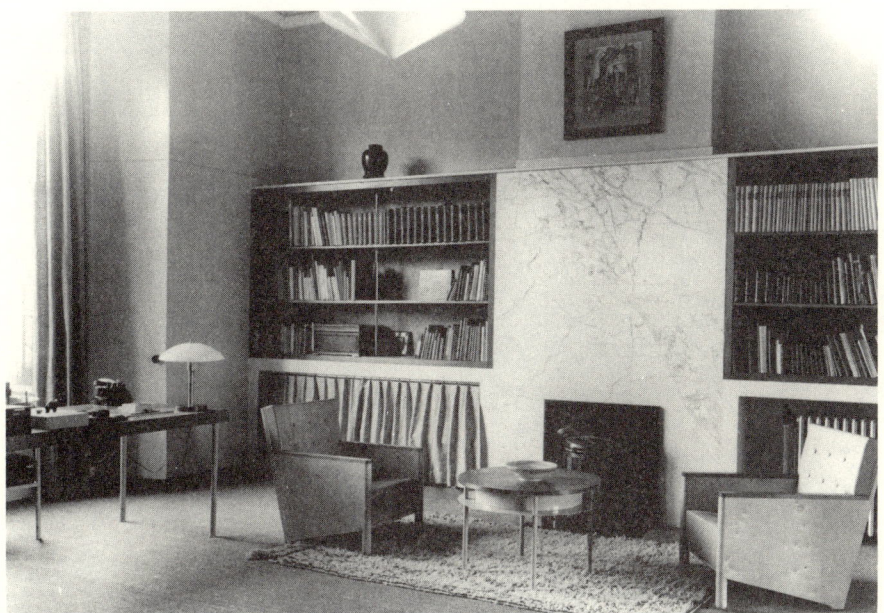

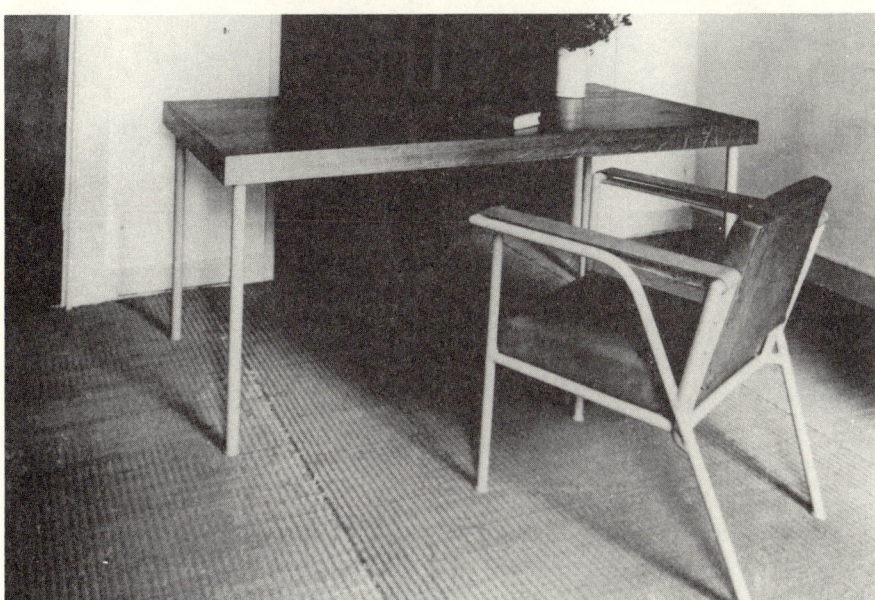

Plate 24 (top). Study interior for M.J.I. de Jonge van Ellemeet, Town Hall, Rotterdam, The Netherlands (now altered). 1930. De Jonge van Ellemeet was then Oud's senior officer in the municipal structure. Jacobus Johannes Pieter Oud, Architect/designer. © JJP Ko Oud 1934 Beeldrecht. Reproduced by Permission of VI$COPY LTD, Sydney 1998.

Plate 25 (bottom). Refurbishment of library interior for D. Hannema, Haringvliet, Rotterdam, The Netherlands. Detail of tubular steel work table and chair. 1934. Jacobus Johannes Pieter Oud, Architect/designer. © JJP Ko Oud 1934 Beeldrecht. Reproduced by Permission of VI$COPY LTD, Sydney 1998.

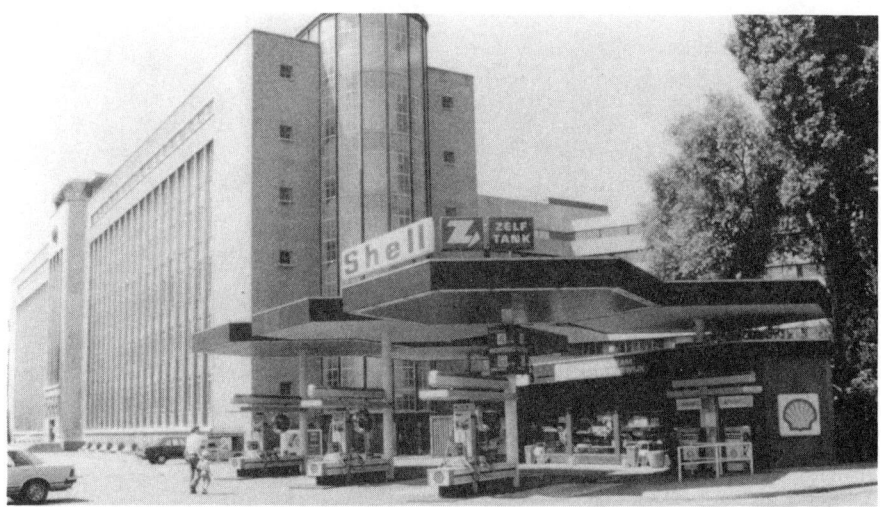

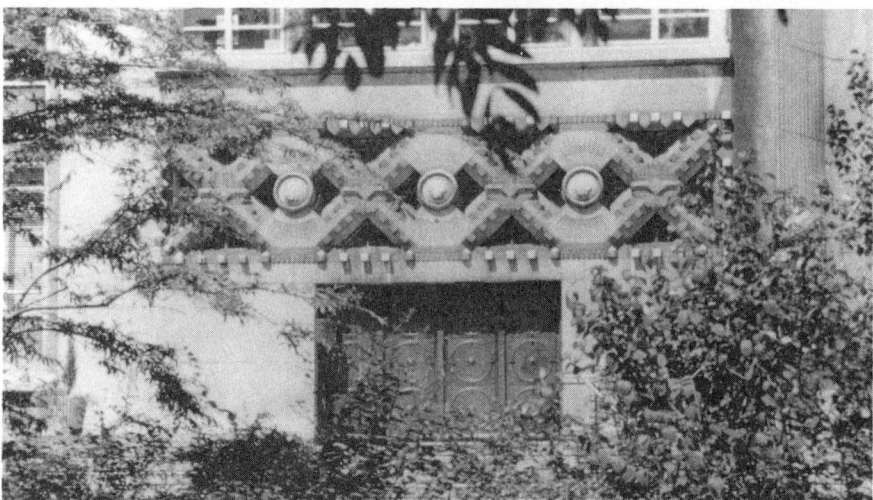

Plate 26 (top). Headquarters Building, B.I.M. (*Bataafsche Import Maatschappij*, later the Shell Co), Wassenaarseweg 80, The Hague, The Netherlands. 1938–42. Jacobus Johannes Pieter Oud, Architect. General view. The building was completed during the German occupation of The Netherlands. Not seen outside of the country until after World War II, it shocked the tranatlantic *aficionados* of International architecture with its abundance of applied decoration, and brought their unjustified censure down upon Oud for forsaking the lofty principles of modernism. Photograph by Donald Langmead, 1981.

Plate 27 (bottom). Headquarters Building, B.I.M. (*Bataafsche Import Maatschappij*, later the Shell Co), Wassenaarseweg 80, The Hague, The Netherlands. 1938–42. Detail of main entrance. Jacobus Johannes Pieter Oud, Architect. In responding to criticism, Oud observed that the building "is an effort to strive again after architecture as a matter of the soul," adding that he "tried to avoid a lot of mistakes such as [he] made in former works which were praised now and then by [his] colleagues from over the Ocean." Photograph by Donald Langmead, 1981.

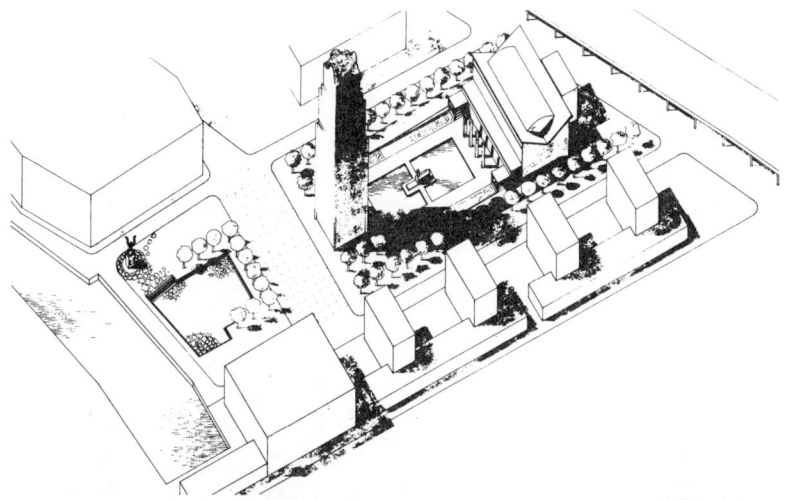

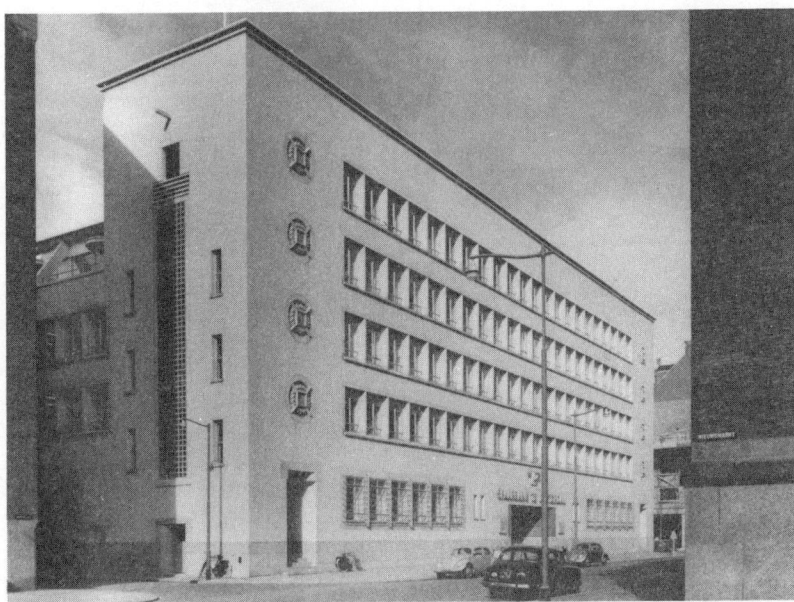

Plate 28 (top). Proposal for redevelopment of St Laurens church and surrounding area, Rotterdam, the Netherlands. 1950. Jacobus Johannes Pieter Oud, Architect. Aerial perspective. An avowed opponent of restoration throughout the post World War II reconstruction era, Oud published this controversial (unrealized) proposal to retain only the tower of the bomb-damaged church and redevelop the site and its surrounds. © JJP Ko Oud 1912 Beeldrecht. Reproduced by Permission of VI$COPY LTD, Sydney 1998.

Plate 29 (bottom). Rotterdam Savings Bank, Botersloot 25, Rotterdam, The Netherlands. 1942–50. Jacobus Johannes Pieter Oud and A. A. van Nieuwenhuizen, Architects. The unremarkable, severely symmetrical building in white glazed bricks replaced offices destroyed in the May 1940 bombing of Rotterdam. © JJP Ko Oud 1950 Beeldrecht. Reproduced by Permission of VI$COPY LTD, Sydney 1998.

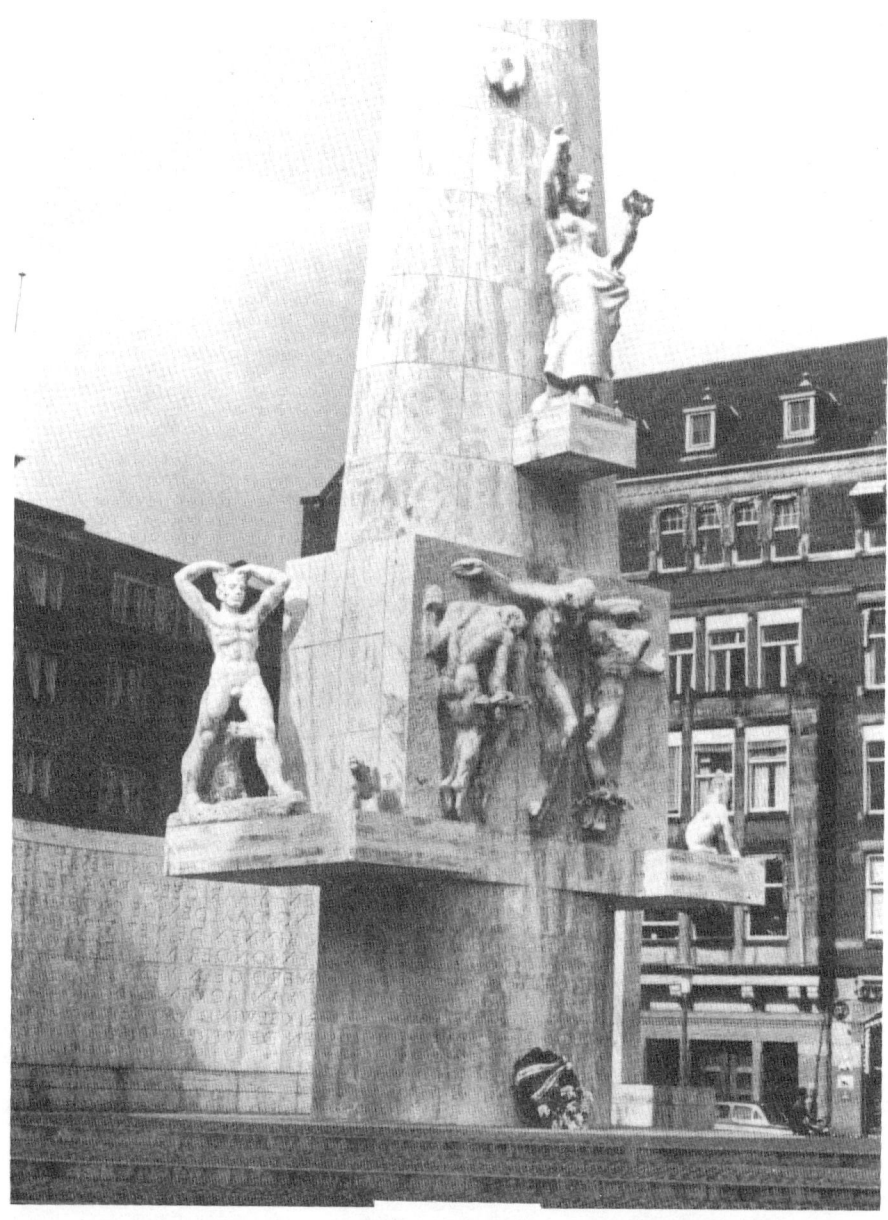

Plate 30. National Monument, Damplein, Amsterdam, The Netherlands. 1949. Jacobus Johannes Pieter Oud, Architect; John Rädecker, Sculptor. Detail of base. The monument stands on concentric circular steps in the center of Amsterdam, facing the sixteenth century palace designed by Jacob van Campen. In 1996 a major restoration was commenced, because of the advanced deterioraiton of the travertine limestone used in the structure. © JJP Ko Oud 1949 Beeldrecht. Reproduced by Permission of VI$COPY LTD, Sydney 1998.

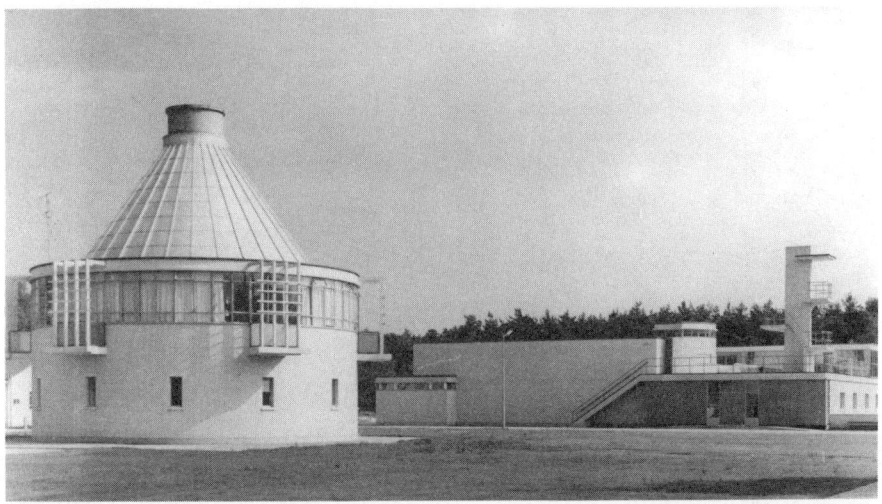

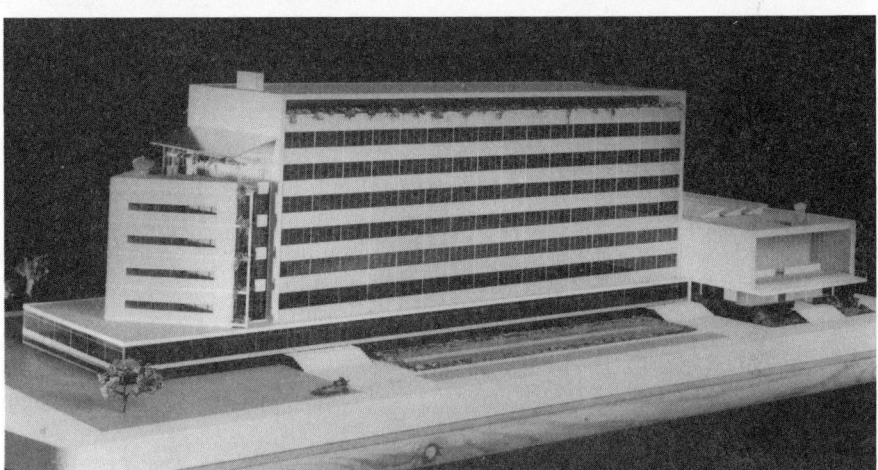

Plate 31. Bioherstellingsord, Wekeromseweg 6, Arnhem, The Netherlands. 1952–60. Jacobus Johannes Pieter Oud, Architect. Boiler house, with sports building and lookout tower in background. Construction of the rehabilitation center for invalid children was financed by a surcharge on cinema tickets, a scheme initiated by the national association of cinema proprietors. The special purpose buildings, all utilitarian in appearance, formed the spine of a formally disposed site, with dormitory blocks for the 120 residents flanking it in forested areas. © JJP Ko Oud 1952–60. Beeldrecht. Reproduced by Permission of VI$COPY LTD, Sydney 1998.

Plate 32. Design for a town hall, Stadhuisplein 1, Almelo, The Netherlands. 1962–73. Jacobus Johannes Pieter Oud, Architect. Photograph of model. The anonymous building was Oud's last design, in what he called his poetic functionalist style. It was executed in 1969–73 under the supervision of Hans Oud and H. Dethmers. © JJP Ko Oud 1962. Beeldrecht. Reproduced by Permission of VI$COPY LTD, Sydney 1998.

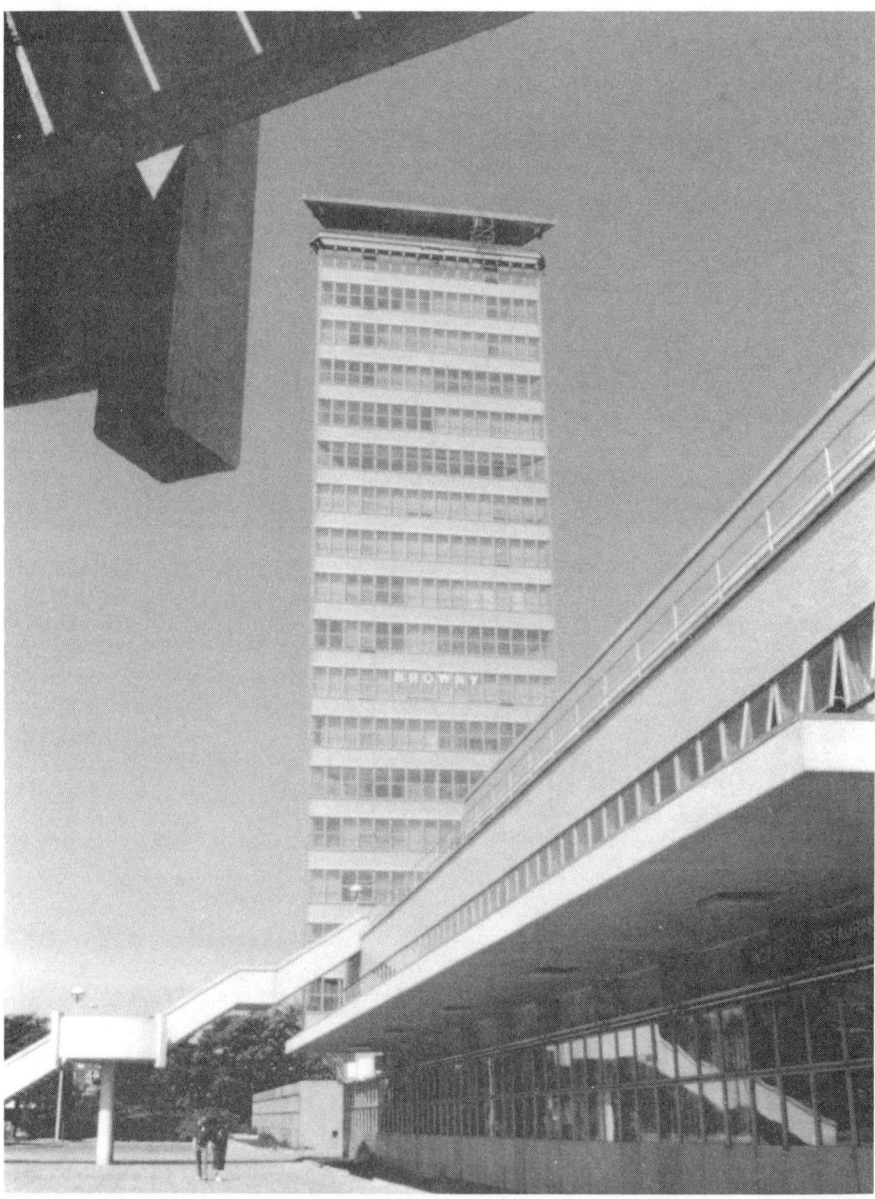

Plate 33. Nederlands Congresgebouw, Churchillplein 10, The Hague, The Netherlands. 1956–69. Jacobus Johannes Pieter Oud and Hans Oud, Architects. View of hotel tower. In the sense of the complexity of its program, the Congress Building is Oud's *magnum opus*, its symmetrical planning redolent of a Roman forum. The center consisted of an exhibition hall, a delegate's hall, a music auditorium and a theater with all their ancillary spaces, as well as the obligatory large open spaces for car parking. Part of his latter day "poetic functionalist" style, it is not his best work. For example, the hotel tower, an equilateral triangular prism (with all the concomitant planning difficulties) and the flying stair propped on a single column border on the mannerist. Photograph by Donald Langmead, 1981.

ANNOTATED BIBLIOGRAPHY

1910-1919

1911
Journals
001. Oud, J.J.P., "Over bouwkunst." *Schuitemakers Purmerender Courant*, 1911, 18 January. Dutch: "About architecture." Oud discusses style in historical and modern architecture, and criticizes historical revivalism.

002. Oud, J.J.P., "Opwekking." *Studenten Weekblad*, 1911, 10 March. Dutch: "Awakening." The short piece encourages cooperation among students at Delft *Technische Hogeschool*. See *ibid.*, 17 March for comments by Oud's peers.

003. Oud, J.J.P., "Arbeiderswoning van J. Emmen." *Technisch Studententijdschrift*, vol 1, 1911, 15 March. Dutch: "Workers' houses by J. Emmen." The piece also mentions the Beet house at Purmerend by Oud himself. Cf. *ibid.*, vol 2, 1912, 1 February, p 28.

1912
Journals
004. Oud, J.J.P., "Schoorsteen in het gebouw der Werkmansvereeniging. 'Vooruit' te Purmerend." *Klei*, vol 4, 1911, pp 338-39. Dutch: "Chimneypiece in the 'Vooruit' Working Men's Association building, Purmerend." In the brick industry journal, a short thorough description accompanies a photograph of the chimneypiece. The panels above the brick dadoes were painted by Jac Jongert.

1913
Journals
005. Oud, J.J.P., "Duitsche kunst." *De Wereld*, 1913, 12 October. Dutch: "German art." Not seen.

006. Oud, J.J.P., "Landhäuser von Hermann Muthesius." *Bouwkundig Weekblad*, vol 33, 1913, p 589. Dutch text, German title. The book review refers to Muthesius' stay in England, and the influences of English domestic architecture on Europe through the publication of *Das Englische Haus* (1906).

007. Oud, J.J.P., "Naar aanleiding van 'Van de Scheepvaarttentoonstelling'." *De Wereld*, 1913, 18 July. Dutch: "Introduction to the Shipping Exhibition." Oud takes issue with an article by H. van Booven. See *ibid.*, 3 October 1913.

008. Oud, J.J.P., "Ons eigen bouwstijl." *Bouwkundig Weekblad*, vol 33, 1913, pp 223-24. Dutch: "Our own architectural style." A letter to the editor criticises an article by G. van Hulzen in *Holland Express*, 5 March 1913.

009. Oud, J.J.P., "Stadsschoon." *Schuitemakers Purmerender Courant*, 1913, 8 June; 3 September. Dutch: "Beauty of cities [idiom]." The piece responds to the published extension plan for Purmerend, Oud's home town.

010. *Klei*, "Woonhuis te Aalsmeer." Vol 5, 1913, 1 November, pp 321-23. Dutch: "Dwelling at Aalsmeer." Abrief description of the construction of the house for Oud's brother Gerrit at 45 Uiterweg, Aalsmeer is accompanied by two views, an elevation and ground floor plan. A German translation in *Nordische Baukunst*, November 1914, p 36 omits the drawings.

1914
Journals
011. Oud, J.J.P., "Bioscooptheater te Purmerend." *Bouwkundig Weekblad*, vol 34, 1914, pp 64-66. Dutch: "Cinema in Purmerend." Most of the short comment praises Willem Brouwer's decorative work on the cinema at 16 Dubbele Buurt. There is a general exterior view, two plans; and a photograph of the monogram on the pilasters, executed in glazed terra cotta

1915
Journals
012. Dudok, Willem Marinus and J.J.P. Oud, "Arbeiderswoning te Leiderdorp," *Bouwkundig Weekblad*, vol 35, 1915, pp 85-87. Dutch; "Workers' housing in Leiderdorp." A letter (June 1915) about the architects' collaborative design of 24 dwellings for the *Dorpsbelang* Housing Association cites cost and rents. Drawings (December 1914) include site plan, street elevations and house types. See Brouwer to the editor, *Leidsche Dagblad*, 19 January 1916, p 2.

013. Oud, J.J.P., "Architecten met de pen." *Bouwkundig Weekblad*, vol 35, 1915, pp 44-45. Dutch: "Architects with the pen." The polemic, dated Leiden 23/1/1915, differentiates between architects who build and those who write and challenges the philosophy of the architectural critic van Hylckama Vlieg.

1916
Journals
014. Oud, J.J.P., "Landhuisje te Blaricum." *Bouwkundig Weekblad*, vol 37, 1916, pp 23-24. Dutch: "Small country house at Blaricum." A few paragraphs illus-

trated by two general views and floor plans describe the building and the evolution of the design of the Mrs. van Essen-Vinckers house. The contractor, G. Dop, is identified.

015. Oud, J.J.P., "De moderne and modernste bouwkunst." *Bouwkundig Weekblad*, vol 37, 1916, pp 341-42. Dutch: "Modern and most modern architecture." The sometimes sarcastic article, dated Leiden, 6 March 1916, defends H.P.Berlage as a founder of modernism against criticism from Michel de Klerk, amongst others. See Frank, "Michel de Klerk (1884-1923), an architect of the Amsterdam School," Columbia University, 1970.

016. Oud, J.J.P., "Over cubisme, futurisme, moderne bouwkunst enz." *Bouwkundig Weekblad*, vol 37, 1916, p 156. Dutch: "On cubism, futurism, modern architecture etc." The article, dated 4 June 1916, is mostly about new developments in painting but links with architecture are established: the confluence of the arts in the "rhythmic relationship of stone to space, in form and color, sound and form." There is a citation from van Doesburg, "De nieuwe beweging in de schilderkunst," originally published in *De Beweging*, vol 12, August 1916 and reprinted as a booklet, 1916.

1917
Journals

017. Doesburg, Theo van, "Bij de bijlagen; II. J.J.P. Oud ontwerp voor een complex van huizen voor een strandboulevard." *De Stijl*, vol 1, 1917, October, pp 11-12, pl 2. Dutch. "Oud's design for a housing complex on an esplanade." A congratulatory piece about the Scheveningen boulevard houses is used as a launching pad for polemic. There is tiny sketch, and an elevation and perspective of the unrealized project. Cf. Huib Hoste, "De Stijl," *De Telegraaf*, 17 November 1917, p 7 and J.P.M[ieras], "*De Stijl,*" *Bouwkundig Weekblad*, vol 38, 1917, p 273.

018. Oud, J.J.P., [Letter to the editor]. *Holland Express*, vol 10, 1917, p 479. Dutch. Oud signed the letter of 29 September 1917 as "collaborator of De Stijl." While couched in the polite Dutch form of address, this is in reality an angry response to a piece by Dirk Roggeveen (*ibid.*, 19 September). For the whole context in sequence see Bernard Canter (editor), "Schilderkunst: vereeniging 'De Sphinx', 1ste tentoonstelling, Leiden," *ibid.*, pp 58-59, 70-71; van Doesburg, "Open brief aan Bernard Canter," *ibid.*, p 441; Canter, [reply to van Doesburg], ibid., pp 441-43; Canter, "Kunst: ter verklaring," *ibid.*, 453-54; Roggeveen, *ibid.*, p 455.

019. Oud, J.J.P., "Gedachten over bouwkunst." *Gedenkboek ter herinnering aan het 10-jaar bestaan der Vereniging van Leerlingen der Rijksnormaalschool van Teekenonderwijzers*, Amsterdam, 1917, pp 36-38. Dutch: "Thoughts on architecture." Not seen. This is a souvenir book of the tenth anniversary of the Student Association of the National School for Art Education, Amsterdam, which Oud attended around 1910.

020. Oud, J.J.P., "Het monumentale stadsbeeld." *De Stijl*, vol 1, 1917, no 1, pp 10-11. Dutch: "The monumental in townscape." Oud's first contribution to the journal, the staccato polemical essay, dated Leiden, 9 July 1917, pleads for integration of the arts, universal esthetic agreement, and the standardization of mass housing. Parts were reprinted *ibid.*, vol 5, 1922, pp 207-08. Also published in Wiekart (ed.), *Ter Wille van een Levende Bouwkunst*, 1962. For Italian and English translations see respectively Polano, "Notes on Oud ...," *Lotus*, no 16, 1977 and Jaffé (ed.), *De Stijl*, London, 1970.

021. S----, "Iets over bouwkunst." *Panorama*, 1917, 30 May, p 4. Dutch: "About architecture." The populist journal publishes images of (i.a.) the Gerrit Oud house, Aalsmeer and the van Essen-Vinckers house, Blaricum.

022. *Nieuwe Rotterdamsche Courant*, "Gezelschap: De Sphinx." 1917, 22 January, p 1. Dutch: "De Sphinx Fellowship." A review of the group's first exhibition in Leiden, 18-31 January mentions the painters, notably Harm Kamerlingh Onnes, and Oud's "tasteful" drawings. See *Leidsch Dagblad*, "Eerste tentoonstelling van 'De Sphinx'," 22 January 1917, p 1 and *Eenheid*, 3 February 1917, p 2.

1918
Journals

023. Doesburg, Theo van, "Aanteekeningen over monumentale kunst ..." *De Stijl*, vol 2, 1918, no 1, pp 10-12. Dutch: "Notes on monumental art ..." While the polemic purports to relate to a photo of the hall of *De Vonk*, in which van Doesburg had a hand, it almost ignores the building. Oud is not mentioned. The plan and exterior are illustrated *ibid.*, no 2, p 20ff. See Gratama, "Vacantiehuis te Noordwijkerhout," *Klei*, vol 12, 15 January 1920, pp 13-19; Hoste, "Het vacantiehuis te Noordwijkerhout," *Telegraaf*, 1 March 1919, avbd, p 2.

024. Hoste, Huib, "Twee villa's aan zee." *Telegraaf*, 1918, 27 April, avbd, p 9. Dutch: "Two seaside villas." The article reviews a villa for B. Ruys at Noordwijk aan Zee (architect, Willem Kromhout, 1916-17) and the rebuilding of the villa *Allegonda*, Katwijk aan Zee by Oud and Menso Kamerlingh Onnes.

025. Oud, J.J.P., "Architectonische beschouwing bij bijlage VIII, woonhuis van Fred C. Robie door F.L.Wright." *De Stijl*, vol 1, 1918, no 4, pp 38-41. Dutch: "Architectural exposition of ... Wright's Robie house." This very important critique demonstrates that Oud understood the pragmatic and formal sources of Wright's domestic architecture, perhaps before anyone else in Europe. The plan of only one floor is reproduced. For not altogether accurate Italian and English translations see respectively Polano, "Notes on Oud ...," *Lotus*, no 16, 1977 and Beckett et al., *The Original Drawings of J.J.P. Oud, 1890-1963*, London, 1963.

026. Oud, J.J.P., "Bouwkunst en normalisatie bij den massabouw." *De Stijl*, vol 1, 1918, no 7, p 77-79. Dutch: "Architecture and standardization of mass building." The essay dated Rotterdam, February-March 1918 rejects historical revivalism and stresses the social, constructional and technological determinants of architectural form to arrive at an acceptable standardized house. For Italian and

English translations see respectively Polano, "Notes on Oud ...," *Lotus,* no 16, 1977; Benton et al., *Form and Function: a Sourcebook for the History of Architecture,* London, 1975.

027. Oud, J.J.P., "Glas in lood van Theo van Doesburg." *Bouwkundig Weekblad,* vol 39, 1918, no 35, pp 199-202. Dutch: "Theo van Doesburg's leadlight." Citing Frank Lloyd Wright on the importance of "light openings," the piece seeks to establish the place of traditional materials and means in the new architecture before appraising several van Doesburg leadlight designs: *Dans I* (1917); *Compositie II* (1917); *Compositie III* (1917); *Compositie V* (1918) and *Motief 'Vrouwekop'* (n.d.). See also Oud to the editor, *ibid.,* p 242.

028. Oud, J.J.P., "Kunst en machine." *De Stijl,* vol 1, 1918, no 3, pp 25-27. Dutch: "Art and the machine." The essay was written in Leiden, December 1917. Some ideas are developed in Oud's later Robie house critique (025) but the piece indicates an awakening to the possibilities and inevitability of a machine based culture and a machine esthetic. Also published in Wiekart (ed.), *Ter Wille van een Levende Bouwkunst,* 1962. For Italian and English translations see respectively Polano, "Notes on Oud ...," *Lotus,* no 16, 1977 and Jaffé (ed.), *De Stijl,* London, 1970, pp 96-98. Cf. Oud, "Kunst, Handwerk und Maschine," *Thuringer Allgemeine Zeitung,* vol 75, 1924, no 190, p 6.

029. Oud, J.J.P., "Verbouwing Huize 'Allegonda', Katwijk aan Zee." *Bouwkundig Weekblad,* vol 39, 1918, p 29. Dutch: "Rebuilding the villa *Allegonda,* Katwijk aan Zee." The piece simply describes the project.

1919
Books and Monographs
030. Doesburg, Theo van, *Drie Voordrachten over de Nieuwe Beeldende Kunst: haar ontwikkeling, aesthetisch beginsel en toekomstigen stijl,* Amsterdam, 1919. Dutch: *Three Lectures on the New Visual Art...* Published by the *Maatschappij voor Goede en Goedkoope Lectuur,* the small book reprints "De ontwikkeling der moderne schilderkunst," "Het aethetische beginsel der moderne beeldende kunst" and "De stijl der toekomst," all of 1916. Van Doesburg uses the interiors of *De Vonk* to illustrate one of the lectures, without mentioning Oud. There are explanatory notes and images at the back. See also *De Stijl,* 1919, no 1, pp 10-12.

Journals
031. Doesburg, Theo van, "Grondbegrippen der nieuwe beeldende kunst, 1915-1918." *Tijdschrift voor Wijsgebeerte,* vol 13, 1919, pp 30-49 and 169-88. Dutch: "Underlying principles of the new visual art." The title describes the content, from van Doesburg's point of view. Part II deals with Oud's cubism and reprints his correspondence with van Doesburg. The villa *Allegonda* and the Spangen and Tusschendijken houses are illustrated. Facsimile, *Grondbegrippen der Nieuwe Beeldende Kunst,* Nijmegen 1983, edited by Cees Boekraad et al. with a postscript by Boekraad (illustrations of *De Vonk* and a discussion of the Oud-van Doesburg relationship) and correspondence between van Doesburg and Laszlo

Moholy-Nagy, 1922-32. The content also appeared as *Bauhausbucher 6: Grundbegriffe der neuen gestaltenden Kunst*, Munich, 1925 (reprinted Mainz and Berlin 1966, ed. Hans Wingler, with an afterword by Hans L.Jaffé). Published in English as *Principles of Neoplastic Art*, Greenwich, Conn., 1968 and London, 1969.

032. Oud, J.J.P., "Architectonische beschouwingen." *De Stijl*, vol 2, 1919, no 7, pp 79-84. Dutch: "Architectural exposition." The first section, "Mass building and street architecture" addresses matters Oud had tackled in "Bouwkunst en normalisatie bij den massabouw," using his unrealized 1918 design for workers' flats as an exemplar. There are small plans, elevation and a perspective drawing. "Reinforced concrete and architecture" lauds the potential of the new material; Oud's ideas are applied to a comprehensively illustrated but clumsy Wrightian design for a double workers' dwelling, also unrealized.

033. Oud, J.J.P., "Dr H.P. Berlage und sein Werk." *Kunst und Kunsthandwerk*, vol 22, 1919, no 6-8, pp 189-228. German: "Dr H.P. Berlage and his work." An extensive, adulatory essay is accompanied by excellent photographs and drawings of Berlage's work.

034. Oud, J.J.P., "Boekbespreking. Dr. Otto Grautauff, *Formzertrümmerung und Formaufbau in der bildenden Kunst* [book review]." *De Stijl*, vol 2, 1919, no 10, pp 113-14. Dutch: "Book review ..." The short piece recommends the book but carefully places recent German achievements in the visual arts in the shadow of Holland, De Stijl and Mondrian.

035. Oud, J.J.P., "Orientatie." *De Stijl*, vol 3, 1919, no 2, p 13. Dutch: "Orientation." This typical polemic is about artistic unity, not yet achieved in architectureas it had been in the design of machines.

1920-1929

1920
Journals
036. Doesburg, Theo van, "Aanteekeningen bij de bijlagen VI en VII." *De Stijl*, vol 3, 1920, October, pp 44-46. Dutch: "Notes on attachments VI and VII." Attachment VI is a perspective of Oud's design for the Purmerend factory; VII is of furniture by Rietveld. The polemic says little of either except to inaccurately point out that Oud is free of Wright's influence.

037. Gratama, Jan, "Vacantiehuis te Noordwijkerhout." *Klei*, vol 12, 1920, 15 January, pp 13-19. Dutch: "Holiday house, Noordwijkerhout." The well-illustrated piece cobbles together several sources, including Oud's description, most of his "Orientatie," *De Stijl*, 1919, no 2, p 13 and excerpts from van Doesburg, *ibid.*, 1919, no 1, pp 10-12. Gratama comments on *zeitgeist*. See *Klei*, 8 January 1920, pp 6-7 for interior photographs, also from *De Stijl*.

038. Oud, J.J.P., "Architectonische beschouwing bij bijlage III." *De Stijl*, vol 3, 1920, no 3, p 25. Dutch: "Architectural exposition of attachment III." There is a clear if prejudiced and sentimental critique (dated Rotterdam, 5 January 1920) of the Futurists, especially Antonio Sant'Elia, based of course upon images alone.

039. Oud, J.J.P., "Het bouwen van woningen in (gewapend) beton." *Bouwkundig Weekblad*, vol 41, 1920, pp 89-94; 131-36. Dutch: "Building (reinforced) concrete houses." In 1920 Oud studied system building in Denmark, Germany and England, where he attended the *Daily Mail* Ideal Home Exhibition in February. The first instalment, dated 16 March and published 10 April, reports on the German *Schnellbau Kossel* system, used in workers' housing. The other, dated

May 1920, covers the English *Dorlonco* steel framed system, and aspects of American technology including the cement gun and *Kahn Pressed Steel Construction*. See also "Betonbouw in Duitschland," *Vaderland*, 17 April 1920, where Oud is partly cited and Oud, "De Building Exposition te Londen," *Tijdschrift for Volkshuisvesting*, vol 1, 1920, pp 97-98.

040. Oud, J.J.P., "Gemeentelijke volkswoningen, polder 'Spangen' te Rotterdam." *Bouwkundig Weekblad*, vol 41, 1920, pp 219-22. Dutch: "Public housing in the Spangenpolder, Rotterdam." The piece provides information about blocks I and V, designed August 1918 and completed April 1920. There is a block plan and plans of housing types, a view along Potgieterstraat and one of a living room interior furnished by Rietveld (see also *Wonen-TA/BK*, vol 6, 1978, no 4, p 10.)

041. *Lumière*, [Photographs of *De Vonk*.] Vol 1, 1920, April, loose plate. French.

042. *De Stijl*, "Ontwerp for een entrepôt met stokerij door J.J.P. Oud. Bijlage no 12." Vol 3, 1920, no 11, p 97. Dutch: "Bonded warehouse and distillery. Attachment 12." Images only (plan, elevations, halftone perspective drawing) of the designs for buildings at Purmerend.

1921
Books and Monographs
043. Berlage, Hendrik Petrus, Arnie Keppler, Willem Kromhout and Jan Wils (eds.), *Arbeiderswoningen in Nederland*, Rotterdam, 1921. Dutch: *Workers' Houses in The Netherlands*. In an overview, Wils introduces a well-illustrated collation of 50 government subsidized housing schemes including Leiderdorp (Dudok and Oud), comparing areas, amenity and costs.

044. Kloot Meijburg, Herman van der, *Landhuisbouw in Nederland*, Amsterdam, 1921. Dutch: *Country Houses in Holland*. The 2 volume work is a kind of manual for country house design. After dealing with the subject in pragmatic sections it illustrates many examples, mostly from the twentieth century. The villa *Allegonda* is included. Cf. Herman van der Kloot Meijburg, *Bouwkunst in de Stad en op het Land*, Rotterdam, 1917 (revised 1930.)

Journals
045. Behne, Adolf, "Architekten." *Frühlicht*, no 2, 1921, winter. German. The general article refers to Oud and illustrates both projects for the Purmerend distillery. Reprinted *Frühlicht 1920-22*, Frankfurt am Main/Berlin, 1963.

046. Oud, J.J.P., "Naar de aanleiding van de Amsterdamsche tentoonstelling voor Woninginrichting." *Tijdschrift voor Volkshuisvesting*, vol 2, 1922, no 7-8, pp 196-99. Dutch: "Introduction to the Amsterdam exhibition of domestic furnishing." The piece is just that.

047. Oud, J.J.P., "Over de toekomstige bouwkunst en hare architectonische mogelijkheden." *Bouwkundig Weekblad*, vol 42, 1921, pp 147-60. Dutch: "On future architecture and its architectonic possibilities." This is the first publication of Oud's basic philosophy, presented as a lecture to the Rotterdam group Opbouw

in February 1921. Voicing frustration at the persistence of architectural formalism, and seemingly overawed by progress and the potential of the machine, Oud expects imminent change. Condemning ornament as the "universal panacea for architectural impotence," he predicts an architecture whose "constructive functionalism attains to beauty." Illustrations include the interior of *De Vonk* and the Purmerend factory design. Reprinted as a booklet. There is a response by Brouwer, *ibid.*, 1921, p 175. The lecture was reported in *Nieuwe Rotterdamsche Courant*, 9 March 1921, p 1; 11 March, p 1. See also *Frühlicht*, no 4, 1922, pp 113-18 (reprinted *Frühlicht 1920-22*, Frankfurt am Main/Berlin, 1963); *Baukunst*, May 1925, pp 98-101; *La Cité,* 1923, no 5, pp 73-85; *Stavba*, 1922, no 10, pp 177-192 and "Architecture and the future," *Studio,* 1928, pp 401-06. The piece was included in Oud, *Holländische Architektur*, Munich, 1926 and reprinted in Wiekart (ed.), *Ter Wille van een Levende Bouwkunst*, 1962 and in part in *Forum,* vol 6, 1951, no 5-6. See also Oud, "Bouwen zonder makeup," *Groene Amsterdammer*, 29 October 1949.

1922
Books and Monographs
048. Leliman, J.H.W. and K. Sluyterman, *Het Moderne Landhuis in Nederland*, The Hague, 1922. Dutch: *The Modern Country House in Holland*. A collection of images and plans of 200 houses includes villa *Allegonda*.

049. Oud, J.J.P., *Het Hofplein-plan van Dr Berlage*, Zwolle, 1922. Dutch: *Dr Berlage's Plan for Hofplein*. Part 1 of a *Nederlandse Instituut voor Volkshuisvesting* series on town planning reviews Berlage's 1922 proposal (his second was in 1927) to redevelop the Rotterdam city square. There are plans, street elevations and perspectives. For a slightly fuller discussion of the project see Egbert J. Hoogenberk, *Het Idee van het Hollandse Stad*, Delft, 1980, pp 145 ff.

Journals
050. Behne, Adolf, "Holländische Baukunst in der Gegenwart." *Wasmuths Monatshefte für Baukunst*, 1922, vol 1, no 1-2, pp 1-33. German: "Contemporary Dutch architecture." A short essay introduces a plethora of images, including Oud's design for the Purmerend factory; interiors of *De Vonk*; Spangen housing; the Scheveningen boulevard designs; and exteriors of villa *Allegonda*.

051. Gratama, Jan, "Een oordeel over de hedendaagsche bouwkunst in Nederland." *Bouwwereld,* vol 21, 1922, pp 217-19. Dutch: "A trial of contemporary architecture in Holland." The article reprints fragments of a lecture from the Belgian journal *De Bouwgids.* A derogatory paragraph naming Oud ("not greatly talented") as "forerunner" of cubism in architecture provoked extended debate. See van Doesburg's petulant, "De architect J.J.P. Oud, 'voorganger' der 'Kubisten' in de bouwkunst?" *ibid.*, p 229; Oud's response, "Bouwkunst en kubisme," *ibid.*, p 245, each with the editor's reply and "Het kubisme voor het laatst," *ibid.,* p 270.

052. Oud, J.J.P., [Review of *Het Woonhuis: Zijn Bouw* by Jan Wils]. *Telegraaf,* 1922, 8 June, avbd p 9.

053. Oud, J.J.P., "Het Haagse raadhuis." *Telegraaf*, 1922, 18 June, 3rd blad, p 9. Dutch: "The Hague town hall." This is a lengthy discussion of the appropriate location of the proposed building. A competition held for the Alexanderveld site in 1932-34 was discontinued; Oud, ill at the time, did not enter.

054. Oud, J.J.P., "Ontwerp voor een woonhuis in Berlijn." *Bouwkundig Weekblad*, vol 43, 1922, p 341. Dutch: "Design for a house in Berlin." Oud's unrealized Kallenbach house project in Berlin-Grünewald won a closed competition, in which Walter Gropius, Adolf Meyer and Ludwig Hilberseimer were among invited entrants. The piece provides a description and rationale, with plans, elevations, site plan and a perspective, all annotated in German.

055. Oud, J.J.P., "Uitweiding bij eenige afbeeldingen." *Bouwkundig Weekblad*, vol 43, 1922, p 418. Dutch: "Enlarging upon a few illustrations." Beginning by summarizing the character of German architecture either side of World War I, much of the essay (dated Rotterdam, October 1922) deals with the designs and writings of Bruno Taut and the Expressionists, especially Carl Krayl.

056. Starý, Oldrich, "Nazory na moderní architekturu." *Stavba*, vol 1, 1922, p 125. Czechoslovakian. Oud is mentioned in a review of contemporary European literature on modern architecture; his February 1921 lecture to Opbouw is cited. The latter is translated in *Stavba*, vol 1, 1922, pp 177-92.

057. Stockmeyer, Ernst, "Monumentale Miethaus-Architektur in Holland." *Schweizerische Bauzeitung,* vol 80, 1922, pp 257-59. German: "The monumental architecture of flat buildings ..." Spangen is used as an example in a discussion of the esthetic questions associated with the building type. There are exterior views.

1923
Books and Monographs
058. Wattjes, Jannes Gerhardus, *Nieuw-Nederlandsche Bouwkunst,* Amsterdam, 1924. Dutch: *New Dutch Architecture.* A second part appeared in 1926, a single volume edition in 1929. A brief essay introduces nearly 200 views and floor plans of contemporary Dutch "isms." Oud's designs for the Kallenbach house and the Purmerend factory are in the earlier editions. In the 1929 version only the Hoek van Holland houses appear. Reviewed Mieras, *Bouwkundig Weekblad*, 1927, p 373 and C.M., *ibid.*, 1929, p 391; *De Kroniek*, 1927, p 18; *Ingenieur*, 1927, p 71; *R.K.Bouwblad*, 1929-30, p 224; *Bouwbedrijf*, 1924, p 12; *ibid.*, 1929, p 466.

Journals
059. Behne, Adolf, "De 'Bauhaus'-tentoonstelling te Weimar." *Klei*, vol 15, 1923, pp 245-53. Dutch: "The Bauhaus exhibition at Weimar." A review of the catalytic *Art and Technics* exhibition mentions Oud's "admirable" 17 August lecture about the development of modern architecture in Holland. See Taverne, "De architect en de huisvrouw," *NRC-Handelsblad*, 13 May 1983; de Wit, *ibid.*, 13 May 1983. Cf. Oud, "Huisvrouwen en architecten," *i10*, 1927, pp 44-47 (Reprinted Lehning and Schrofer, *De Internationale Avant-Garde tussen de Twee Wereldoorlogen*, The Hague, 1963.)

060. Brunius, A., "Tradition och Modernism." *Göteborgs Handels och Selfarts Tidning*, 6 August 1923. Swedish: "Tradition and modernism." Not seen.

061. Hilbersheimer, Ludwig, "De wille zur architektur." *Das Kunstblatt*, 1923, pp 133-40. German: "The will towards architecture." Not seen.

062. Hilbersheimer, Ludwig, "J.J.P. Ouds Wohnungsbauten." *Das Kunstblatt*, 1923, pp 289-93. October. German: "Oud's residential buildings." Not seen.

063. Jakstein, Werner, "Weltbaukunst." *Deutschen Übersee-Zeitung*, 1923, 12 August, p 5. German: "World architecture." In a polemic on the emergence international architecture, Oud's design for the Kallenbach house is illustrated.

064. Oud, J.J.P., "Bij een Deensch ontwerp voor de *Chicago Tribune*." *Bouwkundig Weekblad*, vol 44, 1923, p 456. Dutch: "About a Danish design for the *Chicago Tribune*." A review of Knud Lønberg-Holm's entry in the 1922 competition.

065. Oud, J.J.P., "Gemeentelijke woningbouw 'Spangen' te Rotterdam." *Bouwkundig Weekblad*, vol 44, 1923, pp 15-20. Dutch: "Municipal public housing block 'Spangen' in Rotterdam." This well-illustrated description and rationale (dated December 1922) of Oud's designs for blocks VIII and IX includes plans of housing types, site plans, external view and a photo of a typical fireplace. See Oud, "Gemeentelijke woningbouw in 'Spangen' en 'Tusschendijken'," *Rotterdamsche Jaarboekje*, 1924, pp XLIX-LV.

066. Oud, J.J.P., "Geschakelde aforismen over kunst en bouwkunst." *Het Overzicht*, no 15, 1923, March-April, p 41. Dutch: "Various maxims about art and architecture." Not seen.

067. Oud, J.J.P., "In Memoriam K.P.C.de Bazel." *Bouwkundig Weekblad*, vol 44, 1923, p 513-14. Dutch. This is one of several obituaries (dated 6 December 1923) in a special edition. Cited in part *Forum,* vol 6, 1951, no 5-6.

068. Stam, Mart, "Holland und die Baukunst unserer Zeit." *Schweizerische Bauzeitung,* vol 82, 1923, pp 225-29. German: "Holland and the architecture of our times." The second article in a series (see *ibid.*, p 118) illustrates Oud's design for standardized workers' housing.

069. Veissière, Gabriel, "Les architectes du groupe 'Stijl'." *L'Architecture*, vol 34, 1923, p 370. Not seen. French.

070. *Groot-Rotterdam*, "Gemeentelijke woningbouw 'Oud-Mathenesse'." Vol 1, 1923, 28 September, p 427. Dutch: "Municipal housing at Oud-Mathenesse." Illustrations only: six rare views of the construction of the Witte Dorp.

1924
Books and Monographs
071. Steur, A.J. van der (ed.), *Het Stadwoonhuis in Nederland gedurende de Laatste 25 Jaren*, The Hague, 1924. Dutch: *The Townhouse in the Netherlands*

during the Last 25 Years. This revises and enlarges the volume by J.H.W. Leliman, The Hague, 1920. Oud was not included in the original edition but his Spangen housing blocks VIII and IX are here illustrated with plans and exterior views. Reviewed Wils, *Bouwbedrijf,* 1924, p 131.

072. *Jaarboek van Nederlandse Ambachts- en Nijverheidskunst 1923-1924,* Rotterdam, 1924. Illustration only: site office, Oud-Mathenesse.

Journals
073. Badovici, Jean, "Entretiens sur l'architecture vivante." *L'Architecture Vivante,* 1924, spring/summer, pp 30-34. French. Illustrations of Oud-Mathenesse.

074. Badovici, Jean, "Entretiens sur l'architecture vivante: la couleur dans la nouvelle architecture." *L'Architecture Vivante,* 1924, spring/summer, pp 17-18. French: "... Color in the new architecture." French. The essay is cross-referred to plates 18-21 and 34-37 of the Oud-Mathenesse director's shed and designs for workers' dwellings, the Purmerend factory and the Kallenbach villa.

075. Hilbersheimer, Ludwig, "J.J.P. Oud." *Stavba,* vol 3, 1924, no 5, pp 95-96. Czechoslovakian. Not seen.

076. Meyer, P., "Die Entwicklung der Moderne Baukunst in Holland; Vergangenheit, Gegenwart, Zukunft." *Schweizerische Bauzeitung,* vol 83, 1924, pp 134-37. German: "The development of modern architecture in Holland: past, present and future." This reports Oud's lecture to the Zurich Association of Architects and Engineers, 27 February 1924. See Oud, *Holländische Architektur,* 1926. Cf. "L'evolution de l'architecture moderne aux Pays-Bas," *Stavba,* vol 3, 1924, p 96. See also "Architect J.J.P. Oud te Praag," Nieuwe Rotterdamsche Courant, 1 December 1924, summarizing Oud's lecture to the Stavba Architectural Association, Prague, 26 November 1924. The talk was also given in Berlin, 21 January 1923; at the Weimar Bauhaus, 17 August 1923; and in Rotterdam, 16 October 1923.

077. M-----, M.J.J., "Het Witte Dorp." *Spangen,* vol 3, 1924, 25 September, p 20. Dutch: "The Witte Dorp." The letter to the editor (19 September 1924) defends criticism of the housing estate by one van de B—, in the previous number .

078. Okada, Takoa, Sutemi Hougichi et al., *Sinkentiku,* 1924, 22 March, no 2. Japanese. The issue of the pocketbook format journal is dedicated to Oud's work and includes translations of articles by him. There are 33 illustrations.

079. Oud, J.J.P., "Antwoord van J.J.P. Oud." *Bouwkundig Weekblad,* vol 45, 1924, p 50. Dutch: "Oud's answer." Oud's verbose answer (i.a.) was to a four part question about esthetic monitors proposed for Dutch cities. Results of the whole enquiry can be found in "Schoonheids-commissies," *ibid.,* pp 26-27; 44-52.

080. Oud, J.J.P., "Semi-permanente woningbouw Oud-Mathenesse..." *Bouwkundig Weekblad,* vol 45, 1924, p 418-21. Dutch: "Semi-permanent housing ..." The informative article identifies the contractor, dates the project and describes

materials and construction in detail. There are clear general views, tied to a site plan, and drawings sufficient to explain the estate.

081. Oud, J.J.P., "*Vers une Architecture* van Le Corbusier-Saugnier." *Bouwkundig Weekblad*, vol 45, 1924, pp 90-94. Dutch. This review brought Le Corbusier to the notice of Dutch architects. There are several citations in French. Five illustrations are reproduced. Cf. *De Stijl*, vol 6, 1924, p 109.

082. Oud, J.J.P., "Kromhout en zijn tentoonstelling." *Nieuwe Rotterdamsche Courant*, 1924, avbd B, p 1. Dutch: "Kromhout and his exhibition." This review of a retrospective exhibition of the work of the Amsterdam architect Willem Kromhout (1864-1940) was written on the occasion of his 60th birthday.

083. Oud, J.J.P., "Kunst, Handwerk und Maschine." *Thuringer Allgemeine Zeitung*, vol 75, 1924, no 190, p 6. German: "Art, handwork and machine." Not seen, but cf. "Kunst en machine." *De Stijl*, vol 1, 1918, no 3, pp 25-27.

084. Teige, Karel, "De Stijl a Hollandská moderna." *Stavba*, vol 3, 1924, no 2, pp 33-41. Czechoslovakian: "De Stijl and modernism in Holland." The piece discusses De Stijl *in toto*, then by architect. There are views of the Pieterlangendijktraat facade of the Spangen houses, and the Oud-Mathenesse site office.

085. Vaillat, Léandre, "Le visage moderne de la Hollande." *Illustration*, 1924, 8 November, pp 420-23. French: "The modern face of Holland." In a general article about contemporary Dutch architecture, Oud is called a "remarkable theoretician." Reviewed *Architectura*, 1924, p 113.

086. Kamerlingh Onnes, Menso and J.J.P. Oud, "Maison dans les dunes." *L'Architecture Vivante,* 1924, winter, pl 43-44. French. Illustrations of *Allegonda*.

087. *De Reserveboezem*, "'Het Witte Dorp'." Vol 3, 1924, no 33, p 1. Dutch. The parochial paper prints a short eulogy of the Oud-Mathenesse housing scheme, praising Oud for the healthy quality of its environment.

1925
Books and Monographs
088. Berlage, Hendrik Petrus, *De Ontwikkeling der Moderne Bouwkunst in Holland*, Amsterdam, 1925. Dutch: *The Development of Modern Architecture in Holland.* The transcript of a lecture delivered at the Sorbonne, Paris is reprinted from *Wil en Weg*, 1923-24, pp 559ff, 558ff, 626ff. Oud is not mentioned; there are images of Tusschendijken and the Oud-Mathenesse site office.

089. Fries, Heissenrich de, *Moderne Villen und Landhäuser*, Berlin, 1925. Third edition. German: *Modern Villas and Country Houses.* A brief essay introduces international examples, illustrated by clear photographs and plans. There are two of the villa *Allegonda*, and two of the Oud-Mathenesse site office.

090. Gispen, Willem Hendrik, *Het Sierend Metaal in de Bouwkunst*, Rotterdam, 1925. Dutch: *Decorative Metal in Architecture.* Part 12 of a series *Applied Art in The Netherlands* describes hand and machine fabrication techniques and finishes

is followed by an illustrated account of the work of several architects, including a gate to the Spangen courtyard.

091. Gropius, Walter, *Internationale Architektur*, Munich, 1925. Passau, 1927. German. A very short apologetic is followed by about 100 images, including villa *Allegonda*, Spangen, Tusschendijken, Oud-Mathenesse and the incomplete Hoek van Holland houses. Reviewed Oud, *Bouwkundig Weekblad*, 1925, p 587. The facsimile edition, edited by Hans Wingler, Mainz, 1981, has an afterword by Peter Hahn.

092. Vorrink, Koos (ed.), *Op de Kentering der Tijden*, Amsterdam, 1925. Dutch: *At the Turning of the Tides*. An anthology includes Adolf Behne's "Gewrochte of gekochte schoonheid?" illustrated with Oud's sketches for the Kallenbach house.

093. *L'Art Hollandaise à l'Exposition Internationale des Arts Decoratifs et Industriels Modernes,* Paris 1925. French: *Dutch Art at the International Exhibition of Modern Decorative and Industrial Arts.* There are about 150 plates of the Dutch pavilion and the design presentations it housed: the Tusschendijken housing and the display case for the Domela Nieuwenhuis collection are included.

094. *Typen Neuer Baukunst,* Mannheim, 1925. German. The catalog of an exhibition organised by the Bund Deutscher Architekten at *Stadt. Kunsthalle*, Mannheim was republished when the show moved to the *Staatlich. Kunstgewerbeschule*, Hamburg, May-June 1926, and again for the traveling show at Weisbaden (n.d.) and Oldenburg, 1928. Oud is included.

Journals
095. Badovici, Jean, "Entretiens sur l'architecture vivante." *L'Architecture Vivante,* 1925, spring/summer, pp 10-14, pl 1-15. French. A section "L'urbanisme en Hollande" draws attention to Oud's Spangen blocks VIII and IX and Tusschendijken. A plan of Rotterdam locates them and Oud-Mathenesse; all are illustrated with site plans, drawings (including details) and photographs but there is little description and no criticism.

096. Behne, Adolf, "Blick über die Grenze." *Bausteine,* 1925, no 2-3, pp 3 and 37. German: "A glance over the border." The piece refers to the Oud-Mathenesse, Spangen, and Tusschendijken housing estates.

097. Behrendt, Walter Curt, "Wohungsbau des auslandes: Siedlung Oud-Mathenesse bei Rotterdam." *Neubau*, vol 1, 1925, pp 10-14. German: "Housing abroad: ...Oud-Mathenesse." Not seen.

098. Doesburg, Theo van, "L'evolution de l'architecture moderne en Hollande." *L'Architecture Vivante,* 1925, autumn/winter, pp 14-20; pl. 10, 17, 20, 24-25. French: "Evolution of modern architecture in Holland." The polemic includes references to Oud designs: Scheveningen boulevard houses, *De Vonk*, Café De Unie (in color). See also *The Little Review*, 1927, pp 47-51 (English), where most images are omitted. Similar but not identical pieces appear in *La Construction Moderne*, 1928, 30 December, pp 152-54; *Die Bauschau*, 1928, no 21, p 10, both

of which also illustrate Hoek van Holland and Weissenhofsiedlung houses. Cf. *Le Home*, April 1925 and *La Construction Moderne*, 1928, 8 January, 3 June, 30 December; 1929, 21 April;"The progress of the modern movement in Holland," *Ray*, 1927, p 2; "La actividad de la arquitectura moderna holandesa," *Arquitectura*, 1927, pp 143-49, 213-20; 1928, pp 16-21.

099. Oud, J.J.P., "De *Bauhaus Bucher.*" *Bouwkundig Weekblad*, vol 46, 1925, p 587. Dutch: "The Bauhaus books." This reviews the first Bauhaus books: Gropius, *Internationale Architektur*; Moholy-Nagy, *Malerei, Photographie, Film* and van Doesburg, *Grundbegriffe der Neuen Gestaltenden Kunst*, 1925.

100. Oud, J.J.P., "Een Café." *Bouwkundig Weekblad*, vol 46, 1925, p 397-99. Dutch. An apologetic for the Café De Unie on Calandplein, Rotterdam addresses criticisms by the *Bouwpolitie and Woningdienst* (Building Policy and Housing Service)of the building's lack of contextuality. Views show the streetscape.

101. Oud, J.J.P., "Erziehung zur Architektur." *Soziale Bauwirtschaft*, vol 5, 1925, no 4, pp 25-28. German: "Architectural education." Not seen. The piece was translated into Polish in *Reconstruction Economique* .

102. Oud, J.J.P., "The influence of Frank Lloyd Wright on the architecture of Europe." *Wendingen*, vol 7, 1925, pp 85-91. English. Wright is described as "one of the greatest of this time" yet his European influence was not "happy ... in all respects" because it led to uncritical mimicry. The plasticity of modern architecture is due to Wright *and* De Stijl "cubism." Reprinted in Wijdeveld (ed.), *The Life-work of the American Architect Frank Lloyd Wright*, Santpoort, 1925; New York, 1965 (facsimile); *The Early Work of the Great Architect Frank Lloyd Wright*, New York/Avenal, 1994 (facsimile) and Wiekart (ed.), *Ter Wille van een Levende Bouwkunst*, 1962. See also *Holländische Architektur*, Munich, 1926; "De invloed van Frank Lloyd Wright op de architectura in Europa," *Architectura*, 1926, pp 85-89; "Wplyw Franka Wright'a na architekture europejska," *Architektura i Budownictwo*, 1933, pp 188-89.

103. Oud, J.J.P., "Ja und Nein. Bekenntnisse eines Architekten." *Bouwkundig Weekblad*, vol 46, 1925, p 431. German: "Yes and no: confessions of an architect." Reprinted from *Europa Almanach*, Potsdam, 1925, pp 18-20. The piece also appeared in *Wasmuth's Monatshefte fur Baukunst*, vol 9, 1925, pp 140-47, accompanied by drawings and photos of the Tusschendijken, Spangen and Oud-Mathenesse housing, and bio-bibliographical notes. See also *Das Werk*, vol 11, 1924, p 336; *Kvart*, 1930, no 2; *Forum,* vol 6, 1951, no 5-6 (cited in part). Translated in Wiekart (ed.), *Ter Wille van een Levende Bouwkunst*, 1962 and Beckett, *The Original Drawings of J.J.P. Oud*, London, 1979.

104. Oud, J.J.P., "Von technik und baukunst." *Innen-dekoration*, vol 36, 1925, pp 292-95. German: "Of technology and architecture." A staccato piece about the impact of technology on house design, especially kitchens, accompanies several views of Oud-Mathenesse; an interior of *De Vonk* is mistakenly included.

105. Pontrémolly, ——, "De onderscheidingen op Parijsche tentoonstelling." *Bouwkundig Weekblad*, vol 46, 1925, pp 518-520. Dutch: "Distinctions at the Paris Exhibition." The president of the international jury of the 1925 *L'Exposition Internationale des Arts Decoratifs et Industriels Modernes*, Paris, announces the Dutch entries.

106. Sörgel, Herman, "Reisebericht über Neue Holländische Baukunst." *Baukunst*, vol 1, 1925, May, pp 85-90. German: "Vacation report about new Dutch architecture." Oud is named as the leader of "classicism" in Holland, apparently on the basis of a single remark about the Parthenon. There are clear photographs and architectural drawings of Tusschendijken and Oud-Mathenesse. See also Sörgel, "Holländische Architekten-charakterköpfe," *ibid.*, pp 102-03, an inaccurate half-page biography of Oud, with a portrait.

107. Ss [?], "Gemeentelijke woningbouw Rotterdam." *Klei*, vol 17, 1925, March, pp 65-70. Dutch: "Municipal housing, Rotterdam." Interested Rotterdam associations report on "the realistic possibility of achieving harmony among the new housing estates." Oud's public housing is included; there are views of Spangen and Tusschendijken, and plans of the latter.

108. Vlugt, Leendert Cornelis van der, "De semi-permanente woningen in Oud-Mathenesse..." *Bouwen*, 1925, 21 February, pp 161-64. Dutch. The piece blends praise with a description of the estate. There are general views, tied to a site plan and drawings of the house types, for several pages beyond the text.

109. *L'Amour de l'Art,* [Display case, Boymans museum.] Vol 6, 1925, pp 320-21. French. Oud designed the case for the Domela Nieuwenhuis collection. See also *Bouwen,* 20 June 1925, p 100, where it appears in a photograph of the Dutch section of *L'Exposition Internationale des Arts Decoratifs et Industriels Modernes,* Paris, 1925.

110. *Baukunst*, [View of Oud-Mathenesse.] Vol 1, 1925, March/April, p 50. German. The caption calls the suburb "Oud-Rathenegge."

111. *Bouwkundig Weekblad*, "Het archief van den B.N.A." Vol 46, 1925, pp 505-06. Dutch: "Institute of Dutch Architects' archive." News item about the establishment of a drawings/images archive, including work by Oud, commenced in October 1924.

112. *Odbudowa gospo dar cza*, [Images of Tusschendijken and Oud-Mathenesse.] vol 5, 1925, no 2, p 80. (Polish).

1926
Books and Monographs
113. Badovici, Jean (ed.), *L'Architecture Vivante en Hollande*, Paris 1926. French: *Living Architecture in Holland.* Reprinted from the journal, volume II reproduces plates 18-19, 34-37, 43-45. The 21 issues of the important portfolio-format Paris journal 1923-33 were republished by Da Capo, New York, 1975.

114. Meyer, Erna, *Der Neue Haushalt, Ein Wegweiser zu wirtschaftlicher Hausführung*, Stuttgart, 1926. 1928. German. The book teaches housewives how to "go modern" in the age of the machine, descending to such detail as cutlery design. *De Vonk* and a Weissenhofsiedlung kitchen (second edition) are illustrated.

115. Mieras, J.P. and Francis Rowland Yerbury, *Dutch Architecture of the XXth Century*, London/New York, 1926. English. A collection of 100 Yerbury photographs includes Spangen, Tusschendijken and Oud-Mathenesse houses. Oud is called the "skilful leader [of the] objectivist" group, disapproved by Mieras. Reviewed Wattjes, *Bouwbedrijf*, 1926, p 252; *Architettura e Arti Decorative*, 1926, p 584. Also published as *Holländische Architektur des 20 Jahrhunderts*, Berlin, 1926. See Yerbury, *Modern Dutch Buildings*, London, 1931, intended to update the 1926 edition; reviewed *Connoisseur*, 1931, p 268; *Studio*, 1932, p 308; *Burlington Magazine*, 1932, p 266.

116. Minnucci, Gaetano, *L'Abitazione Moderna Popolare nell'Architettura Contemporanea Olandese*, Rome, 1926. Italian: *Modern Public Housing in Holland.* Not seen. Identified by Fanelli, *Moderne Architectuur in Nederland*, 1978, as an important contribution to Italian historical writing.

117. Oud, J.J.P., *Holländische Architektur*, Munich, 1926. German. No 10 in the *Bauhausbücher* series, the anthology contains "Geständnis"; "The future architecture and its architectonic possibilities"; "The influence of Frank Lloyd Wright in Europe" and "The development of modern architecture in Holland." There are 55 images of a wide range of work, mostly Oud's own. Reviewed S[choenmaker], *Bouwbedrijf*, 1927, p 389; F[riedhoff], *Bouwkundig Weekblad*, 1927, pp 94-96; *Bouwgids*, May 1927, p 102; Zwart, *Vaderland*, 13 October 1927. The second, enlarged edition 1929, added a foreword, "Yes and no: confessions of an architect" and "Whither the New Building? Art and standardisation", an afterword, and several images. Facsimile, Mainz-Berlin 1967, with an afterword by Jaffé, "Über J.J.P. Oud 1890-1963." Translated as *Architettura Olandese*, Milan, 1976; Rome, 1981 with an introduction by Polano; as *Hollandse Architectuur*, Nijmegen, 1983, with an introduction by Barbieri et al and an essay, "J.J.P. Oud: Hollandse architectuur tussen De Stijl en Bauhaus" by Barbieri (reviewed Taverne, "De architect en de huisvrouw," *NRC-Handelsblad*, 13 May 1983).

118. Strasser, Emil E., *Neuere Holländische Baukunst*, München-Gladbach, 1926. German: *Recent Dutch Architecture.* Oud and Wils are named as leaders towards a new architecture in this little book, decorated with Christian symbols. Oud-Mathenesse and Tusschendijken houses, and the Café De Unie are discussed and illustrated with fuzzy photos. Reviewed *Bouwbedrijf*, 1927, p 463.

Journals

119. Behne, Adolf, "Zwei Holländische Architekten." *Bauwelt,* 1926, 20 May, no 20, p 13. German: "Two Dutch architects." The piece discusses Mart Stam and Oud, whose Hoek van Holland houses are included.

120. Doesburg, Theo van, "De architect André Lurcat." *Bouwbedrijf*, vol 3, 1926, pp 152-55. This well-illustrated critical appraisal of Lurcat's work contains references to De Stijl and Oud's writings.

121. Haesaerts, Luc and Paul, "L'architecture Hollandaise." *Selection*, March 1926. French: "Dutch architecture." Not seen. A revised form by A. Raymond Neefs (with Luc and Paul Haesaerts) appeared in the Brussels journal *La Cité*, vol 6, 1927, pp 101-18.

122. Havelaar, Just, "Een kort overzicht der moderne toegepast kunsten in Nederland." *Jaarboek van Nederlandsche Ambachts- en Nijverheidskunst, 1925-26*, pp 11-37. Dutch: "A short overview of the modern applied arts..." Oud is mentioned as "the central figure of a group of Rotterdam architects."

123. Meller, P., "Holland und die neue Architektur." *Die Wohnung der Neuzeit*, vol 9, 1926, no 3, pp 9-10. German: "Holland and the new architecture." Not seen.

124. Meyer, Hannes, "Die neue Welt." *Das Werk*, 1926, July, pp 206-09. German: "The new world." The Café De Unie and Oud-Mathenesse site office are illustrated in this piece about international developments in architecture.

125. Stoffels, A., "Das Kafeehaus 'De Unie' von Architekt J.J.P. Oud." *Österreichische Bau- und Werkkunst*, vol 2, 1926, p 329ff. German. Not seen.

126. Spörhase, Rolf, "Neue wohnbauweisen für Etagen- und Siedlungshauser." *Frau und Gegenwart*, 1926, no 23, pp 8-9. German: "New residential building methods for flat and suburb housing." Spangen and Oud-Mathenesse estates are illustrated and used as examples in a general discussion..

127. *Bau-Rundschau*, [View of Oud-Mathenesse.] 1926, no 10, p 152.

128. *Die Form*, "Architektur des Auslandes. Café-restaurant 'De Unie' vol 1, 1926, January, pp 79-80. German: "Foreign architecture." The descriptive article, which mentions contemporary Dutch buildings, borrows heavily from Oud, "Een Café," *Bouwkundig Weekblad*, 1925. Cf. "Architektur des Auslandes," *Gross-Deutsche Hotel Rundschau*, 1926, October, pp 243-44.

129. *Hamburger Correspondent*, "Holland und die Baukunst." 1926, 5 June. German. This is a brief summary of Oud's April lecture in Hamburg. Cf. *Hamburger Freidenblatt*, 9 June 1926.

130. *Wasmuth's Monatshefte für Baukunst*, [Comment on Oud by Peter Behrens.] Vol 10, 1926, April, p 12. German. Not seen.

1927
Books and Monographs
131. Begeer, Carel J.A. (ed.), *Holland. Arts and Crafts 1900-1926*, Amsterdam, 1927. Dutch/ English/ German/French. Myriad excellent images formed a folio-sized catalog for the Leipzig European *Kunstgewerbe* Exhibition, March-August

1927. There is an introduction by G.Knuttel and a halfhearted bibliography. The Café De Unie and Tusschendijken are illustrated.

132. Burgee, J. (ed.), *Bau und Wohnung. Die Bauten der Weissenhofsiedlung in Stuttgart errichtet in 1927 nach Vorschlagen des Deutschen Werkbundes in Auftrag der Stadt Stuttgart und in Rahmen der Werkbund Austellung 'Die Wohnung'*, Stuttgart, 1927. German. The title describes the content: "the construction of a model suburban housing estate for an exhibition entitled 'The Dwelling,' a collaboration of the Stuttgart municipality and the *Deutscher Werkbund.*" Oud's houses are discussed in N. Miller, "Erlauterungsbericht" (pp 87-94).

133. Hilbersheimer, Ludwig, *Grosstadt Architecktur*, Stuttgart, 1927. German: *Architecture of Large Cities.* Oud's Tusschendijken and Hoek van Holland housing are included in a section "Buildings for housing" in this overview of international city planning. Both are illustrated.

134. Hilbersheimer, Ludwig, *Internationale neue Baukunst*, Stuttgart, 1927. 1928. German: *New International Architecture.* The *Bauhausbuch* has a half-page essay introducing 110 illustrations, without comment, including two of Oud's Hoek van Holland houses. Cf. Hilbersheimer, "Internationale neue Baukunst," *Moderne Bauformen*, vol 26, 1927, pp 325-64. Reprinted 1980.

135. Lauweriks, Johannes Ludovicus Mattheus (ed.), *Nieuwe Nederlandsche Ruimtekunst*, Blaricum, 1927. Dutch: *New Dutch Interior Design.* A general polemical essay (3 October 1927) introduces 60 good quality images, including Oud's Weissenhofsiedlung houses. Reviewed *Klei*, 1928, p 78.

136. Platz, Gustav Adolf, *Die Baukunst der Neusten Zeit*, Berlin/New York, 1927. 1930. German/English: *The Architecture of the Latest Age.* The book champions modernism. Oud is cited in the section on Dutch architecture, linked with Dudok as one of the modern masters. The second, enlarged edition discusses his work at length, illustrated with line drawings of Hoek van Holland, and the Purmerend factory and Rotterdam stock exchange designs. There are photographs of Tusschendijken, Oud-Mathenesse, and Weissenhofsiedlung. Reviewed Hackel, *Beeldende Kunst*, 1931, p 187; *Gazette des Beaux Arts*, 1932, part 2, p 123.

137. Sevenhuijsen, Augustus M.J.(ed.), *Nieuwe Bouwkunst in Nederland*, Blaricum, ca.1927. Dutch: *New Dutch Architecture.* An introduction is followed by over 70 views, mostly of Amsterdam School buildings. The Tusschendijken and Oud-Mathenesse schemes are illustrated with fuzzy photographs. Captions are in German, French and, English. Reviewed *Klei*, 1927, p 235; *Bouwkundig Weekblad*, 1927, p 275; *Bouwbedrijf*, 1927, p 541. Cf. *Neue Holländische Baukunst*, Bremen, ca. 1927, introduced by Gustav Brandes.

Journals

138. Adler, Leo, "Neuzeitliche Miethauser und Siedlungen." *Wasmuth's Monatshefte für Baukunst*, vol 11, 1927, no 1, pp 53-63. German: "Contemporary flat buildings and housing estates." Not seen.

139. Adler, Leo, "Vergleich zwischen grundrizzen von J.J.P. Oud und Le Corbusier..." *Wasmuth's Monatshefte für Baukunst*, vol 11, 1927, no 1, pp 32-38. German: "A comparison of Le Corbusier's and Oud's ground plans." Not seen.

140. B——, "Die Wohnungausstellung Stuttgart 1927." *Das Werk*, 1927, no 9, pp 259-71. German: "The housing exhibition . . ." The *Deutsche Werkbund* held an exhibition, July-October 1927, "The Dwelling", prototype houses built as an estate near Stuttgart to the designs of Europe's fifteen leading architects. This general review includes Oud's row houses. There is a photograph.

141. Boeken, Albert, "La nouvelle architecture dans les Pays-Bas." *L'Architecture*, vol 40, 1927, pp 212-15. French: "New architecture in Holland." Not seen.

142. Giedion, Siegfried, "Ist das neue Bauen eine mode?" *Basler Nachrichten*, 1927, 13 November. German: "Is the New Building a fashion?" Not seen; reprinted Huber (ed.), *Siegfried Giedion: Wege in die Öffentlichkeit*, Zurich, 1988.

143. H——, H., "Werkbundausstellung 'Die Wohnung' Stuttgart 1927." *Moderne Bauformen*, 1927, vol 26, no 8, pp 321-24. German: "Werkbund exhibition 'The Dwelling' Stuttgart 1927." News item, illustrated with views of the site model. See also the polemical, uninformative Werner Gräff, "Werkbundausstellung Die Wohnung," *Die Form*, vol 2, 1927, pp 249-50.

144. Klein, Alexander, "Neue arbeiten von J.J.P. Oud, Rotterdam." *Wasmuth's Monatshefte fur Baukunst*, vol 11, 1927, pp 294-98. German: "New work from ... Oud." In May 1927 the publisher Wasmuth organized a Berlin exhibition "Bauten von J.J.P. Oud," covering work 1917-27. This "follow-up" piece gives an overview of Hoek van Holland (with photos) and Weissenhofsiedlung (drawings) and publishes Oud's unsuccessful entry in the Rotterdam *beurs* competition.

145. Lampmann, Gustav, "Stuttgart 1927 'Die Wohnung'." *Zentralblatt der Bauverwaltung*, vol 47, 1927, no 43, pp 549-52. German: "Stuttgart 1927 'The dwelling'." The piece describes the construction of the Weissenhofsiedlung and its houses. There are plans of Oud's building and a photo of the dining room, with furniture by Ferdinand Kramer. Cf. *Baumeister*, February 1928, pp 52; 64-65; 71.

146. Liefrinck, Ida, "Complexe d'habitations Hoek van Holland: architecte J.J.P. Oud." *7 Arts*, vol 6, 1927, 4 December. French: "Housing complex, Hoek van Holland ..." Images are reprinted from *i10*: no text or captions.

147. Liefrinck, Ida, "J.J.P. Oud—né en 1890 à Purmerend ..." *7 Arts*, vol 6, 1927, 13 November, n.p. French: " ...Oud, born in 1890 at Purmerend ..." Two columns of biography and an inaccurate list of works are illustrated with views of Hoek van Holland, reprinted from *i10*. Oud is dubiously credited with collaboration with Dudok on the *Leidsche Dagblad* offices.

148. Meyer, Erna, "Wohnungsbau und Hausführung." *Baumeister*, vol 25, 1927, no 6, pp B88-95. German: "Residential buildings and household management."

Oud's Stuttgart houses are examined in the light of the modern functional needs of the household and thoroughly illustrated. Reprinted in German, *i10*, vol 1, 1927, pp 166-174, where not all illustrations are included.

149. Neumann, Guido E., "November-ausstellung: moderne bauten." *Hagener Zeitung*, 1927, 22 November. German: "November exhibition: modern building." Oud is one of the major themes of this short review of the Weissenhofsiedlung.

150. Oud, J.J.P., "'Aangepast bij de omgeving'." *i10*, vol 1, 1927, pp 349-56. Dutch: "Adapted to the surroundings." The critiique addresses the water tower at Wassenaar by Cor van Eesteren. Cf van Eesteren, "Naar inleiding van de prijsvraag voor een watertoren te Wassenaar," *ibid.*, pp 286-89. Both reprinted in Lehning and Schrofer, *De Internationale Avant-Garde tussen de Twee Wereldoorlogen*, The Hague, 1963.

151. Oud, J.J.P., "Das flache Dach in Holland." *Das Neue Frankfurt*, vol 1, 1927, no 7. German: "The flat roof in Holland." The largely technical article deals with concrete roof structure and built-up bituminous coverings.

152. Oud, J.J.P., "Huisvrouwen en architecten." *i10*, vol 1, 1927, pp 44-47. Dutch: "Housewives and architects." The essay outlines the importance of creating architecture that meets the needs of its users, bringing art and life together. Drawings of the Hoek van Holland houses are included to little point. An "appendix" (in German) reprints the Stuttgart Housewive's Association report on practical requirements for the Weissenhofsiedlung.

153. Oud, J.J.P., "Internationale architectuur: Werkbund-tentoonstelling 'Die Wohnung' Juli-September 1927, Stuttgart." *i10*, vol 1, 1927, pp 204-05. Dutch. A single page of text announces and explains the purpose of the Weissenhofsiedlung, remarking upon the unity of vision of the participating architects. There is an aerial perspective of the estate. Reprinted Lehning and Schrofer, *De Internationale Avant-Garde tussen de Twee Wereldoorlogen*, The Hague, 1963. Cf. Schwitters, "Stuttgart, 'Die Wohnung', Werkbundausstellung," *ibid.*, pp 345-48. For English translations, see Suzanne S. Frank, "*il0*, commentary, bibliography, and translations," *Oppositions*, winter 1976/77.

154. Oud, J.J.P., [no title.] *De Stijl*, vol 7, 1927, no 79-84, pp 38-40. French. The piece celebrates Oud's involvement with De Stijl within an apologetic for modern architecture. There is a portrait, perspectives of the Scheveningen esplanade housing and Purmerend factory designs, and photos of Hoek van Holland and the Weissenhofsiedlung.

155. Oud, J.J.P., "Richtlijn." *i10*, vol 1, 1927, pp 2-3. Dutch: "Direction." French, German and English summaries. Oud's first essay as architectural editor of the journal promises a serious attempt to bring all creative activity together upon the rational base of modern life. It appeared (i.a.) in Italian translation in Benedetti and Pracchi (eds.), *Antologia dell'Architettura Moderna*, Bologna, 1988. The inaugural issue of *International Review i10* (1927-29), founded by

Arthur Muller Lehning, promised "a documentation of the new streams in art, science, philosophy and sociology [giving] a general view of the renewal ... now accomplishing itself in culture and it is open, international, for all." The following notes are drawn from Frank, "*il0*, commentary, bibliography, and translations," *Oppositions*, winter 1976/77. Volume 1 was reprinted, *il0, de Internationale Avant-garde tussen de Twee Wereldoorlogen,* Amsterdam, 1963 (with an essay by Lehning, "*il0* after 35 years"); The Hague, 1966 and Amsterdam 1974. Facsimile, Kees van Wijk (ed.), *Internationale Revue i10*, Utrecht, 1980. See also Lehning and de Haan, "Een gedachten wisseling over de Internationale Avant-garde tussen de Twee Wereldoorlogen," *De Syllabus*, November 1963 and *Deutsche Zeitung*, 22 November 1963; Lehning, "*il0*: confrontatie met het heden," *NRC Handelsblad*, 15 November 1963; Lehning, "Avante-gardisme van de *il0* weer herleefd," *Overijssel en Zwolse Courant, Haarlems Dagblad* and *Arnhemse Courant*, 5, 19 October 1963. See also Schurer[?], "*il0*," *Friese Koerier*, 5 September 1963; Moholy, "Internationale Avantgarde 1927-1929," *Du*, March 1964 and Wijk, "*Internationale revue* il0," *Nederlandse Kunsthistorisch Jaarboek*, vol 28, 1977.

156. Oud, J.J.P., "Toelichting op een woningtype van de *Werkbundaustellung Die Wohnung*, Stuttgart ..." *il0*, vol 1, 1927, pp 381-384. Dutch: "Explanation of a housing type ..." Oud explains his row houses. There are plans, site plans and section, annotated in German; photographs include exterior and interior views. See also "Erläuterungsbericht," *Bau- und Wohnung*, Stuttgart, 1927, pp 86-95.

157. Oud, J.J.P., "Wohin führt das Neue bauen: Kunst und Standard." *il0*, vol 1, 1927, pp 385-86. German: "Whither the New Building? Art and Standardisation." Illustrated with Stuttgart row houses. Also in *Holländische Architektur*, 1929; *Der Kreis*, 1927, no 12; *Die Form*, 1928, no 2 and *Neue Zuricher Zeitung*, 9 September 1927; K.Wiekart (ed.), *Ter Wille van een Levende Bouwkunst*, 1962.

158. Oud, J.J.P., "Woningbouw te Hoek van Holland." *Het Groen Wit Groene Book,* Rotterdam, 1927. Dutch. The book celebrates the tenth anniversary of the Rotterdam Public Housing Service. Oud's houses appear on pp 38-42.

159. Rood, A.H. van, "De Werkbund-tentoonstelling in Stuttgart." *Bouwkundig Weekblad*, vol 48, 1927, pp 297-98; 305-07. Dutch. "The *Werkbund* exhibition, Stuttgart." This subjective review names Oud, Peter Behrens and Hans Scharoun as "eminently above the rest; those three are architects." See "Werkbundausstellung 'Die Wohnung' Stuttgart, Juli bis September 1927," *ibid.*, p 232.

160. Spörhase, Rolf, "Hausbau einst und jekt." *Niedersachsen*, vol 32, 1927, May, pp 98-102. German: "House building then and now." There is no reference to Oud in the text of this polemic about domestic architecture, but the Oud-Mathenesse and Tusschendijken houses are illustrated.

161. Wedepohl, Edgar, "Die Weissenhofsiedlung der Werkbundausststellung 'Die Wohnung' Stuttgart, 1927." *Wasmuth's Monatshefte fur Baukunst*, vol 11, 1927, pp 391-402. German: "The Weissenhof [exhibition, Stuttgart 1927.]" Oud is ignored in the text but there are two exterior views of his row-houses.

162. Westheim, Paul, "Die Wohnung zur Stuttgarter Austellung." *Das Kunstblatt*, vol 2, 1927, September, pp 333-41. Dutch: "The House at the Stuttgart exhibition." This is a general review of the exhibition.

163. Wolff, Lina, "Die Wohnung." *Die Frau und ihr Haus*, vol 8, 1927, October, pp 290-92. German: "The dwelling." A review of the Stuttgart exhibition compares the interiors of the designs, including Oud's row houses.

164. *L'Architecture*, "Spangen VIII and Tusschendijken [illustrations]." Vol 60, 1927, no 7, p 214.

165. *Baumeister*, "Ein neuer Wohnungsbau." Vol 25, 1927, June, pp 297-301. German: "A recent housing [scheme]." A few paragraphs introduce a profusion of images of the Hoek van Holland houses. There is a part citation of Oud's comment on the Weissenhofsiedlung, from *Die Form*, vol 2, 1927, no 9.

166. *Bouwkundig Weekblad*, [Hoek van Holland houses illustrations." Vol 48, 1927, no 43, pp 384-88. Dutch.

167. *Cahiers d'Art*, "Exposition du 'Werkbund' à Stuttgart; L'Habitation." Vol 2, 1927, pp 287-92. French: "*Werkbund* exhibition at Stuttgart: The Dwelling." An illustrated review comments upon the strength and viability of Oud's row houses.

168. *Cahiers d'Art*, "Maisons ouvrièrs à Hoeck van Holland." Vol 2, 1927, pp 366-68. French: "Workers' housing, Hoek van Holland." A paragraph of text prefaces five large images, including one of the backs of the houses.

169. *L'Effort*, "Houses at Hoek van Holland [illustrations.]" Vol 11, 1927, series 2, 15 November. French.

170. *i10*, "Huizen te Hoek van Holland [illustrations.]" Vol 1, 1927, pp 281-84.

171. *Moderne Bauformen*. "Von der Werkbund-Siedlung in Stuttgart [illustrations.]" Vol 26, 1927, pp 408-12.

172. *De Stijl*, "Principeele medewerkers aan De Stijl, 1917-27." Vol 7, 1927, pp 79-84. Dutch: "Principal collaborators in De Stijl ..." The tabulated list includes Oud as a co-founder and member 1917-20.

1928
Books and Monographs
173. *Ausstellung Neue Baukunst*, Oldenburg, 1928. German: *Exhibition of New Houses*. Tusschendijken, Hoek van Holland and Oud-Mathenesse houses are listed in this unillustrated catalog of an exhibition organized by the *Vereinigung für junge Kunst*, at the Oldenburger Schloss, January-February 1928.

Journals
174. Badovici, Jean et al., [The issue]. *L'Architecture Vivante*, vol 5, 1928, spring/summer, plates 18-22. French: "Concerning Stuttgart." An essay by Badovici, "À propos de Stuttgart," introduces a series of essays and a profusion of images. Siegfried Giedion's "La leçon de l'exposition du *Werkbund* à Stuttgart

1927" will interest the student of Oud. His row houses are documented with drawings (annotated in French and German) and excellent interior and exterior photographs, including one taken during the concrete pour.

175. Behrendt, Walter Curt, "Vom neuen Bauen." *Kunst und Kunstler,* vol 26, 1928, August, p 420-25. German: "Of new building." Oud's initials are given as I.I.P. in the text of this general article, but correctly in the caption to a view of the Hoek van Holland houses.

176. Hitchcock, Henry-Russell Jr., "The architectural work of J.J.P. Oud." *The Arts*, vol 13, 1928, no 2, pp 97-103. English. Written when Oud was little known outside Holland and Germany, the article presents him as reacting against the Amsterdam School's "eclectic romanticism and expressionistic picturesqueness." It discusses Tusschendijken, Hoek van Holland and Oud-Mathenesse with a modernist bias. See Oud, "Tijdschriften," *Nieuwe Rotterdamsche Courant*, 6 June 1928: a strange essay, written in the third person, takes issue with Hitchcock.

177. Hitchcock, Henry-Russell Jr., "Modern architecture: II. The new pioneers." *Architectural Record*, vol 63, 1928, May, pp 453-60. English. This places Oud among the "new pioneers," in contrast to the "new traditionalists" and groups him with Le Corbusier and Gropius as a prophet of the "new manner" whose work "at its best and latest is quite on a par" with theirs. Its theme is developed in *Modern Architecture, Romanticism and Integration*, 1929. There are two views of Hoek van Holland.

178. Oud, J.J.P., "Boekbespreking [Adolf Schneck, *Der Stuhl*]." *i10*, vol 2, 1928, no 15, pp 64-65. Dutch: "Book review." A column positively reviews a catalog/ monograph generated by the 1928 Stuttgart exhibition "The Chair," curated by Schneck for the Deutsche Werkbund.

179. Oud, J.J.P., "Beursproject Rotterdam 1926." *i10*, vol 2, 1928, no 14, pp 25-29. Dutch: "Rotterdam stock exchange project." Oud's explanation of his entry in the Rotterdam stock exchange competition is typical of the *toelichtingen* in contemporary Dutch architectural journals, with location plan, floor plans, sections, a street elevation and an isometric drawing.

180. Oud, J.J.P., "Das fliessende leben." *Innen-dekoration*, vol 39, 1928, May, p 209. German: "The flowing life." The half page of polemic is subtitled, "the natural way of architects"

181. Oud, J.J.P., "Toelichting bij het ontwerp motto x voor een beurs te Rotterdam." *Bouwkundig Weekblad*, vol 50, 1929, pp 41-42. Identical to 179, this piece is less generous with images.

182. Oud, J.J.P., "Wohnhausgruppe in Hoek van Holland." *Die Form,* vol 3, 1928, no 2, pp 38-41. German: "Group of dwellings, Hoek van Holland." The piece is largely descriptive, illustrated with rather clinical photographs and a small site plan. See also *Red*, 1928, October, p 56 (Czechoslovakian).

183. Polasek, J., "De Kiefhoek." *Stavitel,* 1928, no 7-8, p 106. Czechoslovakian. Not seen.

184. "Rogkerus," "J.P.Oud: arbeiterwohnungen mit läden in Hoek van Holland." *Die Bauschau,* vol 3, 1928, no 5, pp 4-9. German: "... Workers' houses with shops ..." Oud is hailed as the leader of Rotterdam architects in a piece than announces a brief exhibition of his work in the Cologne Kunstgewerbemuseum but says little about Hoek van Holland. There are excellent illustrations.

185. Stern, Walter, "Das Wohnhaus der Grosstadt." *Die Werag,* vol 3, 1928, no 43, pp 2 -9. Oud's Spangen and Kiefhoek are used as examples and illustrated in a general article about European high density housing.

186. Westheim, Paul, "Das land ohne wohnungsnot." *Berliner Borsenzeitung,* 1928, 12 August. German: "The land without a housing shortage." Oud is described as "one of the best architects Europe" in this general piece about Dutch housing.

187. Wolf, N.H., "Tentoonstelling A.S.B." *De Kunst,* vol 20, 1928, 18 February, pp 245-50. Dutch: "[Architecture, painting and sculpture] exhibition." The show was held at the Amsterdam Stedelijk Museum in February. This review includes Hoek van Holland (illustrated), Oud-Mathenesse, Tusschendijken and Stuttgart houses and designs for the Hotel Stiassni in Brno, Czechoslovakia.

188. *L'Architecte,* [Illustrations only of Weissenhofsiedlung.] Vol 3, 1928, March, fig 23; plate 18. French.

189. *L'Architecture Vivante,* [Hoek van Holland.] Vol 5, 1928, no 21, pp 7; 18-20, plates 22-25. Dimensioned plans and sections of houses and shops, street plans and elevations, all annotated in Dutch, without comment.

190. *Christian Science Monitor,* "Holland helps landlord who removes slums." 1928, 29 March, p 5. English. A column outlines the development of modern architecture in Holland; there are photographs of Hoek van Holland.

191. *L'Emulation,* "L'architecture Hollandaise des dernieres années." Vol 48, 1928, March, pp 25-31. French: "Dutch architecture of recent years." In the conclusion of this article (see *ibid.,* February 1928) there is a single paragraph on Oud, stressing his objectivity.

192. *Das Kunstblatt,* [Images, Hoek van Holland.] Vol 26, 1928, August, p 226. German.

193. *M.S.A.,* [Images, Hoek van Holland.] Vol 1, 1928, p 106. Czechoslovakian.

194. *Nieuwe Rotterdamsche Courant,* "Stadsontwikkeling en stadsuitbreiding." 27 May 1928. Dutch: City development and extension." The article mentions engineer Th. K. van Lohuizen's collaboration at Oud-Mathenesse.

195. *Stuttgarter Neues Tagblatt,* "Die Stuttgarter Werkbundsiedlung als forbild." 27 September 1928. German: "The Stuttgart Werkbund district." News item.

196. *Tér és Forma*, [Images, Hoek van Holland.] 1928, June, p 48. Hungarian.

197. *De Vrouw*, "Het moderne huis." 1928, February, n.p. This populist review of Oud's Stuttgart houses focuses on the interior design and its advantages for the housewife. There are photographs from Burgee (ed.), *Bau und Wohnung*, 1927.

1929
Books and Monographs
198. Giedion, Siegfried, *Befreites Wohnen,* Zürich 1929. German: *Liberated Houses.* The book drips with modernist polemic. The major part of the short text is an essay "Die Wohnung für das existenzminimum," a theme espoused by CIAM. The Hoek van Holland houses, illustrated with plans and external views, are held out as examples of *existenzminimum* dwellings.

199. Hitchcock, Henry-Russell Jr., *Modern Architecture, Romanticism and Integration*, New York, 1929. Reprinted New York, 1970. English. Oud, De Stijl and the *Nieuwe Zakelijkheid* are dubbed "new pioneers," as against "new traditionalists." There is a discussion of Oud's role in the international scene.

200. Mendelsohn, Erich, *Russland, Europa, Amerika. Ein Architektonischer Querschnitt*, Berlin, 1929. German: *Russia, Europe, America. An Architectural Cross-section.* In a review of the respective architectures, the section on Europe includes Oud with Le Corbusier and Dudok. Reviewed Oud, *i10*, 1929, p 135.

201. Taut, Bruno, *Die Neue Baukunst in Europa und Amerika*, Stuttgart, 1929. German. Published as *Modern Architecture,* London, 1929. Facsimile, 1979. A polemical essay intoduces hundreds of images. Oud is among the handful of Dutch architects included, and there is discussion of his housing schemes. Tusschendijken, Hoek van Holland and the Weissenhofsiedlung are illustrated. Reviewed de Gruyter, *Elseviers Geillustreerd Maandschrift*, 1930, part 80, p 281.

Journals
202. Block, Fritz, "Die Weiterentwicklung der holländische architektur." *Bauwelt*, vol 20, 1929, February 28, p 11. German: "The wider development of Dutch architecture." Hoek van Holland is presented with other Dutch architecture.

203. Otten, Albert, "Rotterdamsche problemen." *Bouwkundig Weekblad*, vol 50, 1929, no 21. Dutch: "Rotterdam's problems." A critique of designs for Rotterdam stock exchange reviews earlier criticism in the Dutch press. Oud's "most radical" proposal was not shortlisted. The site plan and east (Coolsingel) elevation are reproduced. See also *ibid.*, [Jury's report (dated April 1927) on the Rotterdam stock exchange design Motto X (Oud)], p172; Zwiers, "Bespreking ontwerp beurs van J.J.P. Oud en J.F. Staal," *Algemeen Handelsblad,* 21 January 1929; *Vaderland*, "Projecten voor Rotterdams beurs," 2 February 1929, odbd, p 1 and Z[wart], "De plannen voor Rotterdamsche Beurs," *ibid.*, 3 February 1929.

204. Oud, J.J.P., "In memory of Peter van der Meulen Smith 1902-1928." *i10*, vol 2, 1929, p 122. English. This is an obituary for a young American "international" school architect with Dutch connections.

205. Oud, J.J.P., "Boekbespreking." *i10*, vol 2, 1929, pp 135-36. Dutch: "Book review." There is a single paragraph on Erich Mendelssohn [sic], *Russland, Europa, Amerika. Ein architektonischer Querschnitt* and a slightly longer critique of J.Vischer and Ludwig Hilberseimer, *Beton als Gestalter*.

206. *Nieuwe Rotterdamsche Courant*, "J.J.P. Oud." 1929, 29 January. News item about Oud's imminent visit to Princeton University (actually Spring 1930). Cf. *News Bulletin of the Institute of International Education*, vol 5, 1929, no 3.

207. *Nieuwe Rotterdamsche Courant*, "Nieuwe architectuur." 1929, 16 April. A news item announces an exhibition mounted in Vienna by the Austrian *Werkbund*. "Most modern work" was by Dutch architects, including Oud. Corbusier's influence upon him is noted. The identical piece appeared in *Vaderland*, 16 April 1929.

208. *Studio Yearbook*, "The New Movement." 1929, pp 13; 43-45; 48-49. English. The article includes (i.a.) photographs and plans of the Hoek van Holland houses. Captions describe construction, materials and color schemes, but offer no criticism.

1930-1939

1930
Books and Monographs
209. Casteels, Maurice, *Die Sachlichkeit in der Modernen Kunst*, Paris and Leipzig, 1930. German: *Objectivity in Modern Art*. In the brief introduction to a book of pictures, Oud is identified with Wils and Dudok as representative of the new in Dutch architecture, one of the true followers of Berlage and the heirs of Wright. There are clear photographs: Hoek van Holland houses, an interior of the Weissenhofsiedlung houses and the 1927 alterations to villa *Allegonda*. See also Casteels, *The New Style, Architecture and Decorative Design*, London, 1931 (originally *L'Art Moderne Primitif*) where almost every Dutch architect's name is wrongly spelt and which reproduces the same images.

210. Cheney, Sheldon, *The New World Architecture*, London, 1930. English. In a very broad review, Oud is mentioned in the same breath as Brinkman and van der Vlugt, and Dudok as "rationalistic".

211. Ritzen, Jos., *Hedendaagsche Bouwen*, Brussels, 1930. The book is a special issue (vol 29, no 4) of the *Katholieke Vlaamsche Hoogeschooluitbreiding*. The general introductory essay contains references to Weissenhofsiedlung, Tusschendijken and Hoek van Holland houses. There are some insignificant images.

Journals
212. Loghem, Johannes Bernardus van. "Nederlandsche bouwmeesters: 'De Kiefhoek', architect J.J.P. Oud." *Groene Amsterdammer*, 1930, 5 April, pp 8-9. Dutch: "Dutch master-architects: 'De Kiefhoek' ..." The polemic says little about Oud and less about Kiefhoek. There are a few photographs, without captions.

213. Lønberg-Holm, Knud, "Glass." *Architectural Record*, vol 68, 1930, pp 332-50. English. Although not referred to in the text, there are large photographs of shops at Hoek van Holland and Kiefhoek and an aerial view of the latter.

214. Lubinski, P.M., "Wspolczesna architektura Holenderska." *Architektura i Budownictwo*, vol 6, 1930, no 3. Polish. Not seen.

215. Otten, Albert, "De Kiefhoek te Rotterdam." *Bouwkundig Weekblad*, vol 51, 1930, no 45, pp 369-71. Dutch: "The Kiefhoek in Rotterdam." The article by a Rotterdam architect repudiates the suitability of concrete houses in the "land of the brick" before describing the estate. There are typical house plans and views of the Apostolic church and Heer Arnoldstraat. See the heated response from Willem C. Brouwer, *ibid.*, no 46, pp 381-83; and A.J. van der Steur, "Over den architect en het experiment ...," *ibid.*, pp 379-81.

216. *Praesens*, "Mysli." 1930, May, pp 87-91. Polish. Illustrations of Kiefhoek and Hoek van Holland housing estates.

217. Oud, J.J.P., "Die städtische Siedlung 'De Kiefhoek' in Rotterdam." *Die Form*, vol 5, 1930, pp 357-69. German: "The De Kiefhoek urban district in Rotterdam." The descriptive, statistical article is replete with aerial and exterior views (captions also in French and English), including the Apostolic church, site plans, plans and sections. The identical text with edited versions of the images appears in "Eine städtische Siedlung in Rotterdam," *Baumeister*, November 1930, pp 425-32 and "Rotterdam varos 'Kiefhoek' lakótelepe," *Tér és Forma*, January 1931, pp 11-17. For a condensed version see 'Siedlung 'Kiefhoek' in Rotterdam," *Zentralblatt der Bauverwaltung*, 1931, no 10, pp 149-53; *L'Architecture d'Aujourd'hui*, March 1931, pp 2-8.

218. Steur, A.J.van der, "Over den architect en het experiment, een overdenking n.a.v. 'De De Kiefhoek'." *Bouwkundig Weekblad*, vol 51, 1930, p 379. Dutch: "About the architect and the experiment, a consideration on the occasion of De Kiefhoek." The title is self-explanatory

219. *Architectural Record*, "Store fronts, Hoek van Holland [images only]." Vol 69, 1930, p 344. English.

220. *La Casa Bella*, [Kiefhoek.] Vol 8, 1930, pp 79-80. Italian. The item briefly reports a general article in *Baumeister*, November 1930. There is a tiny photo.

221. *La Casa Bella*, [Hoek van Holland.] Vol 8, 1930, no 36. Italian. Not seen.

222. *De Kunst der Nederlanden*, [Images of Kiefhoek.] Vol 36, 1930-31, p 318.

1931
Books and Monographs
223. Adler, Leo, *Neuzeitliche Miethauser und Siedlungen*, Berlin, 1931. German. A short essay introduces over 400 images of residential districts in western Europe. Kiefhoek, Oud-Mathenesse and Hoek van Holland are illustrated with several pages of photographs, site plans and plans.

Annotated Bibliography 1930-1939 59

224. Adler, Leo (ed.), *Wasmuths Lexikon der Baukunst*, Berlin, 1931. German: *Dictionary of Architecture*. The *Lexicon* was published in five volumes 1929-37. The entry on Oud has abrupt biographical notes and a list of built works and projects to 1927. Volume 4 has an article by F.A.Vermeulen, "Niederlandische Baukunst."

225. Giedion, Siegfried et al., *Rationelle Bebauungweisen: Ergebnisse des 3. Intern. Konrgr. für neues Bauen*, Frankfurt am Main, 1930. German/French: *Rational Ways of Town Planning*. The document, of which Cornelis van Eesteren was co-editor, reports outcomes of the third CIAM Congress, Brussels, November 1930. Kiefhoek is used as an example.

226. Hitchcock, Henry-Russell Jr., *J.J.P. Oud*, Paris, ca. 1931. French. This is volume II of *Les Cahiers d'Architecture Contemporaine*, subtitled *The Masters of Modern Architecture*. A bland six-page biographical essay introduces 44 pages of large clear images of Oud's oeuvre to date, including photographs and plans of projects and realized buildings. There is a portrait. Reviewed *Nieuwe Rotterdamsche Courant*, 21 November 1931.

227. Johnson, Philip, *Built to Live In*, New York, 1931. English. This pamphlet announces the forthcoming exhibition of architecture that gave rise to the term "International Style." The Hoek van Holland houses are illustrated.

Journals
228. Giedion, Siegfried, "De Kiefhoek." *Bauwelt,* 1931, no 11, p 11ff. German. A short introduction is followed by large images.

229. Giedion, Siegfried, "La phase actuelle de l'architecture hollandaise." *Cahiers d'Art*, vol 6, 1931, no 1, pp 45-54. French: "The present phase of Dutch architecture." Most of the piece is taken up with the work of the Functionalists. Tusschendijken and Spangen are mentioned in connection with the foundation of Dutch Modernism in the 1920s, but only Kiefhoek is illustrated, with reference to the airy, light interiors of the houses. See the response by Sybold van Ravesteyn, "Architectuur, J.J.P. Oud," *Gemeenschap*, 1932, p 84 and C.M., "Sotternijen van Sybolt [sic]," *R.K.Bouwblad*, vol 3, 1931-32, p 256.

230. Gruyter, W. Jos. de, "Moderne Nederlandsche bouwkunst en J.J.P. Oud. III." *Elseviers Gëillustreerd Maandschrift*, vol 81, 1931, pp 10-26; 168-86; plates 33-40. Dutch: "Modern Dutch architecture and ... Oud." After a "general" and "historical" discussion in the first articles, this conclusion of a two-part series provides biographical information on Oud, examines his sources, and reviews some of the literature. There is plenty of critical comment. Illustrations abound, familiar subjects being supplemented by rare reproductions of 1915 designs for a public bath house. Reprinted as a booklet.

231. Hilding Ekelund, "Hollanti—rationalistista Koristelna ja koristeellista rationalismia." *Arkitekten*, vol 11, 1931, pp 52-54. Finnish: "Holland's rational decoratism and decorative rationalism". The article briefly reviews contemporary

Dutch work, including Kiefhoek. For a partial translation into Dutch and a response, see W[attjes], "Een Finsche beoordeeling van de Nederlandsche bouwkunst," *Bouwbedrijf*, vol 8, 1931, pp 339-40.

232. Jonge van Ellemeet, M.J.I. de, "De gemeentelijke woningbouw 'Kiefhoek' te Rotterdam." *Tijdschrift voor Volkshuisvesting*, vol 12, 1931, no 5, pp 101-06. The well-illustrated (external views and typical house plans), comprehensive article is mostly descriptive, with some details of cost.

233. Lønberg-Holm, Knud, "Planning the retail store." *Architectural Record*, vol 69, 1931, pp 506-07 and 495ff. English. Although not mentioning them in the text, the article contains photos of the shops at Hoek van Holland and Kiefhoek.

234. Malespine, Emile, "L'urbanisme nouveau." *L'Effort,* 1931, p 34, plates 74-75. French: "The new urbanism." The short piece is illustrated by the Hoek van Holland houses and Spangen block VIII.

235. Mesnil, Jacques, [Houses by Oud.] *Monde*, vol 5, 1931, June, p 5. French. Not seen.

236. Oud, J.J.P., "The £213 house," *Studio*, vol 103, 1931, March, pp 175-79. English. The article outlines the rationale of Kiefhoek. The scheme was ruled by cost, although Oud claims that he would have provided more services had the budget allowed. There is a dichotomy between the machines for living in—Oud calls them "dwelling Fords"—and the traditional relationship of houses and church as "a culminating point in the general flatness." Otherwise, the *Hersteld Apostolische Gemeente* church is ignored. There is a site plan. See also *Creative Art*, vol 8, 1931, March, pp 174-79.

237. Retera, W., "Interieurs met stalen meubels." *Het Landhuis*, vol 26, 1931, p 579. Dutch: "Interiors with steel furniture." Not seen.

238. *Architectural Record*, "Hoek van Holland and De Kiefhoek." 1931, June. English. Not seen.

239. *Architettura e Arti Decorative,* [Images only of Hoek van Holland, Kiefhoek houses.] 1931, January-February, pp 198-99. Italian.

240. *Baumeister*, [Images only of Apostolic Church, Kiefhoek.] Vol 29, 1931, January, p 16. German.

241. *La Casa Bella,* [Image only of Kiefhoek church, reproduced from 240.] Vol 9, 1931, March, p 76. Italian.

242. *La Casa Bella,* [Image only of Hoek van Holland, reproduced from *Bouwgids*, January 1931.] Vol 9, 1931, March, p 69. Italian.

243. *La Casa Bella,* [Weissenhofsiedlung.] Vol 9, 1931, no 46. Italian. Not seen.

244. *Klei*, "Kiefhoek--witte dorp." Vol 23, 1931, no 11, pp 125-35. Dutch: "Kiefhoek: white village." The official organ of the Dutch clay products industry

claims that brick construction is better and cheaper than concrete (the houses were designed for either) in an introduction to a series of excellent images.

245. *Klei*, "Het Witte Dorp." vol 23, 1931, no 12, pp 137-42. Dutch: "The white village." The shortest of introductions is followed by excellent images of the Oud-Mathenesse "emergency" housing development.

246. *Die Neue Linie*, "Holland baut." 1931, May, p 20. German: "Holland builds." Illustrates Hoek van Holland houses and villa *Allegonda*.

247. *Neue Preussische Kreuzzeitung*, "Villenviertel?—Arbeitersiedlung." 1931, 23 October. German: "Smart residential district?—workers' suburb." This single page, mostly descriptive review of Kiefhoek presents six photographs.

1932
Books and Monographs
248. Barr, Alfred, Henry-Russell Hitchcock Jr., Philip Johnson and Lewis Mumford, *Modern Architecture*, New York, 1932. English. Oud is the Dutch architect accorded special attention in a 20-page article in this exhibition catalog from the New York Museum of Modern Art, February-March 1932. Reprinted in *Museum of Modern Art Reprints* series, New York, 1980.

249. Berlage, Hendrik Petrus et al., *Moderne Bouwkunst in Nederland*, Rotterdam, 1932-35 (20 parts). Dutch: *Modern Architecture in The Netherlands*. Each of this series of 20 monographs illustrates a building type with views and plans, with a general introduction. The brief texts are in Dutch; captions and keys to plans are also in French, German and English. Oud is mentioned only in passing as a member of De Stijl. There are plans and exterior photographs of Spangen, Hoek van Holland, Kiefhoek (including the Apostolic Church) and interior views of Weissenhofsiedlung houses and unidentified other furniture. For reviews of the various volumes, see *Elseviers Gëillustreerd Maandschrift*, 1932, pp 66, 209, 284, 289, 425; 1933, 426; 1934, p 65, 353; Mieras, *Bouwkundig Weekblad*, 1932, p 463; 1933, pp 123, 322, 445; 1934, p 114, 372; *Holland Revue*, 1934, p 95, 286, 527; Koldewey, *R.K.Bouwblad*, 1932-33, p 247.

250. Gouwe, W.J., *Glas in lood*, Rotterdam 1932. Dutch: *Leadlight*. A comprehensive review of recent stained glass work in Holland (ca. 1890-1930) includes references to the work of van Doesburg and Kamerlingh Onnes in villa *Allegonda*, and the former's windows in Oud's Spangen housing (illustrated to little point in monochrome). Reviewed *Beeldende Kunst*, 1932, p 348; *Elseviers Gëillustreerd Maandschrift*, 1932, part 84, p 362; *De Vrouw en haar Huis*, 1932-33, p 340.

251. Hitchcock, Henry-Russell Jr. and Philip Johnson, *The International Style: Architecture since 1922*, New York, 1932. English. Published to coincide with an exhibition at the New York Museum of Modern Art the biased book reviews ten years of modern architecture. Space enclosed, regularity, and rejection of ornament are essential properties of internationalism. Kiefhoek, Hoek van Holland and Stuttgart houses are illustrated. Oud's De Stijl associations are discussed

and the effect of Dutch Neoplasticism on Gropius is noted. Reprinted 1966 with a foreword by Hitchcock, and in 1995 with a foreword by Johnson. Translated into German, *Der Internationale Stil*, Braunschweig, 1985. See Hitchcock, "The International Style twenty years after," *Architectural Record*, August 1951.

252. Loghem, Johannes Bernardus van, *Bouwen*, Amsterdam, 1932. Dutch; English, French, German summaries. (English title: *Building, Holland; built to live in.*) The introduction is an important document of Dutch modernism. Yet, fraught with allusions to Le Corbusier's *Vers Une Architecture*, 1923, it says nothing new. The work of many Dutch architects is illustrated, including Oud's. Facsimile, Nijmegen, 1980. Reviewed van Ravesteyn, *Gemeenschap*, 1932, p 610; Moens, *R.K.Bouwblad*, 1932-33, p 24; *Bouwkundig Weekblad*, 1932, p 361.

Journals

253. Hecke, Gust.van, "Bouwend Holland." *Vooruit*, vol 48, 1932, 9 October, p 1. Dutch: "Built Holland." Oud is mentioned only in captions to images of Hoek van Holland (wrongly identified as Kiefhoek) and Kiefhoek.

254. Mesnil, Jacques, "Maisons Ouvrièrs." *Monde*, 1932, 11 June, p 5. French: "Open houses." The article is derived from Hitchcock's 1931 monograph. Polemic about the European housing shortage precedes a brief overview of Oud's career. There are small plans of Kiefhoek.

255. Oud, J.J.P., [Obituary for Theo van Doesburg.] *De Stijl*, final number, 1932, pp 46-47. Dutch. The journal was revived by former members as a tribute to van Doesburg. Oud's poetic piece, all fashionably in lower case, was one of many obituaries. See *Nieuwe Rotterdamsche Courant*, 6 February 1935, avbd p 2.

256. Oud, J.J.P., "De 'Nieuwe Zakelijkheid' in de bouwkunst." *De 8 en Opbouw*, vol 3, 1932, pp 223-28. Dutch: "The 'New Objectivity' in architecture." The philosophical, critical article responds to two pieces in the Ghent, Belgium newspaper *Vooruit*: "Kroniek door Henri Polak," 23 January 1932, avbd, and an interview with Berlage, 13 February 1932, avbd; each is cited. Reprinted as a booklet, and in Oud, *Nieuwe Bouwkunst in Holland en Europa*, 1935.

257. Oud, J.J.P., "Ontwerp voor een huis in Pinehurst (USA)." *De 8 en Opbouw*, vol 3, 1932, pp 229. Dutch: "Design for a house in Pinehurst." Oud was commissioned by the American Philip Johnson to design a house for his parents in North Carolina; financial problems led to shelving of the project. The piece is descriptive, illustrated by views of the model and drawings.

258. Rietveld, Gerrit Thomas, *Nieuwe Zakelijkheid in de Nederlandsche Architectuur*, Amsterdam, 1932. Not seen. Originally published in *Vrije Bladen*, vol 9, 1932, no 7, pp 1-27. Reviewed van Ravesteyn, *Gemeenschap*, vol 10, 1934. p 801; Knuvelder, *Roeping*, 1931-32, p 815; *Bouwkundig Weekblad*, 1934, p 550.

259. Rothschild, R[ichard], "Passeggiata architettonica in Olanda." *Rassegni di Architettura*, vol 4, 1932, no 10, pp 419-427. Italian: "An architectural walk in Holland." The "celebrated" Oud is specifically discussed in half a column of this

general piece; some of his other works are mentioned but attention is drawn to Kiefhoek's "optimum esthetic solution." There are views of a corner shop and the Apostolic Church. For an expanded version in German see "Bauen im ausland: Holland," *Deutsche Bauzeitung*, vol 67, 1933, pp 65-74.

260. Torry, Euphemia, "Dutch colour Schemes." *Paint,* vol 4, 1932, no 1, pp 13-15. English. A British traveler observes that the "splashes of brilliance"— orange doors and yellow or green strips of color—overcome the monotony of Oud's "Council Houses" in Rotterdam (Kiefhoek).

261. *De 8 en Opbouw*, "Interieurs van Allegonda." Vol 3, 1932, no 24, p 235. Dutch. Illustrations only, reprinted from *Bouwen*.

262. *Architectural Forum*, "Thirteen housing developments." Vol 56, 1932, pp 261-83. English. It is noteworthy that three of the international developments presented are by Oud: large photographs and plans show Weissenhofsiedlung Kiefhoek and Hoek van Holland. The brief commentary is descriptive, general and full of admiration for the economies of modernism.

263. *Bouwbedrijf,* "Architect J.J.P. Oud." Vol 9, 1932, no 25, p 316. Dutch. The eulogistic half page editorial is about Oud's resignation from the Rotterdam municipal architect's office on 1 April 1932 to set up in private practice.

264. *La Casa Bella*, [Image of Apostolic church, Kiefhoek reprinted from *R.K. Bouwblad*, no 12, 1931.] Vol 10, 1932, no 50, p 72. Italian.

265. *Fortune*, "How much house for a dollar?" Vol 5, 1932, no 4, p 34ff. English. The essay discusses the cost of domestic building in the USA and illustrates Oud's Stuttgart houses with the complicated caption, "A German solution by a Dutch architect of the problem of the house in rows."

1933
Journals
266. Berkovich, Elmer, "Het stalen meubel." *De Delver*, vol 7, 1934, pp 9-14. Dutch: "Steel furniture." The general piece (dated 13 September 1933) by the furniture designer examines the development of steel furniture in Europe, naming Oud among the Dutch architects who took it seriously.

267. Flouquet, P.-L., "Les cités-jardins." *Bâtir*, 1933, no 5, pp 164-69. French: "Garden cities." While the text broadly deals with garden city and garden suburb, for some reason Oud's Weissenhofsiedlung houses are illustrated.

268. Henvaux, E., "L'architecture vivante en Hollande." *La Cité,* vol 11, 1933, no 31, p 47ff. French: "Living architecture in Holland." Not seen.

269. Oud, J.J.P., "The European movement towards a new architecture." *Studio*, vol 105, 1933, April, pp 249-56. English. This sermon defines modernist purpose as "seeking clear forms for clearly expressed needs." It begins with the idea of internationalism, and demonstrates the development of Dutch modernism, expectedly focussing upon De Stijl. Oud claims that Dudok "falsely interpreted" De

Stijl's version of cubism to create "a new Romanticism, a play with cubic masses for the pleasure of playing only." See also *ibid.*, October, p 233, which published Oud's amendments to the text. Reprinted in *Nieuwe Bouwkunst in Holland en Europa*, The Hague, 1935. Oud also tried to have the piece published in *Sowjet-Architektur* and *Shelter*.

270. Oud, J.J.P., "Waarom schoonheidscommissies?" *De 8 en Opbouw*, vol 4, 1933, p 73. Dutch: "Why beauty commissions?" This is Oud's comment on the appointment of municipal aesthetic commissions in Holland.

271. Pétrasch, Charles "L'effort des constructeurs hollandais." *Bâtir,* 1933, no 11, October, pp 401-03. French: "The effort of Dutch builders." The inaccurate piece devotes a single short (but adulatory) paragraph to Oud, "the man of the South," and publishes two large images of Kiefhoek and another of Weissenhofsiedlung.

272. *L'Architecture Vivante* [Images of Kiefhoek.] Vol 11, 1933, Spring, plates 19-25.

273. *L'Architettura*, 1933, p 119. Italian. A single paragraph in the "International Architecture" section accompanies images: Oud, Brinkman and van der Vlugt and J.F.Staal are contrasted with Dudok.

1934
Books and Monographs
274. Anderson, M.L. (ed.), *International Architecture 1924-34*, London, 1934. English. The catalog of the centenary exhibition of the RIBA at the new Portland Place premises, opened by the Princess Royal on 30 November 1934 also includes a number of essays about the practice and profession of architecture. The show included the Kiefhoek and Hoek van Holland houses (illustrated). See also *RIBA Journal*, vol 41, 1934, p 1040; vol 42, 1934, p 151, 203; 241-50.

275. Bauer, Catherine K., *Modern Housing*, Boston, 1934. English. The book sets the background of the failure of 19th century cities, reviews early reforms, and assesses post-World War I housing in Europe and America before examining the Elements of Modern Housing. There are references to the Dutch achievement and the 1901 *Woningwet*. Illustrations (too remote from the text) include views of Hoek van Holland and Kiefhoek. Reprinted New York, 1974. See also Bauer, "The Americanization of Europe," *New Republic*, vol 67, 1931, pp 153-54.

276. McGrath, Raymond, *Twentieth Century Houses*, London, 1934. English. The book represents "the small number of good new houses in twenty different countries." Holland has three paragraphs; examples include Hoek van Holland and Weissenhofsiedlung row houses. External views and plans are provided and there are criticisms in the text, together with a brief biography of Oud, with his "clean sense of form." Reviewed Oud, *De 8 en Opbouw*, vol 6, 1935, pp 11-12.

277. Yorke, Francis Reginald Stevens, *The Modern House*, London, 1934. 1944. English. The 1944 tract varies from earlier editions by replacing some examples, perhaps for the sake of a xenophobic U.S. market. The optimistic introduction is

steeped in *zeitgeist*, owing much to Le Corbusier's *Vers Une Architecture*. Oud's Weissenhofsiedlung houses are illustrated over the caption "Workers' houses at Amsterdam ... a modern standard."

Journals

278. Berkovich, Elmer, "Het meubel in 1934." *De Delver*, vol 8, 1934, December, pp 44-48. Dutch: "Furniture in 1934." Publicizing the Amsterdam exhibition "Steel furniture in 1934," organized by the manufacturers Metz and Co, the piece asserts that Oud's chairs form a "chapter in the historical development" of the genre. There is a photograph of the steel furniture display in Metz's store in The Hague, including Oud's chairs 01, 02, 03 and 04.

279. Gelderen, W. van, "Over de Opbouw-tentoonstelling." *De 8 en Opbouw*, vol 5, 1934, no 12. Dutch: "The Opbouw exhibition." Opbouw mounted an exhibition in May 1934 at the *Studio 32* Theater, Rotterdam. Oud's work was included but there is no discussion of it in the text.

280. H[oste], H[uib], "Metaalmeubelen." *Opbouwen*, 1934, vol 4, 15 January, p 14. Dutch: "Metal furniture." Written in conjunction with the Amsterdam and The Hague exhibitions "Steel furniture in 1934," organized by Metz and Co, the editorial cites Oud's "philosophical declaration" of his chair designs.

281. Hoste, Huib, "Oud's nieuwe metaalmeubelen." *Opbouwen*, vol 4, 1934, 15 May, p 129-31. Dutch: "Oud's new metal furniture." Written as a sequel to 280, the piece offers a little criticism and also cites Oud, "De stalen stoel voortbrengsel van kunstnijverheid?," *Nieuwe Rotterdamsche Courant*, 9 April 1934, avbd. Oud's identical text appears as "Tentoonstelling Liberty," *De 8 en Opbouw*, 1934, p 9, where there is a photograph of the Metz showroom, captioned "New chairs by Oud" and illustrating Oud's chairs 01, 02, 03, 04. Contra. Jan de Meijer, "Vakverrotting [The decay of skill]," *Bouwkundig Weekblad*, 1935, pp 463-64.

282. Lionni, Leo, "La nuova architettura Olandese," *Casabella*, vol 7, 1934, pp 73-78. Italian: "The new Dutch architecture." Oud is mentioned only in passing.

283. Oud, J.J.P., "Dr H.P.Berlage, 1856-1934," *Bouwkundig Weekblad*, vol 55, 1934, no 51, pp 26-27. Dutch. The identical text appears (with illustrations) in *De 8 en Opbouw*, vol 5, 1934, pp 149-52. All the *Weekblad* obituaries were reissued as a book, *H.P.Berlage ter Gedachtenis, 21 Febr. 1856-12 Aug. 1934*. See also *L'Architecture d'Aujourd'hui*, December 1934, p 245.

284. Oud, J.J.P., "Huis 'Allegonda' te Katwijk aan Zee." *Linoleumnieuws*, 1934, no 7, pp 12-14. Dutch: "House *Allegonda* at Katwijk an Zee." Not seen.

285. Oud, J.J.P., "Ik dacht zoo: over Jan Jans en zijn ordeel." *De 8 en Opbouw*, vol 5, 1934, p 140. Dutch: "I thought so: on Jan Jans and his trial." A letter to the editor comments on a piece in the 7 July issue.

286. Oud, J.J.P., "Stadt ohne Denkmaler? Ein Umfrage." *Prager Tageblatt*, no 31, 1934, p 111. German. Not seen.

287. Oud, J.J.P., "Stellung und Aufgabe des architekten." *Deutsche Bauzeitung*, 1934, no 50, pp 975-76. German: "The place and role of the architect." Oud responds to three complex questions about the future of the architect in the face of changing culture and economy, posed in the previous issue. For a Dutch translation see "Plaats en taak van den architect," *Nieuwe Rotterdamsche Courant*, 2 February 1935, p 2 (reprinted *Cobouw*, 12 February 1935, p 1).

288. Révèsz-Alexander, Magda, "Modern epitszet s tradicio Hollandiban." *Magyar Muveszet*, vol 10, 1934, pp 289-305. Hungarian: "Modern architecture and tradition in Holland." Not seen.

289. Tusschenbroek, Otto van, "Bij den cursus: De ontwikkeling van de Bouw- en Beeldhouwkunst." *VU* [*Volks Universiteit*], 1934, 23 November. Dutch. The university newsletter announces a course of lectures, *The Development of Architecture and Sculpture*, to be offered in the new year. Oud's Apostolic Church is held out as an exemplar of the timeless truths about design.

290. Yorke, Frederick Reginald Stevens, "Today." *Architectural Review*, vol 76, 1934, pp 9-16. English. This article summarizes Yorke's *The Modern House* and includes views of the Stuttgart row houses, not mentioned in the text.

291. *Nieuwe Rotterdamsche Courant*, "Bij ons in Hillegersberg." 1934, 13 January, p 1; 20 January, p 1; 24 January, pp 2-3; 27 January, p 3. Dutch: "Near us in Hillegersberg." The sub-heading of the first of four articles in the paper's "Onder de Menschen" column asks, "are we going to lose Oud to America?" Beginning with correspondence from Philip Johnson of the New York Museum of Modern Art, about a visit, the series explores Oud's career. There are citations from him, references to the international literature and small images of Hoek van Holland, the Johnson house model and Oud's living room. The author is probably M.J.Brusse (de Gruyter et al., *J.J.P. Oud, Architect*, 1951, p 31).

292. *Nieuwe Rotterdamsche Courant*, "Metz and Co." 1934, 11 November, ocbd C p 3. News item about new premises in The Hague (architect, Willem Penaat) mentions the tubular steel furniture Oud designed for the interiors firm.

293. *Telegraaf*, "'Enerveerend geluid moet worden geweerd'." 1934, 29 August, p 3. Dutch: "Tiring noise must be averted." The paper publishes Oud's thoughts on the effectiveness of the "*Geluidsstichting*" (lit. Noise foundation)

1935
Books and Monographs
294. Highton, John E., *Working Class Housing on the Continent*, Edinburgh, 1935. English. Commissioned by the Department of Health for Scotland, this report of its Secretary's study tour deals with social issues, economics, housing standards and architecture. An appendix describes (i.a.) Kiefhoek in detail.

295. Oud, J.J.P., *Nieuwe Bouwkunst in Holland en Europa*, Amsterdam/Den Dolder, 1935. Dutch: *New Architecture in Holland and Europe*. The slim book reprints "De 'Nieuwe Zakelijkheid' in de bouwkunst," *De 8 en Opbouw*, 1932 and

"The European movement towards a new architecture," *Studio*, 1933. Reviewed: "Twee boekjes over bouwkunst," *Telegraaf*, 7 July 1935 and "Nieuwe bouwkunst," *Nieuwe Rotterdamsche Courant*, 28 September 1935, p 1. Facsimile Amsterdam, 1981, with an afterword by Bernard Colenbrander.

Journals

296. Berlage, Miep van R., "De moderne keuken." *Wereldkroniek*, 1935, 23 March, pp 407, 413. Dutch: "The modern kitchen." Oud's L-shaped kitchen in the Stuttgart row houses is offered as a model. There is a photograph.

297. Elzas, A., "Theo van Doesburg." *De 8 en Opbouw*, 1935, 17 August, pp 173-182. Dutch. The article is structured as a chronology and provides good background reading for the student of Oud.

298. Gruyter, W. Jos. de, "Het nieuwe gebouw van Metz en Co te Den Haag." *Elseviers Geïllustreerd Maandschrift*, 1935, pp 63-64, plate xv. Dutch: "Metz and Co's new building in The Hague." In a piece praising Willem Penaat's and Bart van der Leck's designs for the new showroom (in a building by Rietveld), Oud's steel furniture is also eulogized. There is a photo of his Metz chairs 01, 02, 03, and 04 in the Amsterdam store. See also Pierre Migeonnes, "La couleur dans la décoration moderne en Hollande," *Art et Décorations*, vol 38, 1935, pp 347-51.

299. Oud, J.J.P., "Comment je conçois ma tache." *L'Architecture d'Aujourd'hui*, February, 1935. French: "How I work." This pragmatic description of Oud's *modus operandi* is illustrated with design drawings of the Blijdorp project, and D. Hannema's work room/library, Rotterdam. Reprinted from *Architektur der U. d. S.S.R.*, no 6, 1933, p 27, for which Oud wrote in German, September 1933 (but see *Nieuwe Rotterdamsche Courant*, 20 January, p 1).

300. Oud, J.J.P., [Greater Amsterdam extension plan.] *Telegraaf*, 1935, 18 June, avbd, p 4; 20 June, avbd p 5. Dutch. This is a serialized article on the Amsterdam extension plan: "Uitbreidingsplan voor Groot-Amsterdam" is a general, polemical commentary; "Toekomstig Amsterdam onder de loupe," just as polemical, purports to consider the detail. Part 3 not seen.

301. Oud, J.J.P., "Men moet het nieuwe bouwen zijn kans geven." *Telegraaf*, 1935, 31 March, p 5. Dutch: "People should give the new building its chance." The article takes the form of a series of questions and Oud's concise answers.

302. Oud, J.J.P., "Het nieuwe bouwen. Landelijke architectuur." *Groene Amsterdammer*, vol 59, 1935, 7 December. Dutch: "The new building. National architecture." The illustrated essay, provoked by a book, *Overijssel, Hoe het Bouwt ...* asserts that "a national architecture is no foundation for the future." A.J. Kropholler, a champion of vernacular, "natural" conservatism, gets a drubbing. It excited a lively response: see *ibid.*, vol 60, 4 January 1936, p 10.

303. Oud, J.J.P., "Van hout tot staal." *Groene Amsterdammer*, vol 59, 1935, 19 January, p 16. Dutch: "From timber to steel." The subtitle "developing directions for the chair" describes the content, and focuses on growing domestic use of

tubular steel chairs. There are images of modern furniture, from Rietveld's red-blue chair to Oud's Metz chair 03. In late 1934-early 1935 there was an exhibition entitled "The chair during the last 40 years" at the Stedelijk Museum Amsterdam, organized by V.A.N.K.

304. Pica, Agnoldomenico, "Nascita e fortuna dell'architettura Olandese moderna" *Emporium*, vol 82, 1935, pp 249-258. Italian: "Birth and fortunes of modern Dutch architecture." Much of the overview is given to Oud: Stuttgart, Hoek van Holland and Oud-Mathenesse are specifically mentioned.

305. Shand, P. Morton, "Scenario for a human drama: vi. *La machine-à-habiter* to the house of character." *Architectural Review*, vol 78, 1935, no 459, pp 61-64. Sixth in a series about the history of the early Modern Movement (*ibid.*, July, August, September, October 1934 and January 1935), the often specious article traces development from Berlage and Cuypers in "The Dutch Contribution." Oud is called a "left-wing" architect and the Villa *Allegonda*, rarely seen in non-Dutch journals, is illustrated but attributed solely to Kamerlingh Onnes.

306. Sijmons, K.L., "Rectificatie." *De 8 en Opbouw,* vol 6, 1935, no 3, p 32. Dutch: "Rectification." The piece discusses a number of the German *siedlungen* of the 1920s, including Stuttgart, emphasizing the durability and economics of the project. It concludes that after eight years Oud's row houses looked the best.

307. S[tam], M[art], "Op Donderdag 20 Juni hield architect J.J.P. Oud voor ons een lezing in het Stedelijk Museum te Amsterdam." *De 8 en Opbouw*, 1935, pp 170-71. Dutch. Oud's lecture at the *De 8* townplanning exhibition is partly cited and reviewed. See also *Nieuwe Rotterdamsche Courant*, "De nieuwe bouwkunst," 1935, 21 June, avbd p 1; *Cobouw*, 25 June 1935, p 6; *Maasbode*, 21 June 1935, avbd p 6. Contra. *R.K. Bouwblad*, vol 6, 11 July 1935, p 400; *ibid.*, vol 7, 28 November 1935, p 144.

308. *Nieuwe Rotterdamsche Courant*, "De nieuwe beurs te Rotterdam." 1935, 6 June, p 1. Dutch: "The new Rotterdam stock exchange." An extensive news item about Staal's winning design evaluates Oud's entry in an earlier competition. See also *Maasbode*, 8 June 1935, avbd p 5.

309. *Nieuwe Rotterdamsche Courant*, [Van Doesburg.] 1935, 2 February, avbd p 2; 6 February, avbd p 2. Dutch. A two-part article, "A soon-forgotten art reformer," provides background for the student of Oud, whose *De Stijl* obituary (1932, pp 46-47) for van Doesburg is cited.

310. *Stavba*, [Houses by Oud.] Vol 13, 1935, no 1, pp 7-9. Czechoslovakian. Not seen.

1936
Books and Monographs
311. Barr, Alfred H., *Cubism and Abstract Art*, New York, 1936. English. The profusely-illustrated (in poor quality monochrome) catalog of an exhibition at the New York Museum of Modern Art presents a short history of De Stijl, inevitably

including Oud, one of the "finest artists of our time." His Hoek van Holland houses and Café De Unie are briefly discussed; the latter and the interior of *De Vonk* are illustrated. The Oud-Mathenesse director's hut appeared in the exhibition. There is a short, misleading biographical note. Reprinted 1964, 1974.

312. Boeken, Albert, *Architectuur*, Amsterdam, 1936. Dutch. Reference is made in this series of polemical essays to Oud's Tusschendijken housing, called a "tusschenstadium." Reviewed *Kroniek voor Kunst en Kultuur*, 1936, p 61. Reprinted 1981, with an afterword by Mabel Hoogendonk.

313. Pevsner, Nikolaus, *Pioneers of the Modern Movement*, London, 1936. English. The book outlines the development of modern design until about 1916. It notices Berlage ("regarded in Holland as of greater European significance than appears convincing") and the rise of Expressionism but emphasis upon the German contribution leads to an underestimation of Dutch achievements. Revised as *Pioneers of Modern Design from William Morris to Walter Gropius*, Harmondsworth, 1949. Second edition, New York, 1949. Revised 1960, reprinted 1964; second revised 1968, reprinted 1972, 1975, with little change of mind. Translated as *I pionieri del movimento moderno*, Milan, 1947.

Journals

314. Buys, H., "Interieurs van architect J.J.P. Oud, Hillegersberg." *Het Landhuis*, 1936, p 156. Dutch: "Interiors by Oud ..." After a brief review of his career and Oud's place in European architecture, the descriptive/critical article concentrates upon his furniture. There are good images of D. Hannema's workroom/library.

315. Hoste, Huib, "Moderne architectuur in Holland." *Nieuw Vlaanderen*, 1936, 10 October. Dutch. Not seen.

316. Koldewey, B.J., "Over den vormwil bij be Nieuwe Zakelijkheid." *R.K. Bouwblad*, vol 8, 1936, 6 September, pp 45-48. Dutch: "Concerning the esthetic willfulness of the New Objectivity." Using Oud's lectures on the New Objectivity and van Ravesteyn's "Architectuur, J.J.P. Oud," *Gemeenschap*, 1932 as springboards, the reactionary polemic attacks internationalism.

317. Merkelbach, Benjamin et al., "Internationale en nationale bouwkunst." *Groene Amsterdammer*, vol 60, 1936, 4 January, p 10. Dutch: "International and national architecture." Merkelbach acts as umpire in a debate sparked by Oud's "Het nieuwe bouwen. Landelijke architectuur," *ibid.*, 7 December 1935. Responses by C.M. van Moorsel, A.J. Kropholler (who bore the brunt of Oud's criticism) and J.A.C.Tillema are followed by Oud's reply and editorial comment.

318. Merkelbach, Benjamin, et al., "Het nieuwe bouwen. Onze raadhuisenquête." *Groene Amsterdammer*, vol 60, 1936, 4 April, p 10. Dutch: "... Our town hall enquiry." The paper publishes Oud's response (i.a.) to questions (*ibid.*, 7 March) about the commissioning of the proposed Amsterdam town hall.

319. Oud, J.J.P., "Atelierwoning te Blaricum van architect F.Hausbrand." *Bouwkundig Weekblad*, vol 57, 1936, p 357. Dutch: "Studio-house at Blaricum..."

Oud takes occasion of the publication of a small house by Frans Hausbrand to criticize the building approvals process of the Blaricum municipality's "beauty commission."

320. Oud, J.J.P., "Bij de dood van Leen van der Vlugt." *De 8 en Opbouw*, vol 7, 1936, p 112. Dutch: "On the passing of Leen van der Vlugt." Obituary.

321. Oud, J.J.P., "Mies van der Rohe." *De 8 en Opbouw*, vol 7, 1936, pp 71-72. Dutch. The eulogy is written in celebration of the German architect's fiftieth birthday (27 March).

322. Oud, J.J.P., "Het nieuwe bouwen. Tegenstanders en meeloopers." *Groene Amsterdammer*, vol 60, 1936, 5 September, pp 10-11. Dutch: "The new building. Resisters and hangers-on." This seems to be Oud's rather belated last word in a long-running debate through *De Groene.* See also ibid., 7 December 1935; 4 January 1936 and 4 April 1936.

323. *Het Landhuis*, [Photograph]. 1936, 11 November. An image of the sitting room of a Bussum house by Penaat features steel framed easy chairs by Oud.

324. *Maasbode*, "De nieuwe bouwkunst." 1936, 28 February. Dutch: "The new architecture." This reports Oud's 27 February lecture to the *Rotterdamschen Kunstkring*, in association with a show of his work. See also *Vaderland*, 28 February 1936; "Architect Oud," *Maasbode*, 3 March; *Telegraaf*, "Ontwerpen van den architect J.J.P. Oud," 1936, 8 April, p 7; "Brieven over bouwkunst," *Nieuwe Rotterdamsche Courant*, 29 February (with view of Weissenhofsiedlung) and P.A.B., "Werken van ... Oud," *Vorwaarts*, 10 March 1936.

325. *Vooruit*, "Voordracht van architect J.J.P. Oud." 1936, 11 March. Dutch: "Lecture by ... Oud." The news item summarizes a lecture " The new architecture and interior design: its beginning and its direction," to V.A.N.K. and the Society for Cultural Cooperation at The Hague on 11 March.

1937
Books and Monographs
326. Agate, Gustave (ed.), *Building in Lancashire*, Preston, 1937. In a book produced by the Council for the Preservation of Rural England, a chapter "Suburban Development" by F.L. Halliday illustrates (unidentified) the Hoek van Holland houses, remarked for their "severely practical" aspect.

327. Behrendt, Walter Curt, *Modern building: its Nature Problems and Forms*, New York, 1937. English. Oud is accorded the highest place in the Modern Movement and cited as spokesman for modernism. His view of the link between Wright's early work and cubism is expanded. Kiefhoek housing is illustrated.

328. Eibink, Adolf, W.J.Gerretsen and J.P.L.Hendricks (eds.), *Dutch Architecture of Today*, Amsterdam, 1937. Dutch/English/German/French. Published under the *aegis* of the BNA, the book provides an overview of Dutch architects—mostly Functionalists. J.P.Mieras provides a polemical introduction to over 200

images, including two photographs and rather stark plans, without annotation, of the Apostolic Church, Kiefhoek. Reviewed *Gids*, 1937, part 4, p 133; *R.K. Bouwblad*, 1937-38, p 92.

329. Retera, W., *Het Moderne Interieur*, Amsterdam, ca. 1937. Dutch: *The Modern Interior*. The profusely illustrated book is preoccupied with the Dutch version of international functionalism. Oud's 1927 retrofit of the villa *Allegonda*, and his own house are included. Reviewed *Architectura*, 1937, p 393; *Gids*, 1939, part 1, p 233; *R.K. Bouwblad*, 1937-38, p 156; *Landhuis*, 1937, p 718.

330. Roos, Frank John Jr., *An Illustrated Handbook of Art History*, New York, 1937. English. There is an indistinct view of Oud's Hoek van Holland housing in this collection of images of world art by the Professor of Art History, University of Ohio. Reprinted 1947; revised, second edition 1954; third edition ca. 1970.

Journals
331. Gruyter, W. Jos. de, "The useful arts in Holland," *Studio*, vol 114, 1937, pp 278-79. English. This deals with interiors and furniture, including Metz and Co's commission of architects and artists as designers. Oud is mentioned but his work is not illustrated.

332. Wiessing, H.P.L. "The development of modern Dutch architecture," *Building*, vol 12, 1937, pp 395-99. English. A broad, objective summary links Oud with Rietveld as a New Objectivist and names him as the sponsor of modernism, "and not only in Holland."

333. Z———, S., "Leelijk Rotterdam: strijd tegen conservatisme en wansmaak." *Groene Amsterdammer*, vol 61, 16 January 1937, p 6. Dutch: "Ugly Rotterdam: resisting conservatism and poor taste." The refers to the despoiling of the Café De Unie and there is a rare photograph of the altered facade (*Restaurant Modern[e]*). Cf. *De 8 en Opbouw*, "Café de Unie, later Café 'Den Ouden'," Vol 7, 1936, no 9, p 102.

1938
Books and Monographs
334. Hoyer, Th.B.F., *Nieuw Amsterdam 1626-1936*, Haarlem 1938. Dutch. The magnificent souvenir book published to celebrate the launching of the flagship of the Holland-America Line is printed on art paper, complete with gatefolds, and bound with a gold cord. There are colored renderings of several interiors, including Oud's first-class swimming pool. See also *Nieuw Amsterdam: Facts and Figures*, published by the Holland-America Line, Rotterdam, 1939; C. van Herk, *De Schepen van de Holland-Amerika Lijn*, Bussum, 1981; van Herk, "De *Nieuw Amsterdam*," *Samenspel*, November 1981, pp 12-18.

335. Mumford, Lewis, *The Culture of Cities*, New York, 1938. 1953. Reissued as *The City in History*, Harmondsworth, 1961, 1966, 1984 The book's scope is too great for attention to detail. Oud receives passing mention, almost in the same breath as the New Objectivists.

336. *Van het Eenvoudigste Landhuis tot het Grootste Schip van Nederland,* Wassenaar[?], n.d. [?1938.] Dutch: *From the Simplest House to Holland's Greatest Ship.* An advertising brochure of VEVO parquetry manufacturers includes photographs of three floors in the *Nieuwe Amsterdam*, including Oud's circular dance floor in the tourist class lounge (with a large detailed plan).

337. Vriend, Jacobus Johannes, *De Bouwkunst van ons Land*, Amsterdam, 1938. Dutch: *The Architecture of Our Land.* The last chapter covers the 19th and 20th centuries. There are short biographical notes on Oud, but the Apostolic church is the latest building mentioned. This original part dealt with the "flat land", the second with the cities. Reissued in three parts in 1939, to which *Het Interieur* was added in 1950, and which illustrates some of Oud's interiors on the *Nieuw Amsterdam*. Reviewed *Amstelodamum*, 1939, p 43; Fischer, *Architectura*, 1939, p 253; *R.K. Bouwblad*, 1938-39, p 290.

Journals
338. Dingemans, C.F.J., "Development of modern architecture in Holland." *AA Journal*, vol 54, 1938, July, pp 39-43. English. Published to prepare members for a 12-day tour of Holland in September, the essay notes that Oud's architectural output "is not accordance with his qualities and reputation." His links to De Stijl are mentioned.

339. H[endriks], J.P.L., "De architect en het scheepsinterieur." *Bouwkundig Weekblad*, vol 59, 1938, pp 417-27. Oud's role in the design of the *Nieuw Amsterdam* is noted, and there are images of his tourist class lounge and smoking room, and first class swimming pool.

340. Oud, J.J.P., "Saenredam en Le Corbusier." *De 8 en Opbouw*, vol 9, 1938, p 217-18. Dutch. Moved by an article in *ibid.*, no 19, 1938, Oud makes a brief comparison (dated October 1938) between Le Corbusier as a painter and the Dutch artist Pieter Saenredam (1597-1665). There is a comment by J.B. van Loghem in the following issue. The publication coincided with an exhibition, *Pieter Jansz. Saenredam*, at the Boymans Museum, Rotterdam.

341. Stam, M[artinus Adrianus], "Het passagiersschip *Nieuw Amsterdam*." *De 8 en Opbouw,* vol 9, 1938, pp 119-28. Dutch. Oud is not mentioned in the essay, illustrated with photographs taken by Eva Besnyö, on the maiden voyage. See also *Elseviers Gëillustreerd Maandschrift*, vol 95, May 1938, pp 302-32. Cf. Guido Hoogewoud, "De *Nieuw Amsterdam*, overal een andere (luxe) vormgeving," *Wonen TA/BK*, 1974, no 5, pp 25-28, which reprints many of Besnö's images.

342. Wiessing, H.P.L., "J.J.P. Oud." *Building*, vol 13, 1938, pp 274-78. English. An often inaccurate biography develops into eulogy as Oud becomes the hero of modernism; indeed, the father of it and inventor of the term "international style." Berlage's and Wright's influences are noted. Illustrations include a portrait; Hoek van Holland; Kiefhoek church (captioned "apartment houses"); Rotterdam stock exchange design; Stuttgart housing; *Nieuw Amsterdam* tourists' lounge; and the "Pinehurst" model.

343. *Nieuwe Rotterdamsche Courant*, "De samenwerking tusschen directie en architecten." 1938, 23 April, p 7. Dutch: "Cooperation between management and architects." A special edition of the newspaper, replete with images, celebrated the completion of the *Nieuw Amsterdam*. The piece reports an interview with Oud about the commission. See *Rotterdamsch Nieuwsblad*, 23 April, 5de blad, p 2; *Maasbode*, 23 April 1938, pp 9-10; *Vaderland*, 27 April 1938, p 1.

344. *Nieuwe Rotterdamsche Courant*, "Het interieur van het D.S.M.S. *Noordam*." 1938, 15 September. Dutch: "The interior of the ... *Noordam*." The *Noordam* was a smaller sister ship of the *Nieuw Amsterdam*. Oud's design for the dining room is described; the dining room on the *Zaandam* was identical. Cf. *Toeristkampioen*, vol 3, 1938, p 1559. See also *Noordam, Zaandam*, Rotterdam, 1939; C. van Herk, *De Schepen van de Holland-Amerika Lijn*, Bussum, 1981; van Herk, "*Noordam, Zaandam*," *Samenspel*, June 1983, pp 14-16.

345. *Schip en Werf, Nieuw Amsterdam* number, n.d. [1938.]Dutch. The issue of the shipping journal provides a thorough documentation, including large foldout deck plans. Cf. *Wereldkroniek*, [*Nieuw Amsterdam* issue.]1938, 23 April.

346. *Studio*, "The *Nieuw Amsterdam*: a floating palace of art," vol 116, 1938, July, pp 3-18. English. The statement, "In comfort and in the quality of its decoration, the *Nieuw Amsterdam* can rightly claim a superlative" indicates the tone of an article stressing the Dutch role in striving for a new European architecture. Oud is specially mentioned. There are many interior and detail views. See *Casabella Costruzioni*, 1939, no 135 (Italian).

347. *Vie a la Campagne*, "Evolution de l'architecture et du mobilier au Pays-Bas." Vol 114, 1938, 15 December, pp 3-5. French: "Evolution of architecture and furniture in Holland." A rather broad article contrasts a view of Lede, Vreewijk (in the traditional style) with Oud's Hoek van Holland houses (in the modern style). Architects and designers, but not locations, are identified.

1939
Books and Monographs
348. Boerhave Beekman, W., *Hout van Oerwoud tot Interieur*, Deventer, 1939. Dutch: *Timber from Forest to Interior*. The book about world timbers by a "wood expert" illustrates Oud's own living room at Hillegersberg.

349. Yorke, Francis Reginald Stevens and Colin Penn, *A Key to Modern Architecture*, London, 1939. English. This jingoistic primer gives a potted history of architecture, before explaining the effect of structural systems upon form. Passing reference is made to the Dutch pioneers: Hoek van Holland is illustrated.

Journals
350. Gelder, H.G. van, "Ontwerpen voor het nieuwe gebouw der Bataafsche Import Maatschappij in Den Haag." *Elseviers Maandschrift*, vol 97, 1939, p 353-54; pl lxv. Dutch: "Design for the new B.I.M. [Shell] building in The Hague." The piece reports Oud's success in the competition for the building, discusses the

relative merits of the schemes of Kropholler, Roosenburg and Friedhoff and prophetically comments upon Oud's change of direction. There are two perspectives. See also "Oud's nieuwe zetel der Bataafsche Import Mij," *Vaderland*, 1939, 26 January. avbd C, p 1; *Voorwaarts*, 26 January; "Kantoorpaleis in de Residentie," *Telegraaf*, 26 January; *De Tijd*, 26 January; "Brieven over bouwkunst," *Nieuwe Rotterdamsche Courant*, 4 April. Most reproduce the perspective drawings. The proposal was reported and monitored in many national and provincial newspapers. Clippings abound in the Oud collection, NAi.

351. Oud, J.J.P., "Een ordeel van J.J.P. Oud, arch." *Cobouw*, vol 83, 24 January 1939. Dutch: "A judgement by ... Oud." A few paragraphs and three sketches set out Oud's opinion about the redevelopment of central Amsterdam around the Palace in the Dam.

352. Pevsner, Nikolaus, "Frank Lloyd Wright's peaceful penetration of Europe." *Architects' Journal*, vol 89, 1939, pp 731-34. English. First outlining Wright's points of contact with the European architectural community until 1911, the article discusses at length his influence upon the Dutch, including Oud. Reprinted in Dennis Sharp, *The Rationalists. Theory and Design in the Modern Movement*, London, 1978.

353. *De 8 en Opbouw*, [Interiors by Oud.] Vol 10, 1939, pp 21-30. Dutch. Gerrit Rietveld and W. van Gelderen each offer comment upon a collection of images of Oud's furniture, which he supplied at the editors' request. There are rarely published interiors of his house at Hillegersberg, as well as the additions to Villa *Allegonda*, Weissenhofsiedlung, the Metz chairs 03 and 04 (1934), the Metz fauteuil 07c (1934) and the tourist class lounge and smoking salon of the *Nieuwe Amsterdam*.

1940–1949

1940
Books and Monographs
354. Hamlin, Talbot Faulkner, *Architecture through the Ages*, New York, 1940. Revised 1953. English. The wide-ranging book does not have much space for Modernism. Oud, first praised for his "precise elegance and ... imaginative use of the simplest forms" is chastised in the second edition for decorating the Shell Building.

355. Richards, James Maude, *An Introduction to Modern Architecture*, Harmondsworth, 1940. English. Among the most widely read books on modernism, the book was reprinted 1941, 1944, 1948; revised 1953 (reprinted 1956, 1959, 1960); revised 1962. Oud is recognized as a major international player, although in such a general work treatment is slight. The Weissenhofsiedlung houses are illustrated. Translated into Dutch: *Moderne Architectuur,* Zeist, 1961.

356. Wattjes, Jannes Gerhardus and W.Th.H. ten Bosch, *Rotterdam en hoe Het Bouwde*, Leiden, 1940. Dutch: *Rotterdam and How it Built.* French, German and English summaries. A populist book, published only months before the bombing of Rotterdam, praises Oud's housing: Tusschendijken, Oud-Mathenesse and Kiefhoek are illustrated. The 1941 edition has German and English summaries.

Journals
357. Hitchcock, Henry-Russell Jr., "Wright's influence abroad." *Parnassus*, vol 12, 1940, pp 11-15. English. The brief, general and jingoistic article claims that Wright "paid off" the architectural debt to Europe. Specific mention is made of Oud's projects at Purmerend.

1941

Books and Monographs

358. Giedion, Siegfried, *Space, Time and Architecture, the growth of a new tradition*, London/Cambridge, Mass., 1941. 1942. 1943. 1947. 1949. 1952. 1963. 1967. English. Developed from Harvard University's Charles Eliot Norton lectures for 1938-39, this is among the century's most important architecture books. Taken together, the references to Oud throughout the book portray a pioneer of modern architecture. Also published as *Ruimte, Tijd en Architectuur*, Amsterdam, 1954; *Raum, Zeit, Architektur*, Ravensburg, 1964; *Spazio, Tempo ed Architettura*, Milan, 1954.

359. Kraayvanger, H.M. (ed.), *Nederland Bouwt in Baksteen 1800-1940*, Rotterdam, 1941. Dutch: *Holland Builds in Brick*. The catalog of an exhibition at the Boymans Museum, Rotterdam 26 July-15 November, is introduced by an essay, "Dutch architecture after Berlage." The Shell Building was included in the show. There are biographical notes, an incomplete list of works and bibliography, and illustrations. Reviewed Pica, "L'architettura olandese dal 1800 al 1940." *Costruzione Casabella*, 1942, April, pp 26-29.

Journals

360. Staal, Arthur, "Het gebouw der B.I.M." 1941, *Telegraaf*, 13 June, avbd p 3. Dutch: "The B.I.M. [Shell] Building." The review combines description with appreciative criticism. It mentions Kropholler's Sint-Paschalis church as a foil. There is a general view, a detail of the main entrance and a portrait. See also *De Standaard*, 3 June 1941.

361. Tusschenbroek, Otto van, "Architect J.J.P. Oud. Verbouwing van een woning te Rotterdam." *Interieur*, vol 58, 1941, no 408, pp 293-96. Dutch: "Oud ...Rebuilding a house in Rotterdam." The mostly descriptive piece reprints rarely published interiors by the photographer van Ojen of Oud's own house (Cf. *De 8 en Opbouw*, 1939, no 3, pp 21-30). The contractor, W. van Yperen, is identified.

362. Tusschenbroek, Otto van, "Werk van J.J.P. Oud voor de *Nieuw Amsterdam* en de *Noordam*." *Interieur*, vol 58, 1941, no 402, pp 115-18. Dutch: "Oud's work on the *Nieuw Amsterdam* and *Noordam*." Five excellent van Ojen photographs are accompanied by an "old news" description.

363. *Costruzione Casabella*, "Analisi degli elementi costituenti l'abitazione." 1941, no 163, pp 34-39. Italian: "Analysis of the elements of the house." The daylighting, ventilation, living rooms, kitchens, bedrooms and service areas of several European examples are examined, illustrated with interior views and plans. There is one view of Kiefhoek, not referred to in the text.

364. *Costruzione Casabella*, "Case a due piani isolate e a schiera." 1941, no 162, pp 15-23. Italian: "Two-story detached and row houses." Two columns of text accompany views and plans of German, Finnish, Swiss and Dutch examples, including Hoek van Holland and Kiefhoek.

1943
Books and Monographs
365. Kromhout, Johan Cornelis, "Architecture" in Barnouw and Landheer (eds.), *The Contribution of Holland to the Sciences*, New York, 1943. English. This propaganda publication lionizes the Amsterdam School and Dudok; other "internationalistic" moderns including Oud, are dismissed in the last paragraph.

366. Pevsner, Nikolaus, *An Outline of European Architecture*, Harmondsworth, 1943. 1945. 1951. 1953. 1957. 1960. 1963 (reprinted 1968 with revised bibliography). English. The influential book changed little throughout several editions: Oud briefly appears, in the shadow of Le Corbusier, and his "excellent ... working class houses near Rotterdam" and the Weissenhofsiedlung are mentioned. Dutch edition: *Geschiedenis van de Bouwkunst in Europa*, Rotterdam, 1949, 1965.

Journals
367. Mulhern, Elvira, "Netherlands architects set the pace." *Knickerbocker Weekly*, vol 3, 1943, no 27, pp 34-37. English. A glib essay, subtitled "Oud followed neoplasticists in functional design," traces Oud's career into the early 1930s. There are photographs of some better-known works.

1945
Journals
368. Oud, J.J.P., "Hoofdkantoor Bataafsche Import Maatschappij te 's-Gravenhage." *Bouwkundig Weekblad*, vol 63, 1945, p 14. Dutch: "Head office of B.I.M. [Shell Co] at The Hague." Oud's *toelichting* accompanies comprehensive general and detail photographs, floor plans, and sections. Reprinted as a booklet, January 1946. Cf. Oud, "Het nieuwe kantoorgebouw voor de B.I.M. ...," *Groene Amsterdammer*, 1945, no 30, p 10.

1946
Books and Monographs
369. *Piet Mondriaan Herdenkingstentoonstelling*, Amsterdam, 1946. Dutch: *Mondrian Memorial Exhibition*. Postwar austerity affected the quality of this catalog of a show at the Stedelijk Museum, Amsterdam, November-December 1946. It includes memorial essays by Oud, van Eesteren, Michel Seuphor, Til Brugman, Peter Alma and a piece by Mondrian himself.

Journals
370. Broek, Johannes Hendrik van den, "Stroomingen en tendenties in de nieuwe Nederlandsche architectuur." *Bouw*, vol 1, 1946, pp 4-11. Dutch: "Streams and tendencies in the new Dutch architecture." This general piece discusses what its title promises. It is claimed that Oud's nature broke through (one assumes) modernist stringency to decorate the Shell Building, which is illustrated.

371. Emden, S. J. van, "Samenspraak der architecten." *Bouw*, vol 1, 1946, pp 12-21. Dutch: "Dialog of the architects." The long, non-specific, polemical piece is about architectural unity: "the path to unity is beaten, but it is long and difficult." A large image of the Shell Building is unrelated to the text.

372. Oud, J.J.P., "Architecture today." *Yearbook of the Institute of Architects in Ireland*, 1946, pp 27-29. English. Oud ("the leading spiritual descendant of Berlage"), Gropius and Wright were each asked for "messages". Oud's short response (11 May 1946) pleads for a revival of modernism's first passion, extended to "make good building into fine architecture." There is a portrait and a view of the Shell Building.

373. Oud, J.J.P., "De Delftsche School en synthese in architecture." *Bouwkundig Weekblad*, vol 64, 1946, p 222. Dutch: "The Delft School and synthesis in architecture." Another of Oud's tirades against architectural conservatism (and conservation), is dated July 1946. The debate continued into 1947.

374. Oud, J.J.P., "Het dictatuur van de 'Delftsche school' en de volkhuisvesting." *Vrij Katheder*, vol 6, 1946, p 3013. Dutch: "The dictator of the Delft School and public housing." Oud's complaints in this polemic are about the conservative esthetic being applied to postwar reconstruction in Holland and the whole question of replicating historic buildings. Current proposals for Middelburg are criticized as a museum-like project. The "dictator" was Professor M.J.Granpré Molière of Delft *Technische Hogeschool.*

375. Oud, J.J.P., "Durven en niet durven in de architectuur." *Bouw*, vol 1, 1946, pp 613-14, 620-21. Dutch: "Daring and not daring in architecture." The journal conducted a forum about attitudes to post-war reconstruction. Oud was among many contributing architects and this essay eloquently encapsulates sentiments, both positive and negative, widely expressed elsewhere. Cf. 374 and 377.

376. Oud, J.J.P., "Vorm en Vrijheid." *Bouw*, 1946, December, special edition, p 5. Dutch: "Form and freedom." Oud responds at length to a *Gemeentemuseum* exhibition of Willem Marinus Dudok's two rebuilding plans for The Hague, greeting the "fresh" plan (in contrast to the contemporary redevelopment plan for Amsterdam) with relief.

377. Oud, J.J.P., "Wij bouwen weer op?" *Groene Amsterdammer*, 1946, 21 December, p 11. Dutch: "Who is rebuilding?" The piece continues Oud's criticism, begun six months earlier, of the *Delftsche School*, whose adherents secured many post World War II rebuilding commissions, and in many cases undertook to reconstruct rather than replace destroyed historical buildings. Oud's argues against anti-modern architecture. Reprinted *De Opbouw*, vol 1, January 1947, pp 11-13 and in Wiekart (ed.), *Ter Wille van een Levende Bouwkunst*, 1962.

378. *Architectural Record*, "Mr Oud embroiders a theme." Vol 100, 1946, December, pp 80-84. English. The Shell Building is reviewed in an inconclusive discussion of the apparent change in Oud's direction, which also criticizes him for "decorating" the design. There are many plans and photographs. Also illustrated are his Hoek van Holland houses, Rotterdam stock exchange design and Rotterdam City Center Project. See "Mr Oud replies ...," *ibid.*, vol 101, March 1947, p 18; for a Dutch translation see "Oud in de Amerikaanse pers," *Forum*, vol 2,

1947, pp 71-73, following editorial comment. See also "Periodical report," *Architectural Record*, November 1952, pp 348-50. Cf. "Das Unbehagen an der modernen Architektur," *Die Neue Zeitung*, 23 July 1951.

379. *RIBA Journal*, "Head office, Shell Company ..." vol 53, 1946, pp 162-66. English. A brief history precedes a general description of the building's construction. The article concludes with a minute resumé of Oud's career. There are general and detail photographs, plans, and a section. Cf. "BIM-building at The Hague," *Architectural Review*, vol 103, April 1947, pp 152-53. See also J.J.Vriend, "Het nieuwe kantoorgebouw voor de BIM door J.J.P. Oud," *Groene Amsterdammer*, 12 January 1946 (reprinted Vriend, *Reflexen,* 1959).

1947
Books and Monographs
380. Hamlin, Talbot, *Architecture: an Art for All Men*, New York, 1947. English. The book names Oud as a pioneer of modernism, but says little more about him.

Journals
381. Haas, H. J. de, "Kantoorgebouw van de Shell Nederland NV te 's-Gravenhage." *Bouwbedrijf,* vol 24, 1947, pp 11-16; 21-24; 31-34. Dutch: "Shell Company office building in The Hague." With a few minor mistakes of fact, the comprehensive series presents a critical and descriptive account from the design competition until completion. There are clear photographs, plans and sections.

382. Granpré Molière, Marinus Jan, "Delft en het nieuwe bouwen." *Katholiek Bouwblad,* vol 14, 1947, pp 146-56. Dutch: "Delft and the New Building." This response to criticism is a clear and concise apologetic for *Delftsche School* architecture. It should be studied in parallel with persistent attacks, including those by Oud through 1946 and 1947. Reprinted as a booklet.

383. Komter, Auke (ed.), "Stand van zaken." *Forum*, vol 2, 1947, pp 181-192. Dutch: "Position of the professions." Oud was among 25 eminent Dutch architects whose opinion was sought about the place and role of the *Architectura et Amicitia* group, of which *Forum* was the public voice. His response (i.a.) is cited.

384. Oud, J.J.P., "Bouwen in het zuiden." *Groene Amsterdammer*, 1947, 14 June, p 3. Dutch: "Building in the south." Oud takes up his theme of the Delft School, its Roman Catholic attachments, and the architecture of the predominantly Catholic southern provinces, especially Limburg. See also Oud, "Delftse school in namaak-antiek [letter to the editor]," *Kampioen*, 1947, p 308; Oud, "Walcheren," *Bouw*, 1947, p 275, with a response by one Gerber.

385. Oud, J.J.P., "Het geloof van een architect." *Groene Amsterdammer*, 1947, 23 August, p 7. Dutch: "The faith of an architect." Review of Ayn Rand's *The Fountainhead.*

386. Oud, J.J.P., "Meeningen over de Delftsche School." *Groene Amsterdammer*, 1947, 22 February, p 7. Dutch: "Opinions about the Delft School." The essay selectively cites some of the supportive correspondence provoked by "Wij

bouwen weer op?" *ibid.*, 21 December 1946. The Delft Student Association executive STYLOS responded ("Het Delftsche bouwen," *ibid.*, 19 April 1947, p 8); *De Groene* printed Oud's reply.

387. Oud, J.J.P., "Vragen en antwoorden over de wederopbouw in ons land." *Bouw*, vol 2, 1947, p 147. Dutch: "Questions and answers about the reconstruction of our land." The editors had asked for the opinions of a "few well-known figures in the architecture world." Oud's responses are concisely stated.

388. Schmitz, Marcel, "Le plan Dudok pour la reconstruction de La Haye." *Les Arts Plastiques*, 1947, no 2, pp 72-78 French: "The Dudok plan for rebuilding The Hague." After a diatribe on the nature of architecture and town planning, this essay reviews the proposals for The Hague, odiously comparing them with Oud's Hofplein proposal in Rotterdam plan and with developments in the center of Brussels. See *Chantiers*, January-February 1948, pp 14-20.

389. *Bouw*, "Toekomstig Almelo." Vol 2, 1947, part II, pp 146-47. Dutch: "Future Almelo." Not seen.

1948
Books and Monographs
390. Giedion, Siegfried, *Mechanization Takes Command: a Contribution to Anonymous History*, New York/Oxford, 1948. English. Reprinted 1955, 1975. The investigation of the impact of mechanization upon life deals with many areas. Rietveld is identified as an important pioneer, among other members of De Stijl. The Dutch contribution to functional houses is also treated: Oud's kitchen in the Stuttgart houses is discussed. Also published as *Die Herrschaft der Mechanisierung: ein Beitrag zur Anonymen Geschichte*, Frankfurt am Maine, 1977. 1987. Cf. "Die Mechanisierung des Haushaltes," *Werk*, 1947, no 9, pp 297-312.

391. Ravesteyn, L.J.C.J. van, *Rotterdam in de 20ste Eeuw,* Rotterdam 1948. Dutch: *Rotterdam in the Twentieth Century*. In the third volume in a series about the city's development, the Kiefhoek and Oud-Mathenesse housing estates are included against a wide backdrop. There are poorly reproduced aerial views.

392. Summerson, John, *Heavenly Mansions and Other Essays on Architecture*, London, 1948. English. Reprinted 1963. In "Architecture, painting and Le Corbusier" (the transcript of a Perry Bequest lecture at Bristol University, 1947), De Stijl is briefly discussed, and the rather specious claim made that Oud's plans are indistinguishable from Mondrian's paintings.

393. *Kantoorgebouw "Shell-Nederland N.V."* Rotterdam, 1948. French/English. This information booklet published by the *Bureau Documentatie Bouwwezen*, provides images, plans, elevations, sections and detail drawings, as well as statistical information about the building, down to color schemes and services.

Journals
394. Kloos, Jan Piet, "The Dutch melting pot." *Architectural Review*, vol 103, 1948, no 646, p 137-56. English. This wide-ranging and well-illustrated article

identifies the "isms" of modern Dutch architecture, summarizing the ideals of each. Among buildings discussed are the Shell offices, classified as an example of the New Empiricism, illustrated with ground floor plan and photographs.

395. Oud, J.J.P., "Drie nieuwe professoren in Delft." *Groene Amsterdammer*, 1948, 17 January. Dutch: "Three new professors at Delft." Oud comments upon the appointment of three senior lecturers at Delft *Technische Hogeschool*: Cor van Eesteren, J.H. van den Broek and G.H.Holt.

396. Oud, J.J.P., "Het gebouwencomplex van de U.N." *Forum*, vol 3, 1948, no 2, pp 38-40. Dutch: "The United Nations building complex." The polemic takes issue with Le Corbusier's *U.N. Headquarters* (New York, 1947) and the building itself. Reprinted Wiekart (ed.), *Ter Wille van een Levende Bouwkunst*, 1962.

397. Oud, J.J.P., "Gedachten over bouwkunst." *Gedenkboek ter Herinnering aan het 10-jarig Bestaan der vereniging Leerlingen der Rijks Normaalschool voor Teekenonderwijzers te Amsterdam*, Amsterdam, 1948. Dutch: "Thoughts on architecture." Not seen.

398. Oud, J.J.P., "Ontmoedigende plaatjes." *Groene Amsterdammer*, 1948, 7 August, p 8. Dutch: "Discouraging little pictures." Oud prefaces a review of an exhibition "New Dutch churches" and its catalog *Nieuwe Nederlands Kerken*, with a wistful summary of the national pre-war architectural scene.

399. Oud, J.J.P., "U.N. Building." *RIBA Journal*, vol 55, 1948, June, pp 363-64; October, p 560. English. In a letter to the editor, Oud uses criticisms of his Shell Building as a beachhead for a critique of the United Nations Building, New York, and to attack "architectural collectivism." He pleads for an architecture of faith, not brains. His comments drew fire (Howard Robertson, *ibid.*, July, p 422; Edward Passmore, *ibid.*, August, p 473). Oud's reply ("United Nations headquarters," *ibid.*, October, p 360) presents a lucid, concise defense of his own philosophical position on the New Architecture: "Functional building is [its basis] but it is not yet ... art-in-building." Reprinted *AIA Journal*, 1948, pp 278-80. See *RIBA Journal*, November 1948, p 38, for Passmore's last word.

400. *Elseviers Weekblad*, [Full page plate of rear view of Shell Building]. 1948, no. 50, p 71.

401. *De Rotterdammer*, "Op 'Oostduin' zal iets groots worden verricht." 1948, 1 May, p 4. Dutch: "Something big will be set up at Oostduin." News item about the *Nederlandse Hervormde* church's intention to construct a multipurpose building near The Hague. Oud 's 1951 designs were never realized.

1949
Books and Monographs
402. Plantenga, J.H. and A.van de Boom, *Viftig Eeuwen Bouw-, Beeldhouw- en Schilderkunst*, Zutphen, 1949. Dutch: *Fifty Centuries of Architecture, Sculpture and Painting*. It is perhaps significant that Oud's Shell Building should be among illustrations in a book that covers 5000 years.

403. Sartoris, Alberto, *Introduzione all'Architettura Moderna*, Milan, 1949. Italian: *Introduction to Modern Architecture*. Oud is bound to be mentioned an any book about modern architecture: this one briefly focuses upon the Weissenhofsiedlung row-houses. There is a photograph.

Journals

404. Mumford, Lewis, "Monumentalism, symbolism and style." *Architectural Review*, vol 105, 1949, April, pp 173-80. English. A response to ideas expressed in Siegfried Giedion's September 1946 lecture to the RIBA, "The need for a new monumentality," cites the Shell Building as evidence that Oud was one of several architects who, "on approaching maturity, promptly reached back for certain elements they had dropped in their first one-sided absorption in expressing technical processes."

405. Niegemann, J., "Vom bauen in Holland." *Der Baubilder*, 1949, pp 495-502. German: "Building in Holland." A short, non-specific article includes two images of the ESVEHA building, Rotterdam.

406. Oud, J.J.P., "Bouwen en pseudo-bouwen." *Groene Amsterdammer*, 1949, 22 January, p 7. Dutch: "Building and pseudobuilding." The essay continues Oud's long battle against the traditionalist philosophies of the *Delftsche School*, His argument is against anti-modern architecture and for the *Nieuwe Bouwen*. Cited in part *Forum*, vol 6, 1951, no 5-6.

407. Oud, J.J.P., "Bouwen zonder makeup." *Groene Amsterdammer*, 1949, 29 October, p 9. Dutch: "Building without makeup." The piece refers to his "Over de toekomstige bouwkunst en hare architectonische mogelijkheden," *Bouwkundig Weekblad*, 1921, and to the reinforced concrete designs of the Swiss engineer Robert Maillart (of the same spirit as Holland's "good old farm architecture")— all to make the point that Delft conservatism is a passing stylistic phase.

408. Oud, J.J.P., "Contemporary English architecture." *Architectural Times*, 1949, p 24. English. Commenting upon the uniqueness of English architecture, Oud identifies the best qualities of English country houses and reveals that his early study of them, and a love for modern painting provoked him "to strive after a functional architecture." English modern architecture, he says, is "the soundest in the world." He blames World War II for the "setback" of Dutch modernism. Cf. "Riesamina sé stesso," *Metron*, 1952, no 45, pp 7-15.

409. Oud, J.J.P., "Duidelijkheid in de stedebouw," *Forum*, vol 4, 1949, pp 127-30. Dutch: "Clarity in town planning." Rejecting the Corbusian idea of towers in parks, Oud promotes 3- or 4-story housing blocks to maintain desirable urban character. An abbreviated form appeared as *U.N. Bulletin 2: Housing and Town and Country Planning*, 1949, revised in *RIBA Journal*, March 1951, pp 193-95. See also *Ruimte*, November 1953; and Wiekart (ed.), *Ter Wille van een Levende Bouwkunst*, 1962. There is comment by Auke Komter, "Duidelijkheid in de stedebouw," *Forum*, 1949, pp 131-36.

410. Oud, J.J.P., "Groot 's-Gravenhage." *Groene Amsterdammer*, 1949, no 12, p 7. Dutch: "Greater The Hague." Oud's review of Dudok's structure plan for rebuilding The Hague includes his "overall impression that with a minimum of drawbacks and a wide view Dudok had made a spacious, beautiful plan that would be relevant for decades." They later came into conflict over the Congress building.

411. Oud, J.J.P., "Restaureren tot er de dood op volgt." *Amsterdams Weekblad*, 1949, 26 February, p 7. Dutch: "Restoration until death follows." The piece sets building restoration against living architecture, citing Gouda town hall as a building whose charm is in the layers of change imposed upon it, as opposed to the "frozen-in-time" approach of self-conscious restoration. See also Oud, "Restaureren tot verhoud." *ibid.*, 2 April 1949, in which he responds to G.C.Bremer's comments on this piece, *ibid.*, 26 March.

412. Vriend, Jacobus Johannes, "De natuur gestyleerd tot monument." *Groene Amsterdammer*, 1949, 8 October, p 9. This is a critique of Oud's proposal for the National monument at Grebbeberg, near Rhenen. There is an aerial perspective of the design, whose publication a few weeks earlier attracted great attention in the national press; see, e.g., "Nog veel nodig voor het nationale monument," *Algemeen Dagblad*, 23 August 1949, almost identical to "Nationaal legermonument Grebbeberg," *Nieuwe Rotterdamsche Courant*, 23 August 1949. Cf. "Stijvol oord van wijding en waardigheid," *Amsterdamse Parool*, 23 September 1950.

413. Wesiecker, Wilhelm, "Zweistimmige Baukunst." *Europäische Illustratierte*, vol 2, 1949, no 18, pp 9-11. German: "Two voices of architecture." A populist piece, subtitled "Dutch architecture, past and present," uses the Shell Building and (ironically) the 20-year-old Kiefhoek, to demonstrate present directions in architecture. The images are clear.

414. Wit, C.P.A. de, "De grondslagen van een toekomstige architectuur." *Bouwbedrijf*, vol 26, 1949, pp 179-83; 189-94; 201-206. Dutch: "The foundations of future architecture." The sweeping (sometimes rambling) polemical series identifies, praises and illustrates Oud's Shell Building as taking the right direction.

415. Zuithoff, J., "Decadentie in de Nederlandse architectuur: een overzicht van de laatste 50 Jaar," *Bouwbedrijf*, vol 26, 1949, pp 123-27; 135-41. Dutch: "Decadence in Dutch architecture; overview of the last 50 years." The title says it all. Oud's Oud-Mathenesse, Kiefhoek and Hoek van Holland houses, and the Shell Building are cited and illustrated.

416. *Nieuw Utrechtse Dagblad,* "'t Is moeilijk van het Vreeburg iets draaglijks te maken." 1949, 2 September, p 2. Dutch: "It's hard to make anything tolerable from Vreeburg." A news item about Oud's commission to produce an urban design proposal for Vredenburg in Utrecht reports an interview with the architect.

417. *Nouvelles Hollandes*, [Photograph of Shell Building], vol 5, 1949, 17 October, p 1.

418. *Rotterdamsche Parool*, "Kunstenaar licht zijn schepping toe." 26 August 1949. Dutch: "An artist explains his creation." A piece about the National war memorial at Grebbeberg reports an interview with Oud about the design. There is an aerial perspective. The identical piece appeared in *Haagsch Dagblad*, *Nieuw Utrechts Dagblad*, and *Dagblad voor Amersfoort* on the same day.

419. *Rotterdamsche Parool*, "Wethouder Meertens zet Witte Dorp in het zonnetje." 26 July 1949. Dutch: "Alderman Meertens puts the Witte Dorp in the spotlight." News item about 25th anniversary of Oud-Mathenesse housing development. Cf. *Rotterdamsch Nieuwsblad*, 27 July; *Nieuwe Rotterdamsche Courant*, 27 July; *Algemeen Dagblad*, 27 July.

1950-1959

1950
Books and Monographs
420. Hill, Oliver, *Fair Horizon: Buildings of Today*, London, 1950. English. In an optimistic view of the modern movement Oud is hailed "a pioneer of modernism" and his Hoek van Holland houses are illustrated.

421. Kaufmann, Edgar Jr., *What is Modern Design?*, New York, 1950. This book in the Museum of Modern Art's *Introductory Series to the Modern Arts* sets out the dogmas of Modernism for the uninitiated; a 1934 tubular steel chair by Oud for "conversing and relaxing" is illustrated.

422. Raynal, Maurice et al., *De Picasso au Surrealisme*, Geneva/Paris, 1950. French. Also published in English as *History of Modern Painting from Picasso to Surrealism*. Oud is mentioned in the passages on De Stijl, but only mentioned.

423. Thienen, F.W.S. van (ed.), *Algemene Kunst Geschiedenis*, Utrecht, 1950. Dutch: *General Art History*. Oud figures in a short analytical section about functionalism in Holland, set in the wider European context. The Purmerend factory (illustrated) is taken as an example of De Stijl cubist aesthetic; Dudok, named Oud's legatee, improved on it. Oud's entry in the Rotterdam stock exchange competition is illustrated, as is the Shell Building, with a comment about its divergence from the modern mainstream.

424. Whittick, Arnold, *European Architecture in the Twentieth Century*, London, 1950, vol I. London, 1953. New York, 1973. London, 1974. English. This huge, poorly-written book is very broadly based. Following a social history, there is a division by building types, an approach which produces more a history of

buildings than of architecture. Oud is cited as "the great architectural exponent and influence" in Rotterdam, and there are spasmodic references—always glib, sometimes inaccurate—to his pre-1930 work. A longer paragraph about the Shell building (illustrated) betrays the lack of research. First edition reviewed *Architectural Design*, December 1953, p 35.

425. Zevi, Bruno Benedetto, *Storia dell'Architettura Moderna*, Turin, 1950. Italian: *History of Modern Architecture*. Oud is placed among the masters of the rationalistic period, with Mies van der Rohe, Le Corbusier and Gropius; accordingly, he is treated as a V.I.P. and referred to throughout the book. There are photographs of Kiefhoek and Hoek van Holland. Later editions 1953, 1955, 1961 and in English as *Modern Architecture: a Visual History*, London, 1982.

426. Zevi, Bruno Benedetto, *Towards an Organic Architecture*, London, 1950. English. In chronicling the trend towards organic architecture, and the influence of Sullivan and Wright upon Europe, Zevi anticipates the decline of modernism. He cites Oud as Holland's modern master, using Kiefhoek as an example. There is an interesting chronology. Reviewed *RIBA Journal*, August 1950, p 402.

Journals

427. Elte, Hans, "The modern movement in Holland." *Journal RAI Canada*, vol 27, 1950, pp 214ff. English. A short essay introduces many photographs. Oud is presented as the most important figure; others are considered praiseworthy. The only pre-1940 example illustrated is the Shell Building, with a ground floor plan, two general views and a detail of the main entrance.

428. G——s, A. [Interview with Oud.] *Elseviers Weekblad*, 1950, 4 November. The piece concentrates upon Oud's views about postwar reconstruction, especially in Rotterdam and the inevitable question arises about the St Laurens church. There is a large aerial perspective of his 1942-43 proposal for Hofplein.

429. Jager, J. de and W.van Someren, "Hoofdkantoor Hoogovens." *Forum*, vol 5, 1950, pp 388-95 Dutch: "Head Office of the Blast Furnace Company." Following a brief history of the steelworks and an outline of the closed architectural competition (September 1947), the piece reviews and illustrates proposals by Oud, Roosenburg, Zwiers and the winner Dudok. Illustrations: location plan; large perspectives, elevation and ground floor plan. Cf. C.Wolterbeek, "Het nieuwe hoofdkantoor der Hoogovens ...," *Ingenieur*, vol 61, 1950, p A581ff, which plagiarizes half a page of this text to introduce images of all the entries.

430. M[ieras], J.P. "Rustig in de golven van te tijd." *Bouwkundig Weekblad*, vol 68, 1950, p 699. Dutch: "Peaceful on the waves of time." A nostalgic paragraph directs attention to the serene architecture of villa *Allegonda*, illustrated with a photograph that (ironically) shows its man-proof barbed wire boundary fence.

431. Oud, J.J.P., "Architectuur-critiek en architectuur." *Groene Amsterdammer*, 1950, 14 January, p 9. Dutch: "Architectural criticism and architecture." The piece, responding to criticisms of a recent exhibition of painting, sculpture and

architecture at the Amsterdam Stedelijk Museum, discusses the complexities of creative processes, none more complicated than architecture. Reprinted *Bouwkundig Weekblad*, vol 77, 1959, pp 405-06, and as "Die Architekten und die Kritiker," *Kontrapunkte, Jahrbuch Freie Akademie der Künste*, Hamburg, 1956, pp 57-61. See also Wiekart (ed.), *Ter Wille van een Levende Bouwkunst*, 1962. Cf. Oud, "Industriële vormgeving," *Groene Amsterdammer*, 1958, 18 January.

432. Oud, J.J.P., "De Commissies en de Instanties." *Groene Amsterdammer*, 1950, 15 April, p 9. Dutch: "The Commissions and the Authorities." The polemic pleads for release from the limitations imposed upon architectural creativity by an increasing number of required "approvals" from statutory bodies.

433. Oud, J.J.P., "Geef Rotterdam zijn kern terug." *Elseviers Weekblad*, 1950, 4 November, p 25. Dutch: "Give Rotterdam its center back." Not seen.

434. Oud, J.J.P., "Moeilijkheden van de dag." *Groene Amsterdammer*, 1950, 11 February. Dutch: "Difficulties of the day." In a critique of Karel Appel's painting in the Amsterdam town hall canteen and Ossip Zadkine's Rotterdam sculpture "The Destroyed City", Oud defends each against attacks made in "Schoonheid of demonie?," *Katholiek Bouwblad*, vol 17, 1950, pp 100-103.

435. Oud, J.J.P., "Otto van Tuss[ch]enbroek, *Achter Blinkende Vensters* [book review]." *Interieur*, vol 63, 1950, p 323. Dutch.

436. Oud, J.J.P., "Rotterdam en de St Laurens." *Groene Amsterdammer*, 1950, 29 July. Dutch: "Rotterdam and St Laurens [Church]." Illustrated by an isometric drawing, this is Oud's rationale of his controversial (and unrealized) proposal to retain only the tower of the bomb-damaged church and redevelop the site and its surroundings. See F.J.Brevet's rejoinder, "Rotterdams St Laurens: een grote kerk?" and Oud's reply, *ibid.*, 19 August 1950. The discussion is briefly commented upon in "Rotterdams St Laurens," *Bouw*, vol 40, 1950, pp 658-59. See also A.Buffinga, "Het voorstel van J.J.P. Oud voor de Sint Laurenstoren te Rotterdam." *Forum*, 1950, pp 307-09. The scheme was widely announced: e.g., "Architect Oud heft nieuwe plan voor herbouw St. Laurens," *De Rotterdammer*, 29 July, p 2; "Rotterdam en de St. Laurens," *Trouw*, 29 July; "Architect Oud: De toren behouden maar een moderne kerk bouwen," *Rotterdamsch Parool*, 31 July; "Een St. Laurensplan van architect Oud," *Rotterdamsch Nieuwsblad*, 1 August 1950, p 1. Ecclesiastical response was immediate and outraged: e.g., "Vergulde armoe surrogaat, zegt ds Den Hartog," *Rotterdamsch Parool*, 1 August; Oud, "Architect Oud beantwoord ds Den Hartog," *ibid.*, 3 August; "Ds. den Hartog en architect Meischke tegen het plan-Oud," *De Rotterdammer*, 4 August, p 5. Public opinion was also aroused: e.g. "De Kijker," *ibid.*, 8 August, p 1; K.A.Boogh, "De kerk-rüine als monument," *Rotterdamsch Nieuwsblad*, 19 August. The reader is referred to *Repertorium betreffende Nederlandse Monumenten van Geschiedenis en Kunst*, vol 3, The Hague, 1962. The church was restored 1952-68: see Blijstra, "Rotterdam heeft beslist: Sint Laurens zal herrijzen." *Vrije Volk*, 20 January 1953, p 3, which rehearses the whole saga.

437. Oud, J.J.P., "Zweden-Nederland 1-0." *Groene Amsterdammer*, 1950, 16 December. Dutch: "Sweden, one—Holland, nil." Responding to comments of the Dutch Minister for Postwar Reconstruction in *Bouw*, that Holland was falling behind Sweden in providing quality housing, Oud asserts that the architectural profession is not to blame but restricted by over-regulation.

438. Vriend, Jacobus Johannes, "L'architecture moderne." *Nouvelles de la Hollande*, vol 6, 1950, no 250, pp 22-28. French. The chronological essay sets out Holland's role in the development of modern architecture. Oud is mentioned as associated with De Stijl. There is a photograph of Kiefhoek.

439. Vriend, Jacobus Johannes, "Het nieuwe nationale monument op de Dam." *Groene Amsterdammer*, 1950, 8 June. Dutch: "The new national monument in The Dam." This descriptive, critical article calls the square in central Amsterdam a "difficult child" in urban planning terms. There is a schematic isometric of the location. Cf. "Het nationaal monument op de Dam." *Bouw,* vol 40, 1950, pp 234-35, which names the working party of the National Monument Commission for War Memorials, and "Het nationaal monument ... gedachten-wisseling tussen ... Oud en G.Bolsius," *ibid.*, p 363. Initiated in 1949, with Oud as architect and John Rädecker as sculptor, the project was to be protracted. Rädecker had made notional designs as early as 1946 (see Dedalo Carasso, "Een monument voor de natie," *Jong Holland*, March 1987). Following publication of the preliminary official design, public interest was intense and sustained. See, e.g., "Ellende, verzet, overwinning verbeeld in Dam-monument," *Parool*, 28 February 1950; "Nationaal monument zal aanzien van Dam grondig veranderen," *Amsterdams Parool*, 27 March 1950, p 1; "Pasquino," "Ons nationaal monument," *Telegraaf*, 4 October 1958; "Het voorlopig ontwerp nationaal monument gereedkomen," *Nieuwe Rotterdamsche Courant*, 27 March 1950, avbd p 1; Oud, "Over het Dammonument," *ibid.*, 2 November 1959, and "Het Dammonument ...," *Algemeen Handelsblad*, 20 December 1960. There is a clippings book (F.a26) in the Oud collection, NAi.

440. *Bouwkundig Weekblad*, "Architect J.J.P. Oud onderscheiden." Vol 68, 1950, p 93. Dutch: "Honors for ...Oud." News item: Oud was honored for his contribution to architecture and post-war reconstruction.

441. *Nieuwe Rotterdamse Courant*, "Spaarbank te Rotterdam krijgt een nieuw Hoofdgebouw." 1950, 13 December, p 2. Dutch: "Rotterdam Savings Bank gets new headquarters." A news item with a photo of the model briefly describes the building proposed to replace the ruined one on Botersloot. The project was initiated in 1942. See also *Rotterdamsch Parool*, 13 December; *Trouw*, 13 December; *Rotterdamsch Nieuwsblad*, 13 December; *De Rotterdammer*, 13 December; Maasbode, 13 December; *Algemeen Dagblad*, 14 December.

442. *Nouvelles de la Hollande*, "L'Architecte J.J.P. Oud." Vol 6, 1950, no 238, p 3. French. The piece was written to celebrate Oud's 60th birthday. Many notices appeared in national and provincial Dutch newspapers, e.g., "Vurig verdediger van moderne bouwkunst," *Parool*, 8 February; cf. *Algemeen Handelsblad*, 8

February; *Vrije Volk*, 9 February. Others are too numerous to list; many can be found in a clippings book (F.a26) in the Oud collection, NAi.

1951
Books and Monographs

443. Argan, Giulio Carlo, *Walter Gropius e la Bauhaus,* Turin, 1951. Italian: *Gropius and the Bauhaus*. The influence of De Stijl members on the philosophy of the Bauhaus is noted. Also published as *Gropius und das Bauhaus*, Hamburg, 1962, 1983; *Walter Gropius et le Bauhaus*, Paris, 1979, *Walter Gropius y el Bauhaus*, Buenos Aires, 1957.

444. Gruyter, W. Jos. de et al., *J.J.P. Oud, Architect*, Rotterdam 1951. Dutch. The catalog of exhibition at the Boymans-van Beuningen Museum, Rotterdam, February-March 1951 has an introductory essay by de Gruyter, a long-time friend of the architect, and a bibliography that seems to be the basis for some later ones. The show was widely reviewed. See, e.g., J.J.Vriend, "Het werk van architect J.J.P. Oud," *Groene Amsterdammer*, 3 March 1951, reprinted Vriend, *Reflexen, Nederlands bouwen na 1945,* 1959; J.P.Mieras, "Tentoonstelling van het werk van J.J.P. Oud in Museum Boymans," *Bouwkundig Weekblad*, 1951, p 131; "De werken van architect Oud," *Nieuwe Rotterdamsche Courant*, 3 March 1951, p 5; F.O., "Tentoonstelling van het werk van ... Oud, representative of our time," *De Maasstad*, 1951, pp 233-36; "J.J.P. Oud, pionier van het nieuwe bouwen," *Algemeen Dagblad*, 24 February 1951, p 7; "Architect Oud in zijn tijd," *De Rotterdammer*, 13 March 1951; de Gruyter, "Architect J.J.P. Oud 1890-1950," *Bouw*, 1951, pp 181-86; C.J. van Mansum, "Het oeuvre van architect J.J.P. Oud," *Bouwbedrijf*, 1951, pp 63-66 (with a previously unpublished portrait of Oud and his wife Annie) and *Vrij Nederland*, 3 March, p 5. There is a book of clippings (F.a26) in the Oud collection, NAi.

445. Oud, J.J.P., *Het Gebouw "Shell Nederland N.V." 's-Gravenhage*, The Hague, 1951. Dutch. The illustrated booklet transcribes Oud's talk to the Congress of the International Association of Art Critics, 9 July 1951.

446. *The "ESVEHA" Office Building, Rotterdam*, Rotterdam, 1951. French/English. An information booklet published by the *Bureau Documentatie Bouwwezen*, provides images, plans, elevations, sections and detail drawings, as well as statistical information down to color schemes and services.

447. *De Stijl*, Amsterdam, 1951. Dutch/German (French and English summaries). The catalog of an exhibition at Amsterdam's Stedelijk Museum, organized by van Doesburg's widow Nelly, Oud, van Eesteren, Rietveld, Hans Jaffé and others reprints essays and manifestoes originally published in *De Stijl,* and contains over 40 illustrations of members' work. Reviewed Salomonson, *Goed Wonen*, 1951, pp 156-58; Vriend, *Groene Amsterdammer*, 14 July 1951; "H.R.", *Burlington Magazine*, 1951, p 300. It was also shown in Venice and at the Museum of Modern Art, New York (reviewed, with a view of Café De Unie, *Architectural Record*, January 1953, pp 10-11.)

Journals

448. Argan, Giulio Carlo, "De tentoonstelling van F.L.Wright te Florence." *Forum*, vol 6, 1951, pp 299-303. Dutch: "The Wright exhibition in Florence." Reviewing the touring "Sixty Years of Living Architecture" show (that Wright later persuaded Oud to organize in Rotterdam), Oud's application of Wright's "spatial and plastic initiatives" to the "problems of society" is underlined.

449. Boeken, Albert, "Een halve eeuw bouwen." *Forum*, vol 6, 1951, pp 4-17. Dutch: "A half-century of building." A photograph of the Shell Building is included in a polemical essay about developments in Dutch architecture through the first half of the century. Oud is mentioned, but only mentioned, in the text.

450. Mayer, Hans F.K., "Manifest der moderne." Vol 4, 1951, pp 57-61. German: "Evidence of the modern." A short article about changes in style since 1900.

451. Oud, Hans E.[Hendrik Emile], "Nieuw hoofdkantoor voor de Spaarbank te Rotterdam." *Bouw*, vol 6, 1951, p 329. Dutch: "New headquarters for the Rotterdam Savings Bank." The building (1942-50) replaced the offices destroyed in the May 1940 bombing of Rotterdam. The piece by Oud's son (also an architect) is largely descriptive, illustrated with plans and photographs of the model. See *Maasstad*, 1950/51, no 11, p 224; 1957/58, no 4, pp 73-75.

452. Oud, J.J.P., "Bouwkunst, verkeer en Amsterdamse binnenstad." *Groene Amsterdammer*, 1951, 8 December. Dutch: "Architecture, traffic and inner city Amsterdam." Citing the example of the impact of increased vehicular traffic in Paris upon perception of detail in urban architecture, Oud concludes that "precious" architectural detail has had its day, a fact that should be remembered in the redevelopment of inner Amsterdam. Partly cited, *Bouw*, 23 February 1952, p 139. Also in Wiekart (ed.), *Ter Wille van een Levende Bouwkunst*, 1962.

453. Oud, J.J.P., "Ruimteproblemen." *Groene Amsterdammer*, 28 April. Dutch: "Space problems." Oud criticizes a block of three shops (now the Ter Meulen/Wassen/van Vorst department store, Binnenwegplein, Rotterdam) by van den Broek and Bakema (1948-51). Also published in Wiekart (ed.), *Ter Wille van een Levende Bouwkunst*, 1962.

454. Oud, J.J.P., "Schilder en architect." *Groene Amsterdammer*, 1951, 13 January. Dutch: "Painter and architect." The essay responds (December 1950) to A.M.Hammacher, "Schilder en architect," *ibid.*, 9 December 1950, setting out the essential differences between the "esthetic" painter and the "idealistic" architect. Oud cites his own "Ja und Nein. Bekenntnisse eines Architekten," *Europa Almanach*, 1925. The discussion was continued by Jan Engelman and Charles Eyck, *ibid.*, 27 January 1951. Also in Wiekart (ed.), *Ter Wille van een Levende Bouwkunst*, 1962.

455. *Forum*, vol 6, 1951, no 5-6, The issue. Dutch. An editorial, "J.J.P. Oud: zestig jaar" introduces a series of tributes in a profusely illustrated special edition to celebrate Oud's sixtieth birthday: Willem van Tijen, "Over de artistieke zijde

van Ouds werk"; Gerrit Rietveld, "Over architect Oud"; Huib Hoste, "Oud"; Siegfried Giedion, "Aan de alleenstaande [unique] J.J.P. Oud..." There are extracts from Oud's own writings, including "Over de toekomstige bouwkunst en hare architectonische mogelijkheden," *Bouwkundig Weekblad*, 1921; "In Memoriam K.P.C. de Bazel," *ibid.*, 1923; "Bouwen en pseudo-bouwen," *Groene Amsterdammer*, 1952 and "Ja und Nein. Bekenntnisse eines Architekten," *Bouwkundig Weekblad*, 1925.

456. *Elseviers Weekblad*, "J.J.P. Oud. Belijder van de architectuur." 1951, 3 March, p 29. Dutch: " ...The confessor of architecture." This short appraisal of his career is published probably to commemorate Oud's sixtieth birthday. There is a portrait.

457. *Hoofd en Hand*, "Architect Oud..." Vol 4, 1951, no 7, pp 16-17. The anonymous overview of Oud's career, giving no hint of its sources, is subtitled "a development which reflects the problems of the *Nieuwe Bouwen*." There is a view of the Hoek van Holland houses.

458. *Werk*, "Hollandische Architektur und kunst der gegenwart." Vol 38, 1951, November, pp 325-60. German: "Contemporary Dutch architecture and art." In a series of related articles, Hendrik Hartsuyker's "Merkmale Holländischer architektur" is a "re-hash" of Dutch modern architectural history. Only the Hoek van Holland houses are illustrated and Oud receives passing mention. He is also briefly discussed in Friedrich Vordemberge-Gildewart, "Zur geschichte der Stijlbewegung, " *ibid.*, pp 349-56.

1952
Books and Monographs
459. Hamlin, Talbot (ed.), *Forms and Functions of Twentieth Century Architecture*, New York, 1952. English. Because the four weighty volumes are about design rather than history and theory (divided as follows: I, Elements of building; II, Principles of composition; III and IV, Building types), the references to Dutch modernism are as examples only. Most critical comment is in the captions to photographs, rather than the text. Kiefhoek is illustrated.

460. *Frank Lloyd Wright*, Rotterdam, 1952. Dutch. The catalog of a traveling exhibition "Sixty Years of Living Architecture" in the Glass hall at *Ahoy-gebouw*, Rotterdam, July-August 1952, under the auspices of the *Academie van Beeldende Kunsten en Technische Wetenschappen* includes Oud's introduction titled simply "FLLW", reprinted as "Wright's betekenis voor het nieuwe bouwen," *Groene Amsterdammer*, 1 July 1952. It was not intended that the show should go to Holland, but Wright met Oud during the Paris showing and persuaded him to organize it. Reviewed Schelling, *Bouwkundig Weekblad*, 1952, pp 231-32; M[us], "Tentoonstelling Frank Lloyd Wright" *Ons Huis*, 1952, pp 757-65. See also Bruce Brooks Pfeiffer (ed.), *Letters to Architects: Frank Lloyd Wright*, Fresno, 1984. Cf. Oud, "Frank Lloyd Wright," *Groene Amsterdammer*, 17 May 1952, a eulogy written (in part) to publicize the imminent exhibition.

461. Oud. J.J.P., *Building and Teamwork*, Rotterdam, 1952. English. This enlightening article (dated January 1952) rebuts Gropius' idea that buildings should be designed by teams. Oud's "provisional conclusion" is that the art of building has been displaced by the business of building, in which architects look to "share risks with others." When an English version of the article was rejected by *Architectural Review* Oud published it independently, as a booklet. It also appeared as, "Building design and teamwork," *AA Journal*, January 1958, reprinted in *The Builder*, 1958, pp 185-86. Cf. "Bouwen en Teamwork," *Groene Amsterdammer*, 1952, 9 February, p 11; "Bauen und Teamwork," *Der Architekt*, June 1952, pp 93-95; "Riesamina sé stesso," *Metron*, 1952, no 45, pp 7-15. Also in Wiekart (ed.), *Ter Wille van een Levende Bouwkunst*, 1962.

Journals
462. Barr, Alfred H. (ed.), "De Stijl, 1917-28." *New York Museum of Modern Art Bulletin*, vol 20, 1952, no 2. English. The issue celebrates an exhibition (December 1952-February 1953) that started in Amsterdam's *Stedelijk* Museum and moved to New York via Venice. Philip Johnson's foreword credits De Stijl with the "basic aesthetic organizational ideas" of the International Style. A history by Barr (from *Cubism and Abstract Art,* 1936) examines De Stijl's influence, particularly upon Gropius, Mies, and Le Corbusier. There is a chronology, and photographs of *De Vonk*'s hall interior and Café de Unie. Reviewed Hess, "The Dutch this century," *Art News*, 1953, no 9, pp 23-25; Coates, "De Stijl, survey at the Museum of Modern Art," *New Yorker*, 27 December 1952, pp 47-48; *Architectural Record*, January 1953, pp 10-11(with a view of Café De Unie); Fitzsimmons, "Modern surveys De Stijl: its contribution to design," *Art Digest*, 1 January 1953, pp 6-7; "De Stijl: a revolution in retrospect," *Interiors*, January 1953, pp 108-13, in which Oud is called the group's most conservative, most influential architect and interiors of villa *Allegonda* and the Stuttgart houses are illustrated.

463. Mus, Cor, "Architectuur: binnenhuis en meubelkunst." *Ons Huis*, vol 10, 1952, no 8, pp 684-90. Dutch: "Architecture: interiors and furniture design." A rambling attempt to put Oud into the bigger picture of Dutch modern architecture is mostly taken up with captions to seven excellent illustrations of the Shell Building, including rarely published interiors of the main stair hall and the rotunda canteen.

464. Oud, J.J.P., "Architect en supervisor." *Groene Amsterdammer*, 1952, 3 May. Dutch: "Architect and supervisor." Oud kept nagging about the conflict between architects van den Broek and Bakema and planning limitations placed upon their design for shops in Velsen by the urban designer Willem Dudok. M.H.Wevers responds with "De functie van de supervisor," *ibid.*, 14 June to which there is a "postscript" by Oud.

465. Oud, J.J.P., "Bouwkunst of industrial design?" *Groene Amsterdammer*, 1952, 1 November, p 12. Dutch: "Architecture or industrial design?" The piece comments upon the first proposals for the UNESCO building in Paris, which

involved a number of architects. Oud reiterates his arguments against "teamwork" in architectural design. Also in Wiekart (ed.), *Ter Wille van een Levende Bouwkunst*, 1962. See van den Broek and Bakema, "Open brief aan ... Oud," *ibid.*, 9 December 1952, pp 9-10. Cf. Oud, "Industrial design en bouwkunst," *Bouw*, 1956, part 2, p 738.

466. Oud, J.J.P., "Riesamina sé stesso." *Metron*, 1952, no 45, pp 7-15. Italian. The piece translates three of Oud's essays: "Contemporary English architecture," *Architectural Times*, 1949; "Bouwen en Teamwork," *Groene Amsterdammer*, 1952 and the transcript of a talk about the Shell Building at The Hague, 9 July 1951. There are aerial views of the Shell Building and Kiefhoek. English summaries appear in *Architectural Record*, November 1952, pp 348-50.

467. Oud, J.J.P., "John Rädecker (1885-1856) en J.J.P. Oud (geb. 1890) Het Dammonument (Amsterdam)." *Openbare Kunstbezit*, 1952, 18c-18d. Dutch: "[Rädecker and Oud]: the monument on the Dam, Amsterdam." Not seen.

468. Oud, J.J.P., "Stationspostgebouw Den Haag." *Forum*, vol 7, 1952, p 320ff. Dutch: "The Station Post Building in The Hague." A positive commentary, especially on the role of G.C. Bremer, engineer for the building, accompanies thorough visual documentation. The architects were Emmen and Engel.

469. Oud, J.J.P., "Die Weissenhofsiedlung." *Stuttgarter Zeitung*, 1952, 4 April, p 2. German. A letter to the editor refers to an article in the *AIA Journal*, January 1952 on Oud's role in the building of the *siedlung* in 1927.

470. *Bouw*, "Stedebouw en architectuur. Nog eens: de kwestie Velsen." Vol 7, 1952, p 346. Dutch: "Town planning and architecture. Once again: the Velsen question." The "question" is about conflict between Dudok's city plan and architects van den Broek and Bakema's design for shops in Velsen. See "Stedebouwkundige tegenover architect ... ," *Nieuwe Rotterdamse Courant*, 24 April 1952; "Bouwen en Teamwork," *Groene Amsterdammer*, 9 February 1952.

471. *Revista Nacional de Arquitecture*, "El arquitecto J.J.P. Oud." Vol 12, 1952, January, pp 27-29. Spanish: "The architect J.J.P. Oud." The sketchy overview of Oud's career reproduces indifferent photographs of the Shell Building, Kiefhoek housing and church, Hoek van Holland, Oud-Mathenesse and Stuttgart.

1953
Books and Monographs
472. Steur, A.J. van der et al., *Building in the Netherlands*, London, 1953. This is the catalog of an exhibition, "strictly post-war in scope," at the RIBA, February-March 1953. There is a preface by Howard Robertson, and essays by van der Steur and J. van Ettinger. Oud's *ESVEHA* offices were included. Reported "Building in the Netherlands," *RIBA Journal*, 1953, p 171. The show moved to Scotland, the second Biennale at Sao Paolo, Brazil and then to the United States. Reviewed Oud, "'Building in the Netherlands'," *Groene Amsterdammer*, 2 October 1954, p 9; *Nieuwbouw Nederland*, April 1953, pp 1-2.

473. Veronesi, Guilia, *J.J. Pieter Oud*, Milan, 1953. Italian. Fanelli calls this sparse pocket book one of the most important works on Oud. It includes an essay, a sketchy biography, a slender bibliography and small illustrations. Reviewed S.van Embden, *Forum*, 1954, p 341.

474. Zevi, Bruno Benedetto, *Poetica dell'Architettura Neoplastica*, Milan, 1953. Turin, 1974. Italian. Also published as *De Stijl: the Poetics of Neoplastic Architecture*, London, 1982. Among the first books to recognize the importance of De Stijl as a "necessary precursor of all modern architecture", it has been claimed that Zevi's "analysis of the group's personalities, aims and achievements has ... become a standard work on the subject." There are plates of Oud's earlier works, including *De Vonk* and Kiefhoek.

Journals

475. Bakema, Jan Berend et al., "Architectuur en 'teamwork'." *Bouw*, vol 8, 1953, pp 57-59. Dutch. In a piece subtitled, "And after that still more on the Velsen question" an outline of the "conflict" between Dudok and the firm of van den Broek and Bakema introduces a letter from Bakema to Oud. Oud replies in "Architectuur: lichtend symbool of grootste gemene deler?," *ibid.*, pp 60-61. See Oud, "Bouwen en 'teamwork'," *Groene Amsterdammer*, 9 February 1952, p 11; "Bouwkunst of industrial design?" *ibid.*, 1 November 1952, p 12; van den Broek and Bakema, *ibid.*, 9 December 1952, pp 9-10.

476. Bakema, Jan Berend, "Dutch architecture today." *Architects' Year Book*, vol 5, 1953, pp 67-82. English. The very general piece claims that Oud's latest works (the ESVEHA building is cited and illustrated) are a reaction against a "too functional interpretation of De Stijl principles."

477. Oud, J.J.P., "Genormaliseerde scholebouw." *Groene Amsterdammer*, 1953, 11 April. Dutch: "Standardized school building." The polemic, attacking the idea of prefabrication of especially schools and houses, is subtitled "a building site is something more than a laboratory." Cf. Oud, "Bouwkunst of industrial design?" *ibid.*, 1952. Van Tijen and Maaskant, who bear some of his criticism, respond in "Het wezen der industriële productie, *ibid.*, 2 May 1953; there is a short rejoinder by Oud.

478. *Bouw*, "Standaardtype arbeiderswoningen." vol 8, 1953, p 270. Dutch: "Model workers' houses." An Oud design of 1947 is published in conjunction with some housing designs for Veendam by architect E. van Linge.

479. Rossi, Vittorio, "Oud e il cubismo." *Il Popolo di Roma*, 1953, 22 August, p 3. Italian: "Oud and cubism." The populist piece makes a giant leap between an exhibition of Cubist paintings at Rome's *Galleria d'Arte Moderna* and Oud's interpretation of Cubism during and after his association with De Stijl.

480. Steur, A.J. van der, "Na-oorlogse bouwkunst in Nederland." *Bouw*, vol 8, 1953, 23 March, p 202-04. Dutch: "Postwar architecture in Holland." The general essay draws attention to English language criticism of the Shell Building.

481. Warnaars, F.H. "Het provinciehuis van Zuid-Holland." *Katholiek Bouwblad,* vol 20, 1953, no 15, pp 225-37. Dutch: "The South Holland Province House." Oud was among five architects invited to submit proposals to replace the building destroyed during the bombing of The Hague. The article outlines the project's history and illustrates the schemes. There are plans and a perspective of Oud's (unsuccessful) design, and the jury's comment. See also *Ingenieur*, vol 65, 1953, part II, no 38, pp B179-90; *Polytechnische Tijdschrift B*, 1953, p 196B; *Bouw,* 1953, p 179-83. Cf. H.G.J. Schelling, "Plannen voor nieuw provinciehuis van Zuid-Holland ...," *Bouwkundig Weekblad*, 1953, pp 165-72.

482. *Groene Amsterdammer*, "Werken van architect J.J.P. Oud." 1953, 16 May. Dutch: "Works of ... Oud." In an anonymous review of a small exhibition of Oud's recent work at the Schielandhuis, Rotterdam, May 1953, special mention is made of the Shell Building and his competition entries for the steel works and the South Holland *Provinciehuis*. There is a perspective of the latter.

483. *Hier Rotterdam,* "Interview met J.J.P. Oud." 1953, 15 May. Dutch. Not seen.

1954
Books and Monographs
484. Guarneri, Libero, *L'Evoluzione dell'Architettura Moderna*, Milan, 1954. The book consists mostly of images, following a short essay. Oud is not mentioned in the text, but the Kiefhoek church and Stuttgart houses are illustrated.

485. Mieras, J.P., *Na-oorlogse Bouwkunst in Nederland*, Amsterdam, 1954. Dutch: *Postwar Architecture in Holland.* English summary. The text of the BNA sponsored publication focuses on postwar events. The only Oud buildings included in a vast array of images are the Kiefhoek Apostolic church, the villa *Allegonda*, and the Shell Building. He is not mentioned in the polemical text.

486. Pluym, Willem van der, *Vijf Eeuwen Binnenhuis en Meubels in Nederland 1450-1950*, Amsterdam, 1954. Dutch: *Five Centuries of Interiors and Furniture in Holland ...* The final chapter refers to the new streams; a whole section is devoted to neo-Plasticism. *De Vonk* and Weissenhofsiedlung interiors are illustrated, and a prototype armchair of 1950.

Journals
487. Banham, Reyner, "Mendelsohn." *Architectural Review*, vol 111, 1954, August, pp 85-93. English. The general Dutch influences upon the German architect are noted in this lyrical but inaccurate essay, and his evaluation of Oud is included.

488. Blijstra, Rien, "De moderne Nederlandse bouwkunst." *De Nieuwe Stem*, vol 9, 1954, pp 517-33. Dutch: "Modern Dutch architecture." The essay rehearses the development of twentieth century architecture, from Berlage's "awakening" until the present. Oud is mentioned—only Kiefhoek is noted—and a passage from his "Het monumentale stadsbeeld," *De Stijl*, 1917, is cited.

489. Jaffé, Hans Ludwig C., "De Stijl." *Art d'Aujourd'hui*, vol 5, 1954, May/June, pp 6-8. French. Oud's role in the foundation of the group, and his architectural products of 1921-25 are discussed in a concise history of De Stijl, by the Associate Director of Amsterdam's Stedelijk Museum. There is a view of the Café De Unie and a photo and drawings of the Oud-Mathenesse site hut.

490. Oud, J.J.P., "Architectuur en prijsvragen." *Groene Amsterdammer*, 1954, 23 January, p 9. Dutch: "Architecture and competitions." An essay examining the relationship between architect, client and building is disposed against architectural competitions. Then, Oud's entries.had not been overly successful. Partly cited in de Haan and Haagsma, *Architects in Competition*, London, 1988.

491. Oud, J.J.P., "Neue Form oder neue Architektur," *Die Spur des Menschen, Jahrbuch Freie Akademie der Kunste,* Hamburg, 1954, p 94. German: "New form or new architecture." Not seen.

492. Oud, J.J.P., "Een monument ontstaat. Het Dam-monument in pantoffels," *Groene Amsterdammer*, 1954, 13 February. Dutch: "A monument arises. The Dam monument in slippers." See also "Nationale monument in 1956 gereed," *Telegraaf,* 12 January 1954.

493. Plaut, James S., "Industrial design in the United States." *Perspectives*, 1954, no 9, pp 118-29, and plates. English. De Stijl is recognized as an influence on American industrial design but the author's knowledge of it is grossly inaccurate. The Café de Unie is illustrated, and the wrong date given.

494. S[chelling], H.G.J., "Film over moderne Nederlandse architectuur." *Bouwkundig Weekblad*, vol 72, 1954, p 309. Dutch: "Film about modern Dutch architecture." Produced by the Ministry of Education, Arts and Sciences, the film had its national premiere on 21 August, and a week later was shown at the Triennale in Milan, Italy. Kiefhoek and the Shell Building are included.

495. Smithson, Peter, "Modern architecture in Holland." *Architectural Design*, vol 24, 1954, pp 225-26. English. The article introduces buildings discussed elsewhere in the issue. A potted history of formative influences upon the Dutch moderns stresses the roles of van Doesburg, De 8 and Opbouw. A number of seminal buildings are illustrated; some dates are omitted, others are inaccurate.

496. Vermeulen, Frans A.J., "Is de moderne bouwkunst wel zo zakelijk?" *Wereld*, 1954, pp 950-60. Dutch: "Is modern architecture really so objective?" The article draws upon international examples to support the idea that modern architects "refer" to other buildings, while protesting that their designs are from grassroots analysis. The Shell Building is (unconvincingly) compared to the Porte Alegre Clinic in Brasilia (architect, J.M.Moriere). Both are illustrated.

497. Slebos, J.C., "Gulden snede en nog iets." *Bouw*, vol 9, part 1, 1954, p 48. Dutch: "The golden mean and then some [idiom]." This is the conclusion of a five-part series on classical proportional geometry (the first appeared on 19 December 1953), which provoked a good deal of discussion in subsequent issues.

See, e.g., *ibid.*, p 55, where Hans Oud enters the lists, and pp 274-75, which prints J.J.P. Oud's argument with Slebos; then the editors closed the discussion.

498. *Bouwkundig Weekblad*, "Wandelen door Rotterdam." Vol 72, 1954, pp 166, 172. Dutch: "Strolling through Rotterdam." A guide to a walking tour of Rotterdam includes some of Oud's inner-city buildings.

499. *Forum*, "Studieprijsvraag voor een Wijkcentrum Amsterdam-Noord." Vol 9, 1954, pp 391-94. Dutch: "Study competition for Amsterdam North district center." This reports the meeting of the working party assembled by *Architectura et Amicitia* to clarify requirements for the project: Oud was there to discuss architectural aspects and his comments are published pp 391-92.

1955
Books and Monographs
500. Korevaar, A. et al., *Bouwkundige Encyclopedie*, Amsterdam, 1955. Dutch: *Encyclopedia of Building*. There is a short paragraph on Oud, "one of the driving forces of De Stijl."

501. *Mondriaan*, The Hague, 1955. Dutch. Oud wrote the introduction to this catalog of an exhibition at The Hague Gemeentemuseum, February-April 1955. There are also essays by Michel Seuphor and Mondrian. The introduction was reprinted as "Mondriaan," *Groene Amsterdammer*, 1955, 12 February, p 9 (which includes an image of Oud's Stuttgart houses); see also "Rectificatie op artikel Mondriaan," *ibid.*, 19 February. Italian version in Palma Bucarelli and Giovanni Carandente (eds.), *Mondrian*, Rome, 1957, when the show moved to *Palazzo Reale*, Milan and the *Galleria Nazionale d'Arte Moderna*, Rome.

Journals
502. Berendsen, Anne, "Lijnen en vlakken van een levenshoud." *Vaderland*, 16 February 1955. Dutch: "Lines and planes of a worldview." Written to celebrate Oud's 65th birthday, the piece is one of many tributes, too numerous to list. There is a clippings book (F.a26) in the Oud collection, NAi.

503. Broek, Johannes Hendrik van den, "J.J.P. Oud; eredoctor in de technische wetenschappen." *Forum*, vol 10, 1955, pp 210-12. Dutch: "Oud. honorary doctor in the technical sciences." This respectful piece noting the awarding of the degree by Delft *Technische Hogeschool* is dated August, 1955. There is a portrait, and a perspective of the Utrecht Life Assurance Company building. The event was widely reported: see, Vriend, "Architect J.J.P. Oud ere-doctor," *Groene Amsterdammer*, 4 June 1955, p 11, reprinted Vriend, *Reflexen, Nederlands bouwen na 1945*, 1959; Blijstra, "Bouwmeester J.J.P. Oud thans ere-doctor," *Vrij Nederland*, 24 September, p 6; R.B., "Architect Oud wordt eredoctor in Delft," *Vrije Volk*, 24 September, p 5; "Bij het ere-doctoraat van arch. J.J.P. Oud," *Algemeen Dagblad*, 24 September; *Nieuwe Rotterdamsche Courant*, 27 September, p 1; *Volkskrant*, 27 September, p 5; *Rotterdamsch Parool*, 26 September, p 9. There is a book of press clippings in the Oud collection, NAi. See also special number of the university's newspaper *Canticlaar*, September 1955.

504. Colijn, A.W., "Er moet een woningen-Kleiboer komen!" *Elseviers Weekblad*, 1955, 17 September, pp 2-3. Dutch: "A housing Kleiboer must come!" Oud is interviewed about Holland's urgent need to build up to 100,000 houses a year.

505. Oud, J.J.P., "Deze sit-down regelingen verstoren de bouw-harmonie," *Algemeen Dagblad*, 1955, 5 August, p 2. Dutch: "These sit-down regulations disturb architectural harmony." The newspaper publishes Oud's response to an article about building and planning regulations.

506. Tusschenbroek, Otto van, "Bij werk van J.J.P. Oud als meubelontwerper en binnenhuisarchitect." *Interieur*, vol 68, 1955, pp 361-65. Dutch: "About Oud's work as a furniture and interior designer." A positive discussion of the oeuvre is generously illustrated with quite rare images: Metz-fauteuil 07c (1934); Metz-chair 04 (1933); Metz-chair 07b (1934); Oud's own work room; Dr D. Hannema's work room; writing room on the *Nieuw Amsterdam*; Shell Building board room; and a chair for the Rotterdam Savings Bank.

507. *L'Architettura,* "Architetto J.J.P. Oud." 1955, pp 343-350. Italian. Not seen.

508. *Bouw,* "Bio Vacantie-oord, nabij Arnhem." Vol 10, 1955, pp 906-07. Dutch: "[Rehabilitation center] near Arnhem." This is the first publication of Oud's designs (begun 1952) for a scheme initiated by the National Association of Cinema Proprietors and completed in 1960, to build a rehabilitation center at Arnhem for child victims of poliomyelitis. Construction was financed by a ten cent surcharge on cinema tickets. The Dutch word for cinema is *bioscoop*, hence the name "*Biovacantieoord*." Illustrations include an aerial perspective and sketches of the administration building, boiler house and pavilion.

509. *Bouw,* "Kantoorgebouw op de Coolsingel." 1955, no 28, pp 574-76. Dutch: "Office building on Coolsingel." The article gives details of Oud's design for the Utrecht Life Assurance Company building to be constructed in the heart of Rotterdam's central business district. There is a perspective.

510. *Bouwkundig Weekblad,* "Rede Prof Ir J.P.Berghoef bij erepromotie J.J.P. Oud." Vol 73, 1955, pp 433-35. Dutch. This is the text of Berghoef's speech when awarding Oud's honorary doctorate at Delft *Technische Hogeschool*, 26 September 1955. The cover has a photograph of the ESVEHA building, and there are perspectives of the Utrecht Insurance Co and Christian High School. Cf. "Ere-promotie van dr J.J.P. Oud," *Bouw*, 1955, p 821, illustrated with the model of Oud's unrealized design for the South Holland Province House.

1956
Books and Monographs
511. Bucarelli, Palma, *Piet Mondrian*, Rome, 1956. Italian. This modest volume is the catalog of an exhibition at the *Galleria Nazionale d'Arte Moderna*, Rome and the *Palazzo Reale*, Milan, between November 1956 and February 1957. An essay by Oud is followed by a chronological catalog, a bibliography and indifferent images.

512. Gropius, Walter, *The Scope of Total Architecture*, New York, 1955. London, 1956. English. The book formed part of a *World Perspectives* series; earlier titles had been in the realm of politics, religion and philosophy. Gropius set out to define "a new set of values" for an integrated architecture and urbanism reflecting the age, by publishing an anthology of his lectures and writings ca 1937-56. Oud is mentioned only in passing as a leader of De Stijl, but Gropius' ideas about "teamwork" provide good contrasting background. Also published in German as *Architektur.Wege zu einer optischen kultur*, Frankfurt am Main, 1956.

513. Jaffé, Hans Ludwig C., *De Stijl 1917-1931: the Dutch Contribution to Modern Art*, Amsterdam, 1956. With a foreword by Oud, this definitive work by the Associate Director of the AmsterdamStedelijk Museum examines origins, character and development, and influence upon the arts of De Stijl movement. There are brief biographies. Images include portraits, Scheveningen esplanade housing project; Oud-Mathenesse site office; projected factory, Purmerend; Stuttgart row houses. There is an extensive bibliography. Reviewed Oud, *Forum*, 1956, pp 355-56. Also published as *De Stijl 1917-1931. Der Niederländische Beitrag zur modernen Kunst*, Frankfurt, 1965 and *Per un'Arte Nuova. De Stijl 1917-1931*, Milan, 1964. Republished in English, Cambridge, Mass./London, 1986 (reviewed Champa, *New Criterion,* vol 6, September 1987, p 45ff; Overy, "Demystifying De Stijl," *Studio*, July 1988, pp 61-62.)

514. Seuphor, Michel, *Piet Mondrian: Life and Work*, Amsterdam/New York, 1956. English. The book deals mostly with painting but provides interesting and valuable background material on De Stijl group, as well as giving insights into the influence of Theosophy upon Dutch art and architecture in the early part of this century. It is replete with illustrations and there is a classified catalog and a list of all his known works. The bibliography is limited to Mondrian. Reviewed Oud, *Forum*, 1956, pp 355-56.

515. Whittick, Arnold, *Eric Mendelsohn*, New York, 1956. English. The author minimizes the Dutch role in the vanguard of modern architecture, although acknowledging the contribution of some individuals. In the single paragraph dealing with impressions of The Netherlands gained by Mendelsohn, 1919-23, Oud is mentioned as an important contributor, but overshadowed by Gropius.

Journals
516. Bakema, Jan Berend, "Het Tweede Vrijzinnig Christelijk Lyceum van Oud (1956) gezien in verband met de architectuurontwikkeling." *Forum*, 1956, pp 229-54. Dutch: "Oud's Second Liberal Christian high school in The Hague seen in the light of architectural developments." A favorable evaluation of Oud's career prefaces a descriptive critique and a plethora of images of the building, many in color. Hoek van Holland, Kiefhoek and the Purmerend factory design are also illustrated. Reprinted as a booklet. For other reviews of the school see Wegerif, "Het Tweede Vrijzinnig Christelijk Lyceum een belangrijk gebouw," *Haagsche Courant*, 4 September 1956 and Vriend, "Nieuwe school van architect Oud," *Groene Amsterdammer*, 29 September 1956 (profusely illustrated).

517. Lewis, David, "De Stijl," *Architectural Design*, vol 26, 1956, p 338. English. The essay identifies De Stijl as founded (like Suprematism in Moscow) upon the notion of synthesis. There follows a loose knit analysis of works, with a few small photographs. Little is said about architecture.

518. Mariani, Leonardo, "Recenti opere di J.J.P. Oud." *L'Architettura,* vol 2, 1956, September, pp 342-51. Italian: "Recent works of ... Oud." A single page overview of Oud's career includes translations of fragments of his writings; it is followed by illustrations of earlier works and the Bioherstellingsord, the South Holland Province House project, the two memorials, the Utrecht Insurance offices, the high school in The Hague and two chairs.

519. Oud, J.J.P., "Nationaal monument op de Dam te Amsterdam." *Bouwkundig Weekblad*, vol 74, 1956, pp 226-28. Dutch: "National monument in The Dam, Amsterdam." An exposition of the design is illustrated with a location plan, perspective and an aerial photograph of the opening ceremony. See Oud, "Het Dam-monument ... ," *Maatstaf,* vol 4, 1956, p 407; "John Raedecker," *Groene Amsterdammer*, 21 April 1956, p 9.

520. Oud, J.J.P., "Viftig jaar moderne kunst in de USA en het ontwerp voor de USA-ambassade in London," *Groene Amsterdammer*, 1956, 16 June. Dutch: "Fifty years of modern art in the USA and the design for the US embassy in London." Not seen.

1957
Books and Monographs
521. Blijstra, Rein, *Nederlandse Bouwkunst na 1900*, Amsterdam, 1957. Dutch: *Dutch architecture after 1900.* Second edition Utrecht/Antwerp 1962. The populist book also appeared as *L'Architecture Néerlandaise aprés 1900*, Amsterdam, 1966 and *Dutch Architecture after 1900*, Amsterdam, 1966 in sometimes clumsy translation, giving an overview of the ideological conflicts between the schools. Blijstra's sympathies lie with the modernists and Oud is given his due place. The Dutch edition has images of Kiefhoek, the Shell Building and the Christian high school, The Hague; only Kiefhoek is illustrated in the English edition. Reviewed *Casabella*, 1957, no 254.

522. Knuttel, G. and J.Kruger, *Bouwkunst*, Amsterdam, 1957. Dutch: *Architecture.* In a book covering 3000 B.C. to the present, detail is slight. The Shell Building is illustrated; Kiefhoek and Hoek van Holland are mentioned in the text.

523. Lotzeler, Heinrich, *Vom Sinn der Bauformen*, Frieburg, 1957. German: *Meaning in Building Forms.* There are two long, inaccurate paragraphs about Oud in this critical history of architecture, and an image of Hoek van Holland.

524. Sartoris, Alberto, *Encyclopedie de l'Architecture Nouvelle--Ordre et Climat Nordiques*, Milan, 1957. French: *Encyclopedia of New Architecture: Northern Order and Climate.* This is the last in a 3 volume set. A few brief chapters, including "Netherlands abstraction," focussing on De Stijl and particularly van

Doesburg, are followed by myriad images. The Hoek van Holland, Kiefhoek (wrongly captioned) and Stuttgart houses are among them. Originally published as *Gli Elementi dell'Architettura Razionale*, Milan, 1932 (1935, 1940, 1941) and revised as *Gli Elementi dell'Architettura Funzionale*, Milan, 1941.

525. Vriend, Jacobus Johannes, *Nieuwere Architectuur,* Bussum, 1957. Dutch: *Recent Architecture.* Oud wrote the foreword, "Ten Geleide" to this overview of international architecture from 1800. Several of his designs and buildings are illustrated and discussed in the chapter on Dutch architecture. Reviewed Oud, *Groene Amsterdammer*, 9 February 1957. The foreword is reprinted, "Nieuwere Architectuur," *ibid.*, 8 February 1958.

Journals

526. Blijstra, Rein, "National monument en erebegraafplaats." *Forum*, vol 13, 1957, p 62-88. Dutch: "National monument and memorial cemetery." The comprehensive, well-illustrated piece provides good background history of the Dam and includes discussion of the monument by Oud and Rädecker.

527. Fischer, Wend, *Bau. Raum.Gerät*, Munich, 1957. German: *Building. Space. Equipment.* This third volume in the series *Die Kunst des 20. Jahrhunderts* (ed. Carl Georg Heise) provides a carelessly researched overview. There is half a chapter on De Stijl and brief discussion of Oud's public housing. Hoek van Holland and the Weissenhofsiedlung are illustrated.

528. Kazemier, G., "Het Tweede Vrijzinnig Christelijk Lyceum te 's-Gravenhage," *Bouwkundig Weekblad*, 1957, pp 29-34. Dutch: "Second Liberal Christian high school in The Hague." The writer was the school's rector and the approving, descriptive piece sets out the educational philosophies expressed in the design. It is illustrated with plans and exterior photographs. See also H. Dethmers, "Tweede Vrijzinnig Christelijk Lyceum ...," *Bouw*, 1957, II, pp 850-59, which gives a detailed description, identifies contractors and consultants and provides interior views; Blijstra, "Oud's Lyceum in Den Haag, evenwichtig, persoonlijk," *Vrije Volk,* 14 September 1957; R. Oxenaar, "Een school van architect ... Oud," *Nieuwe Rotterdamsche Courant*, 8 June 1957, p 2; "Hollande. Collège catholique [sic] a La Haye," *L'Architecture d'Aujourd'hui*, June/July 1957, pp 20-21.

529. Mariani, Leonardo, "Architettura popolare di J.J.P. Oud." *Edilizia Popolare*, 1957, no 15, pp 34-40. Italian: "People's architecture by ... Oud." The critical, descriptive essay "revisits" the mileposts of Oud's career, especially the social housing schemes at Oud-Mathenesse, Kiefhoek and Stuttgart, all illustrated with plans and photographs. Other key works and projects are mentioned, the high school in The Hague is illustrated, and there is a rarely seen image of the Presikhaaf housing estate, Arnhem (with van Hassel, 1951). Cf. Mariani, "Recenti opera di ... Oud," *L'Architettura,* September 1956.

530. Oud, J.J.P., "De Stijl--toen en nu." *Groene Amsterdammer*, 1957, 12 January, p 10. Dutch: "De Stijl--then and now." Written when interest in De Stijl was being revived through books and exhibitions, much of the piece deals with the

relationship between architecture and painting that was explored by the group, and problems associated with collaboration. It draws parallels with the painters who recently contributed to the high school in The Hague; the main stair hall is illustrated, showing Karel Appel's mural. Reprinted in Wiekart (ed.), *Ter Wille van een Levende Bouwkunst*, 1962.

531. Oud, J.J.P., "Is architectuur vogelvrij?" *Groene Amsterdammer*, 1957, 20 July, p 10. Dutch: "Is architecture outlawed?" The essay addresses the problems faced by architects when called upon to alter or rebuild one of their earlier designs. Reprinted in Wiekart (ed.), *Ter Wille van een Levende Bouwkunst*, 1962.

532. Oud, J.J.P., "J.J.P. Oud. Von Ihm selber." *Das Einhorn, Jahrbuch Freie Akademie der Künste*, Hamburg, 1957, pp 57-61. German: "Oud, by himself." The piece needs no description. It was reprinted as "Selbstdarstellung" in Wilhelm Maler (ed.), *Profile: Jahrbuch Freie Akademie der Kunst in Hamburg*, Hamburg, 1967 and reissued as a booklet.

533. Rutgers van der Loeff, M. and J.B. de Boer, "Het nationale monument, Amsterdam." *Polytechnische Tijdschrift B*, 1957, pp 530-34b. Dutch. De Boer was a lighting engineer employed by Philips N.V., and a brief history of the monument project in the Dam precedes a detailed description of the floodlighting installations, illustrated with rather spectacular night photographs of the results.

534. *L'Architettura,* [Congress Building, The Hague.] Vol 2, 1957, pp 626-29. Italian. Not seen.

535. *Visie*, [Illustration of Café De Unie.] 1957, no 5. Dutch.

1958
Books and Monographs
536. Brown, Theodore M., *The Work of G. Rietveld, Architect*, Utrecht/Cambridge, Mass., 1958. English. Derived from Fulbright scholar Brown's doctoral dissertation at the University of Utrecht, the book is among the first to identify Rietveld as an historically important "powerful and independent artist." The text is divided into the phases of his career, but most emphasis is given to the Schröder house. It translates Rietveld, "Inzicht." *i10*, 1928, pp 89-90 and "Levenshouding als Achtergrond van Mijn Werk," and provides a well-researched catalog of works. His relationship with Oud through De Stijl is briefly discussed and there is an attempt to link the design of the Purmerend factory (illustrated) with Rietveld's red-blue chair. Van Doesburg's condemnation of Oud (letter to Rietveld, 10 August 1923) is published. See *Bouwkundig Weekblad*, vol 76, 1958, p 316. Reviewed *Selearte*, vol 9, 1961, no 50, pp 2-13.

537. Everts, F.E.C., *Nederland op de Wereldtentoonstelling Brussel 1958*, The Hague, 1958. Dutch: *Holland at the Brussels World's Fair 1958*. There is a photograph of the model of the Dutch pavilion, by Rietveld et al. See also the subsequent guidebook (1958) for another view of the model. Oud and Ben Merkelbach are cited as architectural "supervisors."

538. Hitchcock, Henry-Russell Jr., *Architecture, Nineteenth and Twentieth Centuries*, Harmondsworth, 1958. 1963. 1977. English. In a sketchy history bordering on the inaccurate, developments in Holland 1890-1957 share a chapter with Austria and Scandinavia, all indebted to Germany. Hitchcock was an *aficionado* of Modernism, a bias shown in his evaluation of Oud—somewhat diminished from his fervent admiration of the 1920s—who is here grouped among the "second generation" of moderns. There are illustrations of Kiefhoek housing and church; Hoek van Holland. Wright's influence is noted.

539. Kultermann, Udo, *Bouwkunst van Deze Tijd*, Amsterdam/Antwerp, 1958. Dutch: *Contemporary Architecture.* An introductory essay is followed by a short history, country by country, and pages of large plates. Kiefhoek is illustrated. Also published in German as *Baukunst der Gegenwart: Dokumente des Neuen bauen in der Welt*, Tübingen, 1958.

540. Pallottino, Massimo (ed.), *Enciclopedia Universale dell'Arte, Rome*, 1958. The modern section was edited by Giulio Carlo Argan; the entry on Oud is by Giuliana Veronesi, who confuses The Hague Congresgebouw with the South Holland Province House. Published as *Encyclopedia of World Art*, London 1965.

541. Ragon, Michel, *Le Livre de l'Architecture Moderne*, Paris, 1958. French: *The Book of Modern Architecture.* Professedly written "*avec passion*," this rather confusingly structured book makes passing reference to Oud and the Dutch, the sole entry in the bibliography being a French work of 1932.

Journals

542. Dam, Herman van, "Geschreven portret dr J.J.P. Oud." *Goed Wonen*, vol 11, 1958, pp 294-95. Dutch: "Written portrait of ... Oud." The populist essay purports to present an image of Oud through his writings (a few scraps are cited) and his buildings (an incomplete list is given, *sans* images) and a few biographical notes. It does not, but there is a photographic portrait.

543. Haas, H.J. de, "Ontwerp voor een congresgebouw te 's-Gravenhage." *Bouwbedrijf*, vol 35, 1958, pp 215-23. Dutch: "Design for a convention center, The Hague." The essay is about the commission, Oud's design, and Dudok's earlier town-planning ideas for Stadhoudersplein and Zorgvliet. There was a subsequent collision between the two architects. The article provides an 18 point "official explication" of the design, fully illustrated with plans, sections, elevations and perspectives. It was followed by an editorial, "Ontwerp voor een congresbouw ...," *ibid.*, pp 227-29, which questions the explication, and "Het ontwerp voor het Haagse congresgebouw," *ibid.*, p 250, a letter from Oud and the editors' response. Cf. *Bouwen en Wonen*, vol 5, 1958, pp 235-38 (with fewer images) and *Polytechnische Tijdschrift B*, vol 14, 1959, pp 182-89b; the identical piece appears in German: *STZ*, 1960, pp 597-606.

544. Mumford, Lewis, "The rebuilding of Rotterdam," *Delta*, vol 1, 1958, no 2, pp 5-17. English. Most of the article deals with the post-World War II period but there are a few allusions to earlier 20th century architecture.

545. Oud, J.J.P., "De architectuur van de Nederlandse afdeling op de Wereldtentoonstelling Brussel 1958." *Forum*, vol 13, 1958, pp 185-214. Dutch: "The architecture of the Dutch section, Brussels World's Fair, 1958." Oud and Ben Merkelbach supervised the project; the architects were Boks, van den Broek and Bakema, and Rietveld. The piece gives a history of the commission, sets out the design philosophy, lists the collaborators and describes the building. There are two photographs. Reprinted as a booklet. See Oud, "Over de samenwerking voor de tentoonstelling in Brussel," *Groene Amsterdammer*, 26 April 1958, a response to J.J.Vriend's comments about "building and teamwork" in the previous issue.

546. Oud, J.J.P., "Het Congresgebouw van 's-Gravenhage." *'s-Gravenhage*, vol 13, 1958, September, pp 32-36. Dutch: "The Hague's Congress Building." With the design drawings and model, the journal published a letter from Oud, rehearsing his career and outlining his rationale for the building. Made public in early September 1958, the scheme was widely reported in the national and provincial press: see, e.g., *Haagse Dagblad*, 10 September; *Het Binnenhof*, 10 September, p 3; *Vrije Volk*, 10 September, p 2; *Haagsche Courant*, 10 September, p 9. Cf. Oud, "Das Kulturelle Zentrum in Den Haag," *Fundamente, Jahrbuch Freie Akademie der Künste*, Hamburg, 1959, pp 108-09. For a chronology, see "Congresgebouwplannen als een geschiedenisboekje," *Vaderland*, 11 July 1959, p 14.

547. Oud, J.J.P., "Henry Ford in Alkmaar," *Groene Amsterdammer*, 1958, 8 November, p 3. Dutch. Oud complains that Bruin's Alkmaar redevelopment plan is determined by vehicular traffic flow and car-parking. Reprinted in Wiekart (ed.), *Ter Wille van een Levende Bouwkunst*, 1962.

548. Oud, J.J.P., "Le Corbusier." *Groene Amsterdammer*, 1958, 12 April, p 9. Dutch. Written to publicize an exhibition of Le Corbusier's architecture, painting, sculpture and tapestries at The Hague Gemeentemuseum, 29 March-1 June, the well-illustrated, rather adulatory piece reviews the Swiss' career. Reprinted in Wiekart (ed.), *Ter Wille van een Levende Bouwkunst*, 1962.

549. Oud, J.J.P., "Nut van auto's in de stad wordt steeds meer twijfelachtig," *Nieuwe Utrechts Dagblad*, 1958, 29 November. Dutch: "Benefit of automobiles in the city is becoming increasingly doubtful." Not seen.

550. Oud, J.J.P., "Rietveld 70 jaar." *Forum*, vol 13, 1958, p 80. Dutch. The piece is one of several warm tributes published for Rietveld's seventieth birthday. See Frits Bless, "Rietveld: myth and reality," *ibid.*, vol 23, 1980-81, no3, p II.

551. Scully, Vincent Jr, "Modern architecture: towards a redefinition of style," *Perspecta*, vol 4, 1958, pp 5-10. English. This transcribes a talk about Wright's influence on De Stijl. While it does not mention Oud, it is included here because it links the "profound impulse towards continuity" found in Wright's pre-1911 houses and De Stijl to the 1920s European developments and the International Style. Reprinted *College Art Journal*, 1958, no 2, pp 140-59. Cf. Scully, *Modern Architecture. The Architecture of Democracy*, New York, 1961 (London 1968) which expands the ideas and in which the Café De Unie is illustrated.

552. *Bouwwereld*, "Het ontwerp voor een Cultureel Centrum te 's-Gravenhage." 1958, pp 1133-39. Dutch: "The design for a cultural center in The Hague." The article gives a history and description of the Congress building. Other incisive essays about the design include Bruno Zevi, "Il ritorno di un artista," *L'Espresso,* 1958, 19 October (Dutch translation: *Bouw,* 1958, p 693.) Cf. *Vaderland,* 3 June 1959, p 5. See also "Kulturzentrum den Haag," *Bauen und Wohnen,* February 1959, pp 56-60 and a descriptive, statistical piece bereft of illustrations: "Ein grossprojekt; Das neue Kongressebäude im Haag," *Schweizer Baublatt,* 23 January 1959, p 19-22. Shorter notices include "Plan voor congresgebouw met hotel." *Hotel-Revue,* 1958, no 38, pp 2-3; "Nouvelle salle de congrès a La Haye," *L'Architecture d'Aujourd'hui,* 1958, no 80, p IX, "Centre culturel et salle de congres a La Haye," *Habitats-Habitations. Documents d'Architecture et d'Urbanisme,* August 1958, pp 95-98; "Hollande. Centre culturel de La Haye," *Techniques et Architecture,* December 1958, pp 70-71; H.G. Franks, "Dutch ink Global Conference Center," *Christian Science Monitor,* 22 October 1958, p 3, "Cultural centre, The Hague, Holland," *Architectural Design,* 1959, p 429, "Cultural center for The Hague," *Architectural Record,* February 1959, p 4; "This is what The Hague Congress Building will look like," *International Associations,* January 1959, p 62; Lisa Ronchi, "Il centro culturale a l'Aja," *Architettura: Cronache e Storia,* 1959, pp 626-29; "Centro cultural de La Haya," *Arquitectura,* September 1960, pp 146-52.

1959
Books and Monographs
553. Broek, Johannes Hendrik van den et al., *Gids voor Nederlandse Architectuur*, Rotterdam, 1959. Dutch/ English: *Guide to Dutch Architecture.* This overview of historic and modern architecture was published for the UIA congress in The Hague. Oud's role is discussed and his major works included.

554. Francastel , Pierre (ed.), *Les Architectes Célébres*, Paris, 1959. French: *Celebrated Architects.* Oud is among architects fêted in a broad-ranging book.

555. Joedicke, Jürgen, *A History of Modern Architecture*, New York/London, 1959. English. Originally *Geschichte der Modernen Architektur*, Teifen/ Stuttgart, 1958, the book expands a thesis about the synthesis of form, function and construction. Special attention is paid to De Stijl's accentuation of formal elements. Oud is included and his Purmerend factory project, Hoek van Holland and Kiefhoek housing are discussed. Second English edition, London, 1961.

556. Oud, J.J.P., *Ja, Eben. Künstler-Erlebnisse, Gedankenvolles und Gedankenleeres*, Wassenaar, 1959. German: *Just So. Artist-experience, Thoughtful and Thoughtless.* Not seen. The comment in Hans Oud's 1984 bibliography reads "mimeographed as a private publication; aphoristic banter about Paul Citroen."

557. Vriend, Jacobus Johannes, *De Schoonheid van Ons Land. Architectuur van deze Eeuw*, Amsterdam, 1959. Dutch: *The Beauty of our Land. Architecture of This Century.* The most extensive work in Vriend's considerable *oeuvre* is one of

a series. It is divided into short chapters, each dealing with an artistic genre. Oud's role in De Stijl and after is noted: "in [his] work can be seen reflected the whole development of western European architecture." There are clear photographs of the villa *Allegonda*, Café de Unie, Oud-Mathenesse, Hoek van Holland, Kiefhoek Weissenhofsiedlung, Shell Building and the high school in The Hague. Cf. Vriend, *De Schoonheid van Ons Land. De Steden*, Amsterdam, 1951.

558. Vriend, Jacobus Johannes, *Reflexen, Nederlands Bouwen na 1945,* The Hague, 1959. Dutch: *Reflections: Dutch Building after 1945* . French, German and English summaries. This anthology from *Groene Amsterdammer*, 1945-58, includes "The work of architect J.J.P. Oud" (1951), "Architect J.J.P. Oud eredoctor" (1955) and "Het nieuwe kantoorgebouw voor de BIM" (1946). Reviewed *Vaderland*, 19 March 1960.

Journals

559. Joedicke, Jürgen, "Strömengun in der Architektur der Gegenwart." *Bauen und Wohnen*, vol 13, 1959, pp 326-332. German: "Directions in contemporary architecture." Oud is mentioned briefly in a wider discourse, and there is a small image of the Kiefhoek houses.

560. Oud, J.J.P., "Frank Lloyd Wright." *Groene Amsterdammer*, 1959, 18 April. Dutch. An "official" obituary by Vriend, is complemented by this warm, (mostly secondhand) anecdotal "personal word" from Oud.

561. Oud, J.J.P., "Kuststad Nederland. Waar de blanke top de duinen. ...," *Groene Amsterdammer*, 1959, 25 July, p 9. Dutch: "Coast City, Holland. Where the white top of the dunes [song title] ..." The piece discusses the possibilities of housing developments along the coast. There was a rejoinder from W. Huygens, burgemeester of the North Holland resort town Bergen: "'De blanke top der Kennemer duinen schittert in de zonnegloed'," *ibid.*, 12 September 1959. See also Oud, "Naschrift," *ibid.* He resumes the theme in "Recreatie-kust-Holland of Manchester aan zee?" *ibid.*, 13 October 1962.

562. Oud, J.J.P., "Het nationale monument op de dam en de politie." *Groene Amsterdammer*, 1959, 11 April, p 3. Dutch: "The national monument in the Dam and the police." The piece pleads for police protection of the monument from inappropriate use and vandalism. Cf. Oud, "Het Dam-monument in de verdrukking," *Algemeen Handelsblad*, 20 December 1960.

563. Oud, J.J.P., "Open brief aan de Raad der gemeente Wassenaar." *De Wassenaarder*, 1959, 6 August. Dutch: "Open letter to the Wassenaar City Council." Not seen.

564. Oud, J.J.P., "Professor L.O.Wenckebach." *Groene Amsterdammer*, 1959, 13 June. Dutch. This introduces an exhibition of Wenckebach's sculpture.

565. Oud, J.J.P., "Verkeer, stedebouw en professor Feuchtinger," *Groene Amsterdammer*, 1959, 12 December. Dutch: "Traffic, town planning and Professor Feuchtinger." Not seen.

566. Oud, J.J.P., "'Zijn er nog architecten?'" *Groene Amsterdammer*, 1959, 7 February, pp 9-11. Dutch: "Are there still architects?" Originally published as a booklet, The Hague, 1959, this lecture presented at Delft *TH* on *Hogeschooldag*, 10 January 1959 revisits Oud's persistent rejection of teamwork. It drew fire: e.g., Schamhart, "Er zijn nog architecten," *ibid.*, 28 March 1959 and Bakema, "Zijn er al architecten, die begrip hebben van de veranderde samenleving," *ibid.*, 13 April 1959. Oud's final word was "Tot slot," *ibid.*, 4 April, p 11. The lecture was reprinted *Katholiek Bouwblad*, vol 26, 1959, pp 136-38 and *Bouwkundig Weekblad*, vol 77, 1959, pp 110-12 and in Wiekart (ed.), *Ter Wille van een Levende Bouwkunst*, 1962. The *Hogeschooldag* was reported in *Zien*, vol 1, 1959, no 4, pp 35-36 and no 5.

567. Vriend, Jacobus Johannes, "Building in The Netherlands," *Delta*, vol 2, 1959, no 1, pp 89-90. English. Written mainly in praise of reconstruction after World War II, the article also deals with the work of Berlage, and mentions Granpré Molière as well as Expressionists and modernists.

568. *Katholiek Bouwblad*, [Image of Shell Building.] vol 26, 1959, p 137.

1960-1969

1960
Books and Monographs
569. Banham, Reyner, *Theory and Design in the First Machine Age*, London, 1960. English. One of the most important architectural history books of this century devotes considerable space to the Dutch. Oud's role in De Stijl is examined, as are his polemics of the 1920s. The Purmerend factory and boulevard housing designs are illustrated. Reprinted 1962, 1967, 1970 (New York), 1972, 1973. Republished Cambridge, Mass., 1980 and as *Die Revolution der Architektur. Theorie und Gestaltung in Ersten Maschinenzeitalter*, Reinbek, 1964.

570. Benevolo, Leonardo, *Storia dell'Architettura Moderna* (2 vols), Bari, 1960. 1964. 1966. Italian. An excellent, copiously illustrated social history contains references to Oud, including associations with De Stijl and the Bauhaus. Tusschendijken, Oud-Mathenesse, Kiefhoek, Hoek van Holland, and Stuttgart houses, the Shell Building and the boulevard housing design are discussed and illustrated. Translated as *Geschichte der Architektur des 19. und 20. Jahrhunderts*, Munich, 1964; *History of Modern Architecture*, Cambridge, Mass./London, 1971 (reprinted 1978, 1979, 1980, 1982).

571. Blake, Peter, *The Master Builders*, London, 1960. English. Long after Oud's fall from the Modernist grace, the book mentions him and the Weissenhofsiedlung only in passing as one of De Stijl architects and a minor contributor.

572. Dorgelo, A., *Modern European Architecture*, Amsterdam/London, 1960. English. Objective, thorough descriptions of a number of buildings, includes the Shell headquarters building. There is a brief history of the project, a briefer

critique and many photographs and construction drawings. Services and construction are described and statistics are provided.

573. Eckardt, Wolf von, *Eric Mendelsohn*, New York/London, 1960. English. Describing Mendelsohn's 1919 visit to Holland, the author identifies "the [*sic*] famous housing development by Oud" as the "quintessence of coldly rational De Stijl cubism." In 1919, none of the "white boxes" had been built!

574. Gorter, Sadi de (ed.), *Cesar Domela*, The Hague, 1960. Dutch. The slim catalog of an exhibition at the Gemeentemuseum, September-October 1960, refers to the four relief murals in the Utrecht insurance offices, Rotterdam.

575. Oud, J.J.P., *Mein Weg in 'De Stijl'*, 's-Gravenhage/Rotterdam, 1960. German: *My Way in De Stijl*. The essay, originally written in German, 1957-58, is Oud's recollection of his involvement with the group and its effect upon his career. It provides insights into his philosophy. Cf. "Mijn weg in De Stijl.," *Plan*, 1981, no 6, pp 16-25, translated by Annie Oud-Dinaux and Carel Dinaux, who repudiate the original publisher's claim that it was translated from the Dutch to German by Kees and Erica de Wit. There are many images. German edition reviewed Baljeu, "De Stijl toen en J.J.P. Oud nu," *Forum,* 1960-61, pp 285-88. Dutch translation (1961), Reviewed Vriend, *Groene Amsterdammer*, 10 June 1961 and Wiekart, "Verslag van een ontwikkeling," *Vrij Nederland,* 16 May 1961. Translated as *Mi Trayectoria en "De Stijl,"* Murcia, 1986; "La mia strada in 'De Stijl'," *Casabella Continuata*, 1961, no 249, p 55ff , with images of the Purmerend factory, Stuttgart housing and the Arnhem rehabilitation center.

576. *Schermers Agenda*, Baarn, 1960/61. The illustrated diary publishes a rare 1904 photograph of Oud, then aged 14, with his brothers P.J.(Pieter), the oldest, who entered politics and Gerrit, the youngest, who became a banker.

Journals

577. Jacobsen, Wouter A., "Voor lichamelijk gehandicapte kinderen bouwde Nederlandse Bioscoopbond herstellingsoord te Arnhem." *Technische Gids voor Ziekenhuis en Instelling*, vol 29, 1960, pp 511-17. Dutch: "The Netherlands Cinema Association built a rehabilitation center at Arnhem for physically handicapped children." An article in a technical journal describes the buildings, focussing on the mechanical services. The illustrations serve a similar purpose.

578. Jonker, Gert, "Esthetica en gordijngevel, vraaggesprek met dr. J.J.P. Oud." *Bouwkundig Weekblad,* vol 78, 1960, p 68. Dutch: "Esthetics and curtain walls, interview with ... Oud." The title explains the content which derives from seeking Oud's opinions on the aesthetic problems of the building system, provoked by examining photographs of international examples.

579. Oud, J.J.P., "Commenta l'editoriale del n. 50." *L'Architettura*, 1960, pp 795-96. Italian/English. Oud responds ("an architect muttering to himself") in English to Zevi's editorial, "Un gesto probante: gli architetti scelgono la critica storia," *ibid.* ,no 50; much of it is about his position *vis à vis* Internationalism.

580. Oud, J.J.P., "De aannemer zij volledig team-lid!" *Bouw*, vol 15, 1960, p 180. Dutch: "The contractor a full member of the team!" The article, among several reviewing the book *Doelmatig Bouwen. Teams voor woningbouw*, Rotterdam, 1959, reiterates much of Oud's previous comment on the subject.

581. Oud, J.J.P., "Architectuur die uitgaat van 'eten, slapen en voeten vegen'." *De Tijd-Maasbode*, 1961, 26 August. Not seen.

582. Oud, J.J.P., "Bio-herstellingsoord te Arnhem." *Bouw*, 1960, pp 1306-11. Dutch: "Cinema rehabilitation center at Arnhem." Construction of the center was financed by a surcharge on cinema tickets, a scheme initiated by the National Association of Cinema Proprietors (the Dutch word for cinema is *bioscoop*, hence "*bio*-herstellingsoord"). Oud's *toelicht* sets out the philosophy and describes the scheme, with a plethora of images. The collaborators are identified. An abridged version appears in *Bouwkundig Weekblad*, 1960, pp 507-15. Cf. *Bouwwereld*, 1960, pp 521-526 and "Bauen für Kinder," *Kontraste, Jahrbuch Freie Akademie der Künste*, Hamburg, 1960. See also Günther Kühne, "Oud und die Klassik," *Bauwelt*, 1961, pp 1163-67. Also reported in "Colonia Bio-holiday ad Arnhem, Olanda," *L'Architettura*, May 1961, pp 37-42 (with some color images); "Bio-Zentrum, Arnhem, Holland," *STZ*, 1962, pp 529-33; "Convalescent Home, Arnhem, Holland," *Architectural Design*, March 1961, p 127 and Rein Blijstra, "Architecture and planning," *Delta*, 1960, no 2, pp 64-65. Populist notices include Paul Man, "Dit is van *uw* dubbeltjes gebouwd," *Libelle*, 1960, no 35, pp 4-7; J.J.Vriend, "Oud's Bioherstellingsoord, Arnhem," *Groene Amsterdammer*, 2 July 1960; Karel Wiekart, "Het nieuwste werk van J.J.P. Oud," *Vrij Nederland*, 22 October 1960, p 7; "Nieuw leven voor 72 kinderen," *Haagsche Courant*, 26 March 1960, p 2;

583. Oud, J.J.P., "Waarom ik van het toepassen van baksteen afstapte en op grond waarvan ik er weer toe terugkeerde," *Baksteen*, 1960, May, pp 1-5. Dutch: "Why I stepped aside from the propriety of brick and why I again returned to it." The title says it all. There are images of the Arnhem Bioherstellingsoord, including a color cover.

584. Seip, Dick, "Geef de mensen toch ruimte, niet blokken." *Algemeen Dagblad*, 1960, 23 February. Dutch: "Give the people yet more space, not [housing] blocks." This reports an interview with Oud, subtitled "a peep at 1980." His opinions about the "Moloch" of traffic and high rise anonymous housing blocks are clearly stated. There is a portrait.

585. Vriend, Jacobus Johannes, "Plan voor een Haags Congresgebouw." *Groene Amsterdammer*, 1960, 23 January. Dutch: "Plan for a Congress Building in The Hague." News item. See also "Moderne congreszaal in Den Haag," *Cobouw*, 17 May 1962.

586. *De Tijd-Maasbode*," De Beurs van Berlage weer in opspraak.," 1960, 4 June, p 23. Dutch: Berlage's stock exchange again compromised." Oud is one of several architects commenting upon the future of the famous Amsterdam building,

threatened with demolition or conversion. The comments were reprinted in *Bouw*, 1960, pp 748-49. Cf. Oud, "In welk door brein is de gedachte opgekomen?" *De Tijd-Maasbode*, 7 June 1960, p 24; "In wat voor wereld leven we toch?" *Haagsche Courant*, 9 February 1960, p 5 and "Voorkeuren," *Elseviers Weekblad*, 19 March 1960, p 27 (Italian translation, *Casabella*, 1961, no 256, pp 24-31).

587. *Bouwkundig Weekblad*, "Een publicatie in het jaar waarin Dr J.J.P. Oud 70 jaar werd." Vol 78, 1960, pp 501-15. Dutch: "... the year in which ... Oud reaches 70 years." The piece has little text and many images, including rarely seen landscape sketches by Oud and interiors of the Rotterdam Savings Bank. Later works are emphasized. Birthdays are major events in the Dutch ethos and the press made much of this one, usually with derivative summaries of Oud's career. Cf. Dimitri Frenkel Frank, "J.J.P. Oud pleit voor persoonlijke bouwkunst," *Telegraaf*, 20 February 1960; J.J.Vriend, "Bouw-meester Oud 70," *Groene Amsterdammer*, 13 February; Cees Doelman, "Bij de 70ste verjaardag van architect dr Oud," *Nieuwe Rotterdamsche Courant*, 6 February; "Bouwmeester Oud Dinsdag 70 jaar," *Haagsche Courant*, 5 February; "J.J.P. Oud, pionier van de nieuwe architectuur, vandaag 70," *ibid.*, 9 February. Others are too numerous to list but see clippings book (F.a26) in Oud collection, NAi.

1961
Books and Monographs
588. Brion, Marcel, *Domela*, Paris, 1961. French. The text, illustrated with a few color images, "sets out a brief sketch of the person and work of ... Domela." There is a desultory bibliography and list of exhibitions and works, including the relief murals for the Utrecht insurance offices, Rotterdam.

589. Huyghe, René (ed.), *L'Art et l'Homme*, vol 3, Paris, 1961. A page of text and photos in Bernard Champigneulle's article, "Art after the First World War" mentions De Stijl; there are small, images of Hoek of Holland housing and the Shell Building. English version, *Larousse Encyclopedia of Modern Art*, Paris/London, 1965. 1967. 1974. Spanish translation, *El Arte y el Hombre*, Paris, 1966.

590. Jones, Cranston, *Architecture Today and Tomorrow*, New York, 1961. English. In this unreliable book there is reference to Oud's important place in European modernism in the chapter "Philip C. Johnson: the return of elegance."

591. Pallottino, Massimo (ed.), *Encyclopedia of World Art*, New York, vol 5, 1961. English. Original edition in Italian, Rome and Venice, 1958. The modern art section of the encyclopedia was edited by Giulio Carlo Argan. The Dutch attract a good deal of attention in Leonardo Benevolo's article "European modern movements" where Oud and De Stijl are dealt with at some length. There are photographs of Kiefhoek and Hoek van Holland housing.

Journals
592. Hofhuizen, Herman, "Dr J.Oud: bouwen in maatschappelijke en individuele zin," *De Tijd/Maasbode*, 1961, 26 August. The piece expounds the ideas in *Zijn er nog architecten?* The Hague, 1959, and cites frequently from Oud's writings.

There is a brief biography, a portrait, and images of the Shell Building, the Congress center model, and the Bioherstellingsoord boiler house.

593. Oud, J.J.P., "Architektur und baudetail heute." *Detail*, 1961, no 1, pp 4-5. German. Oud is among several architects commenting upon technical matters.

594. Oud, J.J.P., "Cooperation between painters, sculptors and architects ..." *Information Bulletin: International Association of Plastic Arts*, 1961, no 41, pp 9-12. English. Oud's invited response is published in full.

595. Oud, J.J.P., "J.J.Vriend 65 jaar." *Groene Amsterdammer*, 1961, 18 March. Dutch: "J.J.Vriend, 65 years old." A short piece celebrates the birthday of the prolific architectural writer and critic.

596. Oud, J.J.P., "De melodie van de ruimte." *Groene Amsterdammer*, 1961, 18 March, p 9. Dutch: "The melody of space." The short essay challenges the idea that "workability" should precede feeling in the design of architectural space. Also in Wiekart (ed.), *Ter Wille van een Levende Bouwkunst*, 1962.

597. Oud, J.J.P., "Tradition in einem Einfamilienhaus," *Traditionen, Jahrbuch Freie Akademie der Künste*, Hamburg, 1961, pp 94-96. German: "Tradition in the single-family dwelling." The short piece describes and explains, with line drawings, the 1960 (unrealized) design for the Plate house, Voorburg.

598. Pevsner, Nikolaus, "Modern architecture and the historian or the return of historicism" *RIBA Journal*, vol 68, 1961, April, pp 230-40. The specious essay contends that Europe is currently undergoing an historical revivalism. Highly imaginative comparisons are biased by a Modernist viewpoint, which slyly and rudely alludes to the Shell Building as "Beton-Rococo." Reprinted Pevsner, *Studies in Art, Architecture and Design*, vol 2, 1968.

599. Tijen, Willem van, "The present state of architecture." *Forum*, vol 15, 1960-61, pp 325-30. The journal reports in Dutch and English the full text of a lecture presented to *Architectura et Amicitia* by van Tijen, and the ensuing discussion. Oud's early work is overlooked and he is lumped with Sybold van Ravesteyn as a neo-classicist, a "sideline that led us back."

600. Wiekart, Karel, "Portret van een verzekeringsmaatschappij." *Vrij Nederland*, 1961, 2 December. Dutch: "Portrait of an insurance company." This is a descriptive critique of the Utrecht Life Assurance Company building in Coolsingel, Rotterdam. There is a detail photograph of the facade. Cf. Wiekart, "Kantoorgebouw 'Utrecht'." *Vrij Nederland,* 18 September 1961; *Nieuwe Rotterdamsche Courant*, 21 November 1961, p 7.

601. *Cahiers de Centre Scientifique et Technique du Batiment*, "Cahiers la polychrome architecturale." 1961, December, pp 4-5. French: "Notes on architectural polychromy." A view of the Café De Unie and a color schematic drawing have captions that comment upon the importance of color information in appreciating the design.

602. *Progressive Architecture*, "Recent works of a pioneer: J.J.P. Oud." Vol 42, 1961, June, p 72. English (USA). The bland, descriptive piece presents images of the Bioherstellingsoord, The Utrecht Insurance building and the model of the Congress Center.

1962
Books and Monographs
603. Banham, Reyner, *Guide to Modern Architecture*, London, 1962. English. The facile book is divided into two sections: theory and practice. It claims in an obscure gloss that Oud was the first to "reveal the temper, ... preoccupations and preferred architectural forms of the budding International Style." Since Banham had earlier made a professedly close study of Oud, it is surprising that he names him "another pre-1914 pupil of ... Behrens." Revised as *Age of the Masters*, London, 1975.

604. Champigneulle, Bernard and Jean Ache, *L'Architecture de XXe Siecle*, Paris, 1962. French: *Twentieth Century Architecture.* Oud is linked with Wright, and also with Dudok as reacting against the willfulness of the Amsterdam School.

605. Conrads, Ulrich and Hans G. Sperlich, *The Architecture of Fantasy: Utopian Building and Planning in Modern Times*, New York, 1962. London 1963. English. The edited and expanded translation by George and Christine Collins of *Phantastische Architektur*, Stuttgart, 1960 demonstrates that not all 20th century architecture was uniform. Illustrations are followed by translated documents including Oud's comment on the Einstein Tower.

606. Wiekart, Karel (ed.), *J.J.P. Oud: Terwille van een Levende Bouwkunst; een keuze uit zijn geschriften*, The Hague, 1962. Dutch: *J.J.P. Oud: In Favor* [idiom] *of a Living Architecture; a selection from his writings.* The following essays appear in the anthology: "Het monumentale stadsbeeld," *De Stijl*, 1917; "Kunst en machine," *De Stijl*, 1918; "Over de toekomstige bouwkunst en hare architectonische mogelijkheden," *Bouwkundig Weekblad*, 1921; "The influence of ... Wright on the architecture of Europe," *Wendingen*, 1925; "Ja und Nein. Bekenntnisse eines Architekten," *Bouwkundig Weekblad*, 1925; "Wohin führt das Neue bauen: Kunst und Standard," *i10*, 1927; "Wij bouwen weer op?," *Groene Amsterdammer*, 1946; "U.N.Building," *RIBA Journal*, 1948; "Bouwen en pseudo-bouwen," *Groene Amsterdammer*, 1949; "Bouwen zonder makeup," *ibid.*, 1949; "Clarity in town planning," *U.N.Bulletin 2*, 1949; *Het Gebouw Shell Nederland N.V., 's-Gravenhage*, The Hague, 1951; "Architectuur-critiek en architectuur," *Groene Amsterdammer,* 1950; "Bouwkunst, verkeer en Amsterdamse binnenstad," *ibid.*, 1951; "Ruimteproblemen" *ibid.;* "Schilder en architect.," *ibid.*; "Bouwen en Teamwork," *ibid.*, 1952; "Bouwkunst of industrial design?," *ibid.*, 1952; "Architectuur en prijsvragen," *ibid.*, 1954; "Studieprijsvraag voor een Wijkcentrum Amsterdam-Noord," *Forum*, 1954; "De Stijl--toen en nu," *Groene Amsterdammer*, 1957; "Is architectuur vogelvrij?," *ibid.*; "Henry Ford in Alkmaar," *ibid.*, 1958; "Le Corbusier," *ibid.*; "Professor L.O.Wenckebach," *ibid.*, 1959; "'Zijn er nog architecten?'," *ibid.*; "De melodie van de ruimte," *ibid.*, 1961.

There is an introduction and afterword by Wiekart, and a few photographs. Announced in J.M.Boersma, "Belangrijk boek op komst," *Vaderland*, 15 October 1960 and Wiekart, "Een collectief of het werk van één architect," *ibid.*. Reviewed, Vriend, *Groene Amsterdammer*, 7 July 1962.

607. Oud, J.J.P. and L.J.F. Wijsenbeek, *Mondriaan*, Zeist, 1962. Dutch. The book consists of two essays (Oud's recollections in "Mondrian, the man" and "Mondrian, painter and thinker" by Wijsenbeek), a bibliography and several pages of color and monochrome plates.

608. Wingler, Hans Maria, *Bauhaus: Weimar, Dessau, Berlin, Chicago*. Cologne 1962. German. There are manifestoes and contemporary essays, and allusions to contemporary Dutch thought. Oud, Stam, van Doesburg and De Stijl are frequently mentioned. Second German edition: *Das Bauhaus*, Bramsche, 1968. See also adapted and supplemented English edition, Cambridge, Mass., 1969.

Journals

609. Cerruti, Marisa, "Palazzo per uffici a Utrecht." *L'Architettura*, vol 8, 1962, May, pp 38-42. Italian: "Palace for Utrecht [insurance company] offices." This thoroughly illustrated review of the building has multilingual captions and a list of collaborating artists. See also van Rooij, "Coolsingel in Rotterdam nu eindelijk compleet," *Volkskrant*, 8 January 1962; "Een nieuwe aluminium gevel aan de Coolsingel," *Constructies*, 1962, no 1, pp 9-13 (with details of the curtain wall system), reprinted in "Kantoorgebouw voor ... 'Utrecht' aan de Coolsingel," *Bouw*, vol 18, 1963, pp 470-75; "Bürobau mit Aluminium-Fassade," *Detail*, 1962, pp 236-37, with construction details and names of contractors.

610. Oud, J.J.P., "Het carnaval der architecten." *Groene Amsterdammer*, 1962, 10 February. Dutch: "The carnival of the architects." The essay deals with changes in architectural philosophy from De Stijl to Brutalism, and questions the sources and quality of contemporary architecture. There is a swipe at Gropius and teamwork, and at Mies van der Rohe's commercialism; the strongest criticism is reserved for contemporary church architecture in which Oud believes that "carnival is the order of the day." That aspect of the piece drew spirited response. See, e.g., "Voor kerkbouw moeten weer spelregels komen," *Dortsch Dagblad*, 19 November; "Stroom van nieuwe kerken," *De Tijd-Maasbode*, 21 July, p 9; *Vaderland*, 16 February; *Cobouw*, 20 November. There is an English translation in *Delta*, vol 5, 1962, no 3, pp 15-21.

611. Oud, J.J.P., "Hoge gebouwen, bouwspreiding en 'architectuur-reservaat'." *Groene Amsterdammer*, 1962, 22 December. Dutch; "Tall buildings, building sprawl and 'architectural reserve'." This is a polemic against the tall apartment block, its social impropriety and its impact upon the architectural character of Dutch cities. Cf. Oud, "Geen hoogbouw." *Televisier*, 6 October 1962, pp 16-17, where he argues with Rietveld, and "Eemshaven," *De Nieuwe Stem*, March 1962.

612. Oud, J.J.P., "Kantoorgebouw voor 'De Utrecht' te Rotterdam," *Bouwkundig Weekblad*, 1962, pp 40-45. Dutch: "Office building for the Utrecht [Life Assur-

ance Co] ..." The architect's *toelichting* of the building is illustrated with plans, sections, perspectives and excellent interior and exterior views.

613. Oud, J.J.P., "Oswald Wenckebach." *Groene Amsterdammer*, 1962, 17 November. Dutch. An obituary for the sculptor, most famous for his *Mannetje Jacques*, provides a critical overview of his career.

614. Oud, J.J.P., "Recreatie-kust-Holland of Manchester aan zee?" *Groene Amsterdammer*, 1962, 13 October. "Holland's leisure coast or Manchester-on-sea?" This is a polemic against high density residential or industrial development of Holland's west coastal resorts. Cf. Oud, "Kuststad Nederland. Waar de blanke top de duinen. ...," *ibid.*, 25 July 1959, p 9.

615. Wiekart, Karel, "De moderne architectuur en wij." *Compositie*, vol 7, 1962, no 1, pp 9-15. Dutch: "Modern architecture and us." The broad apologetic commends the Bioherstellingsoord for achieving "wonderful harmony between the most modern materials and technology, and the ... tradition [of brick]." There is a view of the boiler house and sports building.

616. *Nieuwe Rotterdamsche Courant*, "Een nimmer gepubliceerd plan voor het Hofplein."1962, 1 September. Dutch: "A never-before published plan for Hofplein [Rotterdam]." The paper prints Oud's response to an article in its 23 August issue, setting out the history of his 1942-43 proposal for Hofplein, which he describes. There is an aerial perspective. The headline is inaccurate: the scheme was in fact published in *Elseviers Weekblad*, 4 November 1950.

1963
Books and Monographs
617. Conrads, Ulrich (ed.), *Frühlicht 1920-22. Eine Folge für Verwirckichung des neuen Baugedanken*, Frankfurt am Main/Berlin, 1963. This is a photographically reduced facsimile of four issues of Bruno Taut's short-lived journal *Frühlicht*, which paid some attention to Oud in the early 1920s.

618. Copplestone, Trewen (ed.), *World Architecture*, London, 1963. English. The large, handsome, semi-populist book has a modern architecture section by John M. Jacobus Jr., which mentions Oud as an Internationalist and calls the Kiefhoek Apostolic church (illustrated) a "product of 'De Stijl' movement."

619. Oud, J.J.P., *Architecturalia, voor Bouwheren en Architecten*. The Hague, 1963. Dutch: *Architecturalia, for Building Owners and Architects*. This apologetic was compiled 1961-62 as a reflection upon fifty years of architectural practice. Reviewed Abma, *Bouw*, vol 19, no 1, p 22.

620. Pehnt, Wolfgang (ed.), *Encyclopaedia of Modern Architecture*, London, 1963. 1967. English. An excellent elementary source, this is the English version of *Knaurs Lexicon der Modernen Architektur*, Munich and Zurich, 1963. The introduction points out the tension in the 1920s between Expressionism and Modernism in the Netherlands. There are articles on Oud, Neo-plasticism, and De Stijl. Also published as *L'Encyclopedie de l'Architecture Moderne*, 1964;

Dizionario dell'Architettura Moderna, 1966; Gerd Hatje, *Elseviers Encyclopedie van de Moderne Architectuur*, 1967 (Dutch).

621. Vriend, J.J., *Bouwkunst voor onze Tijd*, Amsterdam, 1963. Reprinted 1967. Dutch: *Architecture for our Time.* The populist volume is part of the *Weten en Kunnen* series. A general essay introduces European architecture country by country and there are a few paragraphs on De Stijl. Café De Unie is illustrated.

Journals

622. Albarda, J.H., "In memoriam Dr J.J.P. Oud," *Bouwkundig Weekblad,* vol 81, 1963, pp 431-40. Dutch. Oud died of a heart attack on 5 April 1963. This profusely illustrated obituary criticizes his work, which "served architecture, and through architecture, humanity." Obituaries proliferated, nationally and internationally; see, e.g., Bakema, "Architect Oud 5 April 1963†." *Forum*, vol 2, 1963, pp 92-95;.Vriend, "Wij verloren een groot bouwmeester," *Groene Amsterdammer*, 13 April 1963, p 9; Buffinga, "Het werk van dr. J.J.P. Oud," *Bouw,* 1963, no 16, p 488; "Een groot kunstenaar ging heen," *Bouwwereld*, vol 59, 1963, pp 556-57; "Bij het overleden van architect dr J.J.P. Oud," *Nieuwe Rotterdammer* 6 April 1963; "In memoriam J.J.P. Oud," *Baksteen,* vol 5, 1963, no 3; Hartsuyker, "In memoriam J.J.P. Oud," *Werk*, 1963, no 7, pp 150-52; and Joedicke, "J.J.P. Oud†," *Bauwelt*, 22 April 1963, reprinted *Für Eine lebendige Baukunst*, 1965; Pica, "J.J.P. Oud," *Domus*, July 1963, pp 10-11.

623. Broek, Johannes Hendrik van den, "Ter herdenking †dr.h.c. J.J.P. Oud, Architect." *Ingenieur*, 1963, 24 May 1963, p 283ff. Dutch: "In memory of ...Oud." Reprinted as a booklet, this personal recollection is illustrated with a wide range of Oud's buildings and projects.

624. Ekstant, S., "In memoriam J.J.P. Oud, het geweten van de moderne architectuur." *TA/BK,* 1963, no 7, pp 149-57. Dutch: "In memoriam J.J.P. Oud, the conscience of modern architecture." Cf. A.J.J. van Rooy, "Oud, het geweten van de architectuur," Vol*kskrant,* 24 February 1964 and K.N. Elno, "J.J.P. Oud: Het geweten der moderne architectuur," *Streven,* vol 14, 1961, pt 2, no 7.

625. Jaffé, Hans Ludwig C., "Wie was J.J.P. Oud?" *Kroniek van Kunst en Kultuur*, 1962/63, no 11/12, pp 13-20. Dutch: "Who was ...Oud?" The tribute traces Oud's career through phases: early work, De Stijl, the early twenties, the New Objectivity from 1926, and finally work after the Shell Building. There are good images of early projects and of the later works. See Jaffé, "In memoriam J.J.P. Oud," *Bouwkundig Weekblad,* vol 81, 1963, pp 431-48.

626. Jordy, William H., "The symbolic essence of modern European architecture of the twenties, and its continuing influence." *Journal Society of Architectural Historians*, vol 2, 1963, no 3, pp 177-87. English (USA). The article seeks to identify the radical theories behind European architecture of the 1920s. De Stijl, is identified as the inmost essence of architecture, and Oud is the only Dutch architect discussed. His use of neo-Platonic, neo-classicist forms is seen as an impingement of history upon "non-historical" architecture; his works were not

merely functional but consciously sought aesthetic qualities as abstract art. Reprinted in *Nineteenth and Twentieth Century Architecture*, New York, 1976.

627. Morgan, Giulio, "Due progetti di J.J.P. Oud." *L'Architettura,* vol 8, 1963, April, pp 824-28. Italian: "Two projects by Oud." English, French, German and Spanish summaries. A short essay introduces designs for the Almelo town hall and the A. Plate house, Voorburg (wrongly located in The Hague), each illustrated with perspectives, plans and a photograph of the model.

628. Ragon, Michel, "*De Stijl.*" *Jardin des Artes*, vol 106, 1963, September, pp 23-31. The article is about the journal rather than the group, and in a section about architecture Oud's contribution is inevitably mentioned. There is a portrait and an image of the Oud-Mathenesse director's hut.

629. Wiekart, Karel, "De drie-eenheid van Ouds architectuur." *Museumjournaal*, 1963, no 3, pp 58-65. Dutch: "The trinity of Oud's architecture." This obituary, falling just short of apotheosis, gives a positive critical overview of Oud's career, set against the background of Dutch modernism. There are citations from his writings and illustrations of major buildings and projects.

630. Wiekart, Karel, "Holländische Architektur von heute." *Bauen + Wohnen*, 1963, April, pp 163-68. German: "Present day architecture in The Netherlands." A general history and appraisal focuses on post-1945 events, with an attempt to divide the discussion by building types. Oud's works are mentioned; the Utrecht offices and the Congress Building model are illustrated.

631. Zevi, Bruno Benedetto, "Jacobus Johannes Pieter Oud è morto." *L'Architettura*, vol 9, 1963, July, pp 146-47. Italian: "Oud's death." English, French, German and Spanish summaries. Zevi boasts that *L'Architettura* did not "write off" Oud because of the Shell Building, like others believed him wrong to think he could design outside of "a cultural context." There is a catalog of *L'Architettura* articles about Oud, a portrait and images of projects and buildings.

632. *Architectural Design*, "The work and writings of J.J.P. Oud." Vol 33, 1963, pp 303-09. English. The obituary includes correspondence between Oud and Peter Smithson (1957), Oud's "Het monumentale stadsbeeld," *De Stijl*, 1917 and "J.J.P. Oud. Von Ihm selber," *Das Einhorn,* Hamburg, 1957. The Scheveningen boulevard houses; Purmerend factory design; Weissenhofsiedlung; Kiefhoek; Café de Unie; Shell offices and later works are illustrated.

633. *Architectural Review,* "J.J.P. Oud: 1890-1963," vol 134, 1963, p 310. English. In an obituary the "convincing modernity" of Oud's earlier work is attributed in part to the influence of van Doesburg and De Stijl. He is accused of lacking vision and it is implied that others (e.g. Gropius and Hitchcock) were more responsible for his success. He is indirectly condemned (with Dudok) for compromising the lofty principles of modernism.

634. *Nederland Nu*, "Van de Amsterdamse beurs tot het Haagse congresgebouw." 1963, June, pp 20-31. Dutch: "From the Amsterdam stock exchange to

Annotated Bibliography 1960-1969   119

The Hague Congress Building." The subtitle reads, "The development of the *Nieuwe Bouwen* in Holland, and Oud's place in it"; that is what the populist piece delivers, purportedly drawing on the writings of van Loghem, Vriend and Gratama. Several works are illustrated.

1964
Books and Monographs
635. Blijstra, Rein, *'s-Gravenhage, Stad aan de Vijver*, Amsterdam, 1964. Dutch: *The Hague:City on the Water.* The Shell Building is briefly mentioned but about a page is given to discussing the Christian high school. Both are illustrated.

636.   Conrads, Ulrich, *Programmes und Manifeste zur Architektur des 20. Jahrhunderts,* Berlin, 1964. Also published in English as *Programmes and Manifestoes of 20th Century Architecture.* There are translations of the seminal documents. The Dutch content, indirectly related to Oud, is: De Stijl Manifesto I (1918); De Stijl Creative Demands (1922); De Stijl Manifesto V (1923), with van Doesburg and van Eesteren's commentary, "Towards collective building"; van Doesburg's "Towards a plastic architecture" (1924).

637. Hammacher, A.M., *Mondrian, De Stijl and their Impact*, New York, 1964. English. Hammacher wrote the introduction to this illustrated catalog for an April 1964 exhibition at the Marlborough-Geerson Gallery, New York. There are insights into the loose structure of the De Stijl group, and a reading list compiled by Joost Baljeu: "Selection of Statements by Mondrian and the De Stijl Artists."

638. Hilberseimer, Ludwig, *Contemporary Architecture: Its Roots and Trends*, Chicago, 1964. The broad history provides a chronological outline into which regional and philosophical "schools" are fitted. Dutch achievements take a back seat to German, but there is a section on Neoplasticism, which is taken to embrace Oud. The works illustrated, but poorly identified, include the Purmerend factory and boulevard housing projects, Tusschendijken and Weissenhofsiedlung.

639. Reygers, Leonie (ed.), *De Stijl*, Dortmund, 1964. German. The catalog of exhibition at Museum am Ostwall, May-June 1964, includes an essay by Hans Jaffé, biographical notes on Oud and some of his De Stijl collaborators, and good quality illustrations: the strand boulevard and Purmerend factory projects, and Kiefhoek (including) the Apostolic Church

640.   Millon, Henry A., *Key Monuments in the History of Architecture*, New York, 1964. English. A collection of images includes Hoek van Holland.

641. Perogalli, Carlo, *Storia dell' Architettura*, Milan, 1964. Italian: *History of Architecture.* A tightly-packed "profile" hardly has space to develop ideas; Oud is allowed four lines. Only the Café De Unie is illustrated.

642. Wiekart, Karel (ed.), *Herdenkingtentoonstelling J.J.P. Oud*, The Hague, 1964. Dutch: *Retrospective Exhibition: J.J.P. Oud.* Catalog of exhibition at The Hague Gemeentemuseum, February 1964. The museum also published a broadsheet with an overview of Oud's career, 1915-58. Reviewed 'TAS', "Expositie ter

herdenking van een te vroeg gestorven architect," *Algemeen Dagblad,* 12 February 1964; "Herdenkingsexpositie J.J.P. Oud," *Nieuw Rotterdamse Courant,* 15 February; Blijstra, "Oud: verzet tegen elk dogma," *Vrije Volk,* 7 March; J.E., "Het nieuwe van Oud," *Vrij Nederland,* 14 March; "Levenswerk van Oud in Gemeentemuseum," *Vaderland,* 8 March; van Rooij, "Oud, het geweten van de architectuur," *Volkskrant,* 27 February; Oudshoorn, "Architect Oud herdacht," *Parool,* 18 February; Keizer, "Architect Oud vond slechts ten dele erkenning," *Haagsche Courant,* 15 February; "Architect J.J.P. Oud 1890-1963," *De Waarheid,* 29 February; Vriend, "Het werk van ... Oud." *Groene Amsterdammer,* 3 March.

643. Wiessing, H.P.L., *John Raedecker,* Amsterdam, 1964. Dutch. The slim volume in the *Nederlandse Beeldende Kunst en Bouwkunst* series is about the sculptor who collaborated with Oud on the Dammonument, Amsterdam.

Journals

644. Gruyter, W. Jos. de, "Oud—één van de grootsten." *Bouw,* vol 20, 1964, pp 394-99. Dutch: "... one of the greatest." This obituary-*cum*-exhibition review (The Hague Gemeentemuseum, February 1964) is a friend's reminiscences, putting Oud's architecture into national context. Illustrations represent his career from the villa *Allegonda* and the Purmerend factory design to the Almelo town hall.

645. Laprade, Albert, "Les R.I.A. précurseurs des U.I.A." *L'Architecture d'Aujourd'hui,* vol 34, 1964, no 113/114, pp 38-39. French: The [*Réunions Internationales d'Architectes*] forerunner of the [International Union of Architects]." The piece notes Oud's presence at the September 1933 gathering in Milan.

646. Maaskant, H.A., "Ir. W. van Tijen." *Bouwkundig Weekblad,* vol 82, 1964, pp 33-35. Dutch. The interview includes Oud's remark to van Tijen: "You are not an architect but an engineer."

647. Veronesi, Giulia, "J.J.P. Oud, 1890-1963." *Zodiac,* 1964, no 12, pp 82-105. Italian. See also *Il Vitruvio,* Florence, 1969, no 3, pp 53-58. The tribute contains a bit of criticism, a dash of biography and a part translation of Oud, "De Stijl 1917-1927," *De Stijl,* 1927. Illustrations include a portrait, the boulevard houses and Purmerend factory projects, *De Vonk* and the South Holland Province House.

648. Wiekart, Karel, "Oud als woningbouwer." *De Woningbouwvereeniging,* 1964, May, pp 96-101. Dutch: "Oud as housebuilder." Oud's housing design 1917-31 is presented as an example of the fusion of artistic expression and social conscience. All the projects are illustrated.

649. Wilson, Colin St John, "Gerrit Rietveld 1888-1964." *Architectural Review,* vol 136, 1964, pp 399-402. Oud is accused, with Lissitzky and van Doesburg, of distorted interpretation of Rietveld's early work.

650. *Bouw,* "Raadhuis voor Almelo." Vol 19, 1964, pp 126-27. Dutch: "Almelo town hall." A brief history of the project identifies collaborators and describes the proposal. There are floor plans and perspectives. See "Almelose raad unaniem achter bouw van nieuw stadhuis," *Dagblad van het Oosten,* 13 April 1969.

651. *Haagsche Courant*, "Congresgebouw: het mooiste 'praatpaleis' te wereld." 1964, 30 June. News item, progress report.

652. *Journal de Chefs-d'oeuvre de l'Art*, "J.J.P. Oud préciseur du fonctionnalisme." 1964, no 44, I and II. French: "Oud, clarifier of functionalism." Not seen.

1965
Books and Monographs
653. Blijstra, Rein, *Dutch Town Planning after 1900*, Amsterdam, 1965 [?]. English. Blijstra emphasizes town planning after World War II but there is an overview of the first forty years as well, and Oud's Rotterdam housing is included. There are images of Kiefhoek and Spangen. The populist book also appeared in French, German and Dutch

654. Collins, Peter, *Changing Ideals in Modern Architecture*, London, 1965. English. Most of the book deals with what many regard as the prehistory of the Modern Movement. It emphasizes the influence of painting upon architecture, 1925-1950, paying particular attention to De Stijl.

655. Fischer, Wend (ed.), *J.J.P. Oud: Bauten 1906-1963*. Munich 1965. German: ...*Oud: Buildings 1906-1963*. The catalog of an exhibition at the Neuen Sammlung, Munich, July-August 1965 includes excerpts by Oud: "On future architecture and its architectonic possibilities"; "The development of modern architecture in Holland"; "The influence of ... Wright on the architecture of Europe"; "Yes and no: confessions of an architect"; "Whither the New Building? Art and Standardization" and "Mijn weg in De Stijl." There is an illustrated list of works. Reprinted 1966 for an exhibition at the *Akademie der Künste, Berlin*. The show is reviewed Landgraf, *Architektur und Wohnform-Innendekoration*, 1965, no 8; *Bauwelt*, 1966, p 152. Cf. Fischer, "Das werk von J.J.P. Oud." *Bauen + Wohnen*, vol 19, 1965, December, pp xii.1-xii.4.

656. Jaffé, Hans Ludwig C., *The 'De Stijl' Group. Dutch Plastic Art*. Amsterdam, 1965. The book is a highly condensed version of *De Stijl 1917-1931: the Dutch Contribution to Modern Art*, Amsterdam, 1956. An essay introduces biographical notes on each member: the boulevard houses and Purmerend factory projects, and Kiefhoek are illustrated. Also in French, English, Spanish and German.

657. Wiekart, Karel, *J.J.P. Oud*, Amsterdam, 1965. Dutch. One of the small books (18 pages of text) in the series *Visual Art and Architecture in the Netherlands*, provides 24 pages of images, including the unrealized designs for Blijdorp. Also in Dutch, French, Spanish and German.

658. *N.V. Nederlands Congresgebouw*, 's-Gravenhage, ca. 1965. Dutch: *Netherlands Congress Building*. Not seen.

Journals
659. Jaffé, Hans Ludwig C., "Die Niederländische Stijl-Gruppe und ihre soziale Utopie." *Jahrbuch für Aesthetik und Allgemeine Kunstwissenschaft*, Cologne, 1965. German: "The Dutch De Stijl group and its social utopia." The essay

examines the social aspirations of De Stijl members van Doesburg, Mondrian, van der Leck and Huszár. Mention is made of the group's architects, including Oud. See also *Stil und Überlieferung in der Kunst des Abendlandes*, Berlin, 1977, pp 46-52.

660. Serenyi, Peter, "Le Corbusier's changing attitude toward form." *Journal Society of Architectural Historians*, vol 24, 1965, no 1, pp 15-23. English. There is frequent reference to De Stijl's influence on Le Corbusier's architecture.

661. Sharp, Dennis, "Progress and tradition in modern Dutch architecture." *RIBA Journal*, vol 72, 1965, no 3, pp 136-41. English. Publicizing a March 1965 exhibition at the RIBA, the brief history devotes a paragraph to Oud. Kiefhoek housing and the *Bioherstellingsoord* are illustrated.

662. Smithson, Alison and Peter, "The heroic period of modern architecture." *Architectural Design*, vol 35, 1965, p 587 ff. English. A compendium of images covering the period 1910-37 is interspersed with citations from European Modernist architects and various books and journals, and correspondence between Oud and Smithson (1957). Reprinted as *The Heroic Period of Modern Architecture*, New York/Milan, 1981. Cf. "Heroic relics," *Architectural Design*, 1967.

663. *Haagsche Courant*, "Gaat Haags congresgebouw het winnen van het Amsterdamse?" 1965, 13 February. Dutch: "Will The Hague's Congress Building beat Amsterdam's?" A parochial piece compares the RAI building in Amsterdam with Oud's building.

664. *Vaderland*, "Het congresgebouw. Zo is het ..." 1965, Weekprogramma 30 June-7 July, pp 12-14. The progress report includes photographs of construction

1966
Books and Monographs
665. Fleming, John; Hugh Honour and Nikolaus Pevsner, *Penguin Dictionary of Architecture*, Harmondsworth, 1966. English. There are articles on Oud,.Dutch architecture, and De Stijl. Enlarged and revised 1972, 1980, 1991 and in large format 1992, with the same text but with a portrait, and images of the earlier works. German edition: *Lexicon der Weltarchitektur*, Munich, 1966, 1971, 1978.

666. Gelderen, W. van et al., *Hedendaagse Bouwkunst in Nederland*, Amsterdam, 1966. Dutch: *Contemporary Architecture in Holland.* Catalog of an exhibition at the Amsterdam Rijksmuseum, October-December 1966. Oud's major postwar works are included, with a brief biography. The entire issue of *Bouwkundig Weekblad*, 25 October 1966 illustrated the show and was reprinted as a booklet.

667. Jacobus, John M. Jr., *Die Architektur unserer Zeit: zwischen Revolution und Tradition*, Stuttgart, 1966. English edition: *Twentieth Century Architecture: the Middle Years 1940-1965* , New York/London, 1966. Oud's "classic International Style" Kiefhoek is illustrated as an example of simplistic "arbitrary and affected" functionalism. Most of the text and illustrations deal with post-1940 movements.

668. Manzoni, Pietro Scurati, *Il Razionalismo*, Milan, 1966. Italian: *Rationalism*. In a book spanning three centuries, a chapter is devoted to De Stijl; Oud's work is noted but not illustrated. He is mentioned in passing throughout the book.

669. Moody, Ella, *Modern Furniture*, London, 1966. 1969. English. The slim volume illustrates, without identification or comment, the Weissenhofsiedlung living room, attributed to *Modern Interiors*, 1931 (not seen).

670. Pischel [-Fraschini], Gina, *Storia Universale Dell' Arte*, Milan, 1966. 1968. 1975. 1978. Italian. English edition: *A World History of Art*, New York, 1968. 1975. Oud's "skilful town planning" at Kiefhoek and Hoek van Holland is commended, but both estates are offered as De Stijl exercises.

671. Praag, M.M.van, *Nederland Bouwt*, Alphen a/d Rijn, 1966. Dutch: *Holland Builds*. Oud is mentioned in a scathing section on the "Stijlgroep" but praised for later including ornament in the Shell Building.

672. Sharp, Dennis, *Modern Architecture and Expressionism*, London, 1966. English. Oud's contribution to Bruno Taut's magazine *Frühlicht* is noted. ("Over de toekomstige bouwkunst ... ," no 4, 1922, pp 113-18).

673. Zervos, Christian, *Domela*, Amsterdam, 1966. Dutch. There is a short essay, biographical notes, a bibliography and a list of exhibitions of Domela's work. It is made clear that his relief murals for the Utrecht Insurance building were an an important part of his oeuvre.

Journals
674. *'s-Gravenhage*, "Congresgebouw wordt markant punt in Den Haag." Vol 21, 1966, no 9, pp 2-19. Dutch: "Congress Building becomes a landmark in The Hague." A progress report reviews the building's history. There are rare images of the construction site, a biography and a portrait.

675. *Holland Herald*, "Watchful widow." Vol 1, 1966, no 2, pp 20-21. A chatty piece claims that Oud's widow Annie Oud-Dinaux had taken over the administration of his office and was "keeping an eye" on progress of the Congress Building.

1967
Books and Monographs
676. Lissitzky-Küppers, Sophie, *El Lissitzky. Proun und Wolkenbügel, Schriften, Briefe, Dokumente*, Dresden, 1967. German. English edition: *El Lissitzky. Life, Letters, Texts*, London, 1968; revised, 1980. There is reference to Oud and Lissitzky's friendship and the impression made upon the artist by Spangen.

677. Sharp, Dennis, *Sources of Modern Architecture*, London, 1967. English. This source book contains a sketchy biography of Oud. The bibliography is slight and mostly English language with few post-1960 references. Revised 1981.

Journals
678. Brown, Theodore M. "Dutch architecture 1907-1917." *Nederlandse Kunsthistorisch Jaarboek*, 1967, pp 227-36. English. The paper, providing excellent

background, begins with a hasty sketch of contemporary world architecture, and proceeds to the thesis that the period was merely formative in Holland. There is scholarship beneath the bias and apparent cynicism.

679. Jaffé, Hans Ludwig C., "Prof C. van Eesteren 4 Juli 70 jaar." *Bouwkundig Weekblad*, vol 85, 1967, pp 213-19. Dutch. Providing good background, the piece examines Oud's relationship with van Eesteren and Léonce Rosenberg, for whom van Doesburg and van Eesteren built a house in Paris in 1923.

680. Leeuwenburgh, A., "Het Nederlandse Congresgebouw te 's-Gravenhage." *Polytechnisch Tijdschrift,* vol 22, 1967, no 2, pp 44-51. Dutch: "The Netherlands Congress Building ..." This comprehensive, extensively illustrated (with drawings) report on the finished design includes biographical material on Oud and a list of contractors. See also A.Uytdehaage, "Das Niederländische Kongresszentrum in Den Haag," *Baumeister*, 1966, pp 1248-50; "Das Niederlandische Kongresszentrum in Den Haag," *Der Afbau,* 1967, pp 185-89 and Zotzmann, "Toneelinstallaties in het Nederlandse Congresgebouw," *Polytechnische Tijdschrift B*, vol 23, 1968, pp 116-19, which is mostly about about stage design.

681. Smithson, Alison and Peter, "Heroic relics." *Architectural Design*, 1967, no 12. The issue. English. A picture essay on the heroic period of modern architecture (*ibid.*, December 1965) includes Hoek van Holland, Kiefhoek and Weissenhofsiedlung. Anecdotal captions often provide information about current condition of buildings; there is little criticism.

682. Tummers, Nico H.M., "De Hagener Impuls." *Bouwkundig Weekblad,* vol 85, 1967, pp 393-465. Dutch. The piece is mostly about the Hohenhagen artists' colony in Germany, but J.L.M.Lauweriks' effect upon Oud is mentioned; the Oud-Mathenesse director's hut is discussed and illustrated. Reprinted and revised as *J.L.Mathieu Lauweriks. Zijn werk en zijn invloed op architectuur en vormgeving rond 1910: de Hagener Impuls,* Hilversum, 1968.

683. T[ummers], N[ico H.M.] (ed.), "Op weg naar 'De Stijl'." *Cobouw*, 1967, 16 June, pp 21-28. Articles include "Uit de inhoud van *De Stijl*"; Baljeu, "Theo van Doesburg en de oprichting van De Stijl"; Tummers, "Rob van 't Hoff en het werk van Wright"; van Dongen, "De Stijl was katalysator" and a "Stijl map" of Holland. References to Oud are many and there is a photo of villa *Allegonda*.

684. Weaver, Mike (ed.), "Great little magazines no 6: *De Stijl.*" *Form*, vol 6, 1967, December, pp 29-39; vol 7, 1968, pp 25-32. English. This fruitful source provides a summary of contents and indexes to the entire run of the journal 1918-32. The second part translates a number of key articles.

1968
Books and Monographs
685. Fanelli, Giovanni, *Architettura Moderna in Olanda 1900-40*, Florence, 1968. Italian: *Modern Architecture in Holland ...* The comprehensive, cursory book provides good background. There are myriad images (mostly small) and,

although there are gaps and flaws, the biographies and bibliography are its most valuable aspect. Dutch edition: *Moderne Architectuur in Nederland 1900-1940*, The Hague, 1978, with a poorly translated English summary.

686. Joedicke, Jürgen, *Architecture since 1945: Sources and Directions*, New York, 1969. Oud is "one of the first of his generation to escape from tradition-bound architecture." There is a minuscule image of the boulevard housing design and a larger one of Kiefhoek. Also published in German, Stuttgart, 1969.

687. Joedicke, Jürgen and Christian Plath, *Die Weissenhofsiedlung*, Stuttgart, 1969. German. The well-illustrated little book begins with an overview of the project before presenting the houses, each with a photograph, plans, elevations and its architect's rationale. Revised in a German/French/English edition 1977.

688. Petersen, Ad (ed.). *De Stijl,* Amsterdam/The Hague 1968. (Mainly) Dutch. Facsimile in two volumes of the entire run of the journal, including the "last number" of 1932.

689. Pevsner, Nikolaus, *Sources of Modern Architecture and Design*, London, 1968. 1975. English. The theme is "a style for the age." Half a page outlines the "development" of Wright's forms in a "new spirit"—Cubism—by De Stijl. The boulevard house design is illustrated, and there are biographical notes.

690. Portoghesi, Paolo (ed.), *Dizionaro Enciclopedico di Architettura e Urbanistica*, Rome, 1968-69. Italian: *Encyclopaedia of Architecture and Town Planning*. There is a long entry on Oud by Marcello Fagiolo, with a list of buildings and projects, a short bibliography and small line drawings of several projects 1917-60.

691. Tafuri, Manfredo, *Teorie e Storia dell'Architettura*, Rome/Bari, 1968. Italian. An English translation *Theories and History of Architecture*, London, 1980, was made from the 4th Italian edition, 1976. The Shell Building is an example of the potential conflict between architectural modernity and history.

Journals
692. Beek, Johan van de, "J.J.P. Oud." *Delftse School*, 1968, pp 373-77. Dutch. The student journal publishes a rather belated review of Wiekart (ed.), *Ter Wille van een Levende Bouwkunst*, 1962. There are poor photos and a cut-away perspective of the Congress building. See Tummers, "Het onvoltooid zelfportret van architect Oud (1890-1963)," *Cobouw*, 16 August 1968, p 18.

693. Housden, Brian, "De Stijl: the other face of tradition." *Design*, vol 231, 1968, pp 26-31. English. Marking an exhibition at the Camden Arts Centre, London (March 1968), the attempt to outline the group's ideas claims that De Stijl's central role in the modern movement was hitherto unrecognized by "all but a few enthusiasts". There is a photo of a Weissenhofsiedlung kitchen.

694. Jaffé, Hans Ludwig C., "The De Stijl concept of space." *Structurist*, vol 8, 1968, pp 8-11. English. While the major theme is painting, the essay examines Mondrian's views about the essential esthetic quality of architecture.

695. Milner, John, "Ideas and influences of De Stijl." *Studio*, vol 175, 1968, pp 115-19. English. Reviewing an exhibition at the Camden Arts Centre, London (March 1968), the essay outlines the group's philosophy and history and examines its impact upon Gropius and Mies (through van Doesburg) and Internationalism (through Oud and Rietveld). The boulevard house designs are illustrated.

696. Pica, Agnoldomenico, "De Stijl: 50th anniversary." *Domus*, 1968, no 450, pp 14-15. The reflective essay is illustrated by a mosaic of *De Stijl* covers, portraits (including Oud's) and works (including the Purmerend warehouse, the Oud-Mathenesse director's hut and the Stuttgart houses).

1969
Books and Monographs

697. Arnason, H.H., *A History of Modern Art*, London/New York, 1969. Revised 1977. In a chapter on De Stijl, an inaccurate page or so is given to architecture, mostly to Oud. The Hoek van Holland houses and Café De Unie are illustrated.

698. Banham, Reyner, *The Architecture of the Well-tempered Environment*, London, 1969. 1973. English. The author challenges Oud's conclusions in "The influence of ... Wright on the architecture of Europe." (*Wendingen*, 1925, p 85ff)

699. Baumgart, Fritz, *Stilgeschichte der Architektur*, Cologne, 1969. Also published as *A History of Architectural Styles*, London, 1970. Oud's only noteworthy contributions are identified as Hoek van Holland houses (illustrated) and the Weissenhofsiedlung, mentioned only in passing.

700. Karsten, Charles J.F., *De Stijl 1917-1931*, Amsterdam, n.d. [1969?] Dutch/English. This slim guide to a traveling exhibition has a 12 page insert in English.

701. Overy, Paul, *De Stijl*, London/New York, 1969. English. The small populist book puts the movement in an international context; its myriad illustrations (some color) include many Oud projects. Cf. Overy, *De Stijl*, London, 1991.

702. Szénássy, István L., *Architectuur in Nederland 1960/67*, Amsterdam, 1969. Dutch: *Architecture in the Netherlands...* In this overview a section is devoted to Oud's works: the *Bioherstellingsoord*, Utrecht Insurance offices, Congress Building and the projected Almelo town hall. All are illustrated.

Journals

703. B[eerends], A., "Het drama Oud." *Katholiek Bouwblad*, vol 36, 1969, no 8, pp 93-99. Dutch: "The Oud drama." The piece takes occasion of the Congress Building opening to examine Oud's "mythical" role in modern architecture.

704. Frampton, Kenneth, "*De Stijl*." *Architectural Design*, vol 39, 1969, pp 614-17. English. Apparently unable to read the text, Frampton confines himself to a "visual appraisal"of the 1968 facsimile of *De Stijl*. He notes milestones in the group's developing philosophy, suggested by the contents of successive editions.

705. Geurtsen, Rein and Jean Piret, "Map Guide 9: Rotterdam 20th century buildings," *Architectural Design*, vol 39, 1969, p 229. English. This well-detailed

small scale map locates 96 Rotterdam buildings, 41 of which were built between 1900 and 1940. The gazetteer gives name, location, date and architect, as well as occasional special comments. There is also an index to architects.

706. Oud, Hendrik Emile, "Open brief aan J.J.Vriend." *Groene Amsterdammer*, 1969, 29 March. Dutch: "Open letter to J.J.Vriend." Not seen.

707. Röntgen, F.E. et al., "Het Nederlands Congresgebouw te Den Haag." *Polytechnisch Tijdschrift*, vol 24, 1969, pp 544-80. Dutch: "The Netherlands Congress Building ..." A collection of (mostly technical) essays presents a brief critique and extended descriptions illustrated with clear drawings and photos of the completed work. Röntgen discusses architecture; G.H. van Boom, construction; R.W.Veenstra, lighting installations; J.H.G.Verhorst and H.Kromhout, mechanical services; H.Stolk, electrical/acoustic installations; H.W.Muller Kobold, catering facilities. An identical piece by van Boom appears as "De Constructies van het Nederlands Congresgebouw," *Bouw*, vol 24, 1969, p 468-73. See also "Het Nederlands Congresgebouw in Den Haag," *Constructies*, vol 11, 1969, no 3, pp 54-60.

708. Zevi, Bruno Benedetto, "Theo van Doesburg morgen." *Bouwkundig Weekblad*, vol 86, 1969, pp 63-64. Dutch: "Theo van Doesburg tomorrow." The transcript of a talk at the opening of an exhibition at Stedelijk van Abbemuseum, Eindhoven, December 1968 mentions Zevi's correspondence with Oud about why the latter left De Stijl. See also *Museumjournaal*, 1969, April, no 2, pp 58-63.

709. Bouw, "Nederlands Congresgebouw te 's-Gravenhage ..." *Bouw*, vol 24, 1969, no 12. The issue. A series of articles provides a comprehensive, well-illustrated description of Oud's largest work. Designed 1956-63, its construction (1964-69) was supervised after his death by his son Hans. Note especially Galjaard, "Moderne maatschappij heeft congresgebouwen nodig," *Bouw*, 1969, p 458ff, to which there is a response: Groenewegen, "De Haag heeft een congresgebouw, maar hoe was de opdracht?" *ibid.*, pp 1097-98. See also Kolk, "Nederlands Congresgebouw," *Baksteen*, 1969, no 2, pp 28-35. The building drew diverse criticism in the national and parochial press; for both sides of the argument see, e.g., "Haagse congresgebouw on-Nederlands," *De Tijd*, 27 June 1968; van den Heuvel, "Het Nederlands Congresgebouw, doolhof voor een zakenman," *Accent*, 22 February 1969; Röling, "Groot gebouw in verwaterde stijl," *Algemeen Handelsblad*, 15 March; Niehorster, "Kunstwereld niet onverdeeld gelukkig met het Nederlands Congresgebouw," *ibid.*, 19 April; Smit, "Gave kroon op het werk van architect Oud," Vol*kskrant*, 22 February. Cf. Vriend, "De onvoltooide symphonie van architect Oud," *Groene Amsterdammer*, 15 March; Wiekart, "Architectuur, voltooid en onvoltooid," *Vrij Nederland*, 15 March; van de Pol, "'De roem heeft hij haast met zijn bloed gekocht'," *ibid.* (reporting an interview with Annie Oud-Dinaux); and Huygens, "Doorkikje in uniek 'praatpark'," *Algemeen Dagblad*, 8 March, p 27; "Nederlands Congresgebouw al door het leven gegrepen," *De Tijd*, 13 March 1969; "Vriendenconcert werd feestelijke vertoning," *Vaderland*, 21 March 1969.

710. *Stedenbouw,* "Het Nederlands Congresgebouw." Hofstadnummer, 1969, pp 2-21. Most of the issue reviews the building. It also includes much technical and statistical information and details of contractors.

1970-1979

1970
Books and Monographs
711. Huyghe, René and Jean Rudel, *L'Art et le Monde Moderne*, Paris, 1970. French: *Art and the Modern World.* Oud is briefly discussed in a broad section on Holland. Several works are mentioned and/or illustrated.

712. Jaffé, Hans Ludwig C. (ed.), *De Stijl*, London, 1970. New York, 1971. English. A translation *Mondrian und De Stijl,* Cologne, 1967, provides English versions of 35 articles from *De Stijl*, 1917-1932 and 24 short biographies. There are images of the Oud-Mathenesse director's hut, Café De Unie, Kiefhoek, and Weissenhofsiedlung.

713. Neumann, Eckhard (ed.), *Bauhaus and Bauhaus People*, New York, 1970. English. Originally *Bauhaus und Dauhäusler*, Cologne 1985. The book gathers recollections of staff and students. In "The Bauhaus style—a myth," Walter Dexel asserts that the modern art of construction matured in the Weissenhofsiedlung inaccurately adding that Oud "had long experience in building such colonies."

714. Oudin, Bernard, *Dictionnaire des Architectes*, Paris, 1970. Revised 1982. French. There is an almost dismissive entry on Jacobus Oud [*sic*].

Journals
715. Jonge, D. de, "Het Haags Congresgebouw: intenties en realiteiten." *De Architect,* vol 1, 1970, no 2, pp 93-99. Dutch: "The Hague Congress Building: intentions and realities." An analytical essay by a sociologist/architectural

researcher evaluates several aspects, including siting, external appearance, interiors, efficiency, profitability and so on. It is replete with images.

716. Rathke, Ewald and Eckhard Neumann, "Constructivism, 1914-1922." *Art and Artists*, vol 5, 1970, July, pp 12-15. An essay publicizing an exhibition at the Annely Juda Fine Art Gallery, London discusses of links between Constructivism and De Stijl. Oud's role is briefly examined.

717. Tijen, Willem van, "Veertig jaar bouwen." *Plan,* 1970, no 9, pp 530-52. Dutch: "Forty years of building." The functionalist review mentions Oud as a member of De Stijl and a non-participant in the New Objectivity.

718. Vickery, Robert, "Bijvoet and Duiker." *AA Quarterly*, vol 2, 1970, no 1, pp 4-10. English. An examination of influences upon Dutch architecture in the 1920s, summarizes conflicting philosophies. Wright's effect upon Oud is explored. The design for concrete semidetached houses and Hoek van Holland shops are illustrated. Cf. Vickery, "Bijvoet and Duiker." *Perspecta*, 1971, no 13, pp 132-61.

719. *L'Architettura*, "Il centro congressi all'Aja di J.J.P. Oud." vol 15, 1970, pp 798-808. Italian: "The Hague Congress Building ..." This is mostly a photo-essay about the "functionally and stylistically faultless" building, with half a page of text. Cf. *ibid.*, January 1959.

720. *Cimaise,* vol 17, 1970, no 99. [Whole issue]. French/English. Reprinted as *De Stijl*, Paris, 1970. Philippe Sers, "The De Stijl movement," pp 12-24, provides good background. Michel Ragon, "The De Stijl movement and architecture," pp 66-75, asserts that Hoek van Holland housing was (after the Schröder house) "the most significant architectural work constructed by De Stijl." There are images of the Oud-Mathenesse site office, Café De Unie and the boulevard house design.

721. *Bouw,* "Opdracht: stadhuis te Almelo." vol 25, 1970, p 155. Dutch: "Contract for Almelo town hall." News item, with photograph of model.

722. *Bouw,* "Verbouw Kongresgebouw." vol 25, 1970, p 1020. Dutch: "Rebuilding the Congress Building." News item.

723. *Plan*, "Jonge monumenten 1900-1940."vol 1, 1970, pp 231-90. Dutch: "Modern heritage buildings ..." This valuable document presents by alphabetical order of architects' names a list of the significant buildings. There are tiny plans and small images of Tusschendijken, Kiefhoek (including the church) and Hoek van Holland.

1971
Books and Monographs
724. Hofmann, Werner and Udo Kultermann, *Hedendaagse Bouwkunst*, Deventer, 1970. Dutch: *Modern Architecture*. Originally *Baukunst unserer Zeit*, Essen, 1969. Hoek van Holland is included among color plates of the works of famous twentieth century architects. There is a short critical analysis.

725. Hoffmann, Gretl, *Architekturführer Stuttgart*, Stuttgart, 1971. German: *Stuttgart Architecture Guide*. A populist book includes the Weissenhofsiedlung.

726. Leering, Jean et al, *Bouwen '20-'40: De Nederlandse Bijdrage aan het Nieuwe Bouwen*, Eindhoven, 1971. Dutch: *Building '20-'40: the Dutch contribution to the New Building*. The catalog of an exhibition at the Stedelijk van Abbemuseum, Eindhoven, September-November 1971 contains a series of essays about the politico-social sources of the *Nieuwe Bouwen*, and the aesthetic influences upon form. Oud's public housing projects are discussed and illustrated. See also Nico Tummers, "Bouwen '20-'40." *TA/BK*, 1971, pp 467-86; Cees Boekraad, *Kritiek en Ontwerp*, Nijmegen, 1982.

Journals

727. Reitsma, Meine, "Congresgebouw zaak van leven en dood." *Vaderland,* 1971, 4 February. Dutch: "Congress Building, a matter of life and death." This reports an extensive interview with Oud's widow.

728. Smets, Marcel et al, "Huib Hoste en de Nederlandse architectuur." *TA/BK*, 1971, pp 308-16. Dutch: "Huib Hoste and Dutch architecture." The Belgian Hoste was an early associate of De Stijl and (in the 1930s) editor of *Opbouwen*. His contact with Oud, and his critiques of Oud's work are outlined.

729. Smithson, Alison and Peter, "Signs of Occupancy." *Architectural Design*, vol 43, 1972, no 2, pp 91-97. In a piece written 1969-70, it is claimed that Oud "built within the common technology of his time, for the social ethos of his time." Kiefhoek is used as an example and there are images of details.

1972
Books and Monographs
730. Bowness, Alan, *Modern European Art*, London 1972. 1983. English. A narrative history of modern art identifies Oud as "the most considerable of De Stijl group and the leading figure in modern Dutch architecture." That is all.

731. Jordy, William H., *The Impact of European Modernism in the Mid-Twentieth Century*, New York, 1972. 1976. 1986. English. Oud's refinement of form is mentioned in a discussion of the Philadelphia Saving Fund Society Building (Howe and Lescaze, 1929-32). Hoek van Holland is illustrated and briefly criticized.

732. Karsten, Charles F.J. and Wim H.Crouwel (eds.)), *De Stijl*, Eindhoven, 1972. Dutch. Reprinted from a catalog for a traveling exhibition, the book consists of fuzzy monochrome reproductions of about 30 panels, two of which refer to Oud. Cf. Karsten, *De Stijl 1917-1931*, Amsterdam, n.d. [1969?].

733. Karsten, Charles F.J. (ed.), *De Stijl*, no location, 1972-73. Dutch. The loose leaf folder published by the *Nederlandse Kunststichting* comprises an essay "De Stijl: logische beginselen" by Cor Blok, facsimiles of the various De Stijl manifestoes and a summary of van Doesburg's 1927 perception of group membership. The problems of the architects are specifically covered.

734. Ragon, Michel, *Histoire Mondiale de l'Architecture et de l'Urbanisme Modernes*, Paris, 1971-1972. French: *World History of Modern Architecture and Urbanism*. The two volume history has a long section on De Stijl which devotes considerable space to Oud. Images include a portrait and the Purmerend factory.

735. Sharp, Dennis, *A Visual History of Twentieth Century Architecture*, London, 1972. Revised 1991. English. This book (mostly pictures) unsatisfactorily traces development by decades, but loses the thread. The preface and the critical text must be read. Major works are illustrated. Oud's post-1930 work is ignored. Also in German: *Architektur im Zwanzigsten Jahrhundert*, Munich, 1973 and French: *Histoire Visuelle de L'Architecture du XX Siècle*, Brussels, 1975.

Journals

736. Curl, James Steven, "Dudok and the modern movement," *Country Life Annual*, 1972, pp 104-07. English. The less than scholarly piece is betrayed by such claims as "In 1912-13 [Dudok] practised with J.J.P. Oud."

737. Jongh, Ankie de, "De Stijl." *Museumjournaal*, 1972, no 17, pp 262-82. Dutch. A special edition is linked with an exhibition, *Het Nieuwe Wereldbeeld. Het begin van de abstracte kunst in Nederland 1910-1925*, at the Centraal Museum, Utrecht. Word portraits of Oud's colleagues provide background.

738. Leitner, Bernhard, "Dutch architecture 1920-1940." *Artforum*, vol 10, 1972, no 10, pp 76-78. English. Written after a show *Bouwen 1920-1940* at the Van Abbemuseum, Eindhoven, the piece attempts to identify the establishment of a new style, ended by the German invasion. Key figures and movements are discussed. Illustrations include Kiefhoek and the Shell Building.

739. Nycolaas, Jacques and Rein Geurtsen, "70 jaar woningwet, nog eens 70 jaar woningnood?" *Plan*, vol 3, 1972, no 9, pp 17-36. Dutch: "70 years of the Housing Act, once again 70 years of emergency housing?" The Witte Dorp is used as an example in a well-researched article about emergency housing. See *Bouwkundig Weekblad*, vol 45, 1924, pp 418-41.

740. Tijen, Willem van, "Prof ir M.J.Granpré Molière." *Plan*, vol 3, 1972, no 6, pp 21-37. Dutch. Marinus Jan Granpré Molière was a major figure ca. 1925-55 when the Architecture Faculty of Delft *TH* provided counterbalance for *Nieuwe Bouwen*, while he was Professor of Engineering. During post World War II reconstruction his "school" was the main target of Oud's polemic, so this article thus provides background to many of Oud's writings of that period.

1973
Books and Monographs
741. Roth, Alfred, *Bergegnung mit Pionieren,* Basel/Stuttgart, 1973. German. Although there are brief chapters on Loos, Hoffmann, Perret, and van de Velde, the book deals mainly with Le Corbusier and Mondrian. Oud's relationship to them is explored, through the Weissenhofsiedlung and De Stijl. Images include a portrait, the Café De Unie, Kiefhoek, and villa *Allegonda*.

742. Rowland, Kurt, *A History of the Modern Movement: Art, Architecture, Design* (vol 1), New York/London, ca. 1973. English. In a comprehensive essay attention to Holland focusses largely upon De Stijl, including less "public" members of the group. Criticism is careful, jargon-free and objective. There are citations from Oud's writings and images of the Café De Unie, the Purmerend factory project, and Hoek van Holland.

743. *H.H. Kamerlingh Onnes 1883-1973*, Voorschoten, 1973. Dutch. Not seen. This is the catalog of an exhibition at the Voorschoten Cultureel Centrum. The painter Harm Kamerlingh Onnes was a fellow member of the Leiden-based art group *De Sphinx*, with whom Oud rebuilt the seaside villa *Allegonda* for Onnes' father, Menso, also an artist.

Journals
744. Kr----, B., "Industriestad Almelo kreeg een aristocratisch stadhuis." *De Tijd*, 1973, 17 September, p 5. Dutch: "The industrial town of Almelo has an aristocratic town hall." A news item reports completion of the building. There is a view, and a portrait of Oud.

745. *Domus*, "Architettura Olandese." 1973, no 529. The issue. Italian. The well-illustrated itineraries include the Hoek van Holland houses.

1974
Books and Monographs
746. Baljeu, Joost, *Theo van Doesburg*, London, 1974. English. The book, structured in episodic sections, outlines van Doesburg's life and works including his collaboration with Oud. There is a monochrome view of the hall of *De Vonk*.

747. Norberg-Schulz, Christian, *Significato nell'Architettura Occidentale*, Milan, 1974. Italian. Also *Meaning in Western Architecture*, London, 1975 (revised 1980, 1983; reprinted 1985.) The Weissenhofsiedlung is used as an example in a discussion of functionalist housing; Oud's row houses are noted as "among the most interesting" and illustrated with a large isometric drawing.

748. Vriend, Jacobus Johannes, *Links Bouwen, Rechts Bouwen*, Amsterdam, 1974. Dutch: *Right Building, Left Building*. This history of the political background of twentieth century Dutch architecture, set in a broad context, discusses the role of the Delft School, especially in relation to post World War II reconstruction. It provides good background to Oud's stand against it. There is a useful chronology.

Journals
749. Hellman, Louis, "Flower and the cube." *Building Design*, 1974, no 197, pp 18-21. English. One of a series reappraising the Modern Movement deals specifically with Holland. Text and captions are replete with errors in names, locations, dates, and facts. The illustrations are too small to be useful.

750. Meijer, J., "Witte Dorp uitbundig in 't goud." *Vrije Volk*, 1974, 2 September. Dutch: *"Witte dorp* exuberant in the gold." News item about rebuilding.

751. Segal, Walter, "Into the '20s." *Architectural Review*, vol 155, 1974, no 923, pp 31-38. English. This transcribes the first of Segal's three lectures—more properly, chats—at University College London, as Professor in the School of Environment Studies. It emphasizes the socialism underlying the artistic revolution. Segal's father was an Expressionist painter, whose exhibitions in Holland had been arranged by Oud.

1975
Books and Monographs
752. Asselbergs, Fons (ed.), *Americana, 1880-1930*, Otterlo, 1975. Dutch; English summaries. This catalog of an exhibition at the Rijksmuseum Kröller-Müller, August-October 1975 includes a foreword by Leonard K.Eaton (reprinted Jan Molema, *The New Movement in the Netherlands*, Rotterdam, 1996); Auke van der Woude, "The new world; variations on a theme, 20 years interest in Frank Lloyd Wright" and Paul Hefting, "Correspondence with America: Berlage, Oud, Wijdeveld." (Essay titles are here given in translation.) Kiefhoek, "Pinehurst," Purmerend distillery and boulevard house designs are illustrated. Reviewed Juffermans, "Hoe Amerika ons bouwkunst beinvloedde," *Algemeen Dagblad*, 12 September 1975; Eaton, "It's hard to beat the Dutch," *Progressive Architecture*, February 1976, p 28; Searing, *Journal of Society of Architectural Historians*, 1978, pp 305-306. See also van der Woude, "Nederland and de nieuwe wereld," *Wonen TA/BK*, 1975, no 17, pp 16-22 and Hefting, "Americana: beschreven door Knud Lønberg-Holm en P.J.J.[sic] Oud...," *Museumjournaal*, 1975, pp 155-60.

753. Benton, Timothy et al, *The New Objectivity*, London, 1975. English. Published for the Open University Course "History of Architecture and Design 1890-1939", this volume deals with the relationship of Dutch architecture and De Stijl with contemporary movements before 1925 in Russia, the United States and Germany. It abounds with illustrations, both in the text and as separate plates.

754. Benton, Timothy, et al., *Form and Function: a Sourcebook for the History of Architecture*, London, 1975. English. Published for the Open University Course, "History of Architecture and Design 1890-1939", the book presents a balanced view through 124 extracts from the writings of key figures, including Oud's "Architecture and standardization in mass construction" (1918).

755. Geest, Jan van, Otakar Mácel and Cees Oorthuys, *Metalen Buisstoelen 1925-40*, Delft, 1975. Dutch: *Tubular Metal Chairs*. This catalog of an exhibition held in Delft, February-March and Haarlem, April-May 1975 has a preface by Willem Hendrik Gispen, an essay and a well illustrated list of exhibits arranged by designer. Six of Oud's pieces 1927-1936 are included. See J. van de Beek, "Buisstoelen '25-'40," *Wonen TA/BK*, 1975, no 8, pp 29-31.

756. Gubler, Jacques, *Nationalisme et Internationalisme dans L'Architecture Moderne de la Suisse*, Lausanne, 1975. French: *Nationalism and Internationalism in Swiss Modern Architecture*. The book mentions Karl Moser's experiences and opinions of Dutch modern architecture, including Oud's.

757. Herbert, Gilbert, *Martienssen and the International Style: the modern movement in South African architecture*, Cape Town/Rotterdam, 1975. English. Attention is drawn to the lectures, journals and books that brought modernism (and the work of Oud) before South African architects in the 1920s and 1930s.

758. Norwich, John Julius (ed.), *Great Architecture of the World*, London, 1975. English. The picture-book has a "Modern Age" section compiled by James Maude Richards and Dennis Sharp. Illustrations include a plan of Kiefhoek among The Netherlands' familiar icons, but the text is negligible. See also the derivative Christine Flon (ed.), *Le Grand Atlas de l'Architecture Mondiale*, Paris, ca. 1981 (English, *World Atlas of Architecture,* Sydney, 1984), which affords Oud hardly any place.

759. Palmes, J.C. (ed.), *Sir Banister Fletcher's A History of Architecture*, London, 1975. English. This was the first edition of the impressive architectural fact book to notice the Dutch moderns' contribution. As in all editions, the text is generally descriptive, never critical. There is only passing reference to Oud and the Hoek van Holland housing is illustrated. See also 19th edition, 1987 (John Musgrove, ed.) and centenary edition, 1996.

Journals
760. Naylor, Gillian, "De Stijl: abstraction or architecture?" *Studio*, vol 190, 1975, no 977, pp 98-102. English. This contribution to the debate demonstrates that artists' verbal articulation enables critics to analyze their work *ad infinitum*. There is an historical narrative plus long citations from the writings of group members, and several images, including the Oud-Mathenesse site office.

761. Grunsky, Eberhard, "Wohnungen für das Existenzminimum; städtische Typenhaussiedlungen in Duisburg." *Deutsche Kunst und Denkmalpflege*, vol 33, 1975, no 1-2, pp 91-109. German: "Existenzminimum houses; municipal housing developments." Not seen.

1976
Books and Monographs
762. Bulhof, Francis (ed.), *Nijhoff, Van Ostaijen,* De Stijl*: Modernism in the Netherlands and Belgium in the First Quarter of the 20th Century*, The Hague, 1976. English. This anthology of six essays read at a symposium "Modernism in the Low Countries 1915-1930," Austin, Texas, October 1973 includes *De Stijl*'s literary content. There are references to Oud's correspondence with group members in Robert Welsh, "Theo van Doesburg and geometric abstraction."

763. Fawcett, Trevor and Clive Phillpot (eds.), *The Art Press: Two Centuries of Art Magazines*, London, 1976. English. Phillpot's essay "Movement magazines: the years of style" refers to *De Stijl*.

764. Haas, C. de, *De Grote Drie,* Bussum, 1976. Dutch: *The Big Three.* A book about Dutch ocean liners includes the *Nieuw Amsterdam.* See Elysa Lewin, "De inrichting van passagiersschepen." *Spiegel Historiae*, vol 12, 1977, pp 416-23.

765. Tafuri, Manfredo and Francesco Dal Co, *Architettura Contemporanea*, Milan, 1976. Italian: *Contemporary Architecture*. A passionate, profusely illustrated, sometimes inaccurate history explores "the political and socio-economic implications of modern architecture, and the larger demands society and government exert upon planning, construction and use." There are frequent references to Oud, especially to do with the Dutch experience of urban reform. The Purmerend factory and distillery, Kiefhoek and Hoek van Holland are illustrated. Published as *Architektur der Gegenwart*, Stuttgart, 1976, 1977; *Arquitectura Contemporanea*, Madrid, 1978; *Modern Architecture*, New York, 1979 and London, 1980.

Journals

766. Baroni, Daniele, "Struttura e linguaggio in De Stijl." *Ottagono*, 1976, December, pp 44-49. Italian: "Structure and language in De Stijl." Not seen.

767. Frank, Suzanne S., "*i10*, commentary, bibliography, and translations," *Oppositions*, 1976/77, winter, pp 65-83. English. This useful document outlines the philosophy and purpose of *i10* (Oud was architectural editor). There is a bibliography with English translations of article titles, a list of independent illustrations, and a bibliographical note on full and partial reprintings, commentaries and reviews. There are translations of Oud, "International architecture: Werkbund Exhibition, 'The Dwelling', July-September 1927, Stuttgart," *i10*, 1927, pp 204-05, and Schwitters, "Stuttgart, 'The Dwelling' ... ," *ibid.*, pp 345-48 .

1977

Books and Monographs

768. Baroni, Daniele, *I Mobili di Rietveld*, Milan, 1977. Italian. Oud is mentioned as a De Stijl member; illustrations include the Café De Unie, Hoek van Holland (captioned Kiefhoek)and a plan of Kiefhoek. Published as *Gerrit Thomas Rietveld Furniture*, London/New York, 1978. The English edition is reviewed Padovan, "The Importance of De Stijl," *Architectural Design*, February 1979, pp 60-63.

769. Burckhardt, Lucius (ed.), *Werkbund: Germania, Austria, Svizzera*, Venice, 1977. Italian. Published in association with the 1976 Venice Biennale, the well-illustrated book contains a series of essays. Hans Eckstein's "Normizzazione standardizzazione costruire per l'existenzminimum" includes references to Oud's Weissenhofsiedlung houses, which are illustrated. Cf. Eberhard Grunsky, "Wohnungen für das Existenzminimum; städtische Typenhaussiedlungen in Duisburg," *Deutsche Kunst und Denkmalpflege*, vol 33, 1975, no 1-2, pp 91-109.

770. Grinberg, Donald I., *Housing in the Netherlands 1900-1940*, Delft, 1977. English. Grinberg's revisionist history exposes the important role of those architects who offered an alternative to the *Nieuwe Bouwen*. Bakema calls it "an essential contribution." It is generously and intelligently illustrated with archival and new photographs, and myriad drawings. Reprinted 1980.

771. Joedicke, Jürgen and Christian Plath, *Die Weissenhofsiedlung*, Stuttgart, 1977. German/French/English. Revised and expanded from its 1968 edition, the

slim volume begins with an overview of the project and presents each house with a photograph, drawings and the architect's rationale. See Joedicke, "Fünfzig Jahre Weissenhofsiedlung." *Bauen und Wohnen*, 1977, pp 405-07.

772. Jonge, Harmen de (ed.), *Stoelen, Chairs, Chaises, Stuhlen, Sedi*, Delft, 1977. This mimeographed multilingual catalog of the furniture collection of the Delft Institute of Technology's *Afdeling Bouwkunde* includes an armchair by Oud (1936), described and illustrated by a photograph and dimensioned drawing.

773. Kultermann, Udo, *Die Architektur im 20 Jahrhundert*, Cologne, 1977. 1980. German: *Twentieth Century Architecture*. Oud is included in this general history; there are images of the Tusschendijken and Kiefhoek housing estates.

774. Wiersma, A. et al, *S. van Ravesteyn*, Amsterdam, 1977. Dutch. The catalog of an exhibition at the Stichting Architectuur Museum, Amsterdam, August-September 1977 and Utrecht Centraal Museum, November 1977-January 1978, includes "Van Ravesteyns toegepast kunst" by Hoost Blotkamp, comparing his furniture design 1918-27 with that of De Stijl members. There is a transcript of proceedings of the "Avegoor weekend," 5-6 June 1937, when over thirty architects gathered to discuss modern architecture. "Hindered from attending," Oud made a submission by letter (8 May 1937).

775. *Tendenzen der Zwanziger Jahre*, Berlin, 1977. German: *Planning and Building in Europe 1913-1933.* Peter Pfankuch et al. (eds.), *Von der futuristischen zur funktionellen Stadt: Planen und Bauen in Europa 1913-1933* (at the Akademie der Kunst, Berlin) is part of the bulky catalog of the 15th European Art Exhibition at various German museums, August-October 1977. It refers to Oud's housing designs, including Blijdorp. There are biographical notes and a bibliography. Cf. "Tendenzen der Zwanziger Jahre: Briefe; Glossen; Kritiken, 1919-31," *Bauwelt,* 1977, pp 1079-110 which reprints Oud's correspondence with Adolf Behne, 1922-26 and illustrates the Purmerend factory and Hoek van Holland.

776. Richards, James Maude, *Who's Who in Architecture*, London, 1977. English. In a short entry on Oud no post-1946 work is mentioned. The Weissenhofsiedlung houses are illustrated.

777. Rotzler, Willy, *Konstructive Konzepte*, Zurich, 1977. 1988. German: *Constructivist Concepts*. The subtitle is "A history of Constructivist art from cubism until the present." Oud is presented as one of the great architectural theorist/writers of his time. Weissenhofsiedlung is discussed at some length.

778. Sutterland, H. and J.H. Pontier, *Geschiedenis der Bouwkunst*, Delft, 1977. Dutch: *History of Architecture*. In a bland, general treatment that borders on the chauvinistic, Oud is given two pages. There are plans and photographs of Kiefhoek, and views of Hoek van Holland and the Congresgebouw.

Journals
779. Polano, Sergio, "Notes on Oud: re-reading the documents," *Lotus,* 1977, no 16, pp 42-54. Italian/English. An article reviewing Oud's role in De Stijl, 1915-20

includes translations of his "more important" contributions to the journal: "Het monumentale stadsbeeld," 1917; "Architectonische beschouwing ... woonhuis van Fred C. Robie door F.L.Wright," 1918; "Bouwkunst en normalisatie bij den massabouw," 1918, and "Kunst en machine," 1918. There are images of his buildings and projects and a list of his articles in *De Stijl.*

780. Rasch, Bodo, "50 Jahre jung." *Deutsche Bauzeitung*, vol 111, 1977, no 11, pp 27-35. German: "Fifty years young." The piece celebrates the fiftieth anniversary of the Weissenhofsiedlung by publishing a general history and illustrating each of the houses. Oud's work has more images than most of the other houses.

781. Rebel, Ben, "Volkswoningbouw van J.J.P. Oud." *Nederlands Kunsthistorisch Jaarboek,* vol 28, 1977, pp 127-68. Dutch: "The public housing of J.J.P. Oud." English summary. A well-researched illustrated article examines the images of Oud created by his publicists and himself and concludes that he was not a "socially-concerned builder of housing," although he had "great merit" in the esthetic sphere. Reissued as a booklet, Haarlem, 1978. For a critical rejoinder, see Hans Oud, *J.J.P. Oud Architekt 1890-1963: feiten en herinnerigen gerangschikt*, The Hague, 1984, pp 115-24.

782. Rouw, J.F.H., "Het Witte Dorp wordt gerenoveerd." *NRC-Handelsblad,* 1977, 7 October. Dutch: "The *witte dorp* to be renovated." News item.

783. Stamm, Günther, "Het jeugdwerk van de Architekt J.J.P. Oud 1906-1917." *Museumjournaal,* vol 22, 1977, pp 260-65. Dutch: "The early work of architect J.J.P. Oud, 1906-17." The title explains the content of a narrative, critical work. Some names and dates vary from later sources. Illustrations include the "Vooruit" building, Schinkel cinema, van Lendt shop, van Bakel house, van Essen house, villa *Allegonda* and *De Vonk*, as well as unrealized designs for a public bath house, nursing home, military housing, a trades school and the *strand boulevard* housing. See also Stamm, "Purmerend bakermat van architectonische wereldgeschiedenis [Purmerend, the cradle of international architectural history]," *Geef Noord-Holland de Ruimte,* September 1977, pp 14-17; "Bakermat 20e eeuwse architectuur ligt in Purmerend [The cradle of twentieth century architecture lies in Purmerend]," *Nieuwe Noordhollandse Courant*, 2 August 1978; and Stamm, "J.J.P. Oud and Walter Gropius: new evidence," *Papers of Southeastern College Art Conference Convention*, Virginia, 1977 (not seen).

784. Ven, Cornelis J.M. van de, "De Rotterdamse bijdrage aan het nieuwe bouwen." *Plan,* 1977, no 2, pp 9-24. Dutch: "The Rotterdam contribution to the new Building." The comprehensive article systematically addresses the theme from proto-modern through closed block, garden suburb housing and the New Objectivity to current approaches. Oud merits a separate section and his Oud-Mathenesse, Spangen and Kiefhoek are analyzed and illustrated.

785. Walden, Russell, "Humanism in Holland," *New Zealand Architect*, vol 44, 1977, no 5, pp 36-49. English. The short piece has little depth. The history is derivative and while photographs are large, captions are inconsistent.

1978
Books and Monographs

786. Campbell, Joan, *The German Werkbund: the politics of reform in the applied arts*, Princeton, 1978. English. Also published as *Der Deutsche Werkbund 1907-34*, Stuttgart, 1981. A study of the *Werkbund* 1907-1934 gives some background information about the setting up of the Weissenhofsiedlung. There is a photograph of the dining room in one of Oud's row houses.

787. Clairet, Alain, *Domela: Catalogue raisonné de l'oeuvre de César Domela-Nieuwenhuis (peintures, reliefs, sculptures)*, Paris, 1978. French/English. Domela was associated with De Stijl and in 1955 he renewed his acquaintance with Oud, who commissioned four relief murals for the Utrecht Insurance building in Rotterdam. This sumptuous catalog of a retrospective exhibition at the Galerie Marguerite Lami, Paris illustrates them among about 250 other works.

788. Fanelli, Giovanni, *Architettura, Edilizia, Urbanistica: Olanda, 1917-1940*, Florence, 1978. Italian: *Architecture, Building Industry, Urbanism: Holland 1917-1940.* The very thick book unsatisfactorily treats the subject as a year-by-year chronology, divided into general socio-political background, architecture, and urbanism. It consists mostly of translated citations, inexactly documented. The illustrations, divorced from the text and grouped at the back, are also chronologically arranged. Many of Oud's early designs and buildings are included, but most images are very small.

789. Kief, Heidemarie, *Der Einfluss Frank Lloyd Wright auf die Mitteleuropaische ein Zelhaus-architektur*, Stuttgart, 1978. German: *Wright's Influence on Mid-European Domestic Architecture.* Revised as Heidemarie Kief-Niederwöhrmeier, *Frank Lloyd Wright und Europa. Architekturelemente, Naturverhaltnis, Publikationen, Einfluss*, Stuttgart, 1983, this is the published version of a thesis from Darmstadt *Technischen Hochschule*. There is a substantial section on De Stijl, and a subsection on Oud, especially his Purmerend factory projects and the Oud-Mathenesse director's hut (illustrated). See also Kief-Niederwöhrmeier, "Frank Lloyd Wright ..." *Baumeister*, vol 81, May 1984, pp 19-27.

790. Sherwood, Roger, *Modern Housing Prototypes*, Cambridge, Mass., 1978. English. The book examines what the author believes to be exemplars of housing design "that set the standard and patterns ... of that which was to follow." Two pages cover the Weissenhofsiedlung houses, illustrated with barely legible plans, an isometric drawing and a single blotchy photograph.

791. Stamm, Günther, *The Architecture of J.J.P. Oud 1906-1963*, Tallahassee, 1978. English. This substantial catalog of an exhibition of documents (including drawings, plans and photographs) from the archives of Oud's widow, mounted at the Florida State University Art Gallery, Tallahassee, May 1978, follows an expected pattern: early work, De Stijl, Internationalism. There is a *curriculum vitae*, a list of works, a bibliography and a translation of "My way in De Stijl." Illustrations are well integrated with the text, which is more chatty than scholarly.

Of great interest is the large number of schematic sketches—"ideas drawings." The book was revised in German by Stamm's sister as Gunther and Brigitte Stamm, *J.J.P. Oud, Bauten und Projekte 1906 bis 1963*, Mainz/Berlin, 1984.

792. Ven, Cornelis J.M.van de, *Space in Architecture,* Assen/Amsterdam, 1978. English. This published version of a 1974 doctoral thesis purports to be "the evolution of a new idea in the theory and history of the modern movements." De Stijl's notion of space and Oud's perceptions of Wright's architecture are discussed. A *De Vonk* interior and the Purmerend factory design are illustrated.

793. Zevi, Bruno Benedetto, *The Modern Language of Architecture*, Seattle/Canberra, 1978. English. In a response to John Summerson's *The Classical Language of Architecture*, Oud is grouped with Le Corbusier, Gropius and Mies van der Rohe, and all are compared with Brunelleschi as "drastic [reducers] of linguistic instruments." The elementary geometry of Kiefhoek (illustrated) is compared with Cola di Caprarola's S. Maria della Consolazione, Todi (1508-12).

Journals
794. Bullhorst, Rainer. "Verwarring, verarming en rijkdom in de architectuur." *De Bouwadviseur,* vol 20, 1978, April, pp 23-26. Dutch: "Confusion, impoverishment and wealth in architecture." The piece asserts that architecture is not an elitist but a popular art. Oud's Congress Building comes in for severe criticism of its utilitarian soullessness.

795. Daldrop, Norbert W., "Weissenhof—fifty years later." *MD (Möbel + Dekoration),* vol 24, no 2, pp 47-56. English. Not seen.

796. Brouwers, Ruud and Hein Reedijk (eds.), "De volkswoningbouw van toen en de betekenis daarvan nu." *Wonen TA/BK*, 1978, no 4, pp 2-18. Dutch: "Early public housing and its meaning for today." The issue was published in association with a changing collaborative *Stichting Wonen* and *Rotterdamse Kunststichting* exhibition "Living in Public Housing"at *De Doelen*, Rotterdam, February-March 1978. There were special shows on Spangen, Oud-Mathenesse and Kiefhoek. The latter two are discussed and illustrated, and there is a photo of Rietveld's furniture in a Spangen "model" house. See F. Haagsma, "Nostalgisch omzien naar de volkswoninkjes van toen," *NRC-Handelsblad,* 18 March 1978, p Z.5.

1979
Books and Monographs
797. Beckett, Jane et al, *The Original Drawings of J.J.P. Oud, 1890-1963*, London, 1979. English. This well-illustrated catalog of an AA exhibition shows Oud's works, with a chronology. There is an introduction by Beckett, a biography and translations of "Architectural comment on the Robie House," *De Stijl*, 1918; "Yes and No: confessions of an architect," *Bouwkundig Weekblad*, 1925, and correspondence about Oud's comments on the U.N. building, New York, *RIBA Journal*, 1948. The show is reviewed *Building Design*, "Functionalism plus," 12 January 1979, p 13, with a drawing of Leiderdorp.

798. Bonta, Juan Pablo, *Architecture and its Interpretation*, London, 1979. English. This examination of architectural criticism refers to several Dutch modernists: Berlage, van Doesburg, Dudok, Oud, and Rietveld.

799. Campbell-Cole, Barbie and Tim Benton (eds.) , *Tubular Steel Furniture*, London, 1979. English. The papers presented at a conference/exhibition at the AA, London, January-February 1977, include Jane Beckett's "W.H.Gispen and the development of tubular steel furniture in the Netherlands," which discusses Oud's associations with the firm and illustrates interiors of the villa *Allegonda* and Weissenhofsiedlung.

800. Casciato, Maristella et al, *Funzione e Senso: Architettura--Casa--Città. Olanda 1870-1940*, Milan, 1979. Italian: *Holland 1870-1940: Cities, Houses, Architecture*. This catalog of a touring exhibition (Turin, Rome and Venice) was revised as *Olanda 1870-1940: Citta, Casa, Architettura*, Milan 1980 and translated into Dutch as *Architektuur en Volkshuisvesting* [*Architecture and Public Housing*], Nijmegen, 1980. It publishes Oud's "Bouwkunst en normalisatie bij den massabouw." *De Stijl*, 1918 and there are references to him throughout. The boulevard and concrete house designs, Spangen and Tusschendijken, Oud-Mathenesse, Hoek van Holland, Kiefhoek and Blijdorp are documented.

801. Heissenbüttel, Helmut (ed.), *Stuttgarter Kunst im 20. Jahrhundert*, Stuttgart, 1979. German: *Art in Stuttgart in the 20th Century*. There is a brief treatment of Weissenhofsiedlung in Frank Werner, "Stuttgart architecture before 1945."

802. Johnson, Donald Leslie, *Australian Architecture 1901-51: Sources of Modernism*, Sydney, 1979. English. The book explores the attractiveness of W.M.Dudok's work for Australian architects in the 1930s, identifying the sources of their forms in general terms. There is passing mention of Oud.

803. Johnson, Philip, *Writings*, New York, 1979. English. In an afterword to the anthology, the architect admits that his conversion to Modernism was provoked by Hitchcock's "The architectural work of J.J.P. Oud," *The Arts*, 1928. See Joost Meuwissen, "Architectuur als conversatie," *Plan,* 1981, no 11, pp 8-17. Cf. the preface in Helen Searing (ed.), *In Search of Modern Architecture ...*, 1982. In 1955, Johnson's story had been slightly different (see John Peter, *The Oral History of Modern Architecture*, 1994, p 225).

804. Mang, Karl, *History of Modern Furniture*, London, 1979. English. Originally *Geschichte des Modernen Möbels*, Stuttgart, 1978. There is reference to Oud's collaboration at Stuttgart with the Frankfurt furniture designer Ferdinand Kramer, and the dining room of one of the "exemplary" row houses is illustrated. See also *Rote Fahne* (Berlin), 1 May 1927.

805. Mansell, George, *Anatomy of Architecture*, London, 1979. English. In this coffee-table attempt at a total history of world architecture Holland is briefly mentioned in a chapter entitled "Twentieth century early modern movements." Oud is identified as *the* Dutch pioneer.

Journals

806. Barbieri, Sergio Umberto, "De vormgeving van de nieuwe wereld." *Vrij Nederland*, vol 40, 1979, 24 February, pp 23-24. Dutch: "The design of the new world." The comment on the AA exhibition "The Original Drawings of J.J.P. Oud" reviews recent literature in the light of Oud's writings and buildings. Kiefhoek is illustrated, but an aerial photo is incorrectly identified as Blijdorp. Reprinted Barbieri and Boekraad, *Kritiek en Ontwerp*, Nijmegen, 1982, with images of the boulevard house designs and Spangen.

807. Beckett, Jane, "Dada, van Doesburg and De Stijl." *Journal of European Studies*, vol 9, 1979, pp 1-25. English. The double issue was reprinted as Richard Sheppard (ed.), *New studies in Dada: essays and documents*, Driffield, 1981. Beckett's well-documented, scholarly exploration of van Doesburg's paradoxical involvement with Dadaism deals mostly with painting and poetry, but there are interesting insights into his relationship with Oud.

808. Campo, Marc à, "Architecten en stoelen/stalenbuismeubelen." *Bouwwereld*, vol 75, 1979, no 9, p 18. Dutch: "Architects and chairs/tubular steel furniture." The essay draws analogies between the development of modern furniture and modern architecture. Oud's association with Metz and Co is mentioned and the sole illustration is of a chair he designed for the firm in 1933.

809. Dettingmeyer, Rob, "Een gebouw als opstelsom van grijpbare elementen en ruimten." *Wonen TA/BK*, 1979, no 24, pp 21-45. Dutch: "A building as a composition of understandable elements and spaces." The general essay includes discussion of Oud's ca. 1951 unbuilt urban design proposals for Vredenburg, Utrecht. There is a plan and a photograph of the model of the scheme.

810. Geest, Jan van, "Re-issue of Oud's and Herbst's furniture." *Architectural Design*, vol 49, 1979, August, p 211. English. This brief article, illustrated with photographs of the reproductions, discusses Oud's furniture designs: chairs for Metz (1933) and the dining room set for Stuttgart. See van Geest, "Her-uitgeven van meubels met industriëlle allure," *Vrij Nederland*, 28 April 1979.

811. Posener, Julius, "Julius Posener: Vorlesung zur Geschichte neuen Architektur." *Arch Plus*, 1979, December, pp 2-80. German. Some of the thirteen lectures, including one on De Stijl, were reprinted in *Aufsätze und Vorträge: 1931-1980*, Braunschweig, 1981. Oud is of course mentioned and some of his correspondence with Bruno Zevi is cited. The boulevard houses and Hoek van Holland are illustrated.

812. Stamm, Gunther, "De Doorbraak (1916-1919) bij J.J.P. Oud." *Bouw*, vol 34, 1979, pp 71-74, 76-79. Dutch: "Oud's breakthrough ..." The essay, based on an analysis of Oud's sketches of the period, is in two parts: "Over de lijnen van geleidelijkheid tussen Velp en Purmerend [Along lines of gradualness between Velp and Purmerend]" and "Kubisme en De Stijl, fasen in een continue ontwikkeling [Cubism and De Stijl: phases in a continuous development]," whose titles reveal their content. Many of Oud's sketches are reproduced.

813. Vermeijden, M., "Wim Wilson maakt van galerie zijn huiskamer." *NRC-Handelsblad,* 1979, 14 November. Dutch: "Wim Wilson makes his living room from a gallery." News item about reproductions of Oud furniture.

814. *Architect*, "Uitbreiding Congresgebouw Den Haag." Vol 10, 1979, no 7/8, p 29. Dutch: "Extensions to the Congress Building ..." A short item with rather meaningless line drawings discusses acoustical problems. See also "Puur waardeloze akoestiek," *ibid.*, no 3, p 21.

1980-1989

1980
Books and Monographs
815. Boasson, Dorien et al., *Kijk Uit, Om Je Heen*, Den Haag, 1980. 1988. Dutch: [idiom] *Look Around You*. Subtitled "the history of modern architecture in the Netherlands," the prolifically illustrated and populist book gives an overview of developments from the late 19th century. Oud is mentioned as one of the important architects in De Stijl and the *Nieuwe Bouwen*. There are tiny images of Spangen, Hoek van Holland and Kiefhoek.

816. Bool, Flip and Kees Broos, *Domela; schilderijen, reliëfs, beelden, grafiek, typografie, fotos*, The Hague, 1980. Dutch: *Domela; paintings, reliefs, sculpture, graphics, typography, photos*. The catalog of an exhibition at The Hague Gemeentemuseum, September-October 1980, includes a reference to the four wall reliefs commissioned by Oud for the Utrecht Insurance offices, Rotterdam.

817. Compton, Michael (ed.), *Towards a New Art: Essays on the Background to Abstract Art 1910-1920*, London, 1980. English. In an anthology published by the Tate Gallery, London, an essay by Jane Beckett, "The abstract interior," touches on De Stijl notion of painting into architecture, using the villa *Allegonda* and *De Vonk* as examples, the latter at greater length and illustrated with three new photographs

818. Cramer, Max, Hans van Grieken and Heleen Pronk, *W.M.Dudok 1884-1974*, Amsterdam, 1980. Dutch. Published in connection with a national touring exhibition, the book forms a valuable overview of Dudok's career. His early collaboration with Oud in Leiden is noted.

819. Frampton, Kenneth, *Modern Architecture: a Critical History*, London, 1980. English. The major part of the book is a series of essays dealing in roughly chronological order with aspects of modernism, 1880-1965. De Stijl is examined in concert with wider European developments in a chapter subtitled "the evolution and dissolution of Neo-plasticism 1917-31." Oud is said to have been "never whole-heartedly affiliated with the movement." Other mentions are just as brief. Revised and enlarged 1985; 1990. Dutch edition: *Moderne Architectuur: een Kritische Geschiedenis*, Nijmegen, 1988.

820. Garner, Philippe, *Twentieth Century Furniture*, London, 1980. English. Oud is mentioned in "The Netherlands: Rietveld" as "exploiting tubular steel and making contact internationally with other progressive designers."

821. Geest, Jan van and Otakar Mácel, *Stühle aus Stahl. Metallmöbel 1925-1940*, Cologne, 1980. German: *Chairs out of steel. Metal furniture.* An introductory essay precedes a folio of designers, in alphabetical order. Oud is given three pages: a brief biography accompanies images of Metz chairs 01, 02, 03 and 04; dining chair for the Weissenhofsiedlung; dining set and armchair for Villa *Allegonda*; Metz fauteuil 07b; and some Metz armchairs of 1938. See Eggink, "De introductie van het stalen buismeubel in Nederland," *Nederlands Kunsthistorische Jaarboek*, vol 31, 1980, pp 563-74, and van Rooy, "W.H. Gispen en de entree van het stalen meubel," *NRC-Handelsblad*, 1 August 1980, for valuable background. Cf. van Geest and Mácel, *The Museum of the Continuous Line*, Amsterdam, 1986.

822. Hedrick, Hannah, *Theo van Doesburg, Propagandist and Practitioner of the Avant-Garde 1909-1923*. Ann Arbor, 1980. English. There is brief discussion of van Doesburg's collaborations with Oud.

823. Lampugnani, Vittorio Magnago, *Architektur und Stadtebau des 20 Jahrhunderts*, Stuttgart, 1980. German. Also published as *Architecture and City Planning in the Twentieth Century*, New York, 1985. The book is divided into the "isms" of twentieth century thought, after an introduction entitled "from the age of enlightenment to Art Nouveau." Oud's association with De Stijl and his work of the 1920s are discussed. Illustrations are small and muddy.

824. Nooteboom, Cees et al., *Nooit gebouwd Nederland*, Amsterdam 1980. 1981. Dutch. A handsome, well documented collection of (mostly) color drawings of 130 years of Dutch unbuilt architectural designs includes Oud's Purmerend factory, his competition entry for the Rotterdam stock exchange, the projected Blijdorp housing estate and the St Laurens church restoration. The captions are informative. Also published as *Unbuilt Netherlands*, 1985 (reviewed Crosbie, *AIA Journal*, September 1986, pp 108ff).

825. *Stoelen*, Delft, 1980. Dutch: *Chairs.* A picture book of international chair design, including examples from preliterate societies, student projects and works by more famous designers, reproduces Oud's tubular steel armchair of 1936. There is a dimensioned perspective drawing.

826. Ebbinge, E., *W.C.Brouwer (1877-1933). Vaatwerk, tuinaardewerk, bouwaardewerk,* Lochem, 1980. Dutch. This is the catalog of an exhibition at the Gemeentemuseum "Het Princessehof," Leeuwarden, January-March 1980 of Brouwer's architectural and garden ceramics. The show moved to the Arnhem Gemeentemuseum, April May 1980 and Gouda Stedelijk Museum, May-June 1980. Brouwer executed the ceramic detail on the Schinkel cinema.

Journals
827. Beckett, Jane, "*De Vonk*, Noordwijk: an example of early De Stijl co-operation." *Art History*, vol 3, 1980, June, pp 202-17. English. The article deals with the co-operation of the artists in building *De Vonk* holiday houses. The philosophies of client and designers are explored. Plans and photographs illustrate the building; also included are Oud's drawings for the De Geus house.

828. Dijk, Hans van (ed.), "Architectuur gids, Rotterdam." *Wonen TA/BK*, 1980, no 5/6. Dutch: "Architecture Guide to Rotterdam." There are brief references to Oud's housing schemes, including Hoek van Holland. Reissued as a booklet.

829. Grinberg, Donald I., "Modernist housing and its critics: the Dutch contributions." *Harvard Architecture Review*, vol 1, 1980, pp 147-60. English. Identifying the Netherlands as "a kind of hot-house for Modernist housing theory," the essay discusses the dialog between architects and critics in a review of Dutch housing from the beginning of the 20th century. Oud's role is mentioned.

830. Heijbroek, J.F., "Her kortstondig bestaan van de Leidsche kunstclub 'De Sphinx'." *Leids Jaarboekje,* 1980, pp 155-62. Dutch: "The brief life of the Leiden art group, *De Sphinx*." The title speaks for itself. Reprinted as booklet

831. Niesten, Joop, "Vormingscentrum, Noordwijkerhout." *Cobouw*, vol 8, 1980, 7 November, pp 51-53. Dutch: "Design Center ..." M. Barkema designed an extension to *De Vonk*; the article describes both schemes and provides photos and a plan. Cf. Barkema, *Vormingscentrum* De Vonk*, Noordwijkerhout*, 1980.

832. Riga, Adina, "J.J.P. Oud's blue furniture." *Domus*, 1980, no 603, pp 38-39. Italian/English. Praising the design of Oud's tubular steel dining set for the Weissenhofsiedlung, this announces that it is being reproduced by Kollector Perpetuel in The Hague. There are color images, an archival photograph of the furniture *in situ*, and detailed construction drawings.

833. Salomons, Izak, "Omgaan met de jonge architectuurmonumenten opgave en noodzak," *Wonen TA/BK*, 1980, no 16-18, pp 44-48. Dutch: "..The need to list recent architectural monuments[idiom]." Claiming that Modernism was not about creating monuments, this is a brief history of the movement in Holland.

1981
Books and Monographs
834. Engel, Henk et al. , *Architectuur van J.J.P. Oud,* Rotterdam, 1981. Dutch. This is the well-designed catalog of the *Rotterdamse Kunststichting* exhibition at the Lijnbaancentrum, December 1981-January 1982. There are essays by Engel,

148 Oud and the International Style

Umberto Barbieri, Sergio Polano, Bernard Colenbrander and Oud himself. The work is divided into three periods, but most attention is given to 1917-30. It is thoroughly illustrated and a touring map was provided, locating 11 Oud buildings in Rotterdam, 1918-61. Italian edition: *J.J.P. Oud*, Rome, 1982. The show was widely publicized and reviewed in Holland: see, e.g., Vermeijden, "Architect Oud: revolutionair en opvoedend," *NRC-Handelsblad*, 23 December 1981; van der Lugt, "Architectonische vormgeving," *Magazijn*, December 1981, p 33; van Rooy, "Met rood moet je voorzichtig zijn. Alleen een toefje," *NRC-Handelsblad*, 31 December 1981, CS; Schenke, "Beeld van een veelzijdig architect," *Algemeen Dagblad*, 30 December 1981; van de Geer, "Bouwen voor de massa's," *Haagse Courant*, 4 December 1981 and "Architect Out tekende voor woonplezier en kwaliteit," *Rotterdamse Nieuwsblad*, 6 January 1982, with an incorrect portrait; Eerhart, "Oud-nieuws," *Wonen TA/BK*, 1982, no 2; "Ontwerp architect Oud uit Purmerend kreeg grote faam," *Noordhollandse Courant*, 5 January 1982; de Jong, "Toonangevend werk van Oud," *Vrije Volk*, 7 January, p 19; Salomons, "Oud, een klassieke moderne architect," *Parool*, 8 January; Burg, "Architectuur van Oud in Lijnbaancentrum," *Cobouw*, 8 January, p 13; Karstkarel, "De 'algemene' architectuur van J.J.P. Oud," *Trouw*, 9 January; Kloos, "Oud: moedig en gewetensvol," *Volkskrant*, 15 January; Bosma, "Oud-Tentoonstelling," *Futura*, February, p 122. Most are illustrated and all have biographies of varying accuracy.

835. Haan, Hilde de and Ids Haagsma (eds.), *Wie Is Er Bang Voor Nieuwbouw?*, Amsterdam, 1981. Dutch: *Who's Afraid of the New Building?* Oud is mentioned in the editors' background sketch to an anthology of philosophical and historical essays by contemporary Dutch architects, scholars and writers.

836. Posener, Julius, *Aufsätze und Vorträge: 1931-1980*, Braunschweig, 1981. German: *Essays and Lectures* ... Oud is mentioned in "De Stijl-Gruppe," and some of his correspondence with Bruno Zevi is cited. The boulevard houses and Hoek van Holland are illustrated. Some lectures appeared in *Arch Plus*, 1979.

837. Rubinger, Krystyna (ed.), *Klassische Moderne. The Classical Moderns*, Cologne, 1981. German/English. The catalog of an exhibition, "Classical Moderns after 1939" at the Galerie Gmurzynska, Cologne, May-August 1981, refers to Oud in the van Doesburg entry and illustrates the monogram the painter designed for him in 1919.

838. Sanderson, Warren (ed.), *International Handbook of Contemporary Developments in Architecture*, Westport, 1981. English. A chapter, "The Netherlands" by H. Wouter Hubers and Heero Meindersma clearly sets out the disagreements between Oud and the Delft School during postwar reconstruction.

839. Selz, Peter Howard, *Art in Our Time*, New York, 1981; London, 1982. English. The book is divided into decades from 1890; within each the arts are treated separately. References to Dutch architecture are desultory and episodic. Mention is made of Oud, Rietveld, and Dudok but there is no attempt to bring ideas together. There are a few small images.

840. Stangos, Nikos (ed.), *Concepts of Modern Art*, London, 1981. English. The book includes a resume of De Stijl by Kenneth Frampton, "The evolution and dissolution of Neoplasticism 1917-31."

841. Tafuri, Manfredo et al., *Nederlandse Architektuur in Internationale Perspektief, 1900-1940*, Amsterdam, 1979. Dutch: *Dutch Architecture in International Perspective* ... The booklet reprints in translation essays from Sergio Polano, *Architettura Socialdemocrazia Olanda 1900-1940*, Venice, 1979, published for an exhibition *Funzione e Senso: Architettura—Casa—Città*, Palazzo Esposizione, Rome, March-April 1979. Oud is mentioned in Tafuri, "Nederland, Weimar, Wenen" and Giorgio Muratore, "De invloed van de Nederlandse architektuur in het buitenland."

842. Wingler, Hans Maria et al., *Bauhaus Archiv-Museum; Sammlungs-Katalog (Auswahl); Architektur, Design, Malerei, Graphik, Kunstpädagogik*, Berlin, 1981. German: *Bauhaus Archive-Museum; select catalog* ... In a documentation of about 500 archival items there is an essay "'Lasste alle Hoffnung fahren!'," by Stephan von Wiese, on the conflict between the Bauhaus and De Stijl. The cover of *Holländische Architektur* (1926) is reproduced, and a model of Weissenhofsiedlung.

843. Wolfe, Tom, *From Bauhaus to our House*, New York, 1981. English. The populist book is drawn from articles appearing in *Harpers Magazine*. The facts are dubious, the generalizations almost stunning, and the socialistaphobia (to coin a word) almost ludicrous. Oud is mentioned in the panorama of modernism. Dutch edition: *Het Geschilderde Woord: van Bauhaus tot ons Huis*, Baarn, 1982.

844. *H.H. Kamerlingh Onnes. Schilder en keramicist*, Leeuwarden, 1981. Dutch: *...Onnes. painter and ceramicist.* Not seen. Kamerlingh Onnes was a fellow member of the art group *De Sphinx*, with whom Oud rebuilt the villa *Allegonda*.

Journals

845. Barbieri, Sergio Umberto, "C. Weeber: urban architecture and housing." *Dutch Art and Architecture Today*, vol 9, 1981, pp 29-38. Dutch/English. Carel Weeber's reference to Michiel Brinkman's Spangen development (1919) is noted in an outline of his own proposals for Dordrecht (1974). An aerial photograph of Spangen, and a perspective of Blijdorp are included.

846. Beckett, Jane, "The styles of De Stijl." *Times Literary Supplement*, 1981, 7 August, p 908. Not seen.

847. Boekraad, Cees (ed.), "Forum discussie." *Plan*, 1981, no 9, pp 48-53. Dutch: "Forum discussion." This reports a discussion about "designer and history, historian and design" involving practitioners in both fields. Oud's name is raised in connection with the Rotterdam Hofplein proposal and Henk Engel draws comparisons between his architecture and van Doesburg's painting

848. Bullhorst, Rainer, "Cultuur-historisch bezit in steigers, waar ligt de grens?" *NRC-Handelsblad*, 1981, 5 December, p 13. Dutch: "Cultural-historical scaffolds,

where is the boundary?" [idiom.] The piece examines the conflicts between pragmatic renovation of public housing and its historic conservation. Oud-Mathenesse (illustrated) and Spangen are used as examples.

849. Engel, Henk, "Van huis tot woning." *Plan*, 1981, no 9, pp 34-39. Dutch: "From house to dwelling." In this "typological analysis of Oud's residential designs" the boulevard project, a street composition, Tusschendijken and Spangen are examined against the background of contemporary European notions and the compositional methods of De Stijl. All are well illustrated.

850. Grassi, Giorgio, "Architectonisch ontwerp en analyse van de stad." *Plan*, 1981, no 9, pp 40-43. Dutch: "Architectural design and analysis of the city." The article uses Oud's work to make its points: Kiefhoek, the Shell Building, the van Essen-Vinckers house and the Rotterdam stock exchange project.

851. Meuwissen, Joost, "Gekozen verwantschap." *Plan,* 1981, no 6, pp 26-31. Dutch: "Selected relationship." Oud was the theme of the issue. This scholarly essay is a critical comment upon a profusely illustrated translation of his "Mijn weg in De Stijl" (see 575), which precedes it, and more particularly on *Architecturalia, voor Bouwheren en Architecten.* There are photos of the Shell Building, the Grebbeberg and Dam monuments, the Bioherstellingsoord and the Utrecht Insurance offices (mostly interiors).

852. Padovan, Richard, "The Pavilion and the court," *Architectural Review*, vol 170, 1981, pp 359-70. English. Subtitled "Cultural and spatial problems of De Stijl architecture," the article expands current discussion of De Stijl, drawing on the writings of van Doesburg and van Eesteren. Several of their projects are illustrated, as well as Oud's Weissenhofsiedlung. Dutch translation "Het paviljoen en het hof ..." *Wonen TA/BK*, 1982, nos 15-16, pp 12-27.

853. Taverne, Ed R.M., "Ouds ontwerp voor het Hofplein." *Plan,* 1981, no 9, pp 30-34. Dutch: "Oud's design for the Hofplein." Oud was the theme of the issue. The illustrated essay identifies the place of Oud's unrealized urban design proposal in the overall rebuilding plan for Rotterdam, initiated soon after the devastating German bombing of May 1940, then analyzes its detail. See 847.

854. Wal, Oege van der, "Hans Magdelijns bracht orde in collectie-Oud." *Nieuws out het Architectuurmuseum*, 1981, no 3. Dutch: "Hans Magdelijns brought order to the Oud collection." The item reports the organization of the Oud Collection held at the museum (now part of the NAi, Rotterdam). See "Guide to Archives" below. There is a portrait of Oud and images of the Kiefhoek church, the Kallenbach house and Amsterdam town hall projects, the Christian High School in The Hague, the Congress Building and a tubular steel chair.

855. Hägele, Rainer and Arno Votteler, "Studienarbeit 'Aqualone." *AIT,* vol 89, 1981, no 1, pp34-35. German: "Aqualone study project." The piece illustrates a student project: hypothetical conversion of Oud's row houses in the Weissenhofsiedlung.

856. *Plan,* "Beelddocumentatie van werk van J.J.P. Oud." 1981, no 6, pp 32-35. Dutch: "Visual documentation of Oud's work." Oud was the theme of the issue (see 847, 849, 850, 851, 853). The title describes the content, which includes only architecture. There are dates, approximate addresses, and images of many of the buildings, with very few plans. For fuller lists of buildings and unrealized projects see Barbieri, *J.J.P. Oud*, Bologna, 1986; Rotterdam, 1987 and Hans Oud, *J.J.P. Oud Architekt 1890-1963...*, The Hague, 1984.

1982
Books and Monographs
857. Beeren, Wim, Paul Donker Duyvis et al. (eds.), *Het Nieuwe Bouwen: Rotterdam 1920-1960*, Delft, 1982. Dutch/English: *The New Building* ... First of a series published by Delft University Press, this is the catalog of an exhibition at the Boymans-van Beuningen Museum, Rotterdam; there were four other (almost) concurrent shows throughout The Netherlands. The focus of this one was Rotterdam's planning and housing developments of the period. There are 200 illustrations, and a bibliography. Reviewed Padovan, *Architectural Review*, January 1985, pp 4-5.

858. Bless, Frits, *Rietveld 1888-1964. Een Biografie*. Amsterdam 1982. Dutch. A selection of Rietveld's writings and speeches is reprinted as an appendix to a mundane, illustrated biography. It is inevitable that Oud should be continually mentioned in any book about one of his erstwhile De Stijl collaborators. That is peripheral to the main thrust of the work. See Bless, "Rietveld: Mythe en werkelijkheid," *Forum*, vol 27, 1980/1981, May, p 41ff, also reprinted as an appendix. Reviewed Kuipers, *Bulletin KNOB*, February 1985, pp 24-26.

859. Blotkamp, Carel et al., *De Beginjaren van De Stijl*. Utrecht 1982. Published in English as *De Stijl: the Formative Years*. MIT Press 1986; 2nd edition 1990; published in Italian as *De Stijl. Nascita di un movimento*, Milan, 1989. This important book consists of a series of well documented, excellently illustrated critical-biographical essays about the earlier members of the De Stijl group. Hans Esser's piece on Oud (to 1922) is no exception, and Oud is inevitably referred to throughout the book. Dutch edition reviewed Yve-Alain Bois, "De Stijl mania (a selective guide to the sudden flood of texts)," *Art in America*, vol 73, 1985, p 13ff. English edition reviewed Bonaventura, *Burlington Magazine*, vol 129, 1987, p 608; Geary, *Structurist*, 1987/88, no 27/28, p 114-15; Woudhuysen, *Design*, September 1987, p 60; Alley, *Apollo*, September 1988, pp 211-212; Stankard, *Design Book Review*, Fall 1988, pp 57-60; Overy, "Demystifying De Stijl," *Studio*, July 1988, pp 61-62; Beckett, "De Stijl," *Journal of Design History*, vol 3, 1990, no 1, pp 63-69. Italian edition reviewed Anzivino, *Domus*, March 1990, pp v-vi.

860. Brederoo, Nico J., *Charley Toorop,* Utrecht, 1982. Dutch. The catalog of an exhibition at Utrecht Centraal Museum contains many references to Oud, especially about his correspondence with Charley Toorop, daughter of the Symbolist painter Jan Toorop, and an artist in her own right.

152   Oud and the International Style

861. Brehm, Burckhard (ed.), *Kindlers Geschichte der Weltkunst*, Munich, 1982. German: *Kindlers History of World Art*. Originally *The Encyclopedia of Visual Art*, Oxford, 1981. Oud is dealt with at some length and in a familiar way in the section on international architecture; there is also a short entry in the lexicon. There is a color image of the Hoek van Holland houses.

862. Curtis, William J.R., *Modern Architecture Since 1900*, Oxford, 1982. English. Parts of the important overview deal with Dutch discoveries and developments. The chapter "Cubism and new conceptions of space" sets out De Stijl's role in modifying Wright's spatial ideas. The town planning and architecture of Berlage, the Amsterdam School, and Oud are discussed.

863. Friedman, Mildred (ed.), *De Stijl: 1917-1931, Visions of Utopia*, Oxford/ New York, 1982. English. Second edition, Oxford 1986. The lavishly illustrated catalog of a traveling exhibition of some 400 items contains essays: "De Stijl: a reintroduction" by Robert Welsh; "De Stijl and the Russian Revolution" by Ger Harmsen; "Painting and sculpture in the context of De Stijl" by Joop Joosten; "Van der Leck and De Stijl 1916-1920" by Rudolf Oxenaar; "De Stijl/architecture—nieuwe beelding" by Sergio Polano; "Neoplasticism and architecture: formation and transformation" by Kenneth Frampton; "The furniture of Gerrit Rietveld: manifestoes for a new revolution" by Martin Filler; "From De Stijl to a new typography" by Kees Broos; "The abstract environment of De Stijl" by Nancy Troy; "De Stijl and the city" by Manfred Bock and "Echoes of De Stijl" by Martin Friedman. The exhibition was first mounted at the Walker Art Center, Minneapolis and moved to the Hirshhorn Museum, Washington D.C. before moving to Holland and being split between the Stedelijk Museum, Amsterdam and the Rijksmuseum Kröller-Müller, Otterlo (see 864). Reviewed *Progressive Architecture*, April 1982, pp 41-42; *Architecture Minnesota*, 1982, no 1, pp 26-31; Denker, *Art Journal*, 1982, no 3, pp 242-46; Abercrombie, *AIA Journal*, 1982, no 2, pp 96-99; Ragon, *Connaissance des Arts*, March 1982, pp 77-81; *Progressive Architecture*, April 1982, pp 41-42; Bois, *Art in America*, 1982, no 10, pp 105-17; Lynton, *Art Book Review*, 1982, no 4, pp 41-43; Michelson, *October*, Fall 1982, pp 5-26; Rousseau, *Arts Magazine*, September 1982, p 2; Shepherd, *Arts Review*, 4 June 1982, p 303; Tapley, *New Art Examiner*, March 1982, p 1, 22; Padovan, *Architectural Review*, February 1983, pp 70-71; Schulz, *Weltkunst*, September 1982, pp 2488-89; Schulze, *Art News*, May 1982, pp 82-86; Larson, *Print Collector's Newsletter*, July-August 1982, pp 78-79.

864. Jaffé, Hans Ludwig C. (ed.), *De Stijl: 1917-1931*, Amsterdam/Otterlo, 1982. This is the Dutch version of the above catalog, with a foreword by Jaffé. Reviewed Overy, *Studio*, 1982, no 997, pp 72-74. Cf. Overy, *New Society*, 1982, pp 384-85.

865. Joosten, Joop (ed.), *De Stijl*, Amsterdam/Otterlo, 1982. Dutch. This is a kind of subsidiary catalog of concurrent exhibitions at the Stedelijk Museum, Amsterdam and the Kröller-Müller Museum, August-October 1982 (see 864). The show included some 30 items about Oud.

Annotated Bibliography 1980-1989   153

866. Lampugnani, Vittorio Magnago, *Architektur unsers Jahrhunderts in Zeichnungen*, Stuttgart, 1982. Also *Architecture of the 20th Century in Drawings: Utopia and Reality*, New York, 1982. The book is about the role of drawings (as opposed to actual buildings) in the communication of architectural ideas. Significantly, Oud's drawings of he Purmerend factory and Blijdorp are reproduced.

867. Porphyrios, Demetri, *Sources of Modern Eclecticism*, London, 1982. English. In a book subtitled "Studies on Alvar Aalto" there are references to Oud in terms of town planning, De Stijl in terms of aesthetic theory.

868. Ratsma, P., *Rotterdam-Centrum in Oude Ansichten; de Landstad*, Zaltbommel 1982. Dutch: *Old Views of Central Rotterdam...* There is an image of the original Café De Unie.

869. Schnitker, M. and Mariet Willinge (eds.), *Het Nieuwe Bouwen: Previous History*, Delft, 1982. Dutch/English. This is the catalog of an exhibition at Amsterdam Architecture Museum; there were four other (almost) concurrent shows in Holland. Essays include "Rational and functional building 1840-1920" by A. de Groot, in which Oud is mentioned. There is also Bernard Colenbrander's "J.J.P. Oud, restrained and careful"—an unbalanced overview of his early career and associations that concludes that his attempts from the mid 1930s to "transcend modernity" ended his "prominent role in the [Dutch] functionalist movement". There are good images of the pre-1928 work. Reviewed Wick, "Neues bauen in Die Niederlanden 1920-1960," *Kunstforum International*, September 1983, pp 176-93; Padovan, *Architectural Review*, January 1985, pp 4-5.

870. *Jac. Jongert 1883-1942. Grafiek tussen kunst en reclame,* The Hague, 1982. Dutch: *...Graphics between art and advertisement.* Not seen. Catalog of exhibition at The Hague Gemeentemuseum. Jongert decorated the interior of the Vooruit Working Men's Association building, Purmerend.

871. *Rijtjes Huizen,* Amsterdam, 1982. Dutch: *Little Rows of Houses.* Poster for an exhibition of Oud's Weissenhofsiedlung row-houses, organized by postgraduate students of the University of Groningen at the *Stichting Wonen*, May-July 1982. There is a history of the Stuttgart project and good images.

872. Andritzky, Michael and Eckhard Stepmann (eds.), *20er Jahre der Deutsche Werkbund*, Berlin/ Darmstadt, 1982. German: *The Deutsche Werkbund in the Twenties.* An anthology of archival and contemporary writings, published by the Werkbund archive, includes forty or so pages about the Weissenhofsiedlung and reprints Oud, "Das flache Dach in Holland." *Das Neue Frankfurt*, 1927, no 7.

Journals

873. Blotkamp, Carel, "Architectuur als utopie, ca. 1916-1944." *Wonen TA/BK*, 1982, March, no 4-5, p 28-41. Dutch: "Architecture as utopia ..." One of a series of articles headed "Mondriaan—architectuur" includes sections about relationships within De Stijl group: "Van Doesburg and Oud in 1916"; "Van Doesburg and Oud in 1917"; "Collaborators abandon De Stijl" and "Mondriaan and Oud."

874. Bois, Yve-Alain, "The De Stijl idea." *Art in America*, vol 70, 1982, no 10, pp 105-17. English. The lavishly illustrated article reviews the exhibition "De Stijl 1917-31, Visions of Utopia" and discusses the question, How can De Stijl be defined? Color studies by Oud are among the images.

875. Doig, Allan, "De architectuur van De Stijl en de westerse filosofische traditie." *Wonen TA/BK*, 1982, no 15-16, pp 45-46. Dutch: "De Stijl architecture and the western philosophical tradition." Oud is briefly linked with Wright in this forerunner of Doig's *Theo van Doesburg. Painting into Architecture, Theory into Practice*, 1986. There are images of the Purmerend factory and *De Vonk* interiors.

876. Es, A. van, "De Stijl en organische architectuur." *Jonas,* 1982, no 6, November, p 16. Dutch: "De Stijl and organic architecture." Not seen.

877. Overy, Paul, "De Stijl." *Studio*, vol 195, 1982, no 997, pp 72-74. English. A review of the exhibition at the Stedelijk Museum, Amsterdam and Kröller Müller Museum, Otterlo looks carefully at the modern movement. Overy loves myth-demolition, and uses the review as a detonator. Cf. Overy, "Putting on De Stijl." *New Society*, vol 61, 1982, pp 384-85.

878. Padovan, Richard, "Dutch functionalism," *Architects' Journal*, vol 175, 1982, pt 3, p 79. English. An historical background to 1980s "functionalist" architecture in Holland explores rationalism in all Dutch schools of the twentieth century. Kiefhoek is illustrated.

879. Postmaa, Casper, "Congresgebouw, onvoltooide symfonie met lange nagalm." *Haagsche Courant*, 1982, 23 March. Dutch: "The Congress Building, an unfinished symphony with a long reverberation time." Drawing mostly upon Hans Oud's doctoral thesis (published as *J.J.P. Oud Architekt 1890-1963 ...*, The Hague, 1984), the piece outlines difficulties faced when realizing the building.

880. Searing, Helen, "J.J.P. Oud." in Adolf Plazcek (ed.), *Macmillan Encyclopedia of Architects,* New York, 1982, vol 3, pp 333-35. The entry follows a standard format: biography, comment upon major works and a bibliography.

881. Troy, Nancy Joslin, "Theo van Doesburg: from music into space." *Arts Magazine*, vol 56, 1982, pt 6, pp 92-101. English. The essay links van Doesburg's use of color in architecture with music and dance. He is cited and images are used to reinforce the arguments. Color schemes for Spangen are discussed.

882. Valk, H. et al., "Zij zochten naar waarheid en klaarheid." *NRC-Handelsblad,* 1982, 1 October, cultural supplement, p 6. Dutch: "They looked for truth and clarity." Not seen.

1983
Books and Monographs
883. Barbieri, Sergio Umberto (ed.), *Architectuur en Planning 40/80*, Rotterdam, 1983. Dutch. The anthology is directed at developments in the Netherlands after 1940. As in any book about Dutch architecture, Oud is mentioned continually in

the text. Tusschendijken and Weissenhofsiedlung are illustrated, and there are biographical notes.

884. Bock, Manfred (ed.), *Van het Nieuwe Bouwen naar een Nieuwe Architectuur: Groep '32: ontwerpen, gebouwen, stedebouwkundige plannen 1925-1945*, The Hague, 1983. Dutch: *From the* Nieuwe Bouwen *to a New Architecture*. Oud's role in contemporary European architecture is set out in "De Nieuwe Architectuur: het streven van Groep '32." Several of his buildings are illustrated.

885. Boekraad, Cees; Flip Bool and Herbert Henkels, *Het Nieuwe Bouwen, Neoplasticism in Architecture. De Stijl*, Delft/The Hague, 1983. Dutch/English. One of a series published by Delft University Press, this is an excellent illustrated catalog to an exhibition at The Hague Gemeentemuseum. Essays include: van Doesburg, "The struggle for the new style" (originally "Der Kampf um den neuen Stil," *Neue Schweizer Rundschau*, 1929, pp 41-46; 171-75; 373-77; 535-41; 627-31); Engel, Fortuyn and de Heer, "Neo-plasticism in architecture and related disciplines, a comparative survey of the period 1917-1931"; Boekraad, "Style and anti-style"; Bois, "De Stijl in Paris" and "Metamorphoses of axonometry"; Barbieri, "The city has style" and Henkels, "Must architecture be inferior to painting?" Reviewed Wick, "Neues bauen in Die Niederlanden 1920-1960," *Kunstforum International*, September 1983, pp 176-93; Padovan, *Architectural Review*, January 1985, pp 4-5.

886. Emery, Marc, *Furniture by Architects: 500 International Masterpieces of Twentieth-Century Design and Where to Buy Them*, New York, 1983. English. The title says it all: reproductions of Oud's dining furniture and stool for the Weissenhofsiedlung are included, illustrated in monochrome.

887. Fanelli, Giovanni, *De Stijl*, Rome/Bari, 1983. Also *Stijl-Architektur. Der niederländsche Beitrag zur frühen Moderne,* Stuttgart, 1985. The book is annoyingly subdivided into little essays. Oud's involvement, including his unbuilt projects, collaborations with van Doesburg and literary contributions to *De Stijl*, are dealt with at length. There is critical analysis of the Oud-Mathenesse site office and the Café De Unie, biographical notes and a selective annotated bibliography. Illustrations abound but they are inconveniently related to the text.

888. Frampton, Kenneth and Yukio Futagawa (eds.), *Modern Architecture 1920-1945*, Tokyo, 1983. English/Japanese. The large format book, divided into ideological-regional sections, includes the Hoek van Holland houses. There is a critique by Frampton, two large photographs and miniscule plans.

889. Geurst, Jeroen and Joris Molenaar, *Van der Vlugt, Architect 1894-1936*, Delft, 1983. This is a picture book of van der Vlugt's oeuvre. The introductory essay includes a section about the architect's link with Oud and *Opbouw*.

890. Jaffé, Hans Ludwig C., *Theo van Doesburg,* Amsterdam, 1983. Dutch. Like any straightforward biography of the turbulent painter, this book inevitably examines his relationship with Oud, through De Stijl. There is a bibliography.

891. Lampugnani, Vittorio Magnago, (ed.), *Lexicon der Architektur des 20 Jahrhunderts*, Stuttgart, 1983. German. Also *Thames and Hudson Encyclopedia of Twentieth Century Architecture*, London, 1986. The primer is a revised and enlarged edition of *Encyclopedia of Modern Architecture*, 1963, from Pehnt, *Knaurs Lexikon der Modernen Architektur*, Munich, 1963. There are articles on The Netherlands (Jacobus) and Oud (Vriend/Hatje). Hoek van Holland, the Shell Building and the Bioherstellingsoord are illustrated.

892. Lange, Eric de, *Geen Officieele, maar Levende Schoonheid*, The Hague, 1983. Dutch: *Not Official, but Living Beauty.* In a book outlining the aesthetic complications of the *Nieuwe Bouwen*, there is brief discussion of the Weissenhofsiedlung; Oud's houses and a typical kitchen are illustrated.

893. Pehnt, Wolfgang, *Das Ende der Zuversicht*, Berlin, 1983. German: *The End of Optimism.* The book is subtitled "Architecture in this century: ideas, buildings, documents." There is a longish study of Kiefhoek and references to Oud throughout the text, as well as biographical notes.

894. Rebel, Bernhard, *Het Nieuwe Bouwen: Functionalism in Dutch Architecture 1918-1945*. Utrecht, 1983. Dutch. This published version of Rebel's doctoral thesis includes couple of sections occupied with Oud. His name constantly recurs and his role as one of the most important figures in the *Nieuwe Bouwen* at the end of the 1920s is stressed. There is an English summary. Reviewed Wick, "Neues bauen in Die Niederlanden 1920-1960," *Kunstforum International*, September 1983, pp 176-93, which illustrates Hoek van Holland houses.

895. Kolling-Dandrieú, Francis Bach and Jet Sprenkels-ten Hoorn, *Index of De Stijl: table of contents and index of names and references*, Amsterdam, 1983. The exceptionally valuable index (published in Dutch despite the English title), described by its authors as "strictly functional", is divided into the following parts: a catalog of volumes, chronological table of contents, alphabetical index of proper names and article titles, list of advertisements, and an index of keywords in Dutch and English. Oud's contributions are of course included.

896. Leidelmeijer, Frans and Daan van der Singel, *Art Nouveau en Art Deco in Nederland*, Amsterdam, 1983. Dutch. After examining the possible sources of Art Nouveau book devotes a chapter to a somewhat augmented De Stijl group. Work of several members is illustrated and Oud's role is outlined.

897. Searing, Helen (ed.), *In Search of Modern Architecture: a Tribute to Henry-Russell Hitchcock*, New York/Cambridge, Mass.,/London, 1982. English. Searing's introduction and Vincent Scully's brief essay ."..Hitchcock and the new tradition" both point out Hitchcock's early propagandizing of Oud's architecture.

898. Straaten, Evert van (ed.), *Theo van Doesburg 1883-1931*, The Hague, 1983. Dutch. The chronologically structured book is subtitled "a documentation based upon material from the Schenking van Moorsel." There are continual references to Oud in the text, and a special section devoted to his collaborations with van

Doesburg at *Allegonda* and *De Vonk*. Of interest are van Doesburg's portraits of Oud, made in 1917. Reviewed Beckett, "De Stijl," *Journal of Design History*, vol 3, 1990, no 1, pp 63-69.

899. Stenchlak, Marian, *Architectuurgids van Nederland*, Rijswijk, 1983. Dutch: *Architecture Guide to the Netherlands*. The populist book is divided into eras before the twentieth century and "isms" within it. There are three pages about Oud, illustrated with drawings of Kiefhoek and the floor patterns in *De Vonk*.

900. Troy, Nancy Joslin, *The De Stijl Environment*, Cambridge, Mass./London, 1983. English. Identified by some critics as the most authoritative study of the use of color in the revolutionary art of the early twentieth century, the thoroughly documented book provides new insights into the impact of De Stijl. It is an expanded version of Troy's dissertation, "De Stijl's collaborative ideal: the colored abstract environment," Yale, 1979. There is extensive discussion of Oud's role in the movement and illustrations of *De Vonk*, designs for Spangen exteriors (in color) and interiors by van Doesburg, and the Stuttgart houses. There is also a valuable bibliography. Reviewed: Bell, *Structurist*, 1983/84, no 23/24, pp 99-101; van Hensbergen, *Burlington Magazine*, vol 126, 1984, pp 367-68; Bois, "De Stijl mania ...," *Art in America*, vol 73, 1985, p 13ff; Padovan, *Architectural Review*, January 1985, pp 4-5.

901. Woud, Auke van der, *CIAM: Het Nieuwe Bouwen International, volkshuisvesting, stedebouw,* Delft, 1983. Dutch/English. One of a series published by Delft University Press, the bilingual book forms an excellent catalog to an exhibition at the Kröller-Müller Museum, Otterlo, April-May 1983; there were four other (almost) concurrent shows in Holland. This one focussed on the work of architects participating in the *Congrès Internationaux d'Architecture Moderne* (CIAM), formed in 1928. There are several articles and a profusion of images. Reviewed Padovan, *Architectural Review*, January 1985, pp 4-5; reviewed and expounded by Rainer Wick, "Neues bauen in Die Niederlanden 1920-1960," *Kunstforum International*, September 1983, pp 176-93 (German) which illustrates Hoek van Holland.

Journals

902. Bijl, Rob van der, "De veranderende architectuur van J.J.P. Oud." *Waarheid*, 1983, 9 August. Dutch: "The changed architecture of ... Oud." Noticing *Hollandse Architectuur*, Nijmegen, 1983, the essay seizes on the old question, Why is the Shell Building different from Oud's earlier work?

903. Botman, A. "De Stijl, van levensstijl in de architectuur, naar een nieuwe levensstijl." *Voorwaarts*, 1983, 25 April, pp 22-27. Dutch: "De Stijl, from lifestyle in architecture to a new lifestyle." Not seen.

904. Cornelis, A., "De inrichting en architectuur van de *Nieuwe Amsterdam*." *De Blauwe Wimpel*, vol 38, 1983, February, pp 54-57. Dutch: "The furnishing and architecture of the *Nieuw Amsterdam*." Not seen. The journal is a monthly publication "for shipping and shipbuilding in the Lowlands."

905. Garrel, B. van, "Ik Ben een zondagskind. Gesprek met Harm Henrik Kamerlingh Onnes." *NRC-Handelsblad,* 1983, 25 February. Dutch: "I am a Sunday's child: conversation with Harm...Onnes." Not seen.

906. Lieshout, Marcel van, "'Bedoeling achter Congresgebouw wordt de genadeslag toegebracht." Vol*kskrant,* 1983, 19 April. Dutch: "Meaning behind the Congress Building becomes the *coup de grace."* The newspaper reports public and professional reactions to The Hague municipality's plans to develop the land around the Congress Building. See also M.J. Veersema, "Schoonheid Congresgebouw bedreigd," *Nieuw Rotterdamsche Courant,* 16 April 1983, p 2; Teun Lagas, "Gepruts aan Oud's Congresgebouw," *Trouw,* 30 June 1983, p 23.

907. Màcel, Otakar, "De legende van de stalen stoel." *Plan,* 1983, no 6, pp 40-46. Dutch: "The legend of the steel chair." An overview of the development of tubular steel furniture illustrates the dining chairs Weissenhofsiedlung houses and the rebuilt villa *Allegonda,* both 1927.

908. Magdelijns, Hans, "Architect Oud en de melodie in de bouwkunst." *Bouw,* 1983, 15 October, pp 28-30; 29 October, pp 26-28. Dutch: "Oud and the melody in architecture." An illustrated critical resumé divides Oud's career into periods, the fifth of which included the Shell Building, called "Oud's revenge."

909. Meindersma, Heero, "Complexity and contradiction in Almelo." *Tube,* 1983, December, no 4, pp 39- 44. Dutch. A critical review of Almelo town hall, (designed shortly before Oud's death and realized 1969-73 by Hans Oud and H. Dethmers) places it within the context of Oud's oeuvre. There is a ground floor plan and three photographs.

910. Searing, Helen, "The Dutch Scene: black and white and red all over..." , *Art Journal,* vol 43, 1983, no 2, pp 170-177. English. Coinciding with several *nieuwe bouwen* exhibitions in The Netherlands, this succinct article, although not altogether accurate, examines the politics of the documents of Dutch architecture, 1920-1940, as well as the bias of histories. It provides excellent background.

911. Smit, Frank, "De Haag in de onvoltooid verleden tijd." *Wonen TA/BK,* vol 11, 1983, no 1, pp 10-26. Dutch: "The Hague in the incomplete past tense." The article examines the twentieth century development of the city. There is reference to Oud's conflict with Dudok over the siting of the Congress Building.

912. Taverne, Ed R. M., "Bouwen zonder makeup: acties van Oud tot behoud van de architectuur." *Wonen TA/BK,* 1983, no 3. Dutch: "Building without makeup; Oud's actions in relation to architecture." This well documented text of Taverne's inaugural professorial lecture (8 February 1983) at the Institute for Art History, University at Groningen examines key issues in Oud's career, especially his involvement with De Stijl and his post-World War II opinions about reconstruction and renovation. Reprinted as a booklet.

913. *Communication Arts Magazine,* [Color illustration of Café De Unie.] Vol 25, 1983, September-October, p 93. English.

914. *Interiors*, "Selections from an international menu," vol 163, 1983, no 143, p 104. English. The article includes a rare photograph of dining furniture for the Weissenhofsiedlung houses, in modern reproduction.

1984
Books and Monographs

915. Dobbelsteen, Hans van den et al. , *Weissenhofsiedlung*, Eindhoven, 1984. Dutch. The outcome of a student project published in connection with an exhibition at Eindhoven Technological University presents an overview of the *siedlung*. The illustrations are of indifferent quality.

916. Dunster, David, *Key Buildings of the 20th Century. Houses 1900-1944*, London, 1984 (New York, 1985). English. The Oud-Mathenesse site office, labeled "temporary house", is inexplicably included with a brief, non-critical description and drawings of doubtful value.

917. Major, Máté, *Geschichte der Architektur*, vol 3, Berlin, 1984. German: *History of Architecture*. First published in Budapest, 1984. A single reference to Oud mentions Kiefhoek (illustrated) and his role in the Weissenhofsiedlung.

918. Oud, Hendrik Emile (Hans), *J.J.P. Oud Architekt 1890-1963: feiten en herinnerigen gerangschikt*, Den Haag, 1984. Dutch: *[Oud]: gathered facts and memories*. French, English and German summaries. The published version of a doctoral thesis (Nijmegen Catholic University) by Oud's son gives unique but biased insights. Images abound and there is a works list, biographical chronology and a poorly organized bibliography. Reviewed Straus, "Een architect getekend in feiten en herinneringen," *Trouw*, 26 April 1984; Kingma, "Het geweten van de architectuur," *Leeuwarder Courant*, 4 May; Jager, "Zoon stelde feiten en herinneringen te boek," *Telegraaf*, 30 November, p 17; Slagter, "Roem naast respect voor Oud," *Ons Erfdeel*, March/April 1986; *PT/Bouwtechniek*, 1984, no 10, p 22; Salomons, "Grote schoonheid in heldere architectuur," *Parool*, 16 May 1984. But for a suggestion that all was not well between father and son, see especially van Rooy, "Een zoon neemt revanche [a son takes revenge]," *NRC-Handelsblad*, 4 May 1984, p CS 7; Colenbrander, "Architecture met een hoofdletter," *Financiëele Dagblad*, 9-12 June 1984, p 17; Kloos, "Hans Oud en de ruzies van z'n vader [Hans Oud and the arguments with his father]," *Volkskrant*, 8 June 1984 and van der Geer, "Oud jr. schreeft onthullend boek over [writes a revealing book about] Oud sr.," *Rotterdamse Nieuwsblad*, 18 May 1984.

919. Pfeiffer, Bruce Brooks (ed.), *Letters to Architects: Frank Lloyd Wright*, Fresno, 1984. English. There are six letters to Oud, and some of his responses.

920. Prak, Niels Luning, *Architects: the Noted and the Ignored*, Chichester, 1984. English. The book discusses the relations between the few "artistic" architects, made famous by critics, art historians and their own publicity, and their more practical colleagues. The author (for reasons that he enunciates) takes Dutch architecture in the 1920s and 1930s as a case study. There is an English translation of selections from *Holländische Architektur*, 1926.

Journals

921. B——, Lewis, "Stuttgart tribute: Architects Le Corbusier, Ludwig Mies van der Rohe, Walter Gropius, Richard Docker, Hans Poelzig, Ludwig Hilbersheimer, Bruno Taut, Max Taut, Adolf Rading, Josef Frank, Hans Scharoun, Mart Stam, and J.J.P. Oud." *Building Design*, 1984, 1 June, p 10. The title hardly leaves room for the text of a short piece about the Weissenhofsiedlung.

922. Irace, Fulvio, " Stuttgart Weissenhof case study." *Domus*, 1984, no 649, April, pp 2-13. Italian/English/French. The article philosophizes about the restoration of modern architecture, noting the "risks of succumbing to a misunderstood reintegrative restoration based of a mythical search for origins." In a detailed discussion of the project; each building is documented, showing "before and after" restoration. See Ruud Brouwers, "Weissenhofsiedlung weer als nieuw." *Wonen-TA/BK*, 1984, no 18, p 7 (news item).

923. Karstkarel, Peter, "Tastbare discussiestukken in Rotterdam en Bologna." *Trouw*, 1984, 23 October. Dutch: "Tangible topics for discussion in Rotterdam and Bologna." A news item about the intended reconstruction of Café De Unie and Le Corbusier's *L'Esprit Nouveau* pavilion in Bologna, gives a brief history of the original and restoration projects. See also "Rotterdam wil café De Unie van J.J.P. Oud herbouwen," *NRC Handelsblad*, 15 June 1984 and "Unie terug," *Vrije Volk*, 11 September 1984 .

924. Moscoviter, Herman, "'n Buiging voor Oud." *Vrije Volk*, 1984, 11 February. Dutch: "Respect for Oud." News item, announcing that the Hoek van Holland houses will not be placed on the national Heritage List until the Rotterdam Public Housing Department pays for renovation.

925. Radovic, Ranko, "Text architects." *Architektura Urbanizam*, vol 24, 1984, supplement, pp 2-68. Not seen.

926. *NRC Handelsblad*, "Rotterdam wil bouwkeet van architect Oud reconstrueren." 31 August 1984. News item about the Oud-Mathenesse director's hut.

1985

Books and Monographs

927. Jaeger, Falk, *Bauen in Deutschland*, Stuttgart, 1985. German: *Building in Germany*. The general architecture guide includes the Weissenhofsiedlung..

928. Kloos, J.P., *Architectuur, een Gewetenszaak*, The Hague, 1985. Dutch: *Architecture, a Matter of Conscience*. An architect makes a "plea in words and images" to the users of the built environment. The discussion inevitably embraces (in passing) the work and writings of Oud.

929. Knobel, Lance, *The Faber Guide to Twentieth Century Architecture: Britain and Northern Europe*, London, 1985. Ten pages of this guide (too bulky to carry) are dedicated to The Netherlands, and 21 monuments are recorded, 17 of the pre-1940 period. Most are in Amsterdam; in Rotterdam: the Hoek of Holland houses. The long captions to dark photographs are informative and objective.

930. Kostof, Spiro, *A History of Architecture: Settings and Rituals*, New York, 1985. English. A ubiquitous but incisive history identifies the two streams of Dutch modern architecture: rational and romantic. There is brief discussion of the Amsterdam School, slightly more about De Stijl, hardly anything about Oud.

931. Mens, Robert, Bart Lootsma and Jos Bosman, *Le Corbusier en Nederland*, Utrecht, 1985. Dutch: *Le Corbusier and Holland*. This is the catalog of an exhibition at the Frans Hals Museum, Haarlem, November 1985-January 1986. Mens' essay, "Documenten rondom Le Corbusier, 1920-1965" compares developments within De Stijl with the Swiss' ideas, and discusses the Weissenhofsiedlung.

932. Naylor, Gillian, *The Bauhaus Reassessed*, London, 1985. English. The book notes the influence of De Stijl upon the Bauhaus and van Doesburg's relationship with the Germans and Oud, when the painter was at Weimar. Oud's participation in the 1923 *Art and Technics* exhibition is also mentioned.

933. Schulze, Franz, *Mies van der Rohe: a Critical Biography*, Chicago/London, 1985. English. There are several insights into the organization of the 1927 Weissenhofsiedlung exhibition, and Philip Johnson's comparative evaluation of Mies and Oud is set down.

934. *J.J.P. Oud: Architectural Drawings 1915-1958*, New York, 1985. This catalog of an exhibition at the Prakapas Gallery, New York City, January-February 1985, illustrates the Café De Unie, the Shell Building and designs for the Purmerend factory, boulevard houses, Rotterdam stock exchange, Hofplein, and "a house for a forester". There are brief biographical notes.

935. *John Rädecker, 1885-1956*, Haarlem, 1985. Dutch. This is the catalog of an exhibition at Teyler's Museum, Haarlem. Not seen. Rädecker was the sculptor of the Dammonument in Amsterdam.

Journals
936. Barbieri, Sergio Umberto, "The housing issue." *Abitare*, 1985, no 236, July-August, pp 37-58. Italian/English. An historical, critical article begins with the effects of the *Woningwet* on housing. Comparison is made between the work of conservative architects, the Amsterdam School and modernists, supported by illustrations of several schemes. Special attention is paid to Kiefhoek.

937. Barbieri, Sergio Umberto, "Spangen: un frammento di Rotterdam." *Casabella*, vol 49, 1985, July, pp 42-53. Italian: "Spangen: a fragment of Rotterdam." Italian/English. The historical review of Spangen naturally includes Oud's contribution. It is illustrated with excellent images.

938. Günther, Roland, "Balance. De Stijl and the tradition of Dutch urban culture." *Daidalos*, 1985, no 15, March 15, pp 83-93. German/English. Based on the assertion that Oud was a frustrated painter, the piece analyzes the composition of the Café De Unie facade, comparing it with works by De Stijl within the broader context of Dutch painting of the urban scene. The argument is extended to the boulevard house project and Oud-Mathenesse.

939. Hoek, Els, "The De Stijl artist." *Structurist*, 1985/86, no 25-26, pp 69-77. English. In an essay is about the De Stijl painters, Oud is mentioned only in connection with correspondence with Mondrian.

940. Nettinga, Willem, "Café De Unie: een 'simple geval' met wereldfaam." *Rotterdamse Nieuwsblad*, 1985, 24 August, p 23. Dutch: "Café De Unie: a 'straightforward case' of world fame." Written in association with the rebuilding, the essay about the original project is based on an interview with Annie Oud-Dinaux. There are portraits of the Ouds and an archival image of De Unie. See also "De Unie nog altijd provocerend," *ibid.*; The project was newsworthy: see, e.g., Karstkarel, "Reconstructie tweebouwwerken van Oud in Rotterdam." *Heemschut*, January 1985, p 10 (mentions Oud-Mathenesse director's hut); "Tweede eerste steen De Unie," *Vrije Volk*, 8 July 1985; "Café De Unie is straks herbouwd," *Trouw*, 10 August 1985; "Eerste steen 'De Unie'," *Vrije Volk*, 28 August 1985 (photo of foundation stone); "Herbouw Ouds café De Unie en feit," *NRC Handelsblad*, 9 September 1985 (news item).

941. Schouten, Martin, "Einde van een stenen strijkkwartet." *Volkskrant*, 1985, 25 May. Dutch: "The end of a brick string quartet." Announcing the proposed demolition of the Oud-Mathenesse estate, the piece rehashes the history of Oud's role in Rotterdam's public housing in the 1920s. For public response see, e.g., "Woningen 'Witte Dorp' rijp voor sloop," *Cobouw*, 15 April 1985; van de Roer, "Witte Dorp wil hechte buurt blijven," *NRC-Handelsblad*, 26 June 1985; Schoonen, "Een wonderlijke combinatie," *Brabants Nieuwsblad*, 28 June 1985; Bullhorst, "Terugkeer van de kaalslag," *NRC-Handelsblad,* 6 July 1985, p 11; Bakker, "'Het palais op de Dam sloop je toch ook niet!'" *Elseviers Weekblad*, 22 June 1985, p 19. See also Günther, *Architekt*, October 1985, p 421.

942. Valstar, Arta, "Een glas-in-loodontwerp van Theo van Doesburg." *Jong Holland*, vol 1, 1985, no 2, pp 2-13. Dutch: "A leadlight glass design by van Doesburg." The essay is about a design for the Provincial Museum of Hanover, of 1925, but contains images of the windows for villa *Allegonda* and Spangen, blocks I and V. See *ibid.*, vol 2, 1986, no 1, pp 53-55.

943. Yamaguchi, Hiroshi et al., "The Netherlands, paradise of modern architecture." *Space Design*, vol 8, 1985, no 251, p 43. Japanese (English captions). There are color images of Hoek van Holland and Kiefhoek, and a drawing of the Café De Unie, with a short text, as well as a chronology of Dutch modern architecture in Japanese/English.

944. *Abitare*. "Rotterdam, Kiefhoek, 1925-1930." 1985, no 236, pp 48-51. Italian/ English. A series of short pieces on "the housing issue" is illustrated with archival and contemporary images and a couple of Oud's characteristically impressionistic sketches in color. The tone is adulatory of Modernism. Reviewed Asselbergs, "Holland gezien door Italianen," *NRC-Handelsblad*, 2 August 1984.

945. *NRC Handelsblad*, [Photograph of demolitions at Kiefhoek].1985, 1 November.

1986
Books and Monographs

946. Barbieri, Sergio Umberto, *J.J.P. Oud*, Bologna, 1986. Italian. Dutch edition, Rotterdam, 1987. The book describes, illustrates and discusses Oud's oeuvre in chronological order. There is a list of works, biographical overview and bibliography. Reviewed van der Woud, *Archis*, February 1988, p 52.

947. Bergvelt, Ellinoor et al., *Industry and Design in The Netherlands 1850-1950*, Amsterdam, 1986. English. Also published as *Industrie and vormgeving in Nederland 1850-1950* (1985), the catalog of an exhibition at the Stedelijk Museum, December 1985-February 1986 mentions Oud's associations with the furniture manufacturers Gispen, Metz and Co and P.G. Duchateau. There is a previously unpublished 1934 citation from Oud.

948. Bollery, Franziska and Kristiana Hartmann (eds.), *200 Jaar Architectuur*, Delft, 1986. Dutch. The two volume work is album of essays and articles reproduced from many sources. There are notes and images of Oud's work.

949. Borsi, Franco, *L'Ordre Monumental: Europe 1929-1939*, Paris, 1986. The Shell Building is discussed and illustrated in a chapter ,"L'esprit des nations."

950. Dearstyne, Howard, *Inside the Bauhaus*, New York, 1986. English. A book recollecting Dearstyne's life as a Bauhaus student (1928-33) recognizes the contribution made to modern architecture by Oud's Rotterdam housing projects.

951. Doig, Allan, *Theo van Doesburg. Painting into Architecture, Theory into Practice*, Cambridge. 1986. English. The well-documented book traces van Doesburg's metamorphosis from painter into architect. His relationship with Oud is referred to throughout; there are many illustrations of *De Vonk* and *Allegonda*. Reviewed Bonaventura, *Burlington Magazine*, 1987, p 608; Stankard, *Design Book Review*, Fall 1988, pp 57-60; Overy, *Studio*, July 1988, pp 61-62; Beckett, *Journal of Design History*, 1990, no 1, pp 63-69.

952. Heer, Jan de (ed.), *Kleur en Architectuur*, Rotterdam, 1986. Dutch: *Color and Architecture*. An anthology produced to connect with an exhibition at the Boymans-van Beuningen Museum, September-November 1986 and Groninger Museum, December 1986-January 1987 contains important essays including Sergio Polano, "De nieuwe kleurbeelding in architectuur. Beschouwing over de Stijl" (see 967) Henk Engel, "Stijl en expressie," sets the De Stijl architects against German contemporaries. Kiefhoek is cited as one of the great examples of color in architecture. Reviewed Boekraad, *Archis*, April 1988, pp 44-51.

953. Jaffé, Hans Ludwig C. et al., *De Stijl Csoport*, Budapest, 1986. Hungarian. Catalog of an exhibition at the Magyar Nemzeti Galeria. Not seen.

954. Kremerskothen, Josef, *Moderne Klassieken: Meubels die Geschiedenis Maken*, Utrecht, 1986. Dutch. Originally *Moderne Klassiker: Möbel, die Geschichte Machen*, Hamburg, 1981. There is reference to the steel furniture used by Oud in the Weissenhofsiedlung houses.

955. Langmead, Donald, *English Language Sources on Dutch Modern Architecture, 1900-1940: Monographs not by Dutch Authors*, Monticello, 1986. English. This is one of a three-part series of annotated bibliographies. See also Langmead, *Journal articles not by Dutch Authors*, 1986 and *Perceptions of Dutch Architects, Writers and Editors*, 1987, all later revised and updated as *Dutch Modernism: Architectural Resources in the English Language*, Westport, 1996.

956. Mook, Jan Willem van et al., *Twee Weken De Singel*, Rotterdam, 1986. Dutch: *Two Weeks of the Singel.* A broadsheet announces the opening of the new Café De Unie in Westersingel, 23 August-7 September. The occasion was widely reported: see e.g., "De Unie," *Nieuws uit Stichting Architectuurmuseum*, 1986, no 4, p 2-3; Janny Kok, "Herbouwd café van Oud in Rotterdam geopend," *Parool*, 29 August; Hans Ibelings, "Een oude bekende reconstrueerd," *ibid.*, 30 August, p 41; Ida Jager, "Verwoest en vervloekt café werd monument van De Stijl," *Volkskrant*, 28 August, p 15; "Muziek, theater en lezingen bij opening van café De Unie," *NRC Handelsblad*, 21 August (cf. "Spiegelwand verbergt in Rotterdams nieuwe versie van De Unie," *ibid.*, 5 July); "Duizenden bij Unie," *Vrije Volk*, 30 August, pp 12-13. The *Rotterdamse Kunststichting* held a month-long "homage to Oud" in the café's upstairs exhibition space: reviewed Schmidt, "Architect Oud had méér te bieden dan café De Unie," *Vrije Volk*, 3 September 1986. See also Nico Tummers, "Herbouw De Unie roept vragen op," *Finançiëele Dagblad*, 23-25 August; "Heropening Café De Unie verloopt niet vlekkeloos," *Volkskrant*, 1 September; "De Unie schiet op, maar de horeca is boos," *Vrije Volk*, 19 April; Lillian Bos and Paulien Caspers, "Pak Oud niet uit," *NRC-Handelsblad*, 29 August 1986.

957. Neret, Gilles, *Panorama de l'Art Moderne: L'Art des Annes 20*, Fribourg, 1986. French: *The Art of the Twenties.* Also published as *Die Kunst der Zwanziger Jahre*, Zurich, 1986. There is a full page color drawing of the Café De Unie facade. Oud is mentioned only in passing.

958. Oud, J.J.P., *Mi Trayectoria en De Stijl,* Murcia, 1986. Spanish: *My Way in De Stijl.* This also translates "The future architecture and its architectonic possibilities," "The influence of Frank Lloyd Wright in Europe" and "Ja und nein: the confessions of an architect." There are over 40 poor quality illustrations.

959. Projektburo Het Witte Dorp, *Programma Meervoudige Studieopdracht Het Witte Dorp*, Rotterdam, 1986. Dutch: *Alternative Programs for the Witte Dorp Study Commission.* The title describes the mimeographed publication, which deals with the rationale for preservation of the Oud-Mathenesse housing development. Original drawings are clearly reproduced, and there is a valuable series of photographs showing the current condition of the "village".

960. Vöge, Peter and Bab Westerveld, *Stoelen: Nederlandse Ontwerpen 1945-1985*, Amsterdam, 1986. Dutch: *Chairs: Dutch designs 1945-1985.* The book puts Dutch furniture design into an international context. Oud's steel framed easy chair of 1950 is illustrated, as well as earlier pieces for Metz and Co.

961. Watkin, David, *A History of Western Architecture*, London, 1986. English. Part of the comprehensive book divides the 20th century into "isms". The Dutch contribution is undervalued and there is passing reference to Hoek van Holland and Kiefhoek as a reaction against the Amsterdam School. Dutch edition: *De Westerse Architectuur: een Geschiedenis*, Nijmegen, 1994.

Journals

962. Brouwers, Ruud, "Dorp in Rotterdam; meervoudige opdracht voor Oud Mathenesse." *Archis*, 1986, no 8, pp 48-52. "Village in Rotterdam: plural commission for Oud-Mathenesse." After setting out the history of Oud's houses the article discusses and illustrates proposals by architects Paul de Ley of Amsterdam, De Nijl of Delft and the Rotterdam firm of Dobbelaar, de Kovel and de Vroom for rebuilding Witte Dorp. There is an aerial view of the original. See Jan Ladenius, "Sloop van Ouds Witte Dorp in Rotterdam is vergissing," *Trouw*, 12 July 1985.

963. Metz, Tracy, "De Stijl distilled." *Architectural Record*, vol 174, 1986, November, pp 75-77. English. Subtitled "A new look at the work of J.J.P. Oud," the piece is prompted by the restoration and rebuilding of the Weissenhofsiedlung and the Café De Unie. It mixes criticism of the new work with an overview of Oud's career. There is an archival image of the Café and a view of Kiefhoek.

964. Metz, Tracy, "Monument op de Dam dertig jaar decor geschiedenis." *NRC-Handelsblad*, 1986, 15 May, p 6. Dutch: "Monument on the Dam thirty years scenic history." A brief history of the monument relates to a May-June exhibition at the Amsterdam Historical Museum .

965. Metz, Tracy, "De zeven duivelen." *NRC-Handelsblad*, 1986, 29 August. Dutch: "The seven devils." A celebration of the new Café De Unie goes beyond it to discuss the history and the resurrection (in one way or another) of the Weissenhofsiedlung, Oud-Mathenesse and Kiefhoek. Archival images include a perspective of Blijdorp. Reprinted as a booklet.

966. *Oase*, 1986, no 14. Dutch. An issue devoted to Oud-Mathenesse includes Roy Bijhouwer, "Oud-Mathenesse, tussen straatbeeld en woning," a discussion of Oud's approach to urban design, illustrated with drawings of his Stuttgart houses; Jan Geuskens, "Meervoudige studie-opdracht Witte Dorp, addressing current plans for replacing Oud's "semi-permanent" housing (cf. Brouwers, "Dorp in Rotterdam; meervoudige opdracht voor Oud Mathenesse," *Archis*, no 8, 1986); Projektburo Het Witte Dorp, *Programma Meervoudige Studieopdracht ...*, 1986; Wytze Patijn, "De nieuwe plannen," a critique of the three proposals; Erwin Zantman, "De idee van een dorp," with explanations of the plans by their architects: Paul de Ley of Amsterdam, De Nijl of Delft and the Rotterdam firm of Dobbelaar, de Kovel and de Vroom. The exercise was reported in the national press: see, e.g., Gert Riphagen, "Bewoners Het Witte Dorp krijgen mooi nieuw dorp," *Volkskrant*, 10 February 1989; "Sloop en herbouw: Witte Dorp forever," *NRC-Handelsblad*, 10 February (cf. "Het Witte wordt gesloopt. Leve het Witte Dorp!" *Van Huis Uit*, December 1987, pp 9-11); Henrico Prins, "Buiten is ook

een verblijfsruimte," *Volkskrant*, 17 February 1989; Canis Zijlmans, "Het Witte Dorp wint de eerste slag," *Vrije Volk*, 16 September; "Weduwe Oud berust in verdwijnen Witte Dorp," *Algemeen Dagblad,* 25 December.

967. Polano, Sergio, "De nieuwe kleurbeelding in architectuur. Beschouwing over De Stijl." In Jan de Heer, (ed.), *Kleur en Architectuur*, 1986. Dutch: "The new color visualization in architecture. Consideration of De Stijl." An examination of the relation between color and architecture includes Oud's early collaborations with van Doesburg and his own Café de Unie. The latter two are illustrated, as is van Doesburg's color schematic drawing (dated October 1921) for the Potgieterstraat elevation of Oud's Spangen housing.

968. *Parool*, "Rotterdamse woningen van Oud gerenoveerd: 'van de buitenkant zijn ze leuk'." 13 February 1986. Dutch: "Oud's Rotterdam dwellings renovated: 'they are nice on the outside'." News item about the renovation of Kiefhoek .

1987
Books and Monographs
969. Blotkamp, Carel, *Mondriaan in Detail,* Utrecht/Antwerp, 1987. Dutch. The book reprints four essays. "Mondriaan--architectuur" (*Wonen TABK* , 1982, no 5, pp 12-51) discusses relationships between van Doesburg and Oud, and Mondrian and Oud. Some of Oud's earlier works are illustrated.

970. Colenbrander, Bernard (ed.), *Oud-Mathenesse, Het Witte Dorp 1923-1987*, Rotterdam, 1987. Dutch. The catalog of an exhibition, "Het Monument in de Woningbouw," at Rotterdam's Boymans-van Beuningen Museum, May-June 1987 includes a history noting the estate's place in Rotterdam's public housing, an essay about its colors, and a general essay on heritage issues. It is illustrated with the architect's drawings and archival and current photographs and there are English and German summaries. The show is reviewed Metz, "Het Witte Dorp wordt met al..le egards uitgeleid," *NRC-Handelsblad*, 13 June 1987; Jager, "Witte Dorp van oud krijgt laatste eer in Boymans," *Volkskrant*, 19 June 1987. See "Het Witte Dorp zal worden gesloopt," *Heemschut*, vol 64, 1987, no 1, p 17.

971. Groenendijk, Paul and Piet Vollaard, *Guide to Modern Architecture in The Netherlands*, Rotterdam, 1987. Dutch/English. The necessarily concise captions in this ubiquitous, well-organized book are nevertheless thoughtful and constructive. All of Oud's extant works 1917-69 are illustrated and discussed. There are limited biographies and bibliographies. Also published in parts: *Guide to Modern Architecture in Amsterdam*; *Guide to Modern Architecture in Rotterdam.*

972. Kuipers, Marieke, *Bouwen in Beton*, The Hague, 1987. Dutch: *Building in Concrete.* The carefully researched book deals with experiments in public housing before 1940. Unrealized De Stijl designs are listed and Oud's double workers' dwellings are illustrated.

973. Musgrove, John (ed.), *Sir Banister Fletcher's A History of Architecture* London, 19th edition, 1987. English. Oud is barely mentioned in the single page of text on the Dutch modernists by David Dunster. His 1920s work is identified

in the greatly improved 20th (centenary) edition, where the 1900-1945 material is revised by Andrew Saint.

974. Sluijs, F. van der, *Haagse Stedebouw: mijn ervaringen in de jaren 1946-1983*, Utrecht, 1987. Dutch: *Town Planning in The Hague: My Recollections of the Years 1946-83.* There are insights into the conflict between Dudok and Oud over the Congress Building in a book by the former Director of the City Development Department.

975. Staal, Gert, *Between Dictate and Design*, Rotterdam, 1987. English. Published in Dutch as *Bouwheer en -meester.* The book reviews the "exceptional cases in which the architecture of the office building" is more than the joint wishes of architect and client. The Shell Building is discussed; there are color images.

976. Stimson, Miriam, *Modern Furniture Classics*, London, 1987. English. A brief discussion of De Stijl prefaces a range of illustrated designs, including Oud's simple blue-lacquered tubular steel dining set for the Weissenhofsiedlung, and manufactured by Escart International of Paris.

977. Witt, Dennis and Elizabeth de, *Modern Architecture in Europe*, London, 1987. English. The guide book includes Hoek van Holland and Kiefhoek (with brief critical notes) and Weissenhofsiedlung. There are excellent photographs. Reviewed Young, *Architecture New Jersey*, vol 27, 1991, no 2, p 26 ff.

978. *J.J.P. Oud 1890-1963: Dokumentation zur Ausstellung der Architektur-Galerie am Weissenhof in Stuttgart*, Stuttgart, 1987. German: A catalog for an exhibition at the restored Weissenhofsiedlung includes an introduction by Hans Oud, reprints of "Mein weg in De Stijl," "Orientatie" (*De Stijl*, 1919), "Ja und Nein. Bekenntnisse eines Architekten" (*Bouwkundig Weekblad*, 1925), and poor images of several projects and buildings. There is chronology and a bibliography.

Journals
979. Albarda, Jan H., "Herinneringen aan Oud." *Jong Holland*, vol 4, 1987, pp 21-23. Dutch: "Remembering Oud." Personal recollections from 1937-42, when Albarda worked for Oud give insights into the architect's character and family life.

980. Arets, Wiel; Wim van den Bergh and Sergio Umberto Barbieri, "Modernita ambigue: l'opera di F.P.J. Peutz." *Casabella*, vol 51, 1987, no 534, pp 36-39. Italian: "Modern ambiguities: the work of .... Peutz." Includes Oud's opinions of Peutz's Heerlen town hall and an English summary of Barbieri's thoughts on Dutch architecture. Captions are in English.

981. B[arbieri], Sergio Umberto, "A Rotterdam, Oud-Oud." *Casabella*, vol 51, 1987, May, pp 30-31. Italian: "Old Oud at Rotterdam...." The piece comments on the new Café de Unie and the proposal to rebuild Oud-Mathenesse.

982. Bois, Yves-Alain, "Mondrian and the theory of architecture." *Assemblage*, 1987, no 4, pp 102-30. English. The article cites correspondence between Oud and Mondrian.

983. Bollery, Franziska and Kristiana Hartmann, "Das kleine Land und die grossen Monumente." *Baumeister*, vol 84, 1987, no 4, pp 24-31. German: "A small country and its great monuments." The piece bemoans the gradual loss of Holland's 20th century architectural icons, including Spangen and the Witte Dorp (Oud's design and the proposals are illustrated.) English summary.

984. Carasso, Dedalo, "Een monument voor de natie." *Jong Holland*, vol 3, 1987, March, pp 2-24. Dutch: "A monument for the nation." An historian at the Amsterdam Historical Museum, then planning an exhibition about the Dammonument provides a well-documented history, illustrated with design sketches and photo. See Carasso, "De wording van he Dammonument. Het Nationaal Monument van J.J.P. Oud en John Rädecker," *Ons Amsterdam*, vol 38, 1986, pp 96-97.

985. Franssen, Bert, "Witte Dorp van Oud ten grave gedragen." *Heemschut*, vol 64, 1987, July, p 10. The piece announces a symposium to discuss the issues of heritage conservation of residential quarters.

986. Furse, John, "J.J.P. Oud," in Ann Lee Morgan and Colin Naylor (eds.), *Contemporary Architects,* London/ Chicago, 1987, pp 668-69. The unsatisfactory note deals only with the early part of Oud's career, although there a reasonable list of works. See also the first edition, edited by Muriel Emanuel (1980).

987. Langmead, Donald, "In Holland staat een huis." *Conference Papers of the Society of Architectural Historians, Australia and New Zealand*, Adelaide, 1987. English. The paper examines the reception of Dutch modernism in the English language press.

988. Lugt, Reyn van der, "Reconstruction of the Café De Unie, Rotterdam." *Domus*, 1987, April, pp 74-80. Italian/English. Profusely illustrated with plans, archival images and photographs (some in color), a brief history of the building, includes Oud's description of the original color scheme. The reconstruction (1985-86) is described in detail. Cf. van der Lugt, "Die Wiedergeburt eines Denkmals der moderne; das Café De Unie ...," *Baukultur*, 1990, May, pp 22-23.

989. Reinhartz-Tergau, Elisabeth, "Een 'Gispenlamp' van J.J.P. Oud." *Jong Holland*, vol 3, 1987, no 1, pp 34-37. Dutch: "An Oud lamp for Gispen." The short illustrated piece demonstrates that Oud made the major design contribution to W.H. Gispen's piano lamp GISO no 404, of 1927. There are also interiors of villa *Allegonda* and the Stuttgart houses. See André Koch, *Gispen Lampen 1926-1949*, Amsterdam, 1980; Max van Rooy, "W.H. Gispen en de entree van het stalen meubel," *NRC-Handelsblad,* 1 August 1980.

990. Schneider, Jos., "De bende van Does." *H.P.*, 1987, 29 August, pp 28-34. Dutch: "The van Doesburg gang." Dutch. The article describes the establishment of the De Stijl group. There are a few reminiscences of Annie Oud-Dinaux.

991. Timon, Kalman, "Kulfold kialltasok." *Magyar Epitomuveszet*, vol 78, 1987, no 4, pp 90-99. Hungarian: "Exhibition review." Not seen.

992. Veldhoen, Lex, "De Kiefhoek: eenvoudige vormen en frisse kleuren." *Magazijn*, 1987, April, pp 38-39. Dutch: "Kiefhoek: simple forms and fresh colors." The piece notes that Oud-Mathenesse will be demolished and Kiefhoek will be renovated. There are a couple of familiar images and notes of an interview with Annie Oud-Dinaux.

993. *L'Architecture d'Aujourd'hui*, "Rendezvous avec Oud." 1987, September, p 78. French: "Meeting with Oud." This is a rather belated news item about restoration of Café De Unie.

994. *Designers' Journal*, "Oud revived." 1987, September, p 6. English. The piece describes the reconstruction program for the facade of the Café De Unie, but emphasizes the new interiors, designed by the firm *Opera*. There are several small images and a plan.

995. *Haagsche Courant*, [Aerial view of Congress Building.] 1987, 17 June. The caption announces proposed extensions to the exhibition hall, by architect Flip Rosdorff. See "Uitbreiding congresgebouw Den Haag," *Cobouw*, 16 March 1987; "Congresgebouw vernieuwd," *Haagsche Courant*, 16 April 1988.

996. *NBT Koerier*, "Achter die gevel, zit gewoon een beetje gek café-restaurant." 1987, February, p 10. Dutch: "Behind the facade sits a normal, slightly mad café-restaurant." The piece announces the rebuilt Café De Unie as an undiscovered but eye-catching tourist attraction. There is a good photograph.

1988
Books and Monographs
997. Gallotti, Alicia (ed.), *Annual of Commercial Spaces*, Barcelona, 1988. French/English/Spanish. There is a brief report of the reconstruction of the Café De Unie, thoroughly illustrated with good color images and a floor plan.

998. Gustmann, Kurt, "De Stijl," in Josef Kremerskothen and Horst Rasch (eds.), *Grosse Architekten*, Hamburg, 1988. German: *Great Architects*. The comprehensive chapter discusses Oud's involvement. His collaborations with van Doesburg are discussed, and some pre-1930, post De Stijl works are illustrated.

999. Haan, Hilde de and Ids Haagsma, *Architects in Competition*, London, 1988. English. The subtitle is "International architectural competitions for the last 200 years." Oud's criticism of competitions in "Architectuur en prijsvragen," *Groene Amsterdammer*, 23 January 1954, and part of his "Bij een Deensch ontwerp voor de *Chicago Tribune*." *Bouwkundig Weekblad*, 1923, p 456, are cited.

1000. Hollingsworth, Mary, *Architecture of the 20th Century*, London, 1988. English. A lightweight book addresses a few paragraphs to Oud and De Stijl, and includes archival images of Hoek van Holland and the Café De Unie.

1001. Koch, André, *Industrieel Ontwerper W.H.Gispen (1890-1981); een modern eclecticus*, Rotterdam, 1988. Dutch: *Industrial Designer ...Gispen ... a modern eclectic*. English summary. The study of Gispen's furniture and furnish-

170   Oud and the International Style

ings notes Oud's influence on him and refers to Oud's design involvement. His nickel-plated piano-lamp (July 1927) is illustrated. See Koch, "Gispen" in *Industrie en Vormgeving in Nederland 1850-1950*, Amsterdam, 1985; Reinhartz-Tergau, "Een 'Gispen-lamp' van ... Oud," *Jong Holland*, 1987, no 1.

1002.   Meuwissen, Joost, *Architectuur als Oude Wetenschap*, Amsterdam, 1988. Dutch: *Architecture as Old Science*. An English translation of the introduction, "Some theoretical remarks on rationalism in Dutch architecture" defines rationalism as "an indication to a certain approach" to Dutch architecture. There are constant references to Oud: indeed, the book is dedicated to his widow, Annie.

1003.   Norberg-Schulz, Christian and Yukio Futagawa, *Roots of Modern Design*, Tokyo, 1988. English/ Japanese. The handsome book claims that, influenced by Wright, Oud's main contribution to architecture was at the Weissenhofsiedlung.

1004.   Pommer, Richard et al. , *Ludwig Hilbersheimer: Architect, Educator and Urban Planner*, Chicago/New York, 1988. English. Hilbersheimer's unrealized 1924 design for row houses is convincingly linked to Oud's boulevard house design. See Hilbersheimer, *Grosstadt Architecktur*, Stuttgart, 1927, p 44.

1005.   Rosenburg, H.P.R. et al. , *Architectuurgids Den Haag 1800-1940*, The Hague, 1988. Dutch: *Architecture Guide to The Hague...* A rather loose introductory essay accompanies a list of building arranged alphabetically by streets. Oud has a biographical paragraph. The Shell Building is illustrated.

1006.   Saliga, Pauline, *The Modern Movement*, Chicago, 1988. English. This catalog of an exhibition at the Art Institute of Chicago, April-November 1988, includes a perspective of Oud's entry in the Rotterdam *beurs* competition.

1007.   Straaten, Evert van, *Theo van Doesburg, Painter and Architect*, The Hague, 1988. English. Also published in Dutch, in connection with an exhibition at the Boymans-van Beuningen Museum, December 1988-February 1989. The book deals at length with van Doesburg's collaboration with Oud. There are rare color images of the floor designs for *De Vonk* and the facades of Spangen.

Journals
1008.   Dupuits, Petra, "De tijden veranderen. Bij de heropening van het eerste Haagse filiaal van Metz en Co." *Jong Holland*, vol 4, 1988, pp 15-22. Dutch: "Times change. On the reopening of the first branch of Metz and Co in The Hague." Oud is included in this piece about architects' and artists' collaboration with the furniture company. An account of the November 1934 opening of the Metz shop publishes his speech. There is a 1934 portrait of him in a timber chair of his own design; photos of a steel armchair and office chair (both 1933) and his 1933 sketch for a lounge chair, all for Metz. See also Dupuits-Timmer, "Metz and Co" in *Industrie en Vormgeving in Nederland 1850-1950*, Amsterdam, 1985.

1009.   Fisher, Thomas, "P/A technics: low cost, high design." *Progressive Architecture*, vol 69, 1988, October, pp 98-109. English. An uninformed essay about the restoration of the Weissenhofsiedlung focuses on the economies of construction methods. There are excellent images: a site plan, and views of the row houses: one of construction, others of post-restoration exteriors.

1010. Harfield, Stephen, "The myth of cult harmony in De Stijl." *Conference Papers of the Society of Architectural Historians, Australia and New Zealand*, Sydney, 1988. English. The paper explains that van Doesburg created the illusion of group harmony by manipulation of the journal. See also Donald Langmead, "Distilling De Stijl," *ibid.*: a brief response that attempts to set De Stijl into Holland's wider artistic context after World War I.

1011. McKinsey, Kristan H., "Not just buildings: 20th century architects' design." *Decorative Arts Society Newsletter*, vol 14, 1988, summer, pp 4-5. English. A discussion of the development of industrial design mentions initiatives that embraced architects: the *Deutscher Werkbund*, Bauhaus and De Stijl.

1012. Moscoviter, Herman, "De Kiefhoek krijgt museumwoning." *Het Vrije Volk*, 1988, 10 February. Dutch: "Kiefhoek gets a museum-house." News item about the restoring one house to its original condition and detail, as a museum in the face of imminent redevelopment of the housing estate. There is a photo of the architect Wytze Patijn with architectural models. See Hanny Vroegh, "Plan voor vernieuwing Kiefhoek ligt klaar," *Rotterdamse Nieuwsblad*, 25 July 1988; Herman Moscoviter, "Museumwoning wordt trekpleister in Kiefhoek," *Vrije Volk*, 30 October 1989. "'De Kiefhoek', manifest van het Nieuwe Bouwen ...," *Bulletin KNOB*, vol 89, 1990, no 2, p 3, announces the opening on 1 September 1990. The event was widely celebrated: "Museum-woning Kiefhoek toont wonder van weleer," *ibid.*, 18 September 1990; Lex Veldhoen, "De Kiefhoek: een museum woning, maar verder?" *Magazijn*, November 1990; "Museumwoning geopend," *Algemeen Dagblad*, 21 September 1990; "Museumwoning De Kiefhoek staat model voor Nieuwe Bouwen," *Bouwwereld*, 19 October 1990, p 10; Ida Jager, "Een T-ford met ruimte voor een eikehouten vitrinekast," *Volkskrant*, 18 September 1990.

1013. Postmaa, Casper, "'Liever de foto's en de herinneringen dan verval'." *Haagsche Courant*, 1988, 1 July. Dutch: "'Rather photos and memories than ruin'." This reports an interview with Annie Oud-Dinaux. There is a view of Kiefhoek and the original gas station beside the Shell Building. The identical text appeared as "'Ik heb liever de foto's en de herinneringen dan verval'," *Rotterdamse Nieuwsblad*, 6 July 1988.

1014. Reinhartz-Tergau, Elisabeth, "Vier mozaïekreliëfs van Domela voor architect J.J.P. Oud." *Beelding*, 1988, November, pp 8-10. Dutch: "Four of Domela's mosaic-reliefs for ... Oud." A well documented essay sets out the relationship in the 1950s between Oud and César Domela, who designed decorations for the Congress Building and four mosaic reliefs for the Utrecht Insurance building. See *Een Nieuwe Synthese. Geometrische-abstracte Kunst in Nederland, 1945-1960*, The Hague, 1988 (exhibition catalog) and Welling, "'Een Nieuwe Synthese' in de Lakenhal," *Beelding*, September 1988, p 11.

1015. *Haagsche Courant*, "Steun for uitbreiding plan van Congresgebouw." 1988, 1 September. Dutch: "Support for Congress Building extension plan." News item.

1989
Books and Monographs
1016. Hofstede, Annigje C.H., *Meubelkunst*, place unknown, 1989[?] Dutch: *Furniture History*. Oud's relationship with Gispen is mentioned and two of his chairs, 1933 and 1936, are illustrated.

1017. Hoogveld, Carine et al. (eds.), *Glas in Lood in Nederland 1817-1968*, The Hague, 1989. Dutch: *Leadlight in Holland* ... The catalog of a traveling exhibition, April-June 1989, has essays on De Stijl by Evert van Straaten that examine van Doesburg's collaborations with Oud and Jan Wils. *De Vonk* is discussed in a biographical sketch of Harm Henrik Kamerlingh Onnes, and his stained glass window is illustrated (in monochrome). Reviewed Esmeijer, *Jong Holland*, vol 2, 1989, no 6, pp 33-36.

1018. Joedicke, Jürgen, *Weissenhofsiedlung Stuttgart*, Stuttgart, 1989. German/English. An essay, "The Weissenhofsiedlung in Stuttgart, past and present," is followed by a section of each of the participants. Oud is afforded three color exterior photos, plans, elevations and an isometric drawing, and his explanation of the design is published. There is a history of the restoration, 1981-87.

1019. Kirsch, Karin, *Kleiner Führer durch die Weissenhofsiedlung*, Stuttgart, 1989. German: *Small Guide to the Weissenhofsiedlung*. French and English summaries. The semi-populist guide provides a background to the project before dealing briefly with each building. Oud's row houses occupy a double page, with tiny line drawings and one interior view. For a scholarly treatment see Kirsch, *The Weissenhofsiedlung: Experimental housing built for the Deutscher Werkbund, Stuttgart, 1927*, New York, 1989 (originally published Stuttgart 1987.)

1020. Klotz, Heinrich (ed.), *Architektur des 20. Jahrhunderts*, Stuttgart, 1989. German. Also published as *20th Century Architecture: Drawings, Models, Furniture* London, 1989. Published for an exhibition at the Deutschen Architektur Museum, Frankfurt am Main, March-May 1989, the beautifully illustrated book mentions the De Stijl architects and calls Oud a master of the modern movement.

1021. Richardson, Sara, *J.J.P. Oud: a Bibliography*, Monticello, [1989.] English. A derivative essay prefaces a partially accurate bibliography.

1022. Strasser, George (ed.), i10 *et son epoque*, Paris, 1989. French: i10 *and its Era*. The catalog of an exhibition at the *Institut Neérlandais*, March-April 1989 includes essays "The lesson of *i10*" by Yve-Alain Bois; "Traces de l'avant-garde: *i10* et l'architecture" by Maristella Casciato and a translation of Oud's "Richtlijn" and some of his correspondence. There is a biography.

1023. Wilson, Vicky (ed.), *Travels in Modern Architecture*, London, 1989. Andrew Higgott's introduction examines the importance of Howard Robertson and F.R.Yerbury's tours, making the plausible claim that they brought architects like Oud to the attention of the British through *Architect and Building News*.

1024. *De 8 en Opbouw*, Amsterdam, 1989. Dutch. This is a reprint in 6 volumes of the modernist journal, 1932-1943—about 5000 profusely illustrated pages, Indexes and appendices are also in English.

Journals

1025. Barbieri, Sergio Umberto, "The demolition of a modern icon; Oud's *Witte Dorp* in Rotterdam." *Domus*, 1989, no 707, pp 16-19. Italian/English. Illustrated with Gabriele Basilico's graphic photographs, the piece mourns the fact that demolition had already started. There is a brief illustrated history of the project.

1026. Fisher, Thomas R., "In the Dutch Modernist tradition." *Progressive Architecture*, vol 70, 1989, December, pp 86-89. English. An article about a pair of semi-detached houses in Rotterdam by Rem Koolhaas speciously identifies "references" to Oud, among others.

1027. Groenendijk, Paul, "Naeve schoonheid in de scheepsbouw: lelijke scheepsontwerpen voorbeeld voor nieuwe architectonische esthetik." *AB Architectuur Bouwen*, vol 5, 1989, no 5, pp 33-39. Dutch. The title gives the content: "naive beauty in shipbuilding: ugly ship designs give way to a new architectural aesthetic." Oud's work for the Holland-America Line is included in this review.

1028. Heuvel, Wim van, "Jonge monumenten in Stuttgart en Wenen; restauraties woningen Oud, Stam en Rietveld." *AB Architectuur Bouwen*, vol 5, 1989, no 1, pp 9-14. Dutch: "Newer heritage buildings in Stuttgart and Vienna: restoration of houses by Oud [et al..]..." The piece gives a little space to the Weissenhofsiedlung, illustrated with drawings and archival and recent photos.

1029. Mik, Edzard, "Allemaal dezelfde voordeur." *De Tijd*, 1989, 15 September, pp 24-26 Dutch: "Everywhere the same front door" The article discusses the restoration of Dudok's "De Burgh" garden suburb, Eindhoven: an "architectural, but for all that, a social success." There is a claim that this "witte dorp" owed something to Oud. Cf. Bernard Hulsman, "Fraaie woonwijk wordt tot monument," *NRC-Handelsblad*, 18 September 1989, p 7.

1030. Selier, Herman et al., "Monumentenzorg." *Architect*, vol 20, 1989, themanummer 37, pp 6-49. Dutch. "Conservation of buildings." Special issue.

1031. Trebbi, Giorgio, "Rinnovo urbano: due episodi Olandesi." *Parametro*, vol 20, 1989, no 174, pp 10-11. Italian. Not seen.

1032. *Arquitectura*, "Weissenhofsiedlung Stuttgart 1927." Vol 70, 1989, May-August, pp 278ff. Spanish. English summary. An essay introduces a series of excellent photographs by Uwe Rau of the restored *siedlung*. There are front and rear views, plans, elevations and an isometric.

1990-1998

1990
Books and Monographs

1033. Bernini, Beatrice and Timo de Rijk, *Het Nieuwe Wonen in Nederland 1924-1936*, Rotterdam, 1990. Dutch: *The New Dwelling in Holland 1924-1936*. Published for an exhibition at the *Expositiecentrum Gooiland*, September-November 1990, the book includes the Stuttgart houses as examples of functionalist design; there are plans, an isometric of the kitchen, and an interior of *De Vonk*.

1034. Celant, Germano and Michael Govan (eds.), *Mondrian e De Stijl*, Milan, 1990. Italian: *Mondrian and De Stijl*. The lavish catalog contains several essays, including Carel Blotkamp's "Mondrian e l'architettura" (*Wonen TA/BK*, March 1982) and Sergio Polano's "Il colore dello stile," both pertinent to the study of Oud. *De Vonk* and Spangen are illustrated.

1035. Cusveller, Sjoerd (ed.), *De Kiefhoek: een Woonwijk in Rotterdam*, Naarden/Laren, 1990. Dutch: *The Kiefhoek: a Residential District in Rotterdam*. Publication coincided with the announced "restoration" (architect, Wytze Patijn) which involved converting pairs of houses into single dwellings. Essays establish socio-historic context, describe and criticize the conversion project, and hail Oud as an "international master-architect." Archival and contemporary photographs proliferate, including color images of restored interiors. Cf. Cusveller, "Renovatie van een straatbeeld; woonwijk-monument Kiefhoek verbouwen," *Architect*, November 1989, Themanummer 37, pp 17-21; Piet Vollaard, "Is Kiefhoek nu voldoende gespaard?" *AB Architectuur/Bouwen*, vol 6, 1990, no 10, pp 45-47 (with color images of the "trial block"). See also "Renovieren eines Stadtbildes," *Baukultur*, May/June 1990, pp 18-21.

1036. Joedicke, Jürgen, *Architekturgeschichte des 20. Jahrhunderts; von 1950 bis zur gegenwart*, Stuttgart/Zürich, 1990. German: *Architectural History of the 20th Century: 1950 to the Present*. Oud is mentioned only in connection with his pre-World War II work; Kiefhoek is illustrated.

1037. Johnson, Donald Leslie, *Wright versus America*, Cambridge, Mass., 1990. English. The book deals with Frank Lloyd Wright's career during its "barren" period in the 1920s and early 1930s. His influence upon the Dutch is touched upon, and Oud's remark that Wright's influence in Europe had not been "a happy one" is expounded.

1038. Lemoine, Serge (ed.), *Theo van Doesburg Peinture, Architecture, Theorie*. Paris 1990. French: *Theo van Doesburg: Painting, Architecture, Theory*. The anthology addresses aspects of van Doesburg's career. See especially Jaffé, "...van Doesburg et la fondation du Stijl" and Doig, "Les transformations géometriques et leur signification dans les prèmieres oeuvres néoplastiques de van Doesburg." The color designs for *Allegonda* and *De Vonk* are illustrated in monochrome.

1039. Martinius, Warna Oosterbaan, *Schoonheid, Welzijn, Kwaliteit: Kunstbeleid en Verantwoording na 1945*, Den Haag, 1990. Dutch: *Beauty, Wellbeing, Quality: Arts Administration and Accountability after 1945*. A chapter on national monuments gives a matter-of-fact history of the Military Monument at Grebbeberg and the National Monument, Amsterdam.

1040. Mual, M., *Design Gedokumenteerd. Gispen buismeubelen en verlichting 1920-1940*, Nijmegen, 190. Dutch: *Design Documented. Gispen tubular furniture and lighting ...* The catalog of selected W.H.Gispen designs includes the piano lamp no 404 designed by Oud.

1041. Reinhartz-Tergau, Elisabeth, *J.J.P. Oud: Meubelontwerpen en Interieurs/ Möbelentwurfe und Inneneinrichtngen*, Rotterdam, 1990. Dutch/German...*Oud: Furniture Designs and Interiors*. The well-documented catalog of an exhibition at Museum Boymans-van Beuningen, Rotterdam, August-September 1990 is a monograph abounding in black and white images. The show was announced *De Architect*, July-August 1990, p 10. For reviews see e.g., Schenke, "Meubelair uit de kelder," *AD Kunst/Media*, 8 August 1990; "De schatbewader van Oud," *Vrije Volk*, 9 August; "Onbekende kastjes van een bekend ontwerper," *Provincieele Zeeuwse Courant*, 11 August; "'Ieder moment geniet ik er nog van," *Utrechts Nieuwsblad*, 11 August; Jager, "Meubelen van Oud: mollig en zacht," *Volkskrant*, 18 August; de Wolff, "Meubelontwerpen uit een zakelijkheidscultus," *ibid.*, 20 August; Adriaansz, "Meubels van Oud geïsoleerd," *Financiëele Dagblad*, 10 September; Metz, "Weerstand tegen het wippend zitten," *NRC-Handelsblad*, 30 August, p 7; Schoone, "Meubels van Oud," *Magazijn*, summer 1990; de Wagt, "Oud's stoelen zaten niet lekker," *Typhoon*, 9 August; Wagemans, "Meubels van Oud in Boymans," *Brabants Dagblad*, 11 August; "Meubels van J.P.Oud in Boymans-van Beuningen," *Eindhovens Dagblad*, 11 August and "De Pijngrens van J.J.P. Oud," *De Tijd*, 24 August. Cf. Moscoviter, "Meubels 'van den mensch uitgegaan," *Dagblad Tubantia,* 6 August; "De vergeten meubels van architect Oud," *Arnhemse Courant,* 7 August; "Met kussens van in rubber gedrenkt motvrij paardehaar," *Vrije Volk,* 4 August 1990, and the identical text in "Meubelontwerper uit noodzaak," *Brabants Nieuwsblad,* 10 August. The catalog is reviewed Collotti, *Domus,* July 1991, p xi.

1042. Schaal, Rolf et al., *Baukonstruktion der Moderne aus heutiger Sicht; Siedlungen,* Berlin, 1990. German: *Building Construction of the modern ...; Suburbs.* There is a chapter on Weissenhofsiedlung.

1043. Woodham, Jonathan M., *Twentieth-century Ornament,* London, 1990. English. Respective approaches to ornament by De Stijl and the Amsterdam School are reviewed in a cursory discussion. Oud is mentioned as a main player in the international arena.

Journals

1044. Allan, John, "Instruments or icons?" *Architectural Review,* vol 187, 1990, no 1125, pp 4-7. English. A review of the first international conference for Documentation and Conservation of Buildings, Sites and Neighborhoods of the Modern Movement (DOCOMOMO), Eindhoven, September 1990 is illustrated with photos and plans of Oud's Kiefhoek houses and Patijn's changes to them, taken as a case study for the conference. See Murray Fraser, "Docomomo is a new group ...," *Architects' Journal,* vol 192, 1990, September 26, pp 76-77.

1045. Barbieri, Sergio Umberto and Hella van der Ploeg, "Avantegarde und Monumentalität." *Baukultur,* 1990, May/June, pp 6-10. German: "Avant garde and monumentality." A well-illustrated overview of Oud's career introduces an issue devoted to him. See 1049, 1050, 1053, 1057, 1059.

1046. Barbieri, Sergio Umberto, "Oud e l'Olanda." *Domus,* vol 62, 1990, January, pp xiii-xviii. Italian/English. An "Oud itinerary" includes a short bilingual introduction, a series of enigmatic, useless location maps, and a list of 16 works, illustrated with small views and plans.

1047. Buchanan, Peter, "Paul de Ley." *Architectural Review,* vol 187, 1990, no 1116, pp 78-89. English (UK). A profile of the Amsterdam architect includes proposals for rebuilding Oud-Mathenesse. There is an aerial view taken during demolition. See Liesbeth Melis, "Ingetogenheid in vorm en kleur; twee woningbouwprojecten Paul de Ley," *Architect,* vol 20, June 1989, pp 80-85.

1048. Casciato, Maristella and Toke van Helmond, "*i10*: lettera documenti immagini." *Casabella,* vol 54, 1990, July, pp 40-58; 62-63. Italian: "*i10: letters, documents, ideas*." The subheading tells the story: "fragments of the international review [*i10*] published in Amsterdam from January 1927 until June 1929."

1049. Günter, Roland, "Die Holländische Tradition von J.J.P. Oud." *Baukultur,* 1990, May-June, pp 26-29. German: "Oud's Dutch tradition." The essay exposes ways in which some of Oud's oeuvre, for all its feted avant garde qualities, derives from long standing norms in Dutch architecture. None of the work cited as evidence is post-1925. The main source is Stamm, *J.J.P. Oud, Bauten und Projekte...*, Mainz, 1984 (cf. Stamm, *The Architecture of ... Oud 1906-1963*, Tallahassee, 1978).

1050. Hartmann, Kristiana, "J.J.P. Oud: biographische Notizen." *Baukultur*, 1990, May-June, pp 24-25. German: "... biographical notes." The notes result from a student project at Braunschweig Technological University. Several posters are illustrated, including a portrait, the Café De Unie and Hoek van Holland.

1051. Heuvel, Wim van, "Honderdste geboortedag van architect J.J.P. Oud vergeten." *Cobouw*, 1990, 7 February. Dutch: "Centenary of Oud's birth forgotten." The illustrated essay, in an annotated list of the major Oud exhibitions and publications over several decades, reproves Holland's forgetfulness.

1052. Langmead, Donald, "Evanescent architect: Robert van 't Hoff 1887-1979." *Exedra*, vol 2, 1990, no 1, pp 6-15. English. Only the second attenuated English-language study of van 't Hoff, this affirms his importance as a carrier of "Wrightiana" to Holland, and traces his brief career including contact with Oud.

1053. Leering, Jean, "J.J.P. Oud. Gestaltung zwischen Neoplastizismus, Neue Sachlicheit und Neoklassizismus." *Baukultur*, 1990, May-June, pp 30-33. German: ."... Oud. [Designing] between Neoplasticism, New Objectivity and Neoclassicism." The essay compares Oud's designs, notably the Congress Building, with the work of Karl Freidrich Schinkel. Reference is made to other buildings, projects and furniture designs.

1054. Locatelli, Vittorio, "Mondrian and De Stijl: between abstraction and architecture." *Abitare*, 1990, November, no 290, pp 211-15. Italian/English. A discussion of architectural space as an extension of planes refers mostly to van Doesburg and van Eesteren's projects. There is some discussion of the former's conflicts with Oud and an image of the Café De Unie.

1055. Moscoviter, Herman, "En nu weer J.J.P. Oud onder de slopersbol." *Vrije Volk*, 1990, 21 September. Dutch: "Once again: Oud under the wrecker's ball." An announcement of the imminent demolition of Spangen Block IX gives a history of the estate and Oud's collaboration with van Doesburg. Cf. Maandag, "Oppassen, daar gaat traks weer een stuckje oud Spangen (IX)," *Rotterdamse Nieuwsblad*, 29 June 1990; "Nieuw variant Jan Luykenblok is 'afschuwelijk'," *ibid.*, 30 August 1990; "Nieuw onderzoek naar renovatie Oud-complex," *Vrije Volk*, 6 July 1990. See also ten Cate, "In Rotterdam rammelt het," *Bouw*, vol 46, 15 March 1991, pp 8-9; "Sloopvergunning voor blok van Oud," *Rotterdams Nieuwsblad*, 15 February 1991; Duivesteijn and Colenbrander, "Rotterdamse oplossing monumentenvraagstuk," *Rotterdams Dagblad*, 10 July 1992.

1056. Schmuck, Friedrich and Hildegarde Kalthegener, "Rekonstruktion des Café De Unie." *Deutsche Bauzeitschrift*, vol 38, 1990, January, pp 101-04. German: "Reconstruction of ... De Unie." This is a belated account of the 1985 project, set in the context of De Stijl. There are archival and current photographs.

1057. Stock, Wolfgang Jean, "Poetischer Funktionalismus." *Baukultur*, 1990, May-June, pp 15-17. German: "Poetic functionalism." This critical review of the Weissenhofsiedlung houses is well illustrated and thoroughly documented from secondary sources.

1058. Swieten, Peter van, "Restauratie of reconstructie van jong monument." *R en O; Renovatie en Onderhoud*, vol 15, 1990, September, pp 14-17. Dutch: "Restoration or reconstruction of recent heritage buildings." The well-illustrated critical article addresses the question in relation to Kiefhoek and Patijn's "trial block" on Hendrik Idoplein: where are the lines to be drawn defining restoration, renovation, reconstruction and replication? See van Heuvel, "Rotterdamse wijk Kiefhoek: restauratie of reconstructie?," *Cobouw*, 12 October 1990.

1059. Werner, Frank R., "Oud und die Gnade der Maschine." *Baukultur*, 1990, May-June, pp 11-14. German: "Oud and the grace of the machine." The subtitle reads, "the Dutch contribution to a socially acceptable minimum house in the first half of the twentieth century" and the piece cites liberally from Oud's "Kunst en machine," *De Stijl*, 1918. Several of his works are referred to; designs for a semidetached house for workers and Kiefhoek are illustrated.

1060. *Gelderlander*, "Switzers in spoor van meester-architect." 25 April 1990. Dutch: "Swiss on the trail of a master-architect." The provincial newspaper reports a study visit to the Biostellingsoord by architecture students from Geneva. An exhibition of their findings followed at the Minerva Academy, Groningen, March-April 1992.

1061. *Haagsche Courant*, "Congresgebouw wil nieuwe toren." 1990, 6 December. Dutch: "Congress Building to have a new tower." News item.

1991
Books and Monographs
1062. Camp, D.L. and D. de Vries-Hermansader, *Rotterdam Architecture: 40 Buildings Documented*, Rotterdam, 1991. Dutch/English. Three boxes of loose-leaf studies include Kiefhoek, the Spaarbank and Utrecht Insurance building, each with six pages of critical text, archival and contemporary photos, and drawings.

1063. Kähler, Gert (ed.), *Architektour: Bauen in Stuttgart seit 1900*, Braunschweig/Wiesbaden, 1991. German: *Architectour: Building on Stuttgart since 1900*. A well-documented guide includes several pages on the Weissenhofsiedlung. It translates an article from *i10* (no 10/27), also published in *Bauwelt*. There are small plans and an isometric drawing of Oud's houses.

1064. Leuthäuser, Gabriele and Peter Gössel, *Functional Architecture*, Cologne, 1990. German/ French/English. After reprinting the text of Hitchcock and Johnson, *The International Style*, 1932, the book sets out monochromatic images by country. Weissenhofsiedlung, Kiefhoek and Hoek van Holland are included.

1065. Overy, Paul, *De Stijl*, London, 1991. English. The well-documented book puts De Stijl in a national and international context and examines its effects. It admits to being a construct of De Stijl, not its reality. Oud's work before 1932 is discussed, much of it illustrated (some in color). Reviewed Pavitt, *Design*, November 1991, pp 58-59; Padovan, *Architectural Review*, October 1991, p 12; Hughes, *Arts Review*, March 1992, pp 82-83.

1066. Patijn, Wytze and Katrien Overmeire, "Restoration of the Kiefhoek in Rotterdam ..." in H.J.Henket et al. (eds.), *Conference Proceedings of the First DOCOMOMO*, Eindhoven, 1991. English. This is the architects' rationale of proposals for the controversial modernization of Kiefhoek, setting out the project parameters, the design and execution, illustrated with archival and contemporary images. For reportage of progress and financing see e.g., Bol, "Reconstructie tot in de finesses," *Bouwwereld*, 25 January 1991, pp 38-41; "Minister laat woonwijk De Kiefhoek restaureren," *Volkskrant*, 18 July 1991; "Vier miljoen van rijk voor restauratie van De Kiefhoek," *Zuiderpost*, 22 August; "Overheid draagt bij aan restauratie volkswoningen Kiefhoek ...," *Bouwwereld*, 23 August, p 7; "Rijkssubsidie voor restauratie van zes monumenten," *NRC Handelsblad*, 20 July; "Restauratie Kiefhoek mogelijk met geld uit kanjerpot," *R en O; Renovatie en Onderhoud*, September, pp 14-16; "Jubelstemming in woon-monument," *NRC Handelsblad*, 18 July. There was international interest: see Polito, "Modern conservation policies in Holland," *L'Industria delle Costruzioni*, June 1991, pp 36-41; Mácel, "Die sanierung der Oud-Siedlung in Rotterdam," *Bauwelt*, 1991, pp 474-75; van der Hoeven, "De Kiefhoek ... Experiment Modelhaus Museumswohnung," *ibid.*, pp 2324-29; Slawik, "Museum-woning," *Deutsche Bauzeitung*, no 1, 1991, pp 132-34:"De Kiefhoek behouden; reconstructie woonhuismonument," *Bouwwereld*, February 1992, p 2.

1067. Pommer, Richard and Christian F. Otto, *Weissenhof 1927 and the Modern Movement in Architecture*, Chicago/London, 1991. English. A well-documented socio-historical study begins with political background before descending to detail. The work is set out by building types, so Oud and Stam are discussed together. The many archival illustrations are inconveniently grouped at the back.

1068. Prak, Niels Luning, *Het Nederlandse Woonhuis van 1800 tot 1940*, Delft, 1991. Dutch: *The Dutch Dwelling, 1800-1940.* The sequel to Meischke and Zantkuyl, *Het Nederlandse Woonhuis van 1300-1800*, 1969, is divided into three periods, each addressing a number of organizational, socio-political and technical issues. Kiefhoek and Spangen (i.a.) are taken as case studies.

1069. Straaten, Evert van, *Theo van Doesburg: Painter and Architect*, New York, 1991. English. The re-issued catalog of an exhibition at the Boymans-van Beuningen Museum, Rotterdam, December 1988-February 1989 includes a list of van Doesburg's paintings and architecture, and another of his writings and a bibliography. It includes projects on which he collaborated with Oud.

1070. Warncke, Carsten-Peter, *The Ideal as Art. De Stijl, 1917-1931*. Cologne, 1991. English. Also published as *Das Ideal als Kunst. De Stijl 1917-31*, Cologne, 1990. An excellent chapter "Ideals in practice" examines Oud's role within the group, discussing his collaborations with van Doesburg and his own projects. It is replete with photographs of *Allegonda, De Vonk* (including color images of interiors); color schematics for Spangen, the Oud-Mathenesse director's shed, and Café De Unie. There are accurate biographical notes, with a portrait.

1071. Wörner, Martin and Gilbert Lupfer, *Stuttgart: ein Architekturführer*, Berlin, 1991. German: *Stuttgart: an Architectural Guide*. There is extensive coverage of the Weissenhofsiedlung illustrated with small images.

Journals

1072. Barbieri, Sergio Umberto, "Renovation and tradition: the reconstruction of Rotterdam." *Abitare*, 1991, February, pp 126-31. Italian/English. There are passing references to the city's modern architectural monuments, including Spangen, Kiefhoek and the rebuilt Café De Unie, each with a small image or two.

1073. Bliek, Nicole, "Terug naar Allegonda." *Algemeen Dagblad*, 1991, 21 August, p 13. Dutch; "*Allegonda* revisited." The populist, nostalgic history of the house through considerable change, identifies successive owners and uses. There is a 1930s photograph and a current one from the same point.

1074. Kroes, Jan Jaap de, "Stadhuis Almelo groter dan vermoed." *Bouw*, vol 46, 1991, 15 November, pp 14-16. Dutch: "Almelo town hall larger than supposed." Oud designed Almelo town hall shortly before his death; it was realized 1969-73 by Hans Oud and H. Dethmers. This piece reports a space study of the building by architects Twijnstra Gudde and DEGW. There are plans and two photographs.

1075. Overy, Paul, "Carpentering the classic: a very peculiar practice. The furniture of Gerrit Rietveld." *Journal of Design History*, vol 4, 1991, no 3, pp 135-66. The generously illustrated, well documented essay refutes the idea that Rietveld reached an *impasse* in chair design, from which it was rescued by the tubular steel "movement" of the late 1920s. His collaborations and correspondence with Oud are noted.

1076. Rosa, Giancarlo, "Serramenti nei movimento moderno: il quartiere Kiefhoek di ... Oud." *Frames, Porte e Finestre*, April-May, 1991, pp 28-35. Italian/English: "Frames in the Modern Movement." The thoroughly illustrated piece combines history and criticism of the original Kiefhoek with a derivative biography of Oud, and an overview of his contemporary work.

1077. Verhagen, Hans, "Getouwtrek om woning van weduwe architect Oud." *Haagsche Courant*, 1991, 18 June, p 9. Dutch: "Tug-of-war over ... Oud's widow's house." The item reports problems with the sale of the Oud family home in Wassenaar. Cf. "Villa weduwe architect Oud verkocht aan hoogste bieder," *ibid.*, 26 June 1991.

1078. *Arkitekturtidskriftet*, "Projekt: Witte Dorp." 1991, no 47-48, pp 175-77. Danish/English. (Denmark). The piece thoroughly reports and illustrates a design for new Witte Dorp, Oud Mathenesse, by Dobelaar, de Kovel and de Vroom, with fold-out pages. There is praise for Oud's design, which is illustrated.

1992
Books and Monographs

1079. Baaij, Hans and Jan Oudenaarden, *Monument uit Rotterdam*, Rotterdam, 1992, Dutch: *Monuments of Rotterdam*. A populist book provides images and short histories of heritage listed buildings, including Oud's Savings Bank.

1080. Barbieri, Sergio Umberto et al., *Visitors' Guide, Randstad Holland*, Delft, 1992. 1996. English. The guide was published for the ACSA European Schools of Architecture Conference. Kiefhoek is described in a single page of text, with a location map, plans and photographs.

1081. Boddaert, Joris, *Roterodamum: Architectuur van Vroeger in het Rotterdam van Nu* .. Rotterdam, 1992. Dutch: *Roterodamum: Earlier Architecture in Today's Rotterdam* ... The book reprints installments of a column appearing in *De Havenloods/Het Zuiden*, 1991-92. Three deal rather nostalgically with Oud's housing blocks in Pieter Langendijkstraat, Tusschendijken.

1082. Groenendijk, Paul and Piet Vollaard, *Moderne Architectuur in Nederland. Zuid Holland*, Rotterdam, 1992. Dutch. This populist booklet includes a brief essay about Oud and De Stijl, illustrated by miniscule images of Café De Unie and the Oud-Mathenesse director's shed. Oud's housing schemes and the Shell Building are also discussed and illustrated. Cf. Groenendijk, and Vollaard, *Guide to Modern Architecture in The Netherlands*; *Supplement*. Rotterdam, 1992 and *Guide to Rotterdam,* Rotterdam, 1992.

1083. Jansens, Johan et al., *Witte Dorp Forever*, Rotterdam, n.d. [1992?] A broadsheet published by the Oud-Mathenesse residents' association celebrates the rising of the estate from the ashes.

1084. Küper, Marijke and Ida van Zijl, *Gerrit Rietveld: the Complete Works*, New York, 1993. Originally published in Dutch, Utrecht 1992. The catalog for the "Gerrit Thomas Rietveld 1888-1964" exhibition has a scholarly text and copious illustrations, many in color. One review claims it to be "indispensable for any further study" of Rietveld. The show started in the Centraal Museum, Utrecht before moving to the Centre Georges Pompidou, Paris and then to the Solomon R. Guggenheim Museum, New York. Oud is referred to throughout.

1085. Möller, Werner and Otakar Mácel, *Ein Stuhl macht Geschichte*, Munich, 1992. German: *A Chair Makes History*. This well-illustrated catalog of an exhibition at Bauhaus Dessau, August-October 1992 chronologically treats the tubular steel stair, dealing with the designers and the commercial developments of the type. Oud is frequently mentioned, and his designs for Metz (1933) are shown. The show later moved to Wiel am Rhein and Hamburg.

1086. Nägele, Hermann, *Die Restaurierung der Weissenhofsiedlung 1981-87*, Stuttgart, 1992. German: *Restoration of the Weissenhofsiedlung, 1981-87*. This thorough study of the project is illustrated with plans, construction details, and "before" and "after" elevations. Oud's houses are discussed in 20 pages, and there

Annotated Bibliography 1990-1998   183

are good photos of the restored building. Reviewed van Heuvel, "Gewetensvolle restauratie woningen Oud in Stuttgart," *Cobouw*, 11 December 1992. See Wurth, "Die Weissenhofsiedlung in Stuttgart," *Bauwelt*, vol 82, 1991, pp 2314-18.

1087. Riley, Terence, *The International Style: Exhibition 15 and the Museum of Modern Art*, New York, 1992. English. This catalog of an exhibition at Columbia University recreating the MoMA *International Style* show of 1932 gives a history of that event. Weissenhofsiedlung, Hoek van Holland, the Kiefhoek church and the model of the unrealized "Pinehurst", North Carolina are illustrated. See Frampton, "Shadow of the enlightenment." *Building Design*, 6 March 1992, pp 12-13, an edited version of a lecture delivered to mark the occasion.

Journals

1088. Flagge, Ingeborg, "Die Grossen Architekten: J.J.P. Oud." *Häuser*, 1992, 23 November, pp 51-62. German: "The great architects: Oud." Not seen.

1089. Fuchs, Hans, "Nu documentatiecentrum; Sikkens reconstrueert de Keet van Oud." *Bouwwereld*, 1992, no 13, pp 8-9. Dutch: "Now a documentation center; Sikkens rebuild Oud's site hut." The copiously illustrated piece announces the rebuilding (architect Wytze Patijn) in Sassenheim of the Oud-Mathenesse site hut for a paint company, Akzo Coatings. The 100,000 guilder project attracted notice: see, e.g., Pronker, "Keetje krijgt herkansing om monument te worden," *Cobouw*, 12 May 1992, p 5; Oosterman, "Oud nieuws: herbouw bouwkeet," *Archis*, February 1992, p 9 (with an illustration of a card model kit); "Keetje van Oud," *Architect*, vol 23, July-August 1992, p 14; "Reconstructie Ouds bouwkeet," *Cobouw*, 3 February 1992; Smits, "Uit de verf," *Financiëele Dagblad*, 12 May; Metz, "Reconstructie van een keetje," *NRC-Handelsblad*, 12 May (with a color photo); "Keet van Oud is terug," *Rotterdamse Dagblad*, 13 May; "Witte Dorp claimt de 'Keet van Oud'," *ibid.*, 15 May; Zijlmans, "Keet van Oud naar het Witte Dorp," *ibid.*, 23 May. The shed was later moved to the rebuilt Witte Dorp; see "Keet van oud terug van weggeweest," *Rotterdams Dagblad*, 7 October 1993.

1090. Meurs, Paul, "Vormgeven aan de herinnering; restauratie en bewaarzucht." *Architect*, vol 23, 1992, no 2, pp 25-59. Dutch: "Design in the memory; restoration and the need to preserve." Not seen.

1091. Yashiro, Masaki, "J.J.P. Oud and his work." *Process: Architecture,* 1993, no 112, pp 112-119. Japanese/English (Japan). In an issue devoted to "collective housing in Holland: traditions and trends," a shallow essay outlines Oud's public housing 1918-1932, illustrated with difficult-to-read plans and color photographs set out in confusing photomontage.

1092. *AB Architectuur Bouwen*, "Omstreden 'reconstructie' monument De Kiefhoek haalbaar." Vol 8, 1992, no 5, p 17. Brief item about reconstruction of Kiefhoek shows small scale plans for converting two houses into one.

1093. *Rotterdams Dagblad*, "Meubelair Oud naar NAi." 1992, 25 September. Dutch: "Oud furniture at Netherlands Architecture Institute." News item.

1993

Books and Monographs.

1094. Brouwers, Ruud, Hans Ibelings and Arjen Oosterman (eds.), *Architectuur in Nederland*, Utrecht/ Rotterdam, 1993. Dutch. Also published in German and English. The book places past and present Dutch architecture within an international context, presenting a series of essays on social, aesthetic and technological aspects. Specific references to include Kiefhoek and the Shell Building.

1095. Colenbrander, Bernard, *Style: Standard and Signature in Dutch Architecture in the Nineteenth and Twentieth Centuries*, Rotterdam, 1993. Dutch/English. Oud figures in an analytical overview of stylistic concepts in Dutch architecture. There are project-oriented demonstrations of ideas. Oud's 1921 lecture "On future architecture and its architectonic possibilities" is reprinted; his Amsterdam city hall competition entry and the Congress Building are illustrated in color.

1096. Groenendijk, Paul and Piet Vollaard, *Moderne Architectuur in Nederland*, The Hague, 1993. Dutch. The slim populist volume has a few pages devoted to De Stijl, giving a history of the group and its ideas an illustrating "typical" work. There are "before and after" images of the Café De Unie.

1097. Hoeven, Ernst-Philip van der et al., *J.J.P. Oud en Bruno Taut; Ontwerpen voor een Nieuwe Stad Rotterdam-Berlijn*, Rotterdam, 1993. Dutch: ... *Designs for a New City, Rotterdam-Berlin.* In a catalog of an exhibition at the NAi, March-April 1994 both men are held out as "master-architects for a new era" and their careers examined against the socio-architectural background of their respective countries. Some of Taut's letters to Oud are included. Oud's public housing is illustrated with drawings and archival photographs. Reviewed Colenbrander, "Met het ene been in de negentiende eeuw: ..." *Archis*, March 1994, pp 46-52; van Bergeijk, "Oud en Taut met elkaar vertrouwd?" *AB Architectuur Bouwen*, vol 10, 1994, no 2, pp 12-13; Adriaansz, "Monumentale stadsbeelden in Rotterdam en Berlijn," *Financiëele Dagblad*, 12 March 1994; Spaninks, "De geduldige worstelaar en de kleurrijke visionair," *Het Nieuwsblad*, 1 February; van Heuvel, "Kleurrijke woningbouw van Bruno Taut," *Cobouw*, 4 February; Ellenbroek, "Al te bruusk van de foto geknipt," *Volkskrant*, 9 February; Cohen, "Systematische worstelaar," *Vrij Nederland*, 19 February; "Oud en Taut bij het NAi," *Architect*, vol 25, February, p 17; "Oud en Taut, en de rol van de stadsarchitect," *Blauwe Kamer Profiel*, March 1994, pp 10-11.

1098. Kultermann, Udo, *Architecture of the 20th Century*, New York, 1993. English. Also published as *Architektur im 20. Jahrhundert*. A 5 page section, "De Stijl and the School of Amsterdam." cites *Mein Weg in De Stijl*, and offers critical comment on Oud's early work (Kiefhoek and Tusschendijken are illustrated). There is a passing reference to Stuttgart with an image of the row houses.

1099. Liesbrock, Heinz and Susanne Blumberger, *Die Neue Stadt. Rotterdam im 20. Jahrhundert: Utopie und Realität*, Munster, 1993. German: *The New City. Rotterdam in the Twentieth Century: Utopia and Reality.* In a short section: "The new building as a basis for a new architecture: the work of J.J.P. Oud", his proposals for Hofplein are published.

1100. Ockman, Jane and Edward Eigen (eds.), *Architecture Culture 1943-1968: a documentary anthology*, New York, 1993. English. The anthology includes "Mr Oud replies," *Architectural Record*, 1947, set in the context of the debate over the "modernity" of the Shell Building. The offending page from the *Record*, December 1946 is reproduced.

1101. Rowe, Peter G., *Modernity and Housing*, Cambridge, Mass, 1993. English. Kiefhoek is included among profusely illustrated case studies. An appendix summarizes salient information about the scheme.

1102. Taverne, Ed R. M., "Neo-De Stijl of Neo-Monumentalisme?" in Wim Denslagen (ed.), *Bouwkunst. Studies in Vriendschap voor Kees Peeters*, Amsterdam, 1993, pp 515-27. This learned essay is the harbinger of Taverne and Broekhuizen, *Het Shell-gebouw van J.J.P. Oud: ontwerp en receptie*, 1995.

1103. Vöge, Peter, *The Complete Rietveld Furniture*, Rotterdam, 1993. English. Essays "From icon to prototype" by Paul Overy and "Space, simplicity, relativity" by Vöge introduce the realized and unrealized designs, chronologically arranged. There are continual references to Oud.

Journals
1104. Dijk, Hans van, "Collective housing in Holland: traditions and trends. Part 1." *Process: architecture*, 1993, no 112, pp 5-97 and Masaki Yashiro, "Collective housing in Holland: traditions and trends. Part 2." *ibid.*, pp 98-152. Not seen.

1105. Henkes, Peter, "Het monument der monument." *Vrij Nederland*, 1993, 8 May, p 32. Dutch: "the monument of monuments." The piece reports an interview with "Nouki" Rädecker, nephew of the Dam monument's sculptor, and George van der Wagt.

1106. Taverne, Ed R.M. and Dolf Broekhuizen, "In de schaduw van Mondriaan: brieven van R. van 't Hoff aan J.J.P. Oud (1945-1947)." *Jong Holland*, vol 9, 1993, no 1, p 38-53; 63-64. Dutch: "In the shadow of Mondrian: letters from [van 't Hoff to Oud ...]." A short essay (with English summary) introduces letters written 1945-47. There is a 1961 portrait of Oud (from *Visie*) and images of the Shell Building and the Rotterdam Savings Bank.

1107. Verbaan, Danny, "'Toren van Oud' wordt woongebouw." *Haagsche Courant*, 1993, 10 July. Dutch: "Oud's tower becomes a residential building." News item about the tower of the Congress Building being converted to apartments. Other proposals followed: see, e.g., Rosenberg, "Toren van Oud wordt verkocht," *Haagsche Courant*, 7 January 1995; Postmaa, "Voor het Congresgebouw is inderdaad the sky the limit," *Haagsche Courant*, 27 March 1995 and "'Bouwen hotel is onaanvaardbaar'," *ibid.*, 18 April 1995 which quotes Hans Oud's reaction. Cf. "Verzet tegen hotel mogelijk," *ibid.*, 18 April 1995. See Vink, "Toren Oud," *ibid.*, 21 January 1995, p 4b; "Nieuw hotel bij het Congresgebouw zeker." *ibid.*, 18 March 1995; "Bouw van hotel op dak Congresgebouw begonnen," *ibid.*, 2 April 1996; Maas, "Lichtvoetige 'Toren van Oud' voor eigenzinnige bewoners," *Cobouw*, 23 May 1996, p 5.

1108. *Rotterdams Dagblad*, "Gedenksteen voor nieuwbouw Kiefhoek." 1993, 8 November. Dutch: "Memorial stone for rebuilt Kiefhoek." News item.

1994
Books and Monographs.
1109. Blotkamp, Carel, *Mondriaan: Destructie als Kunst*, Zwolle, 1994. Dutch: *Mondrian: Destruction as Art.* Oud's collaboration in the "painting into architecture" experiments of De Stijl are discussed.

1110. Buch, Joseph and Tjeerd Boersma, *A Century of Dutch Architecture 1880/1990*, Rotterdam, 1994. English. Also published as *Een Eeuw Nederlandse Architectuur...*, 1993 (Dutch). The book is beautifully designed and thoroughly illustrated. But the English text—always arduous, sometimes glib—is mostly descriptive, repeating the information of the images, and the "underlying thesis" about continuity over the century is self-evident. Oud and De Stijl are included.

1111. Hartveld, Cita, *Moderne Zakelijkheid: efficiency in wonen en werken in Nederland 1918-1940*, Amsterdam, 1994. Dutch: *Modern Objectivity: efficient living and working in The Netherlands ...* Only passing reference is made to Oud in a section about the organization of the architectural profession and a page and a half given to the Witte Dorp and Kiefhoek in a discussion of the *Nieuwe Zakelijkheid.*

1112. Helmond, Toke van (ed.), *i10 Sporen van de Avant-garde*, Heerlen, 1994. Dutch: *i10 Tracks of the Avant-garde.* The collection of essays by and about the journal includes Oud's "Richtlijn" from the first issue.

1113. Hooff, Dorothee van, Jouke van der Werfe and Guy Goethals, *Langs Moderne Architectuur (1945-heden); architectuurroutes in Nederland en Belgie*, Utrecht, 1994. Dutch: *Following Modern Architecture (1945-present); architectural tours in Holland and Belgium.* The Shell Building (with a color photo of a detail); the Congress Building and the Christian High School are included in the tour of The Hague.

1114. Moscoviter, Herman, *Kwetsbare Schoonheid: monumenten in Rotterdam*, Delft, 1994. Dutch: *Fragile Beauty.* The semi-populist book is a sort of plea for preservation. Oud's important role in the city is set out; there are good images, including the rebuilt Café De Unie and the Oud-Mathenesse director's hut.

1115. Peter, John, *The Oral History of Modern Architecture*, New York, 1994. English. The well-illustrated book claims to be "the story of modern architecture in the words of those who created it." Transcribed extracts from a 1961 interview with Oud are cobbled together in a disconcerting way. There is a biographical note, a short track on the accompanying compact disc, a portrait and a view of Hoek van Holland.

1116. Schulze, Franz, *Philip Johnson. Life and Work*, New York, 1994. English. A rather cloying biography makes continual reference to Oud, his influence upon Johnson, and Johnson's evaluation of the Hollander's work. See Hilary Lewis and John O'Connor, *Philip Johnson. The architect in his own words*, New York, 1994.

1117. Vermeer, Gerrit and Bernard Rebel, *Historische Gids van Rotterdam*, The Hague, 1994. Dutch: *Historical Guide to Rotterdam*. A worthwhile guide includes Oud's Utrecht Insurance building and housing schemes, described in historical detail.

Journals
1118. Colenbrander, Bernard, "Anti-academic concepts. J.J.P. Oud's mock battle against eternal values." *Daidalos*, 1994, no 52, pp 98-107. German/English. The paper examines the philosophical influences upon Oud, mostly through his own reading, which returned him to "eternal values" in architecture. The Shell Building and Spangen (with an unrealized van Doesburg color design) are illustrated.

1119. Günther, Roland, "De Stijl and the tradition of Dutch urban culture." *Daidalos*, 1994, no 52, pp 83-93. German/English. Not seen.

1995
Books and Monographs
1120. Bergeijk, Herman van, *Willem Marinus Dudok*, Naarden, 1995. Dutch. The first comprehensive work on Dudok for 15 years is replete with archival illustrations, many in color, and a biography. It includes the Leiderdorp housing and also names Oud as collaborator on the *Leidsche Dagblad* building, a distinction he never claimed. Reviewed Dettingmeijer, *Jong Holland*, 1996, no 3.

1121. Bosma, Koos and Cor Wagenaar, *Een Geruisloze Doorbraak: de Geschiedenis van Architectuur en Stedebouw tijdens de Bezetting en de Wederopbouw van Nederland*, Rotterdam, 1995. Dutch: *A Silent Breakthrough: the History of Architecture and Urbanism since the Occupation and the Reconstruction of The Netherlands*. Most of this daunting book is concerned with regional developments 1945-1960. Oud is mentioned, although not as a major player.

1122. Es, Rob van, *'t Heb Wel Wat: De Kiefhoek, De Reconstructie van een Rijksmonument*, Rotterdam, 1995. Dutch: [idiom] ... *Kiefhoek. The Reconstruction of a National Monument*. The slim, populist book, illustrated with block plans, plans and monochromatic photographs, celebrates the event.

1123. Galfetti, Gustau Gili, *Casas Refugio/Private Retreats*, Barcelona, 1995. Spanish/English. The attractive book illustrates the notion of private retreats in terms of assembly, framing, siting and camouflaging by reference to buildings and projects by several architects. Oud's projected standardized holiday cottage for Beye and Co at Renesse is included.

1124. Gerwen, J.L.J.M. van and N.H.W. Verbeek, *Voorzorg en de Vruchten. Het Verzekeringsconcern AMEV: Zijn wortels en Vertakkingen van 1847 tot 1995*, Amsterdam 1995. Dutch: *The Fruits of Looking Ahead. The AMEV Assurance*

Company: Its roots and branches 1847-1995. In an indulgent book celebrating the company, P.J.J. [sic] Oud is identified as architect of the Utrechtse Life Insurance offices in Rotterdam. There is a view of the Coolsingel facade.

1125. Haar, Gert ter, *Vier Architectuurwandelingen door de Rotterdamse Binnestad*, Rotterdam, 1995. Dutch: *Four Architectural Walks in Inner Rotterdam.* There is a brief history of the former Spaarbank.

1126. Ibelings, Hans, *20th Century Architecture in The Netherlands*, Rotterdam, 1995. English. Also published as *Nederlandse Architectuur van de 20ste Eeuw* and *Niederlandische Architektur des 20. Jahrhunderts*, Munich. An attractive picture book sets out the century by decades, each series of color and monochromatic images being introduced by a few jargon-free paragraphs. Several of Oud's buildings are illustrated and there is a inaccurate paragraph of biography.

1127. Kleijn, Koen, Jos Smit and Claudia Thunnissen, *Nederlandse Bouwkunst*, Alphen a/d Rijn, 1995. Dutch: *Netherlands Architecture.* The semi-populist book contains a longish passage about Kiefhoek (illustrated in color) and further references to Oud.

1128. Küper, Marijke, *Het Stadhuis van Almelo: het laatste ontwerp van J.J.P. Oud*, Almelo, 1995. Dutch: *Almelo Town Hall: Oud's last design.* A carefully researched little book sets out the history of the project and evaluates the building. There are many illustrations, some in color.

1129. Lange, Eric de, *Sober en Solide*, Rotterdam, 1995. Dutch: *Sober and Solid.* The book is about reconstruction in the Netherlands after World War II. Oud's contribution to the polemic, but not the architecture, is noted in passing.

1130. Mattie, Erik and Jan Derwig, *Functionalism in The Netherlands*, Amsterdam, 1995. Dutch/ English. The slim volume contains more than 50 of Derwig's color photographs of many restored buildings beside archival images. It discusses the nature of the *Nieuwe Bouwen*, exposing Oud's apolitical stance and his views on the informants of design, and giving a brief overview of his career 1918-late 1930s. Illustrations include Kiefhoek, Hoek van Holland and the rebuilt De Unie.

1131. Perrée, Rob and Sonja Herst (eds.), *Honderd Jaar Nederlands Stoelontwerp*, Breda, 1995. Dutch: *One Hundred Years of Dutch Chair Design.* As the novel catalog of an exhibition at *De Beyerd*, Breda, July-August 1996, an essay introduces color postcards of the exhibits, including Oud's *fauteuil* of 1934.

1132. Postma, Frans and Cees Boekraad, *26, rue du Départ. Mondriaans atelier Parijs 1921-1936.* Berlin, 1995. Dutch. A study of Mondrian's Paris atelier includes several pages of letters to Oud, 1921-22. Oud's projects for boulevard housing, the Purmerend factory and the Kallenbach house are illustrated

1133. Taverne, Ed R.M. and Dolf Broekhuizen, *Het Shell-gebouw van J.J.P. Oud: ontwerp en receptie*, Rotterdam. 1995. Dutch/English: *Oud's Shell Building: design and reception.* The title describes the approach and content of this thorough, illustrated monograph which addresses the commission, design, and construction. The building is evaluated and there is an examination of public, and national and international professional response. Reviewed Roos, "Verfoeilijke ornamentiek!" *Trouw*, 19 December 1995; Postmaa, "Een schelp als steen des aanstoots," *Haagsche Courant*, 23 December 1995, p 3; "Het Shell-gebouw in Den Haag van J.J.P. Oud," *Architectuurkrant*, January/February 1996.

1134. Timmer, Petra, *Metz & Co: de Creatieve Jaren*, Rotterdam, 1995. Dutch: *Metz and Co: the Creative Years* (English summary). The well-designed, extensively illustrated history of the furniture and furnishings company includes. Oud among many architects who designed for Metz. Several of his tubular steel chairs are illustrated and discussed, as is his relationship with the principals.

Journals

1135. Bosshard, Hans Rudolf, "Aussenbeschriftungen; Wahrnemung und Lebsbarkeit von Schrift in Stadbild." *Archithese*, vol 25, 1995, January-February, pp 8-13. There is passing reference to Oud, and the Café De Unie is illustrated.

1136. Fernandez-Galiano, Luis et al., "Vivienda Europea." *A&V Monografias*, 1995, no 56, pp 2-110. Special issue.[European housing.] Not seen.

1137. Koekebakker, Olof, "Monumenten koesteren: dilemma's bij het behoud van moderne monumenten." *Items*, vol 14, 1995, no 2, pp 52-58; 64-65. Dutch: "Cherishing architectural heritage: the dilemmas of preserving modern examples." The rebuilding of Kiefhoek is cited as an example of Holland's problem with the universal issues of integrity, re-use, economics and so on.

1138. Meurs, Paul, "Neo-Oud or Neo-Modern?" *Archis*, 1995, January, pp 4ff. Dutch/English. The essay explores the validity of demolition and reconstruction as a "radical form of architectural conservation." There is a photograph of the reconstructed Kiefhoek. See Beerda, "Rotterdam: restauratie van een jong monument." *Stedenbouw*, vol 46, 1994, no 512, pp 29-31; "Kiefhoek officieel opgeleveerd," *Rotterdams Dagblad*, 29 December 1995. For populist assessment see e.g., van Es, "De Kiefhoek staat weer," *Vrij Nederland*, 21 October 1995; Maandag, "De Kiefhoek van Oud is weer een wijk van vlees and bloed," *Rotterdams Dagblad*, 23 December 1995.

1996
Books and Monographs

1139. Bergvelt, Ellinoor et al. (eds.), *From Neo-renaissance to Post-modernism*, Rotterdam, 1996. English/Dutch. The lush book is subtitled "A hundred and twenty-five years of Dutch interiors." Marijke Küper, "Space dissolved in color," discusses De Stijl , including Oud's collaboration with van Doesburg in *De Vonk*. There are several references to Oud.

1140. Blotkamp, Carel (ed.), *De Vervolgjaren van De Stijl, 1922-1932*, Amsterdam/Antwerp, 1996. What may be taken as a sequel to *De Beginjaren van De Stijl* deals with the subsequent careers of members in a number of discrete essays, including Taverne and Broekhuizen, "The dissident architects: [...Oud, Wils and van 't Hoff]." Oud's name recurs throughout the well-researched, appropriately illustrated book.

1141. Ibelings, Hans, *The Modern Fifties and Sixties*, Rotterdam, 1996. Dutch/ English. The catalog of an exhibition at the NAi, Rotterdam, June-July 1996 includes an essay on post-war modernity, accompanying images to demonstrate the "spread of contemporary [sic] architecture over The Netherlands." Oud's Utrecht Insurance offices, Rotterdam are illustrated.

1142. Knorre, Alexander von and Gudrun Peltz (eds.), *Niederländsche Architektur von 1900 bis 1940*, Herne, 1996. German. *Dutch Architecture 1900-1940*. The catalog of an exhibition at the Städtische Galerie, Herne, June-August 1996 includes Michael Henning, "Niederländsche Architektur im Umkreis von De Stijl und Neuer Sachlichkeit (1917-1940)."

1143. Kurrent, Friedrich (ed.), *Raummodelle: Wohnhauser des 20. Jahrhunderts*, Salzburg, 1996. German: *Architectural Models. 20th Century Houses*. The book documents 200 architectural "massing" models of significant works. There are brief notes about each; Oud's Weissenhofsiedlung houses are illustrated.

1144. Langmead, Donald, *Willem Marinus Dudok: a Dutch Modernist*, Westport, 1996. English. The 1,200 bibliographic entries in this work are presented alphabetically by decades and further by genres. Each is summarized, described, and evaluated in the context of a critical overview of Dudok's career. There is a critical introductory essay, a list of works and a guide to archival sources

1145. Langmead, Donald, *Dutch Modernism: Architectural Resources in the English Language*, Westport, 1996. English. A critical guide to the English-language literature demonstrates the importance of the Dutch contribution to twentieth century architecture; it summarizes, describes, and evaluates 1,250 references in the light of contemporary theory and practice. There is an introductory essay, and a list of key works of the period 1900-1940.

1146. Molema, Jan, *The New Movement in the Netherlands*, Rotterdam, 1996. English. The well illustrated book contains useful notes on the historiography of Modernism by Maristella Casciato, and two essays on the American connection: Christopher Vernon, "Berlage in America" and Leonard Eaton's introduction to the catalog *Americana* (1975). Six pages, mostly images, are dedicated to Oud.

1147. Nerdinger, Winfried and Cornelius Tafel, *Architectural Guide Germany. 20th Century*, Basel, 1996. English. Also published as *Guida all' Architettura Novocento Germania*, Milan, 1996. The Weissenhofsiedlung is included in this useful book. The brief text is clear and there are plans and an external view of Oud's row houses.

1148. Laan, Barbara et al., *Collectie Gispen: meubels, lampen en archivalia in het NAi, 1916-1980,* Rotterdam, 1996. Dutch: *The Gispen Collection: furniture, lamps and archivalia at the NAi.* This is the catalog of an exhibition held at the

NAi. Historical essays about the firm W.H.Gispen and Co and its successors follow an introduction about the admissibility of utilitarian objects into the realm of design. Oud's pianolamp is included. There are biographies.

1149. Weston, Richard, *Modernism*, London, 1996. English. The book begins with a disclaimer: it is not a history. Although it is stunningly designed and replete with images, its organization is difficult to discern. Most of De Stijl artists are identified and illustrated, including Oud's Café De Unie and Weissenhofsiedlung; there is a cohesive section on the group in chapter 3.

Journals

1150. Adam, Hubertus, "Die Rückkehr der runden Formen." *Bauten*, 1996, May, p 64-65. German: "The return of the round forms." The article emphasizes Hitchcock's role in establishing Oud's international reputation in modern architecture. Several works are mentioned but the piece focuses upon Hoek van Holland, of which there are six views and a site plan.

1151. Fuchs, Hans, "Soepel omgaan met de grenzen van het bouwbesluit; toren gerenoveerd in de geest van Oud." *Bouwwereld*, vol 92, 1996, 22 November, pp 14-15. Not seen.

1152. Stigter, Bianca, "Dibbets: Monument op de Dam moet menselijker." *NRC-Handelsblad*, 1996, 27 February, pp 1, 7. Dutch: "Dam monument must be more humane." The piece reports artist Jan Dibbets' proposal for altering the National Monument. For a response from Hans Oud, see de Lange, "'Het is geen Lego dat anders in elkaar kan'," *Parool*, 29 February; der Nederlanden and Verkerk, "Op zoek naar respect," *ibid.*, 2 March and van de Wint, "Monument is meer dan een kunstwerk," *NRC-Handelsblad*, 5 March. See also "Fuchs wil 'gedateerd' monument vervangen," *Haagsche Courant*, 5 February; "Verandering van Dam-monument niet uitgesloten," *NRC-Handelsblad*, 28 February.

1153. Wagt, Wim de, "'Restauratie Nationaal Monument wordt kostbare geschiedenis'." *Rotterdamsche Dagblad*, 1996, 16 January. Dutch: "Restoration of the National Monument is becoming costly history." A news item about the deterioration of the travertine used on the Dam monument is one of many. See, e.g., Schenk, "Ontwerper monument kende risico's steensoort," *Volkskrant*, 11 January 1996, p 7; "Monument op de Dam brokkelt af," *Parool*, 9 January 1996; "'Beeld vervangen of in hars zetten'," *Parool*, 10 January; "Monument op de dam in verval," *Utrechts Nieuwsblad*, 10 January; "Kalksteen monumentale blunder?," *Telegraaf*, 10 January; "Monument wordt weer onderzocht," *Parool*, 12 January; Huyskens, "Monument," *Algemeen Dagblad*, 13 January. An idea of the emotional issues (including the engagement of a German contractor), the practical and logistical problems and the restoration can be gained from e.g., Bosman and Koelewijn, "Onderdelen monument anders dan bouwtekening," *Parool*, 8 June; "Monument op de Dam wordt deels gesloopt," *Parool*, 7 June; "Monument wordt gedemonteerd," *NRC-Handelsblad*, 8 June; "National Monument op Dam in de steigers," *Cobouw*, 29 February 1996.

1997

Books and monographs

1154. Johnson, Donald Leslie and Donald Langmead, *Makers of 20th Century Modern Architecture*, Westport, 1997. English. The most influential twentieth century architects espousing modernism are brought together in critical discussion and independent profiles through a short examination of the design work of each, an essay outlining the historical course that confirms his or her vital position, and a bibliography at the end of each profile.There is a four page entry on Oud, and connections are made with his De Stijl associates.

Journals

1155. Vries, Jan de, "Allen in alles aan één problem." *Jong Holland*, vol 13, 1997, no 2, pp 48-53. Dutch: "All in all a single problem." English summary. The piece is about correspondence between members of the European avant-garde, 1919-22. Some of van Doesburg's letters to Oud are included.

1156. Wagenaar, Cor, "J.J.P. Oud: 'Ich pfeife auf die Wohnmachine!'" *Jong Holland*, vol 13, 1997, no 2, pp 54-58. Dutch: ... "Oud: 'I whistle on the machine-for-living!'" English summary. The author is presently making (1998) a serious study of Oud's voluminous correspondence; the essay deals with housing design around the end of the 1920s and publishes letters to Edgar Wedepohl (October 1927) and one Schneider (September 1930). Both are in German. The Kiefhoek church and the Weissenhofsiedlung are illustrated.

1157. Scrivano, Paolo, "J.J.P. Oud and Dutch architecture in the writings of Henry-Russell Hitchcock." *Zodiac*, no 18, 1997-98, September-February, pp 90-103. English/Italian. The title explains the content of a well documented essay. There is a portrait of Oud from Hitchcock's 1931 monograph and other poor quality illustrations.

Guide to Archives

Introduction

The archives of J.J.P. Oud have been widely dispersed. However, by far the largest amount of material is housed at the *Nederlands Architectuurinstituut* (NAi), Museumpark, Rotterdam.

Other minor collections, mostly fragmentary assemblings of drawings, blueprints and photographs sold off by Oud's widow, are held by the Canadian Centre for Architecture, Montreal, Quebec and the library of the Royal Institute of British Architects, London. Other minor collections are located at The Hague *Gemeentemuseum*, the *Letterkundig Museum*, also in The Hague and the *Fondation Custodia, Institut Néerlandais*, Paris. These latter hold mostly letters. Oud's prodigious correspondence is widely scattered.

Oud archive, *Nederlands Architectuurinstituut*

The Oud collection at the NAi has been painstakingly accessioned and a substantial series list prepared. It is, of course, in Dutch. The following brief history of the archive is based upon that document.

The materials came into the possession of the Institute and its antecedent organization, the *Stichting Architectuurmuseum*, in four stages through the gift of Mrs. Annie Oud-Dinaux. In 1973 letters and other written material were donated, followed by drawings and photographs in 1974 and more drawings in 1978. After Mrs. Oud's death the remainder of the archive was passed in 1991 to the newly established NAi.

Sorting of the material began as early as 1973, when V.Kuiper, an art history student at the University of Amsterdam prepared a broad inventory of Oud's correspondence. Nothing more was done until 1980-81, when R.M. (Hans) Magdelijns of the Art History Institute at Leiden University and students from Groningen University's Institute for Art and Architectural History, Bernard Colenbrander and S. Hiddema completed the inventory of the written and printed materials. In the event, it seems that Magdelijns was given most of the credit.[1] In 1987 another art history student, S. Zeilich-Jensen, worked with Mrs. Oud to compile a descriptive list of drawing remaining in the Oud's Wassenaar house. There were the five separate lists of materials of various kinds that were then reworked and supplemented by two other lists by M. Boon to produce the comprehensive and very useful finding aid entitled "Plaatsinglijst Archief J.J.P. Oud," now available to researchers in the Study Hall of the NAi.

Organization of the collection

The *plaatsinglijst* was developed for two principal, connected reasons. The significant amount of material, especially drawings, stored out of order (probably because they were misfiled after use) and the poor physical condition of most of precluded further unnecessary handling by researchers. Rather than completely reorganizing the archive, material was "let lie", so to speak, indexed in separate lists. So for example, drawings related to a particular project may be found on up to four lists, indicating storage in different places. The *plaatsinglijst* provides an extremely useful double-page spread listing projects alphabetically and pinpointing the location of relevant documents in each part of the archive.

An introduction explains the idiosyncrasies of each list. There is little point in translating it here. It will suffice to describe its structure and the broad content of each part of the collection. The Oud archive is presently ordered as follows

List A   Mislocated drawings and photographs
List B   Correspondence
List C   Articles, lectures, reports of travel, personalia, etc.
List D   Publications etc. by and about Oud
List E   Drawings
List F   Drawings and general fragments; some exhibition material
List S   Drawings and general fragments; some exhibition material

In addition, there are architectural models by Oud, listed in the *Maquettecatalogus*, located in the NAi Study Hall, and several pieces of furniture he designed, simply in current use throughout the NAi building.

List A   Mislocated drawings and photographs

The section contains boxes of drawings and (blue)prints, boxes of colored architectural renderings; original drawings in mounts; large format photographs; small format photographs; drawings in portfolios; and rolled drawings in tubes. The material covers Oud's professional career, 1906-1962. The chronological series list indicates how many items of each kind relate to each project.

A. Oud-Hartog residence, Venediën 7, Purmerend
Residence, Herengracht 14, Purmerend
Beets residence, Purmerend
Brand residence, Beemster
Tennis clubhouse, Purmerend

Houses and Premises for *Vooruit* Laborers' Association, Purmerend
Residence, Julianastraat 54, Purmerend
Gerrit Oud residence, Aalsmeer
Schinkel Cinema, Purmerend
Van Lendt shop-house, Heemstede
Van Bakel shop-house, Heemstede
Houtman residence, Beemster
Moerbeek residence, Wheere
Workers' housing, Leiderdorp, Leiden (with W.M. Dudok)
Van Essen-Vinckers residence, Blaricum
Public bath house, Blaricum (design)
Nursing home, Hilversum (design)
Military accommodation, Den Helder (design)
Warehouse for G Oud Pzn & Co (design)
W de Geus residence, De Erven 3, Broek-in-Waterland
Renovation, Villa *Allegonda*, Katwijk aan Zee
Row houses, Strandboulevard, Scheveningen (design)
De Vonk holiday house, Noordwijkerhout
Emergency housing under railway viaduct, Rotterdam (design)
Spangen housing estate, Rotterdam
Double workers' housing in reinforced concrete (design)
Standardized housing for workers, Rotterdam (design)
Factory and bonded warehouse, Purmerend (design)
Spangen housing estate, Rotterdam
Tusschendijken housing estate
Dr Kallenbach residence, Berlin-Grünewald (design)
Emergency housing, Oud-Mathenesse
Director's site office, Oud-Mathenesse
Hoekwoningen (corner houses) (design)
Small transformer (design)
Row houses, Hoek van Holland
Café De Unie, Coolsingel, Rotterdam
Workers' housing, *Kiefhoek*, Rotterdam
Display case for Domela Nieuwenhuis Collection, Boymans-van Beuningen Museum, Rotterdam
Grave for E.T.J. Dinaux, Heemstede
Rotterdam Stock Exchange, (design)
Hotel Stiassni, Brno, Czechoslovakia (design)
Row houses, Weissenhofsiedlung, Stuttgart, Germany
House for three families, Brno, Czechoslovakia (design)
Apostolic Church, Kiefhoek, Rotterdam
Study interior for M.J.I. de Jonge van Ellemeet, Rotterdam
Johnson Villa, Pinehurst, North Carolina, U.S.A.
Blijdorp housing estate, Rotterdam
Chair and armchair designs for Metz & Co, Amsterdam

Architect's own study, Hillegersberg
Standard summer cottages for Beye and Co, Renesse
House on a deep allotment (design)
Group of six dwellings (design)
C.J.E. Dinaux residence, Haarlem
Residence, Blaricum
Pfeffer-De Leeuw residence, Blaricum
Renovations to library, Hannema residence, Rotterdam
Town hall, Amsterdam (design)
Interiors, S. S. *Nieuw Amsterdam*
Shell Building, The Hague
Reconstruction plan for Hofplein, Rotterdam (design)
Shops, dwellings and *Olveh* offices, Parkweg, Rotterdam (design)
Rotterdam Savings Bank
Commercial premises for Meddens & Co, Blaak, Rotterdam
Nederlandse Bank voor Zuid-Afrika Building, Pretoria, South Africa (design)
Offices, *Koninklijke Nederlandse Hoogovens en Staalfabrieken*, IJ-muiden (design)
Standardized workers' housing (design)
Meeting hall for the *Vrijzinnig Hervormden* Association, The Hague
National Military Monument *Grebbeberg*, Rhenen
ESVEHA office building, Delftsestraat, Rotterdam
National Monument, Amsterdam
Second *Vrijzinnig Christelijk* Lyceum, The Hague
Semidetached houses, Bloemendaal (design)
Redevelopment of St Laurens church and environs, Rotterdam (design)
Nationale Levensverzekeringsbank, Arnhem (design)
Service building, *Nederlandse Hervormde Kerk*, The Hague (design)
Polder clock tower, Emmeloord (design)
Zuid-Holland Province House, The Hague (design)
Presikhaaf housing estate, Arnhem (with van Hassel)
Renovations to office-factory *De Adelaar*, Apeldoorn
Development, Vredenburg, Utrecht
Bio-Vacantieoord, Arnhem
Office building for *De Utrecht* Life Insurance Co, Rotterdam
Development plan for Gemeentemuseum, The Hague (design)
Nederlands Congresgebouw
Municipal Library, Kiefhoek, Rotterdam (design)
Park keeper's house, *De Hoge Veluwe*, Otterloo (design)
Development plan for *Shell* offices
Town hall, Rhenen (design)
E. Plate residence, Voorburg (design)
Plan for an ideal city (design)

Development plan for Groningen town hall (design)
Almelo town hall

List B   Correspondence

The list identifies 210 cartons containing some 15,000 pieces of correspondence, January 1910-February 1963. It has been chronologically sorted, each bundle normally containing two months' worth of letters. Dr Cornelis Wagenaar of the Institute for Art and Architectural History at the University of Groningen is presently (1998) cataloging in detail the letters; his preliminary lists (not yet publicly available) summarize most items, and in some cases include citations.

List C   Articles, lectures, reports of travel, personalia, etc.

There are 78 boxes of diverse material in the series. Sixteen contain dated manuscripts of many of Oud's articles, 1922-1963. There are two more of undated manuscripts. Specific identified manuscripts include "Die Entwicklung der Moderne Baukunst in Holland; Vergangenheit, Gegenwart, Zukunft," first delivered as a lecture in Zurich, 1924 and *Architecturalia, voor Bouwheren en Architecten*, published in The Hague, 1963. There are also transcripts of lectures, interviews and radio and television talks, as well as documents and publications relating to professional associations, commissions, exhibitions of Oud's work, and assorted pieces by other writers. Descriptions are brief and general.

List D   Publications, etc. by and about Oud

The 123 items (some packets of material) are divided into six sections, although the basis for separation is difficult to discern. The list describes each in fine detail and attempts to date them. It thus facilitates research. As a general indication of content, the series includes offprints and clippings from Dutch and foreign architectural journals and newspapers, brochures and folders. There are critiques and book reviews, and several packets of photographs and postcards, mostly of architectural subjects, as well as such things as souvenir menus and concert programs. Some pieces Oud seems to have collected because they interested him; e.g., articles on Le Corbusier, Frank Lloyd Wright and other architects and artists.

List E   Drawings

The list covers fifty projects, described in adequate detail but arranged in no particular order. An example will serve to demonstrate the structure of classification: the first building in the series is The Netherlands Congress Building, The Hague, of 1956-63; it is among the best documented. The major division is into phases of the project: first design, 1956-58; second design, 1959; definitive design, 1960-63; studies; site building (*directiegebouw*), 1959. Drawings for each phase are then described and dated: for example, under first design, "plans and elevations, February-May 1957 (unnumbered), 9 sheets." The system serves to pinpoint the nature and extent of each item, and serves the researcher well. Where they are available, drawing numbers are recorded: working drawings, as opposed to design drawings, are also indicated. As well as various minor projects, the following are included (in the order in which they appear on the list):

Netherlands Congress Building, The Hague
Netherlands Bank for South Africa, Pretoria (preliminary design)
Shell Building, The Hague
Hofplein, Rotterdam (design)
Interiors, S.S. *Nieuw Amsterdam*
De Vonk, Noordwijkerhout
Gravestone for E.T.J. Dinaux and N.T. Oud-Jansen
Urban design for Vredenburg, Utrecht
Competition entry for Royal Dutch Steelworks offices
Kiefhoek housing
Apostolic Church, Kiefhoek
Tusschendijken housing
Spangen housing
Hoek van Holland housing
Weissenhofsiedlung row houses, Stuttgart
Rotterdam Savings Bank
National Military Monument *Grebbeberg*
National Monument in The Dam, Amsterdam
De Kleine Komedie, Voorburg
Plate house, Voorburg (design)
Almelo town hall
Rhenen municipal offices (design)
Secondary school, Delft (design)
Extensions to The Hague *Gemeentemuseum* (design)
Competition for polder tower, Emmelord
Villa *Allegonda*, Katwijk aan Zee
Semidetached houses, Bloemendaal (design)
Competition for South Holland Province House, The Hague
Pfeffer-de Leeuw residence, Blaricum
ESVEHA office building, Rotterdam (design)
Witte Dorp, Oud-Mathenesse
Second *Vrijzinnig Christelijk* Lyceum, The Hague
Shop house for Meddens and Son, Rotterdam (design)
Service building for *Hervormde* church, Oostduin (design)
Gatekeeper's house, Hoge Veluwe (design)
Presikhaaf housing estate, Arnhem (with van Hassel)
Double workers' housing in reinforced concrete (design)
Interiors for S.Ss. *Zaandam* and *Noordam*
De Utrecht Insurance Co offices, Rotterdam
Standardized workers' housing (design)
Olveh offices, Rotterdam (design)
Bio-Vacantieoord, Arnhem
 Study interior for M.J.I. de Jonge van Ellemeet, Rotterdam
Chair designs for Metz/Hannema/Trousselot
Design for architect's own house

List F   Drawings and general fragments; some exhibition material
The material covered by this list passed to the NAi after the death of Mrs. Oud. It was, according to the compiler of the *plaatsinglijst*, "roughly documented and packed." It is divided into six sections, containing a total of 135 cartons and packets. The following summarizes their content.

Section AD
Drawings, photographs, technical brochures and correspondence relating to several commissions, 1948-62.
Nine boxes of journal and newspaper clippings, including some in albums, relating mostly to Oud, but some to others. All are carefully identified in the list.
Texts and manuscripts of Oud's writings, some in albums.
Sketc.hbooks with portraits and holiday sketc.hes.
Family photo album.

Section VD
Five boxes of photographs, glass negatives, color transparencies and printed postcards of projects, realized buildings and furniture by Oud, arranged in no particular order; the subjects are listed box by box.
Four boxes of correspondence, photographs and documents of Mrs. Oud-Dinaux.

Section PD
Miscellaneous sketches of projects, realized buildings and furniture by Oud.
Exhibition material, including mounted photographs of projects, realized buildings and furniture by Oud.

Section PF
Drawings, sketches, ornament design and other documentation and accounts relating to the Shell Building, 1938-48
Miscellaneous design sketches.
Chair designs, 1933-35, 1947 and 1954.
Presentation drawings and design sketches for the *Nieuw Amsterdam, Zaandam* and *Noordam.*
Preliminary sketches for mostly domestic commissions, 1916-35.
Drawings and paintings made for Oud by Vilmos Huszar, John Rädecker and others, 1925-1942.
Mounted photos of several projects, realized buildings and furniture.

Section KK
Drawings of the Second *Vrijzinnig Christelijk Lyceum*, The Hague.

Section SB
Exhibition material, comprising 56 drawings from the period 1914-62 (buildings, typographical designs and life studies) and 15 photographs of major projects, 1920-41.

200 Oud and the International Style

List S   Drawings and general fragments; some exhibition material
The material covered by this list passed to the NAi after the death of Mrs. Oud. It is described in the *plaatsinglijst* as "loose fragments" and consists of miscellaneous incomplete manuscripts, unsorted correspondence, information about exhibitions and a few unidentified sketc.hed and design drawings.

As this bio-bibliography goes to press, the Oud archive at the NAi is being re-processed by Martien de Vletter and others, as part of a major Oud *manifestatie,* a joint venture of the NAi and the *Instituut voor Kunst en Architectuur Geschiedenis* of the University of Groningen, consisting of a number of publications and a major exhibition proposed to take place in The Netherlands towards the end of 2000.

The Canadian Centre for Architecture
The Centre has a substantial holding of Oud's work: almost 450 drawings, about 90 prints and 150 photographs.[2] The buildings and projects covered include

    Houses and Premises for *Vooruit* Laborers' Association, Purmerend
    Gerrit Oud residence, Aalsmeer
    Schinkel Cinema, Purmerend
    Van Lendt shop-house, Heemstede
    Van Bakel shop-house, Heemstede
    Workers' housing, Leiderdorp, Leiden (with W.M.Dudok)
    Van Essen-Vinckers residence, Blaricum
    Nursing home, Hilversum (design)
    Blaauw residence, Alkmaar
    Technical school, Den Helder
    W. de Geus residence, Broek-in-Waterland
    Renovation, Villa *Allegonda,* Katwijk aan Zee
    Row houses, Strandboulevard, Scheveningen (design)
    Spangen housing estate, Rotterdam
    Double workers' housing in reinforced concrete (design)
    Standardized housing for workers, Rotterdam (design)
    Factory and bonded warehouse, Purmerend (design)
    Tusschendijken housing estate
    Emergency housing, Oud-Mathenesse
    Director's site office, Oud-Mathenesse
    Row houses, Hoek van Holland
    Café De Unie, Coolsingel, Rotterdam
    Workers' housing, Kiefhoek, Rotterdam
    Rotterdam Stock Exchange (design)
    Hotel Stiassni, Brno, Czechoslovakia (design)
    Row houses, Weissenhofsiedlung, Stuttgart, Germany
    House for three families, Brno, Czechoslovakia (design)
    Apostolic Church, Kiefhoek, Rotterdam
    Study interior for M.J.I. de Jonge van Ellemeet, Rotterdam

Johnson Villa, Pinehurst, North Carolina, U.S.A.
Blijdorp housing estate, Rotterdam
Chair and armchair designs for Metz & Co, Amsterdam
Architect's own study, Hillegersberg
C.J.E. Dinaux residence, Haarlem
Pfeffer-De Leeuw residence, Blaricum
Interiors, S. S. *Nieuw Amsterdam*
Shell Building, The Hague
Reconstruction plan for Hofplein, Rotterdam (design)
Shops, dwellings and *Olveh* offices, Parkweg, Rotterdam (design)
Rotterdam Savings Bank
Offices, *Koninklijke Nederlandse Hoogovens en Staalfabrieken*, IJ-muiden (design)
National Military Monument *Grebbeberg*, Rhenen
National Monument, Amsterdam
Second *Vrijzinnig Christelijk* Lyceum, The Hague
Redevelopment, St Laurens church and environs, Rotterdam (design)
Polder clock tower, Emmeloord (design)
Almelo town hall

There are also thirty drawings of chairs, 1933-34, a further selection of forty-seven unidentified drawings and almost 200 issues of various architectural journals of the period 1915-65.

Royal Institute of British Architects, London
The holdings of the RIBA are relatively minor. The drawings, all of unexecuted designs, were presented to the library by Mrs. Oud-Dinaux in 1968.[3] There are three perspectives of the Kallenbach residence in Berlin-Grünewald, a single interior perspective of the living/dining area of the Johnson residence, Pinehurst, North Carolina and a site plan of the proposed Blijdorp housing development.

NOTES

1. Oege van der Wal, "Hans Magdelijns bracht orde in collectie-Oud," *Nieuws uit het Architectuurmuseum*, 1981, no 3.
2. I am indebted for this information to drs Dolf Broekhuizen of the Institute for Art and Architectural History, University of Groningen (McAtee to Broekhuizen, 30 May 1995).
3. James Bettley and Richard Raper (eds.),*Catalogue of the Drawings Collection of the Royal Institute of British Architects: a cumulative index*, Aldershot, 1989, pp 11-12.

List of Works

The list is compiled from three main sources: Hans Oud, *J.J.P. Oud Architekt 1890-1963: feiten en herinnerigen gerangschikt*, Den Haag, 1984; Umberto Barbieri, *J.J.P. Oud*, Rotterdam, 1987; and Giovanni Fanelli, *Moderne Architectuur in Nederland 1900-1940*, The Hague, 1978. Variations are noted. Numbers below the listed works refer to relevant bibliography entries.

Early Career 1906-1918

1906	A. Oud-Hartog residence, Venetiën 7, Purmerend. Barbieri gives Oud-Hertog.
1907-08	Residence, Herengracht 14, Purmerend. Omitted by Hans Oud.
1910	Beets residence, Herengracht 23, Purmerend. 003.
1910-12	Brand residence, Zuiderweg 89, Beemster. Barbieri gives Southeastern Beemster.
1911	Houses and premises for *Vooruit* Laborers' Association, Julianastraat, Purmerend. Barbieri gives Wilhelminalaan 10. 004, 782, 870.
	Tennis clubhouse, Purmerend (design only). Omitted Barbieri.
1912	Residence, Julianastraat 54, Purmerend.
1912	Gerrit Oud residence, Uiterweg 45, Aalsmeer (altered). 010, 021.
1912	Schinkel cinema, Dubbele Buurt 16, Purmerend (altered). 011, 782, 826.

204 Oud and the International Style

1913
: Van Lendt shop-house, Kerkstraat, Heemstede (demolished). Barbieri gives Raadhuisstraat.
783.

1914
: Van Bakel shop-house, Binnenweg 41, Heemstede (altered).
783.

Houtman residence, Zuiderweg 110, Beemster (demolished). Barbieri gives Zuiderweg 9, South-eastern Beemster.

Moerbeek residence, Wheere, Purmerend (demolished).

1914-15
: Workers' housing, Leiderdorp, Leiden (with W.M.Dudok) (demolished). Barbieri gives 1914-16, Fanelli 1915-16.
012, 043, 797, 1120.

1915
: Van Essen-Vinckers residence, Mathijssenhoutweg 37, Blaricum. Barbieri gives address as Houtweg 37.
014, 021, 850.

Public bath house, Blaricum (competition entry; design only).
230, 783.

Nursing home, Hilversum (competition entry; design only).
783.

Military housing, Den Helder (competition entry; design only).
783.

1915-16
: Warehouse for G. Oud Pzn & Co, Purmerend (design only).
696.

1916
: W. de Geus residence, De Erven 3, Broek-in-Waterland. Fanelli gives design only.
827, 952, 967.

Blaauw residence, Alkmaar (design only).

Three row houses, Zutphensestraat 11-15, Velp (altered). Fanelli gives design only.
812.

Technical trade school, Den Helder (competition entry; design only). Barbieri gives 1916-17.

1916-17
: Renovation/conversion, villa *Allegonda*, Boulevard 1, Katwijk aan Zee (with Menso Kamerlingh Onnes and Theo van Doesburg). Barbieri gives 1917-27 but see below.
024, 029, 031, 044, 048, 050, 086, 089, 091, 209, 246, 250, 284, 305, 329, 353, 420, 462, 485, 557, 644, 683, 741, 743, 783, 799, 817, 820, 844, 899, 908, 942, 951-952, 967, 990, 1038, 1070, 1073.

List of Works 205

1917 Renovation jhr. A. Rappard residence, Rapenburg 45, Leiden.

Row houses, Strandboulevard, Scheveningen (design only).
017, 050, 066, 098, 569, 570, 638-639, 647, 691, 720, 752, 783, 790, 806, 811, 837, 849, 934, 938, 1004, 1132.

1917-18 *De Vonk* holiday house, Westeinde 34, Noordwijkerhout (with Theo van Doesburg and Harm Kamerlingh Onnes).
023, 030-031, 041, 047, 050, 098, 104, 114, 311, 462, 474, 486, 647, 746, 826, 791, 817, 827, 831, 875, 899-901, 951-952, 967, 1007, 1017, 1033-1034, 1038, 1070, 1139.

Chief Housing Architect, Rotterdam Municipality, 1918-1933
Oud's private commissions are shown in bold type.

1918 Spangen housing estate, Blocks I and V, Spaanse Bocht, Rotterdam. Barbieri gives street names.
031, 040, 050, 057, 065, 085, 090, 091, 096, 103, 107, 115, 126, 185, 229, 249-250, 643, 676, 784, 786, 800, 806, 815, 844-845, 848-849, 882, 901, 938, 942, 952, 983, 967, 1007, 1034, 1068, 1070, 1072, 1118.

Double workers' housing in reinforced concrete (design only).
032, 039, 074, 168, 718, 797, 800, 972, 1060.

Standardized housing for workers (design only).
020, 026, 068, 754.

Emergency housing under railway viaduct, Rotterdam (design only).

1919 **Studio in the sand dunes, Katwijk aan Zee, for Theo van Doesburg** (design only). Barbieri gives date as 1924.
024, 029, 284, 844.

Factory and bonded warehouse, Purmerend (design only).
047, 050, 058, 074, 136, 154, 423, 513, 516, 536, 555, 569, 575, 632, 638-639, 644, 647, 656, 711, 734, 742, 765, 789, 791, 823, 866, 875, 926, 1132.

1919-20 Spangen housing estate, Blocks VIII and IX, Spaanse Bocht, Rotterdam, (demolished). Barbieri gives all street names.
071, 095, 164, 234, 1055.

1920-23 Tusschendijken housing, Rösener Manzstraat and side streets, Rotterdam (with van Doesburg and Rietveld) (demolished). Barbieri gives dates as 1920-21 and Fanelli as 1920.
031, 065, 088, 091, 093, 095-096, 103, 106-107, 112, 115, 118, 131, 133, 136-137 160, 164, 173, 176, 186, 201, 211, 229, 312, 356, 570, 638, 723, 773, 800, 849, 884, 1098.

206   Oud and the International Style

1922	**Dr Kallenbach residence, Berlin-Grünewald** (design only). 054, 058, 063, 074, 092, 617, 854, 1132.
1922-23	Emergency housing, Oud-Mathenesse (the *Witte Dorp*), Schiedamseweg, Rotterdam (demolished). Barbieri gives date as 1922 and Fanelli as 1922. 070, 073-074, 077, 080, 087, 091, 097, 106, 108, 110, 112, 115, 118, 126-127, 136-137, 160, 173, 176, 187, 194, 223, 244-245, 304, 351, 356, 375, 379, 471, 529, 557, 570, 712, 739, 750, 782, 784, 796, 800, 848, 938, 941, 959, 962, 965-966, 970, 981, 983, 996, 1025, 1029, 1047, 1078, 1083, 1089, 1111.
1923	Director's site office, *Witte Dorp*, Rotterdam (demolished). 072-074, 084, 089, 311, 489, 513, 628, 682, 696, 712, 721, 760, 789, 888, 917, 940, 1070, 1082-1083, 1089, 1114. *Hoekwoningen* (corner houses) (design only). (Noted Barbieri, omitted by Hans Oud. Small transformer house (design only). (Noted Barbieri; omitted by Hans Oud.
1924-27	Row houses, 2de Scheepvaartstraat 91-113, Hoek van Holland. Barbieri gives 1924. 058, 091, 098, 119, 133-134, 136, 144, 147, 152, 154, 158, 165-166, 168-170, 173, 175-177, 181, 184, 187, 189-190, 192-193, 196, 198, 201-202, 208, 211, 213, 216, 219, 221, 223, 227, 233-234, 238-239, 242, 246, 249, 251, 253, 262, 274-276, 291, 304, 311, 326-327, 330, 338, 339, 342, 347, 349, 364, 375, 380, 425, 457-458, 471, 516, 522-524, 527, 538, 555, 557, 570, 581, 640, 670, 681, 697, 699, 718, 720, 723-724, 731, 742, 745, 759, 765, 768, 775, 778, 800, 811, 815, 828, 835, 861, 869, 886, 889, 892, 895, 902, 924, 943, 961, 977, 1000, 1060, 1087, 1115, 1130, 1150.
1924-26	**People's University, Rotterdam** (design only). Barbieri gives 1924-27.
1925	**Café De Unie, Coolsingel, Rotterdam** (demolished). Rebuilt on new site 1986. Both Barbieri and Fanelli give date as 1924. 098, 100, 118, 124-125, 128, 131, 311, 333, 447, 462, 489, 493, 535, 551, 557, 601, 621, 632, 641, 696, 712, 720, 741-742, 768, 868, 888, 914, 923, 934, 938, 940, 943, 952, 956-957, 963, 965, 967, 981, 988, 993-994, 996-997, 1000, 1050, 1054, 1056, 1070, 1072, 1082, 1096, 1114, 1130, 1135, 1149.
1925-29	Workers' housing, Kiefhoek, Groene Hilledijk, Rotterdam (altered). Barbieri gives Kiefhoekstraat and Lindtstraat. 182, 185, 213, 215-218, 220, 222-223, 225, 228, 231-233, 236,

238-241, 244, 247, 249, 251, 253-254, 259-260, 262, 264, 271-272, 274, 294, 327, 328, 342, 356, 363-364, 351, 373, 375, 425-426, 438, 444, 459, 466, 471, 474-475, 488, 494, 516, 521-522, 524, 529, 538-539, 555, 557, 559, 570, 591, 618, 632, 639, 653, 656, 661, 667, 670, 681, 686, 639, 742, 753, 759, 764, 768, 773, 778, 784, 793, 796, 800, 806, 815, 850, 879, 894, 900, 918, 936, 943-944, 952, 961, 963, 965, 968, 977, 992, 1032-1033, 1035-1036, 1044, 1058, 1060, 1042, 1064, 1066, 1068, 1072, 1076, 1080, 1092, 1094, 1101, 1108, 1111, 1122, 1127, 1130, 1137-1138, 1156.

Display case for Domela Nieuwenhuis Collection, Boymans Museum, Rotterdam.
093, 109.

Tomb for E. T. J. Dinaux, Heemstede.

1926 **Rotterdam Stock Exchange, Coolsingel, Rotterdam** (competition entry; design only).
136, 144, 179, 203, 242, 308, 338, 824, 850, 934, 1006.

Hotel Stiassni, Brno, Czechoslovakia (competition entry; design only).
187.

1927 **Row houses, Weissenhofsiedlung, Stuttgart, Germany.**
098, 114, 132, 135-136, 144-145, 148-149, 152-154, 156, 161, 163, 165, 188, 201, 209, 211, 243, 249, 262, 267, 271, 276-277, 324, 353, 363, 366, 469, 484, 486, 513, 527, 557, 571, 632, 589, 687, 699, 712, 713, 726, 748, 769, 791, 756-757, 780, 786, 790, 799, 801, 821, 832, 842, 855, 871, 884, 887, 893, 908, 915, 916, 916, 922, 927, 931, 933, 954, 963, 965, 976-978, 1003, 1009, 1018-1019, 1028, 1032-1033, 1042, 1056, 1063-1064, 1071, 1086-1087, 1143, 1147, 1149, 1156.

1927-31 **Renovations villa *Allegonda*, Boulevard, Katwijk aan Zee.**

1928 **House for three families, Brno, Czechoslovakia** (design only).

1928-29 **Restored Apostolic Church, Eemstein 23, Kiefhoek.**
217, 236, 240, 249, 259, 264, 289, 328, 337, 342, 471, 485, 484, 538, 557, 618, 632, 639, 656, 681, 723, 854, 1087, 1156.

1930 Study interior for M.J.I. de Jonge van Ellemeet, Rotterdam (demolished). Barbieri gives 1931; Fanelli incorrectly gives H.J.I. as client's initials.

1931 **Johnson Villa, Pinehurst, North Carolina, U.S.A.** (design only).
257, 342, 752.

208 Oud and the International Style

1931-32   Blijdorp housing estate, Rotterdam (design only). Both Barbieri and Fanelli give date as 1931.
299, 648, 657, 775, 802, 806, 824, 845, 866, 965.

Private practice 1933-1963

1931-35   Chair and armchair designs for Metz & Co, Amsterdam.

1933   Architect's own study, Hillegersberg, Rotterdam (demolished).
291, 314, 348, 353, 361.

Standard summer cottages for Beye and Co, Renesse (design only).

House on a deep allotment (design only).

1934   Group of six dwellings (design only).

C.J. E. Dinaux residence, Haarlem (design only).

Letterbox and doorknob for Koninklijke Begeer, Voorschoten (design only). Omitted by both Barbieri and Fanelli.

1934-35   Studio houses, Hillegersberg, Rotterdam (design only).

1935   Residence, Blaricum (design only). Omitted by both Barbieri and Fanelli.

1936   Pfeffer-De Leeuw residence, Blaricum (design only).

Polderhuis entrance, Wilhelminapolder (with Hans Richters) (design only). Omitted by both Barbieri and Fanelli.

Renovations to library, Hannema residence, Haringvliet, Rotterdam (demolished). Fanelli gives "design for a house," 1934-36. Omitted Barbieri.
299, 314, 506.

1937   Town hall, Amsterdam (competition entry; design only).
318, 434, 854.

1937-38   Interiors, S.Ss. *Nieuw Amsterdam*, *Noordam* and *Zaandam* for the Holland-America Line (scrapped). Barbieri and Fanelli both give the *Nieuw Amsterdam* only.
334, 337, 339, 341-342, 344-346, 362, 506, 722, 862.

1938-46   Headquarters Building, B.I.M. (*Bataafsche Import Maatschappij*), later the Shell Co), Wassenaarseweg 80, The Hague. Barbieri and Fanelli both give 1938-42.
354, 359, 360, 338, 339, 341, 350, 354, 359, 360, 362-363, 368, 370-375, 377, 423-424, 427, 449, 463, 466, 471, 480, 482, 484, 485, 503, 506, 521-522, 557, 568, 570, 572, 589-590, 598, 606, 625, 631-632, 635, 671, 691, 738, 850, 851, 892, 903, 909, 934,

List of Works 209

            949, 975, 1005, 1013, 1082, 1094, 1100, 1102, 1106, 1113, 1118, 1133.

1941-43   Reconstruction plan for Hofplein, Rotterdam (design only). Both Barbieri and Fanelli give 1942-43.
            049, 348, 428, 616, 847, 853, 934, 1099.

1942-43   Shops, dwellings and *Olveh* offices, Parkweg, Rotterdam (design only). Omitted by Fanelli.

1942-50   Rotterdam Savings Bank, Botersloot 25, Rotterdam (with A. A. van Nieuwenhuizen).
            441, 451, 506, 587, 1079, 1106.

1944   Commercial premises for Meddens & Co, Blaak, Rotterdam (design only). Omitted by Fanelli.

1946   Bank building for *Nederlandse Bank voor Zuid-Afrika*, Pretoria, South Africa (consultancy; design only). Omitted by Fanelli.

1947-48   Offices, *Koninklijke Nederlandse Hoogovens en Staalfabrieken*, IJmuiden (competition entry; design only).
            89, 482.

            Standardized workers' housing (design only).

1948   Meeting hall for the *Vrijzinnig Hervormden* Association, The Hague. (design only).

            National Military Monument *Grebbeberg*, Rhenen.
            372, 378, 891, 1039.

1948-50   *ESVEHA* office building, Delftsestraat, Rotterdam. Barbieri gives 1947-50.
            365, 444, 446, 472, 476, 510.

1949   National Monument, Damplein, Amsterdam (with sculptor John Rädecker).
            372, 439, 519, 526, 562, 984, 1039, 1152, 1153.

1949-56   Second *Vrijzinnig Christelijk* Lyceum, Goudsbloemlaan/ Segbroeklaan, The Hague.
            516, 528, 635.

1950   Redevelopment of St Laurens church and surrounding area, Rotterdam (design only).
            388, 396, 824, 913.

1950   Semidetached houses, Bloemendaal (design only).

1951   *Nationale Levensverzekeringsbank*, Velperplein, Arnhem (design only).

210 Oud and the International Style

Service building, *Nederlandse Hervormde Kerk*, Oostduin, The Hague (design only).
361.

Polder clock tower, Emmeloord (design only).

South Holland Province House, The Hague (design only).
481, 482, 503, 510, 518, 540, 642, 647.

1951-53	Woonwijk Presikhaaf housing estate (360 houses), Arnhem (with van Hassel)
1951-52	Renovations to office-factory *De Adelaar*, Apeldoorn. Barbieri gives 1951, design only. Omitted by Fanelli.
1951-61	Development, Vredenburg, Utrecht (supervision) (demolished). Barbieri gives 1951-63, design only. Omitted by Fanelli. 376, 809.
1952-60	*Bioherstellingsord*, Wekeromseweg 6, Arnhem. 518, 711, 892.
1954-61	Office building for *De Utrecht* Life Insurance Co, Coolsingel 75-77, Rotterdam. 503, 509, 510, 518, 574, 588, 600, 602, 612, 630, 673, 702, 816, 851, 1014, 1062, 1117, 1124, 1141.
1956-62	Development plan for The Hague Gemeentemuseum, (consultant). Barbieri gives 1956-59, design only. Omitted by Fanelli.
1956-69	*Nederlands Congresgebouw*, The Hague. (Executed under supervision of Hans Oud.) Barbieri gives 1956-63, Fanelli 1956 -. 540, 543, 546, 552, 585, 634, 651, 648, 663, 664, 674, 680, 707, 709, 710, 715, 727, 778, 814, 880, 907, 974, 995, 1015, 1061, 1107.
1957	Library, Kiefhoek, (design only). Omitted by Fanelli.
1958	Park keeper's house, *De Hoge Veluwe*, Otterloo (design only). 934.
1959	Development plan for *Shell* offices, Wassenaarseweg 80, The Hague, (with Hans Oud). Omitted by both Barbieri and Fanelli.
1959-60	Town hall, Rhenen (design only). Omitted by Fanelli.
1960	E. Plate residence, Park Leeuwenstein, Voorburg (design only).
1961	Plan for an ideal city (design only). Omitted by Fanelli.
	Development plan for Groningen town hall (design only). Omitted by Fanelli.

1962-73 Town hall, Stadhuisplein 1, Almelo. Both Barbieri and Fanelli give design dates only as 1962-63.

J.J.P. Oud's Library

Oud and his wife Annie moved to the fashionable town of Wassenaar near The Hague in 1953. She continued to live there after his death in 1963 until she also passed away in 1990. The house was sold at auction in June 1991.[1] Some time in the 1980s the *Rijksdienst voor de Monumentenzorg* (National Service for the Preservation of Monuments) commissioned the architectural historian Bernard Colenbrander and a student assistant to list the titles in Oud's library in the Wassenaar house. A handwritten inventory, rather quaintly identifying the location of the books by reference to the decor of the room, was prepared. Since then there has been a major reorganization of the Service's constituents, one of which has metamorphosed into the *Nederlands Architectuur-instituut* (NAi).

After some delay the list was passed to a contract secretarial firm for typing, and the NAi temporarily lost track of it. Pressure of business meant that when it eventually recovered there were no resources available to check its accuracy as to the spelling of authors' names, dates of publication and so on. They were many, because the transcription was made by people with little or no knowledge of the fields covered by the books.

For those reasons it remained very much a provisional list and the NAi intended to revise it when (as they optimistically and mistakenly expected) the library would pass to them after Mrs. Oud-Dinaux's death. That did not happen, although part of the collection is now in the Oud archive at the NAi, Rotterdam.[2] It has not been accessioned or even sorted at the time of writing (early 1998); indeed, some of slimmer volumes and offprints remain in cartons.

Thus, the information that follows is based on the provisional list. A few editorial changes have been made—correction of misspelt names and addition of bibliographical details when available and unambiguous—by consulting the catalogs of the Delft Technological University Library and the Library of Congress of the United States of America.

According to his widow, Oud was an avid book collector.[3] That is borne out by the diversity of the nearly 3,000 volumes on the list. While about half are about art, architecture and design—around 500 on architecture—there are also poetry anthologies, psychiatric treatises, and fiction including English language detective stories and the children's books of A.A.Milne. About 170 titles were added after Oud's death but there is now no way of knowing whether any professional literature was appropriated by his son H.E. (Hans) Oud, also an architect.

The organization of the following partial list, covering only architecture, art and related fields, is self-evident. Publications are classified in the language in which they were published, not by the nationality of the author.

NOTES
1. Verhagen, Hans, "Getouwtrek om woning van weduwe architect Oud." *Haagsche Courant*, 1991, 18 June, p 9. See also "Villa weduwe architect Oud verkocht aan hoogste bieder," *ibid*, 26 June 1991.
2. I am indebted to drs. Mariet Willinge of the NAi for this summary of events (letter to the author, 9 October 1997).
3. ———, "Watchful widow," *Holland Herald*, vol 1, 1966, no 2, p 20-21.

A. ARCHITECTURE

1. PUBLICATIONS IDENTIFIED AS EXHIBITION CATALOGS

Dutch
Constructionism in Poland, 1923-1936, Museum of Folkwang, Essen/Kröller Müller, Otterlo, 1923.
De Stijl, 1917-1931, n.d., n.l.
F.Ll.W., Museum Boymans, 1952.
J.J.P. Oud, Rotterdam, 1951.
Nederland bouwt in baksteen 1800-1940, Museum Boymans, Rotterdam, 1941.

German
Amerikanische Architektur seit 1947, Stuttgart, 1951.
Bauhaus, Stuttgart, 1960.
Bauten in Deutschland seit 1948, Darmstadt, 1959.
Industriebau. Entwicklung und Gestalt, Wiesbaden, 1953.
Neue Baukunst, Oldenburg, 1928.
Typen neuer Baukunst, Hamburg, 1926.
Typen neuer Baukunst, Mannheim, 1926.
Typen Neuer Baukunst, Wiesbaden, 1926[?].

English
Aalto, architecture + furniture, Museum of Modern Art, New York, 1930.
Arthur Segal memorial exhibition, London, 1945.
Frank Lloyd Wright, Sixty years of living architecture, New York, 1951.
The Mars Group exhibition, London, 1938.

French
Frank Lloyd Wright, Ecole Nationale Supérieure des Beaux Arts, Paris, 1952.

2. BOOKS, MONOGRAPHS, OFFPRINTS FROM JOURNALS

Dutch
Ahlberg, Hakar, *Architect Gunnar Asplund*, Amsterdam, 1943.
Alings, H.W., *Amsterdamsche gevelsteenen*, Amsterdam, 1943.
Arnau, Frank, *Brasilia*, Rotterdam/The Hague, ca. 1960.

Bakhuizen, J.N. et al, *Protestantse kerkbouw*, The Hague, n.d.
Bakker Schut, P., *Dr.ir. F. Bakker Schut, Planologie*, Gorinchem, 1944.
Berlage, H.P. et al, *24 schetsen, zwervende en reizende toch thuis*, Rotterdam, 1948.
——, *Mijn Indische reis*, Rotterdam, 1931.
——, *Over Stijl in bouw- en meubelkunst*, Rotterdam, 1908.
——, *Schoonheid in samenleving*, Rotterdam, 1919.
Beyerman, J.J., *De historische schoonheid van Dordrecht*, Amsterdam, 1943.
Bijhouwer, J.T.P., *Nederlandsche tuinen en buitenplaatsen*, Amsterdam, 1942.
Blijstra, Rein, *Nederlandse bouwkunst na 1900*, Amsterdam, 1957.
——, *Nederlandse bouwkunst na 1900*, Utrecht, 1962.
Boer, M.G. de, *Een wandeling door een oud-Nederlandsche stad, Amsterdam*, Amsterdam, 1915.
Bogtman, W., *Nederlandsche glasschilders*, Amsterdam, 1944.
Bos, A., *De stad der toekomst, de toekomst der stad*, Rotterdam, 1946.
Broek, J.H. van den, *Creatieve krachten in de architectonische conceptie*, Delft, 1948.
Brom, Gerard, *Barok en Romantiek*, Groningen, The Hague, 1923.
Bromberg, Paul, *Doelmatig bouwen en wonen*, New York, 1945.
——, *Praktische Woninginrichting*, Amsterdam, 1933.
Brouwenstijn, Gré, *Met en zonder make-up*, Bussum, 1971.
Brugsma and v.der Heide, *Gewapend beton in theorie en toepassing*, Amsterdam, n.d.

Cleerdin, Vincent, *Het Brabantsche dorp*, Amsterdam, 1944.
Croce, B., *Bresser van aesthetics*, Arnhem, 1926.

Duintjer, M., *Bouwen met hart en ziel*, Amsterdam, 1956.

Elno, K.N., *J.J.P. Oud; het geweten der moderne architectuur* (reprint from *Streven* April 1961).
Emck, J.H., *Groei naar een nieuwe bouwkunst*, Groningen, 1950.
Erve, W.S. van der, *Le Corbusier, idealistisch architect*, Utrecht, 1951.

Feltkamp, W.C., *B.A. van der Leck*, Leiden, 1956.
Franquinet, E., *Boerderijtypen in Middelburg*, Maastricht, 1931.

Gelder, H.E. van, *De historische schoonheid van The Hague*, Amsterdam, 1943.

Granpré Molière, M.J., *Delft en het Nieuwe Bouwen*, (reprint from *Katholiek Bouwblad*), 1947.
——, [Report of a lecture] *Over de gedaante van toekomstig Rotterdam*, 1958.
——, *De moderne bouwkunst en haar beloften*, Delft, 1924.
——, *Woorden + werken*, Heemstede, 1949.
Graswinckel, D.P.M., *Nederlandsche hofjes*, Amsterdam, 1943.
Gratama, Jan, *Dr. H.P.Berlage, bouwmeester*, Rotterdam, 1925.
Gruyter, W. Jos. de, *Moderne Nederlandsche bouwkunst en J.J.P.Oud* (reprint from *Elseviers Geïllustreerd Maandschrift*, 1931).
Gugel, E., *Architectonische vormleer*, Amsterdam 1880.
——, *Geschiedenis van de bouwstijlen*, Rotterdam, 1902.
Hartog, Jan de, *Feestelijke Ondergang, leven + werk van Johan C.P. Alberts*, Amsterdam, 1950.
Heybroek, J.F., *Het kortstondiae bestaan van de Leidse kunstclub "De Sphinx"* (reprint from *Leids Jaarboekje*, 1980).
Hoste, Huib, *Ontstaan en betekenis der moderne architectuur*, Brussel, 1952.
Jaffé, Hans L.C., *De Stijl, 1917-1931*, Amsterdam, 1956.
Jans, Jan, *Bouwkunst en cultuur*, Amsterdam, 1934.
——, *Volkscultuur en bouwkunst*, Amsterdam, 1938.
Jelsma, O., *Het maken van begrootingen voor de bouwwereld*, The Hague, 1944.
Kalf, Jan, *Het wonderbaarlijke werk van den architect*, Amsterdam, 1938.
Kalff, L.C., *Kunstlicht en architectuur*, Amsterdam, 1941.
Kerckhoff, E. van, *Oud-Italiaansche villas, tuinen en parken*, Rotterdam, 1928.
Kerkmeyer, J.C., *De historische schoonheid van Hoorn*, Amsterdam, 1942.
Kessen, A., *De historische schoonheid van Maastricht*, Amsterdam, 1943.
Kloos, W.B., *De stedebouwkundige ontwikkeling in Nederland*, Amsterdam, 1947.
Kloot Meijburg, H. van der, *De Nieuwe Kerk te Delft*, Rotterdam, 1923.
——, *Landhuisbouw in Nederland*, Amsterdam, 1921.
Knuttel Wzn., G., *Beknopte ontwikkelings geschiedenis der bouwkunst*, Amsterdam, 1943.
Kok, A.A., *Amsterdamsche woonhuizen*, Amsterdam, 1941.
——, *Edam*, Amsterdam, 1948.
——, *De historische schoonheid van Amsterdam*, Amsterdam, 1941.
Kok, Ijsbrand, *De Hollandse tegel*, Amsterdam, 1949.
Kroes, J.A. van der, *Oude bouwmaterialen, glas, verfwaren en behangsels*, Maassluis, n.d.
——, *Oude bouwmaterialen, hout*, Maassluis, n.d.
——, *Oude bouwmaterialen, kunststeen*, Maassluis, n.d.
——, *Oude bouwmaterialen, metalen*, Maassluis, n.d.
——, *Oude bouwmaterialen, mortels en beton*, Maassluis, n.d.
——, *Oude bouwmaterialen, natuursteen*, Maassluis, n.d.
Krom, N.J., *De tempels van Anghor*, Amsterdam, n.d.

Kropholler, A.J., *Bouwkunst in de 20e eeuw*, Amsterdam, 1933.
——, *Het licht en de kleuren in de bouwkunst en kunstnijverheid*, Amsterdam/Antwerp, n.d.
——, *Kunst en leven; lijn en vorm, licht en kleur in de bouw- en aanverwante kunsten*, Amsterdam/Antwerp, 1938.
——, *Onze Nederlandsche baksteen bouwkunst*, The Hague, 1941.
——, *Over Bouwstijl vroeger en nu*, Amsterdam, 1941.
Kuile, E.H. ter, *De dom van Utrecht*, Maastricht, 1942.
——, *De drie oude kerken van Zutphen*, Maastricht, 1942.
——, *De torens van Nederland*, Amsterdam, 1941.
Kuipers, E., *Brugge, die schoone*, Brugge, n.d.
Kultermann, Udo, *Bouwkunst van deze tijd*, Amsterdam, 1958.

Lamschot, F.J. van, *De kathedraal en het stadhuis*, Amsterdam, 1942.
Lauweriks, J.L.M., *De houtschneden van K.P.C. de Bazel*, Amsterdam, 1925.
——, *Nieuwe Nederlandse ruimtekunst*, Blaricum, 1927.
Leliman, J.W.H., and Sluyterman, *Het moderne landhuis in Nederland*, The Hague, 1916.
Lemaire, Kan R., *Beknopte geschiedenis van de meubelkunst*, Amsterdam, 1942.
Leurs, Stan, *De groote markt van Brussels*, Antwerp, 1942.

Manes, W. et al, *De Nederlandse monumenten van geschiedenis en kunst*, The Hague, 1962.
Martin, W., *Herleefde Schoonheid, 25 jaar Monumentenzorg in Nederland*, Amsterdam, 1943.
Meyer, Jan de, *Bruggen*, Amsterdam, 1946.
Mieras, J.P., *Liber Amicorum Bloemlezing uit de geschriften van J.P. Mieras*, Amsterdam, 1958.
Mulder, J. and H. Boes, *Materialenkennis voor loodgieters en fitters*, Amsterdam, 1941.

Neurdenburg, E., *De historische schoonheid van Groningen*, Amsterdam, 1942.
Nispen tot Sevenaer, E. van, *Nederlandsche Kasteelen*, Amsterdam, 1942.

Oud, J.J.P., *Architecturalia voor bouwheren en architecten*, The Hague, 1963.
——, *Building and teamwork*, Rotterdam, 1952.
——, *Hollandse architectuur*, Nijmegen, 1983.
——, *Nieuwe bouwkunst in Holland en Europa*, The Hague, 1935.
——, *Ter wille van een levende bouwkunst*, The Hague, 1962.
——, *Zijn er nog architecten?* The Hague, 1959.
——, *Bestek en voorwaarden voor kantoor aan de Wassenaarscheweg*, The Hague, 1939.
——, *Over de toekomstige bouwkunst en hare architectonische mogelijkheden* (reprint from *Bouwkundig Weekblad*, 1921).

Pevsner, Nikolaus, *Geschiedenis van de bouwkunst in Europa*, Rotterdam, 1949.
Plantenga, J.H., *Verzamelde opstellen*, Amsterdam, 1926.

Plate, A., Ms for catalog *Nederland bouwt in baksteen*, Rotterdam, 1941.
Pluym, W. van der, H*et Nederlandsche binnenhuis en zijn meubels 1650-1750*, Amsterdam, 1946.
Poptie, A., *Handboek voor den stucadoor*, Amsterdam, 1943 and 1948.
Radinger, Jan, *Kantoren en priëlen*, Amsterdam, n.d.
Rand, Ayn, *De eeuwige bron*, Amsterdam, n.d.
R.C.M.B., *Nederlandsche monumenten van geschiedenis en kunst in beeld*, Amsterdam, 1941.
——, *Kunstreisboek voor Nederland; I, Noord-Holland, Zuid-Holland*, Amsterdam, 1954.
R.C.M.B., *Kunstreisboek voor Nederland; 1, Noord-Holland, Zuid-Holland*, Amsterdam, 1940.
——, *Kunstreisboek voor Nederland; II, Friesland, Groningen, Drenthe*, Amsterdam, 1942 and 1958.
——, *Kunstreisboek voor Nederland; III, Overijssel, Utrecht, Gelderland*, Amsterdam, 1949 and 1954.
——, *Kunstreisboek voor Nederland; IV, Zeeland, Noord-Brabant, Limburg*, Amsterdam, 1953.
Retera Wzn., W., *Het moderne interieur*, Amsterdam.
——, *Nederlandsche bouwmeesters, P. Kramer*, Amsterdam, 1927.
Révész, G., *Creatieve begaafdheid*, The Hague, 1946.
Richards, J.M., *Moderne architectuur*, Zeist, 1961.
Rietveld, Gerrit Th., *Rietveld, 1924. Schröder huis*, Amsterdam, 1963.
Rooy, A.J.J. van, *Nederlandse kerkbouw op een keerpunt*, Haarlem, 1959.
Royen, J.I. van, *Over het geluidsvraagstuk in ziekenhuizen*, Zaltbommel, 1920.

Scharroo, P.W., *Inleiding tot de studie van het gewapend beton*, Amsterdam, 1916.
Sevenhuijsen, A.M.J., *Nieuwe bouwkunst in Nederland*, Blaricum, 1928[?].
Sleeswijk, C. W., *Beschouwingen over architectonische vormleer*, Haarlem,
Slothouwer, D.F., *Amsterdamsche huizen 1600-1800*, Amsterdam, 1928.
——, *Bouwkunst der Nederlandse renaissance in Denemarken*, Amsterdam, 1924.
Sluyterman, K., *Huisraad en binnenshuis in Nederland*, The Hague, 1925.
Sterck-Proot, J.M., *De historische schoonheid van Haarlem*, Amsterdam, 1942, 1946.
Streuvels, Stijn, *De landsche woning in Vlaanderen*, Amsterdam, n.d.

Theunisz, Joh., *Het Stadhuis te Enkhuizen*, Assen, 1927.
Tillema, J.A.C., *Richtlijnen voor de beoordelingen ... Nieuwe Haagse Raadhuis*, The Hague, 1938.
Tusschenbroek, Otto van, *Achter blinkende vensters*, Leiden, 1950.

Unger W.S., *De monumenten van Middelburg*, Maastricht, 1941.

Valderpoort, W., *Beschouwingen over de mogelijkheid van wederopbouw van de Rotterdamse binnenstad*, Rotterdam, 1948.

Various authors, *De Schoonheid van ons land. De steden*, Amsterdam, 1941.
——, *De Schoonheid van ons land. Het landschap*, Amsterdam, 1941.
——, *Duizend jaar bouwen in Nederland*, Amsterdam, 1948.
Vasalis, M., *Parken en woestijnen*, The Hague, 1941.
Vermeulen, F., *ABC van de bouwstijlen in de Nederlanden*, The Hague, 1953.
Vriend, J.J., *Bouwen*, Antwerp/Amsterdam, 1952.
——, *De Bouwkunst van ons land, de steden*, Amsterdam, 1949.
——, *De Bouwkunst van ons land, het interieur*, Amsterdam, 1950.
——, *De Bouwkunst van ons land, het platteland*, Amsterdam, 1949.
——, *De schoonheid van ons land, architectuur van deze eeuw*, Amsterdam, 1959.
——, *De schoonheid van ons land, de steden*, Amsterdam, 1951.
——, *Nederland bouwt in natuur- en baksteen*, Utrecht, 1951.
——, *Nieuwere architecture*, Amsterdam, 1935.
——, *Nieuwere architectuur*, Bussum, 1957.
——, *Reflexen. Nederlands bouwen na 1945*, Amsterdam, 1959.

Wall, V.L. v.d., *Oude Hollandsche bouwkunst in Indonesië*, Antwerp, 1942.
Wattjes, J. and Warners, *Amsterdams bouwkunst en stadsschoon 1306-1942*, Amsterdam, 1943.
Wattjes, J. and ten Bosch, *Rotterdam en hoe het bouwde*, Leiden, 1940.
Weissman, A.W., *Geschiedenis der Nederlandse bouwkunst*, Amsterdam, 1912.
Wiekart, Karel, *J.J.P. Oud*, Amsterdam, 1965.
Wieland, J., *Aluminium in de gevel*, AmsterdamJAntwerp, 1956.
——, *Stalen ramen en deuren*, Amsterdam/Antwerp, 1952.
Wisse, L. and van der Weel, *Centrale verwarming*, Deventer, 1942

Zandstra, Evert, *Shell boerderijengids*, n.l., n.d.

German
Andt, Adolf, *Democratie als Bauherr*, Berlin, 1961.
Angerer, Fred, *Bauen mit hagenden Flächen*, Munich, 1960.
Antworten, Jahrbuch Freie Akademie der Künste in Hamburg, Hamburg, 1963.
Argan, Guilio Carlo, *Gropius und das Bauhaus*, Hamburg, 1962.
Arnau, Frank, *Brasilia*, Munich, 1960.

Baum, Julius, *Baukunst und dekorative Plastik der Frührenaissance in Italien*, Stuttgart 1926.
——, *Die schöne Deutsche Stadt; Süddeutschland*, Munich, 1912.
——, *Romenische Baukunst und Skulptur in Frankreich*, Stuttgart, 1928.
Behne, Adolf, *Der Moderne Zweckbau*. Munich/Vienna/Berlin, 1926.
Behrendt, Walter Curt,*Alfred Messel*, Berlin, 1911.
——, *Die Architektur auf der grossen Berliner Kunstausstellung*, 1924 (reprint from *Kunst*).
Bernoulli, Hans, *Die organische Erneuerung unserer Städte*, Basel, 1942.
Brinkmann, A.E., *Stadt baukunst*, Berlin, 1920.
Brödner, Erika, *Modernes Wohnen*, Munich, 1954.

Clemen, Paul, *Götische Kathedralen im Frankreich*, Zurich/Berlin, 1937.
Coulin, Claudius, *Architekten zeichnen*, Stuttgart, 1962.

David, C.W. et al, *Moderne Küche*, Zurich, 1957.
Deuel, Grete and W., *Das Wohnhaus von Heute*, Leipzig, 1928.

Fengler, M., *Skelettbauten mit Fassadenelementen*, Stuttgart, 1962.
Fischer, Friedrich, *Nadeutscher Ziegelbau*, Munich, 1944.
Fischer, Theodor, *Goethes Verhältnis zur Baukunst*, Munich, 1948.
Fischer, Wend, *Bau, Raum, Gerät*, Munich, 1957.
Forbat, Fred, *Wohnungsbauten, 1930-1931* (reprint from *Bauwelt*, 1931).

Gatz, Konrad and Hierl, *Treppen und Treppenhäuser*, Munich, 1954.
Giedion, Siegfried, *Befreites Wohnen*, Leipzig, 1929.
——, *Spätbarocher und Romentischer Klassizismus*, Munich, 1922.
Graul, Richard, *Schöne Möbel aus funf Jahrhunderts*, Leipzig, 1938.
Gregor, Joseph, *Weltgeschichte des Theaters*, Zurich, 1933.
Gruyer, S., *Venidig, Bauten und Bildwerken*, Augsburg/ Cologne/ Vienna, n.d.

Hagen, Werner, *Die Bauten des deutschen Barocks*, Jena, 1942.
Hawranck, Alfred, *Zur Asthetik des Ingenieurbauwesens* (reprint from *Zeitschrift des Deutschen Vereines für die Geschichte Mährens und Schlesiens*, no 4, 1924).
Hess, Friedrich, *Konstruktion und Form im Bauen*, Stuttgart, 1942.
Hilberseimer, Ludwig, *Internationale Neue Baukunst*, Stuttgart, 1927.
Hiort, Esbjorn, *Contemporary Danish Architecture*, Copenhagen, 1949.
Hoffmann, Herbert et al, *Garten und Haus*, Stuttgart, 1941.
——, *Sitzmöbel aus 6. Jahrhunderten*, Stuttgart, 1938.
Hoffmann, Kurt, *Büro- und Verwaltungsgebäude*, Stuttgart, 1956.
Hofmann, Hans, *Baugesinnung*, Zurich, 1942.

Joedicke, Jürgen, *Geschichte der Modernen Architektur*, Teufen, 1958.

Kahlefeld, Rolf, *Friedrich Jacques, Garagen und Tankstellen*, Munich, 1956.
Katz, Richard, *Drei Gesichter Luzifers; Vorm, Maschine, Geschaft*, Leipzig, 1934.
Kienzle, Hermann, *Karl Moser 1860-1936*, Zürich, 1937.
Kinder, W. and Böckler, *Die Stadt, Ihre Pflege und Gestaltung*, Munich, 1939.
Knapp, F., *Balthasar Neumann, der grobe Architekt seiner Zeit*, Leipzig, 1937.
Kratz, Walter et al, *Das Buch van eigenen Haus*, Berlin, 1937.
Krook, L., *Architektur der Niederlande Lieferung*, Leipzig, 1894.

Lafond, Jean, *Die Kathedrale von Rouen*, Berlin, 1913[?].
Larck, Carl van, *Balthasar Neumann*, Königsberg, 1940.
Lauweriks, J., *Architektur und Kunstgewerbe in Alt. Holland*, Munich, 1924.
Le Corbusier, *An die Studenten, Die "Charte d'Athenès"*, Hamburg, 1962.
Le Corbusier, *Mein Werk*, Stuttgart, 1960.
Lehwess, Walter, *Englische Arbeiter Wohnungen*, Berlin, 1904.

Leitl, Alfons, *Von der Architektur zum Bauen*, Berlin, 1936.
Leurs, Stan, *Alte Baukunst in Flanderen*, Jena, 1942.
Lodders, Rudolf, *Bilderbuch eines Architekten*, Hamburg, 1961.
Lukomshij, G., *Andrea Palladio*, Munich, 1924.
Luth, Erich et al, *Gustav Oelsner, Porträt eines Baumeister*, Hamburg, 1960.

Manteuffel, K.Z. von, *Die Künstlerfamilie Van de Velde*, Leipzig, 1927.
Mayer, H.K.F., *Der Baumeister Otto Bartung und die Wiederentdeckung des Raumes*, Heidelberg, 1951.
Mayr, Otto, and Hierl, *Hotelbau*, Munich, 1962.
Melchers, Bernd, *China, Der Tempelbau, die Lochan van king-yän-sï*, Hagen, 1921.
Mendelsohn, Erich, *Briefe eines Architekten*, Munich, 1961.
Meursen, Theodor, *Geestige Landerkunde Holland*, Nuremburg, 1956.
Moser, Werner M., *Frank Lloyd Wright*, Zurich, 1952.
Müller-Rehm, Klaus, *Wohnbauten von heute*, Berlin, 1955.
Mumford, Lewis, *Vom Blockhaus zum Wolkenkratzer*, Berlin, 1925.
Müthesius, Hermann, *Kleinhaus und Kleinsiedlung*, Munich, 1918.
——, *Wie bane ich mein Haus?*, Munich, 1917.

Nervi, Pier Luigi, *Bauten und Projekte*, Teufen, 1957.
Nestler, Paolo, *Neues Bauen in Italien*, Munich, 1954.
Neuenschwander, E. and C., *Finnische Bauten Atelier Alvar Aalto*, Zurich, 1954.
Neutra, Richard, *Auftrag für Morgen*, Hamburg, 1962.

Otto, Frei, *Das Hängende Dach*, Berlin, 1954.
Otto, Karl, *Die Stadt van Morgen*, Berlin 1959.
Oud, J.J.P., *Holländische Architektur*, Munich, 1926.
——, *J.J.P. Oud von ihm selber* (reprint from *Das Einhorn*, 1957-1958).
——, *Mein Weg in De Stijl*, The Hague, 1959[?].

Patzak, Bernard, *Die Renaissance und Barock villa, Die Villa Imperiale in Pesaro*, Leipzig, 1908.
Pée, Herbert, *Die Palastbauten des Andrea Palladio*, Würzburg, 1941.
Pfamätter, Ferdinand, *Betonkirchen*, Zurich, 1948.
Platz, Gustav Adolf, *Die Baukunst der neuesten Zeit*, Berlin, 1927, 1930.
Ponten, Josef, *Architektur die nicht gebaut wurde*, Stuttgart, 1925.

Rasmussen, Steen Eiler, *Nördische Baukunst*, Berlin, 1940.
Rave, Paul Ortwin, *Griechische Tempel*, Marburg, 1924.
Reichow, Hans B., *Die autogerechte Stadt*, Ravensburg, 1959.
——, *Organische Stadbaukunst*, Braunschweig, 1948.
Ricci, Corrado, *Romenische Baukunst in Italien*, Stuttgart, 1925.
——, *Baukunst und dekorative Plastik der Hoch- und Spätrenaissance in Italien*, Stuttgart, 1923.
Rimpl, Herbert, *Verwaltungsbauten*, Berlin, 1959.
Rittich, Werner, *Architektur und Bauplastik der Gegenwart*, Berlin, 1938.

Rodin, A., *Französische Kathedralen*, Berlin, n.d.
Ruskin, John, *Die sieben Leuchter der Baukunst*, Leipzig, 1900.

Scheffler, Karl, *Die Architektur der Grossstadt*, Berlin, 1913.
——, *Der Geist der Gotik*, Leipzig, 1922.
——, *Deutsche Baumeister*, Berlin, 1939.
——, *Form als Schicksal*, Leipzig, 1939.
——, *Leben, Kunst und Staat*, Leipzig, 1920.
——, *Moderne Baukunst*, Leipzig, 1908.
Schiebring, Paul, *Die Architektur der Italienischen Frührenaissance*, Munich, 1923.
Schmittkenner, Paul, *Baukunst in neuen Reich*, Munich, 1934.
Schneider, Alfonds Maria, *Die Hagia Sophia zie Konstantin*, Berlin, 1939.
Schultze-Naumburg, P., *Kulturarbeiten: Städtebau*, Munich, 1909.
——, *Kulturarbeiten: Hausbau*, Munich, 1912.
Schumacher, Fritz, *Die Klein Wohnung, Studien zur Wohnungsfrage*, Leipzig, 1919.
——, *Grundlagen der Baukunst*, Munich, 1916.
——, *Probleme der Grossstadt*, Leipzig, 1940.
——, *Strömungen in Deutscher Baukunst seit 1800*, Leipzig, 1955.
Schwate, D. A. et al, *Bauen mit Kunststoffen*, Berlin, 1959.
Siegel, Curt, *Strukturformen der modernen Architektur*, Munich, 1960.
Sill, Otto, *Parkbauten*, Berlin, 1961.
Sitte, Camillo, *Der Städtebau nach seinen Kiinstlenschen Grundsätzen*, Vienna, 1909.
Sörgel, Herman, *Theorie der Baukunst*, Munich, 1921.
Spannagel, Fritz, *Der Möbelbau*, Ravensburg, 1939.
Styron, William, *Und legte Feuer an dies Haus*, Frankfurt, 1961.

Taut, Bruno, *Die Neue Wohnung, die Frau als Schöpferin*, Leipzig, 1925.
Tessenow, Heinrich, *Handwerk und Kleinstadt*, Berlin, 1919.
——, *Hausbau und der glucken*, Berlin, 1928.
Thiede, Klaus, *Deutsche Bauernhäuser*, Leipzig, 1941.
Troost, Pr. Gerdy, *Das Bauen in neuen Reich*, Bayreuth, 1938.
Tusschenbroek, Otto van, *Achter blinkende vensters*, Leiden, 1950.

Valendas, B., *Die Garten stadt beweging in England*, Munich/Berlin, 1912.
Lindner, Werner (ed), *Das Dorf, Seine Pflege und Gestaltung*, Munich, 1938.
Various authors, *Die Weissenhofsiedlung*, Stuttgart, n.d.
Vasari, Giorgio, *Lebensbeschreibungen der ausgezeichnetsten Maler, Bildhauer und Architekten der Renaissance*, Berlin, 1911.
Völckers, Otto, *Bauen mit Glas*, Stuttgart, 1948.
——, *Glas als Baustoff*, Eberswalde, 1944.

Wedepohl, D.E., *Bewerkunosverfahren, von Decken konstruktionen*, n.l., n.d.
Werner, Bruno E., *Neues Bauen in Deutschland*, Munich, 1952.
Weyres, W. et al., *Kirchen, Handbuch für den Kirchenbau*, Munich, 1959.

Wingler, Hans M., *Das Bauhaus*, Berlin, 1962.
Witte, Irene, *Die Rationelle Haushalffführung*, Berlin, 1922.
Wolf, Gustav, *Die schöne Deutsche Stadt; Mitteldeutschland*, Munich, 1912
Wolters, Rudolf, *Albert Speer*, Oldenburg, 1943.
——, *Neue Deutsche Baukunst*, Berlin, 1941.

Ziller, Hermann, *Schinkel*, Leipzig 1897.

English
Agate, C. Gustave, *Building in Lancashire*, Preston, 1937.
Arcambeau, Edme, *The cathedrals of France*, London/Glasgow, 1912.

Baker, G., *Windows in modern architecture*, New York, 1948.
Batsford, Harry and Fry, *The English cottage*, London, 1944.
Bauer, Catherine, *Modern housing*, Boston, 1934.
Beckett, Jane, *The original drawings of J.J.P. Oud*, London, 1979.
Blake, Peter, *Marcel Breuer architect and designer*, New York, 1949.
Brett, Lionel, *The things we see: houses*, Middlesex 1947.
Bromberg, Paul, *Architecture in the Netherlands*, New York, 1944.
Brown, Theodore M., *The work of G. Rietveld, architect*, Utrecht, 1958.
Bush-Brown, Albert, *Louis Sullivan*, New York, 1960.

Carter, E.J. and Goldfinger, *The County of London plan*, London, 1945.
Chatterton, Frederick, *English architecture at a glance*, Aberdeen, 1945.
Coles, W.A. et al, *Architecture in America*, New York, 1961.
Creighton, T. H. et al, *Homes*, New York, 1947.
Cross, Kenneth M.B., *Modern public baths*, London, 1938.

Dorgelo, A., *Modern European architecture*, Amsterdam, 1960.

Eckardt, Wolf von, *Eric Mendelsohn*, New York, 1960.
Elder-Duncan, J.H., *Country cottages and weekend homes*, London, 1906.

Fitch, James Marston, *Walter Gropius*, New York, 1960.
Ford, James and Katherine, *Design of modern interiors*, New York, 1942.
——, *The modern house in America*, New York, 1940.
Ford, K.M. and Creighton, *The American house today*, New York, 1951.

Gibberd, Frederick, *The Architecture of England*, Kingston on Thames, 1938.
Goodwin, Philip L., *Brazil builds. Architecture new and old, 1642-1942*, New York, 1943.
Gropius, Walter, *The scope of total architecture*, London, 1956.

Harada, Juo, *The lesson of Japanese architecture*, London, 1936.
Hill, Oliver, *Fair horizon, buildings of today*, London, 1950.
Hitchcock, Henry -Russell, *In the nature of materials*, New York, 1942.
——, *Latin American architecture since 1945*, New York, 1955.
——, *Painting toward architecture*, New York, 1948.
——, *The architecture of H.H. Richardson and his times*, New York, 1936.

Hitchcock, Henry -Russell and Drexler, *Built in USA: post-war architecture*, New York, 1952.
Hulten, Bertil, *Building modern Sweden*, Middlesex, 1951.
Hussey, Christopher, *The life of Sir Edwin Lutyens*, New York, 1950.

Kaufmann, Edgar, *What is modern design?*, New York, 1950.
—— et al, *Frank Lloyd Wright, an American architecture*, New York, 1955.
Kidder Smith, G.E., *The new architecture of Europe*, Cleveland, 1961.
Kishida, Hideto, *Japanese architecture*, Tokyo, 1936.
Kondo, Ichitaro, *Toshusai Sharaku*, Tokyo/Russia/Vermont, 1955.

Le Corbusier, *The Marseilles block*, London, 1953.
Lutyens, Edwin, *Houses and gardens*, London, 1925

Martin, Arthur, *The small house*, London, 1909.
McCoy, Esther, *Richard Neutra*, New York, 1960.
McGrath, Raymond, *Twentieth-century houses*, London, 1934.
Mendelsohn, Erich, *Eric Mendelsohn*, San Francisco [?], 1955.
Mills, Edward D., *The modern church*, London, 1956.
——, *Architects' detail sheets*, London, 1952.
Mock, Elizabeth B., *If you want to build a house*, New York, 1946.
Morrison, Hugh, *Louis Sullivan*, New York, 1935.
Mumford, Lewis, *Art and technics*, London, 1952.
——, *City development*, New York, 1945.
——, *The brown decades 1865-1895*, New York, 1931.
——, *The city in history*, London, 1961.
——, *The culture of cities*, New York, 1938.
——, *The story of Geddes*, New York, 1947.
Myerscough-Walker, R., *Choosing a modern house*, London, 1939.

Nervi, Pier Luigi, *Structures*, New York, 1956.

Orni, N. and Toba, *Castles in Japan*, Tokyo, 1935.
Ostberg, Ragnar, *The Stockholm town hall*, Stockholm, 1929.

Papadaki, Stamo, *Oscar Niemeyer*, New York, 1960.
Pevsner, Nikolaus, *An outline of European architecture*, Harmondsworth, 1945.

Rand, Ayn, *The fountainhead*, New York, 1943.
Richards, J.M., *Modern architecture*, Middlesex, 1946, 1947, 1959.
Richardson, A.E., *The old inns of England*, London, 1934.
Robertson, Howard, *Architecture arising*, London, 1954.
Rosenauer, Michael, *Modern office buildings*, London, 1955.
Roth, Alfred, *The new school*, Zurich, 1950.
——, *The new architecture*, Zürich, 1940.

Saarinen, Eliel, *Search for form*, New York, 1947.
Sharp, Thomas, *The anatomy of the village*, Harmondsworth, 1946.
——, *Town planning*, Harmondsworth, 1945.

Spanowed, W. Shaw, *The British home of today*, London, 1904.
——, *The modern home*, London, n.d.
Stamm, Günther, *The architecture of J.J.P.Oud, 1906-1963*, Tallahassee, 1978.
Storrs, Lewis jr., *The key to your new home*, New York, 1938.
Sullivan, Louis H., *The autobiography of an idea*, New York, 1924.

Tayla, G.C., *The modern garden*, London, 1936.

Various authors, *Building in Cheshire*, Chester, 1939.
——, *Modern architecture in England*, New York, 1937.
Voyce, Arthur, *Russian architecture*, New York, 1948.

Weaver, Lawrence, *Lutyens Houses and Gardens*, London, 1921.
——, *Small country houses of today*, parts 1 and 2, London, 1922.
——, *The* Country Life *book of cottages*, London, 1913.
West, G.H., *Gothic architecture in England and France*, London, 1911.
Whittick, Arnold, *War memorials*, Glasgow, 1946.
Wright Frank, Lloyd, *An autobiography*, London, 1946.
——, *Genuis and the mobocracy*, New York, 1949.
——, *On architecture*, New York, 1941.
——, *Drawings for a living architecture*, New York, 1959.
——, *The future of architecture*, New York, 1953.
——, *When democracy builds*, Chicago, 1945.

Yerbury, F.R., *Old domestic architecture of Holland*, London, 1924.

Zevi, Bruno, *Toward an organic architecture*, London, 1950.

French
Béclt, Marie, *Vézelay*, Paris, 1948.
Bergson, Henri, *L'évolution créatrice*, Paris, 1948.
Bourgeois, Victor, *Architecture, 1922-52*, Brussels, 1952.
——, *L'architecte et son espace*, Brussels, n.d.

Casteels, Maurice, *Esthétique*, Brussels, 1921.
Chaghtai, Muhammed, *Le Taj Mahal d'Agra*, Brussels, 1938.
Champigneuille and Ache, *L'Architecture de XXe siècle*, Paris, 1962.

Donné, André le, *L'Architecte dans la cité*, Paris, 1945.

Giedion, Siegfried, *Walter Gropius*, Paris, 1931.

Jardot, Maurice, *Le Corbusier*, Paris, 1955.

Le Corbusier, *Quand les cathédrales étaient blanches*, Paris, 1937.
Lurcat, André, *Architecture*, Paris, 1929.
——, *Formes Composition et lois d'harmonie*, Paris, 1933.

Mayer, Marcel, *Les albums d'art druet 16, A. et G. Perret*, Paris, n.d.

Petit, Jean, *Un couvent de Le Corbusier*, Paris, 1961.

Various authors, *Le maténau verre dans la construction*, Paris, n.d.

Italian
Americi, Gino, *Palladio*, Firenze, 1949.

Berenson, Bernard, *Palladio Veronese e Vittoria a Maser*, Milan, n.d.

Carli, Enzo, *Brunelleschi*, Firenze, 1949.

Jaffé, Hans L.C., *Il Gruppo "De Stijl"*, Amsterdam, n.d.

Maxiani, Leonardo, *Recenti opere di Jacobus Johannes Pieter Oud* (reprint from *l'Architettura*, 1956).
Minnucci, Gaetano, *L'abitazione moderna popolare*, Rome, 1926.
Moretti, Bruno, *Ville*, Milan, 1937.

Pevsner, Nikolaus, *Charles R. Mackintosh*, Milan, 1950.
Pica, Agnoldomenico, *Nuova architettura Italiani*, Milan, 1936.
——, *Nuova architettura nel monde*, Milan, 1938.

Sartoris, Alberto, *Antonio Sant'Elia*, Milan, 1930.
——, *No posizione dell' architettura e delle arti in Italia*, Florence, n.d.

Travi, Elisa Manan, *Baudelaire, Rembaud et l'architettura*, Bari, 1982.

Venturi, Adolfo, *Architetti dal XV al XVIII secolo, Leon Battista Alberti*, Rome, 1923.

Zevi, Bruno, *Poetica del architettura neoplastica*, Milano, 1953.

Other
Lettshäm, Gustav, *Nordisk arkitektur, 1946-1949*, Stockholm, 1950.
Lüning, Orjan, *Uppsats om arkitektur*, Stockholm, 1948.

B. VISUAL ARTS AND DESIGN

1. PUBLICATIONS IDENTIFIED AS EXHIBITION CATALOGS

Dutch
Beeldhouwwerken en tekeningen van Barbara Hepworth, Otterlo, n.d.
Bonnard, Rotterdam, 1953.

Campigti, Amsterdam, 1955.
Cesar Domela, The Hague, 1960.
Charley Toorop en Wolf Demeter, Amsterdam, 1933.
Charley Toorop, The Hague, 1934.
Claude Monet, The Hague, 1952.
Collectie Ragna Moltzan, The Hague, 1957.
Collectie Thompson uit Pittsburgh, The Hague, 1961.
Collection Urvater, Otterlo, 1957.
Corneille, The Hague, 1961.

De Helsche + de Fluweelen Bruegel en hun invloed op de kunst in de Nederlan den, Amsterdam, 1934.

Engelse landschapsschilders van Gainsborough tot Turner, Rotterdam, 1955.

F.Ll.W., Museum Boymans, 1952.
Facetten 2, The Hague, 1955.
Franse meesters uit het petit palais, Rotterdam, 1952.

Gerrit Beuner, 1945-1955, Eindhoven, 1955.

Herman Kruyder, tekeningen-aquarellen, The Hague, 1961.
Heropenina, 1945, Afbeeldingen oude meesters, Boymans Museum, Rotterdam, 1945.
Het stilleven, Amsterdam, 1933.
Het tekenwerk van Paul Citroen, The Hague, 1956.
Hollandsche winterlandschappen uit de 17e eeuw, Rotterdam, 1932.

Jan Toorop, Charley Toorop, Edgar Fernhout, schilderijen, n.l., 1972.
Japanese art, The Hague Gemeentemuseum, 1958.
Johannes Itten, Amsterdam, 1957.
John Raedecker 1885-1956, Amsterdam, 1956.
Joseph Zaritsley, Amsterdam, 1955.
Julio Gonzales, Amsterdam, 1955.
Julius Bissier, The Hague, 1960.

Karel Appel, Stedelijk Museum Amsterdam, 1965.
Krsto Hegedusic, The Hague, 1960.

Léger, de bouwers, Amsterdam, n.d.

Manessier, The Hague, 1959.
Marino Marini, Rotterdam, 1955.
Massino Campigli, Boymans Museum, Rotterdam, 1947.
Max Beckmann, The Hague, 1956.
Meesterwerken uit vier eeuwen 1400-1800, Boymans Museum, Rotterdam, 1930.
Mondriaan, Gemeentemuseum, The Hague, 1955.
Mosha '54, Rotterdam, 1954.

Nieuwe kunst rond 1900, The Hague, 1960.

Odilon Redon, The Hague, 1957.
Oskar Kokoschka, The Hague, 1958.

Paul Cézanne 1839-1906, The Hague, 1956.
Picasso, Guernica, Amsterdam, n.d.
Piet Mondriaan, Stedelijk Museum Amsterdam, 1946.
Pieter Jansz. Saenredam, Rotterdam, 1938.
Pieter Jansz Saenredam, Utrecht Centraal Museum, 1961.

Sonsbeek '55, Wageningen, 1955.

Soulages, The Hague, 1961.

Vincent van Gogh 1853-1953, Otterlo/Amsterdam, 1953.
Vincent van Gogh, The Hague, 1953.

German
Bildhauer-Zeichnungen, Berlin, 1962.
Curt Wittenberger, Bremen, 1959/1960.
Die Albertine-Drucke und Schrolls Farbendruche, Vienna, n.d.
Fotomontage, Berlin, 1931.
Für Berlin Geplant und nie gebaut, Akademie der Kunste, Berlin, 1957.
George Grosz 1893-1959, Berlin, 1962.
Germania VII, Marländer Trienal, 1940.
Henry Moore, Berlin, 1961.
Internationale Pantomime, Berlin, November 1962.
Italienische Kunst in XX. Jahrhundert, Berlin, 1957.
Japanische Malerei der Gegenwart, Berlin, 1961.
Meisterwerke des Deutschen Expressionismus, Stuttgart, 1960.
Panorama, Basel, 1961.
Paul Klee, Berlin, 1960.
Rudolf Belling, Berlin, 1962.
Signum 62, Berlin, 1962.
Theodor Werner, Berlin, 1962.
Werner Gilles 1894-1961, Berlin, 1962.

French
Corneille, Paris, 1954.

Fernand Léger 1881-1955, Musée des Arts Decoratifs, Paris, 1956.

Karel Appel, Paris, n.d.

Other
Hartung, Madrid, 1961.

2. BOOKS, MONOGRAPHS, OFFPRINTS FROM JOURNALS
Dutch
Adama v. Scheltema, C., *Kunstenaar en samenleving*, Rotterdam, 1922.
Andriesse, E. and de Gruyter, *De wereld van Van Gogh*, The Hague, 1953.
Argan, Guilio Carlo, *Martini*, Amsterdam, 1956.
Arntzenius, L.M.G., *Amerikaansche kunstindrukken*, Amsterdam, n.d.
Arondeus, W., *Matthijs Maris, de tragiek van den droom*, Amsterdam, 1945.

Baljeu, Joost, *Mondrian of Miro?* Amsterdam, 1958.
Berden, J.W.H., *De kunstnijverheid*, Haarlem, 1905.
Blad, Nijpels, *Boek en band*, Utrecht, n.d.
Boer, Julius de, *Jan Toorop*, Amsterdam, 1911.
Bogtman, W., *Nederlandsche glasschilders*, Amsterdam, 1944.

Bolland, G.J.D.J., *De loggia*, Leiden, 1912.
——, *De teekenen des tijds*, Leiden, 1921.
——, *Esthetische Geestelijkheid*, Leiden, 1907.
——, *Het schoone en de kunst*, Amsterdam, 1923.
——, *In den voorhof der schoonheid*, Leiden, 1906.
Bosman, Anthony (ed), *Jaarboek der Nederlandse kunst*, Leiden, 1947.
Bouman, A., *Orgels in Nederland*, Amsterdam, 1943.
Breduis, A., *Rembrandt, schilderingen*, Utrecht, 1935.
Bremmer, H.P., *P. Saenredam*, The Hague, 1938.
——, *Vincent van Gogh, inleidende beschouwingen*, Amsterdam, 1911.
Brinkmann, A.E., *Italianen, Franschen, Duitsers en hun nationale kunst*, The Hague, 1941.
Busken Huet, C.D., *Het land van Rembrandt*, Haarlem, 1920.

Casteur, H. and Smeets, *Inleiding tot de hedendaagse schilderkunst*, Brussels, 1959.
Citroen, Paul, *Jacob Bendien 1890-1933*, Rotterdam, 1946.
Cladel, Judith, *Maillol*, n.l., n.d.
Claudel, Paul, *Inleiding tot de Hollandse schilderkunst*, Rotterdam/Amsterdam, 1944.
Claus, Hugo, *De metsiers*, Brussels, 1948.
Coremans, P., *Van Meegerens fahed, Vermeers and De Hooghs*, Amsterdam, 1949.
Cornette, A.H., *Petrus Paulus Rubens*, Antwerp, 1940.
Croce, B., *Bresser van aesthetics*, Arnhem, 1926.

Degener, F. Schmidt, *Frans Hals*, Amsterdam, 1924.
Deventer, S. van, *Kröller-Müller, de geschiedenis van een cultureel levenswerk*, Haarlem, 1956.
Doelman, C., *Inleiding tot de kunst van Picasso*, Assen/Amsterdam, 1955.
Doesburg, Theo van, *Daumier als schilder* (reprint from *Oude Kunst*, 1918).
——, *Drie voordrachten over de nieuwe beeldende kunst*, Amsterdam, 1919.
——, *Grondbegrippen van de nieuwe beeldende kunst*, Nijmegen, 1983.
——, *Klassiek—barok—modern*, Antwerp, 1920.
Donk, P., *De vrije mens en de gebonden kunsten oratie Delft,* Haarlem, 1958.
Duinkerken, Anton van, *Ascese der schoonheid*, Amsterdam, 1945.
Dürer, Albrecht, *Zijn dagboek van zijn reis door de Nederlanden*, Maastricht, n.d.
Duterle, Jean, *Jean-Baptiste Corot*, Amsterdam, 1960.

Eesteren, Cornelis van, *De conceptie van onze hedendaagse nederzettingen, cultuurlandschappen ...* , Amsterdam, 1958.
Elling, P., *De ontwerper en zijn tijd*, oratie Amsterdam, 1957.
Enzinde, Willem, *Limburgse beeldende kunstenaars*, The Hague, 1949.

Flenner, James T., *Amerika schildert*, The Hague, n.d.
Fore, Milton S., *Pierre-Auguste Renoir*, Amsterdam, 1955.

Foudraine, Jan, *Wie is van hout ...*, Bilthoven, 1972.

Gabriels, J. and Mertens, *De constanten in de Vlaamsche kunst*, Antwerp, 1941.
Gelder, H.E. van, *De historische schoonheid van The Hague*, Amsterdam, 1943.
——, *Rembrandt*, Amsterdam, 1948.
——, *Hendrik Chabot*, Amsterdam, n.d.
Gelder, H.E. van, and Beets, *Kunstgeschiedenis der Nederlanden*, Utrecht, 1936.

Gill, Eric, *Over Typografie*, Amsterdam, 1955.
Gils, J.B.F. van, *Een andere kijk op Pieter Bruegel den Ouden*, The Hague, 1940.
Glavemans-Doeve, A.,*Zestig reproducties van zijn werk*, Amsterdam, 1949.
Glück, C. and Vogelsang, *De schilderingen van Pieter Bruegel den Oude*, Antwerp, 1936.
Gogh, Vincent van, *Brieven aan Ridder van Rappard*, Amsterdam, 1937.
——, *Brieven aan zijn broeder*, Amsterdam, 1914.
Gratama, G.D., *Frans Hals*, The Hague, 1943.
Grohmann, Will, *Expressionisten*, Amsterdam, 1957.
——, *Paul Klee*, Amsterdam, 1955.
Groot, J.H. de, *Van compositie, contrapunt*, Bussum, 1926.
Gruyter, W. Jos de, *Beeldhouwkunst*, The Hague, 1939.
——, *De Europese schilderkunst na 1850*, The Hague/Antwerp, 1954.
——, *Nederlandse schilderkunst uit de Gouden Eeuw*, Amsterdam, 1941.
——, *Wezen en ontwikkeling der Europese schilderkunst na 1850*, Amsterdam, 1935.
——, *Schilderijen zien,* Amsterdam, 1934.
——, *Lajos d'Ebneth*, The Hague, 1946.

Hammacher, A.M, *Jeroen Bosch*, n.l., n.d.
——, *John Raedecker*, Amsterdam, 1940.
——, *Amsterdamse Impressionisten en hun kring*, Amsterdam, 1946.
——, *Charley Toorop in haer werken* (reprint from *Elseviers Geëillustreerd Maandschrift*, 1939).
——, *Mendes da Costa; de geestelijke boodschap der beeldhouwkunst*, Rotterdam, 1941.
——, *Stromingen en persoonlijkheden*, Amsterdam, 1955.
——, *Zadkine*, Amsterdam, 1954.
Hampe, G. and Hahndieck, *Beeldhouwers in beeld*, Utrecht, 1961.
Hana, Herman, *Vijf eeuwen schilderkunst*, Amsterdam, 1957.
——, *De schoonheid in de Schilderkunst*, Baarn, n.d.
——, *Roeland Koning, een beeld van zijn werk*, Baarn, n.d.
Hannema, D., *Van Daumier tot Picasso*, Almelo, 1956.
Hannema, Fr., *Gerard-Terborch*, Amsterdam.
Havelaar, Just, *De religie der ziel*, Arnhem, 1938.
——, *De symboliek der kunst*, Haarlem, 1918.
Havelaar, Just, *Oud-Hollandsche figuurschilders*, Haarlem, 1915.

——, *Vincent van Gogh*, Amsterdam, 1943
——, *Het portret door de eeuwen*, Arnhem, 1930.
——, *Hoogtepunten der Oud Hollandsche landschapskunst*, Bilthoven, 1942.
——, *Vincent van Gogh*, Amsterdam, 1946.
——, *De Nederlandsche landschapskunst tot het einde der zeventiende eeuw*, Amsterdam, 1931.
Helbig, J., *Meesterwerken van de glasschilderkunst in de oude Nederlanden*, Antwerp, 1941.
Hennus, M.F., *J.B. Jongkind*, Amsterdam , 1945[?].
Henseling, Robert, *Omstreden wereldbeeld*, Amsterdam, 1944.
Hilaire-Germain, Edgar, *Degas*, Amsterdam, 1955.
Hoenderdaal, G.J,*Religieuse existentie en aesthetische beschouwing*, Arnhem, 1948.
Huebner, F.M., *Nederlandse en Vlaamse rococo-schilders*, The Hague, 1943.
——, *De romantische schilderkunst in de Nederlanden*, The Hague, 1942.
——, *De romantische schilderkunst in Vlaanderen*, The Hague, 1946.
Huizinga, J., *Het aesthetische bestanddeel van geschiedkundige voorstellingen*, Haarlem, 1905.
Hulzen, A. van, *Utrecht,* Amsterdam, 1944.

Jaffé, Hans L.C.,*De Stijl, 1917-1931*, Amsterdam, 1956.
——, *Het probleem der werkelijkheid in de beeldende kunst der XXe eeuw*, Amsterdam, 1958.
Janssen, Miek, *Jan Toorop*, Amsterdam, 1916[?].
Janssen, Pierre, *Kunstgrepen*, Amsterdam, 1961.
Jolles, André, *Bezieling en vorm*, Haarlem, 1923.
Jongh, Johanna de, *Het Hollandsche landschap in ontstaan en wording*, The Hague, 1903.

Kaas, A.J.W., *August Strindberg*, Arnhem, 1948.
Kirst, Hans Hellmut, *Kultura 5*, Baarn, n.d.
Kist, J.R., *Daumier, verslaggever van zijn tijd, 1832-1872*, Utrecht, 1971.
Kloos, W.B., *De stedebouwkundige ontwikkeling in Nederland*, Amsterdam, 1947.
Knoef, J., *Tusschen rococo en romantiek*, The Hague, 1943.
——, *Van romantiek tot realisme*, The Hague, 1947.
Knuttel, G., *De Nederlandsche schilderkunst . . .*, Amsterdam, 1938.
Knuttel, G. Jr., *Japansche prenten*, Maastricht, 1942.
Knuttel Wzn.,G., *De letter als kunstwerk*, Amsterdam, 1951.
——, *Hercules Seghers*, Amsterdam , 1941.
Konijnenburg, W.A. van, *De aesthetische idee*, The Hague, 1916.
Korevaar-Hesseling, E.H., *Het Nederlandse volkskarakter weerspiegeld in de Nederlandse schilderkunst*, The Hague, 1941.
Kröller-Müller, Hélène, *Beschouwingen over problemen in de ontwikkeling der moderne schilderkunst*, Maastricht, n.d.[1925].

Langui, Em., *Marino Marini*, Amsterdam, 1954.
Lassaigne, Jacques, *Picasso*, Amsterdam, 1949.
Leerink, Hans, *Oude monumentale kunst in Bretagne*, Amsterdam, 1949.
Lepchetz, Jacques, *Amedeo Modigliani*, Amsterdam, 1955.
Loeser, Norbert, *Ortega y Gasset*, The Hague, 1949.
Loon, Hendrik van, *De mens en zijn kunst*, The Hague, 1938.

Mander, Carel van, *Het schilderboek*, Amsterdam, 1936.
Martin, W., *Frans Hals en zijn tijd*, Amsterdam, 1942.
——, *Herleefde schoonheid, 25 jaar monumentenzorg in Nederland*, Amsterdam, 1943.
——, *Rembrandt en zijn tijd*, Amsterdam, 1942.
——, *Van Nachtwacht tot Geeststoet*, Amsterdam/Antwerp, 1947.
Marx, Claude Roger, *Dufy op de renbaan*, The Hague, 1957.
Millar, Oliver, *Thomas Gainsborough*, Amsterdam, 1949.
Muls, Jozef, *Schilders van gisteren*, Utrecht, n.d.
Müseler, Wilhelm, *Europeesche kunst*, Amsterdam, 1940[?].

Naso, P. Oorduis, *De Kunst der Vrijage*, Amsterdam, 1941.
Neurdenburg, Elisabeth, *Delftsch aardewerk*, Amsterdam, 1943.
——, *De Zeventiende eeuwsche beeldhouwkunst in de noordelijke Nederlandse*, Amsterdam, 1948.
Nicolas, Joep, *Wij glazeniers*, Utrecht, n.d.
Norderfalk, Carl, *Vincent van Gogh*, Amsterdam, n.d.

Olman, P., *Huizinga als Kultuurhistoricus*, Haarlem, n.d.
Oratino, P., *Ontaarde kunst,* 's-Graveland, 1945.
Ortega y Gasset, José, *Het gezichtspunt in de kunsten*, (reprint from *Vrije Bladen*, 1937), The Hague, 1937.
Ottema, Naune, *Het kunstambacht en de volkskunst in Friesland*, Amsterdam, 1942.
Oxenaar, R.W.D., *De schilderkunst van onze tijd*, Zeist, 1958.
Ozinga, M.D., *Daniël Marot*, Amsterdam, 1938.

Pen, J., *Harmonie en conflict*, Amsterdam, 1962.
Pilo, Giuseppe M., *Canaletto*, Deventer, 1961.
Pit, A., *Denken en beelden*, Amsterdam, 1922.
Plantenga, J.H. et al, *Vijftig eeuwen bouw-, beeld-, houw- en schilderkunst*, Zutphen, 1949.
Plasschaert, Albert, *Johannes Vermeer en Pieter de Hooch*, Amsterdam, 1924.
Platschek, Hans, *Nieuwe figuratieve kunst?* The Hague, 1960.
Platte, Hans, *De Franse Impressionisten*, Zeist/Arnhem, 1962.
Polak, Henri, *Het kleine land en zijn groote schoonheid*, Amsterdam, 1940.
Poortenaar, Jan, *Rembrandt teekeningen*, Naarden, 1944.
Praag, S. van, *Japanse Prentkunst*, Amsterdam/Antwerp, n.d.

Raaf, K.H. de, *Hoffmann von Fallersleben*, The Hague, 1943.

Rana, Herman, *Het schouwtooneel der schilderkunst*, Nijkerk, 1930.
Rathenau, Walther, *Op nieuwe banen*, Amsterdam, 1919.
Redeker, Hans, *De dagen der artistieke vertwijfeling*, Amsterdam, 1950.
——, *Existentialisme*, Amsterdam, 1949.
Révész, G., *Creatieve begaafdheid*, The Hague, 1946.
Révész-Alexander, M., *Byzantijnsche kunst in Italië*, Amsterdam, 1938.
Rewald, John, *Camille Pissarro*, Amsterdam, 1955.
Ridder, André de, *Remy de Gourmont*, Leiden, n.d.
Rijn, Theo van, *Beeldhouwen*, Amsterdam, 1936.
Rilke, Rainier Maria, *Brieven over Cézanne*, The Hague, 1945.

Sandberg, W. and Jaffé, *Kunst van heden in het Stedelijk*, Amsterdam, 1961.
Scheer, P.A., *Honderd jaren Nederlandsche schilder en teekenkunst*, The Hague, 1946.
Schuurman, K.E., *Carel Fabritius*, Amsterdam, 1947.
Seuphor, Michel, *Mondriaan, Composities*, The Hague, 1958.
Sinninghe, J.R.W., *Over volkskunst*, Amsterdam, 1943.
Söderhjëhn, T. and W., *De Italiaansche renaissance*, Utrecht, 1909.
Staal, Arthur, *Hellas*, Amsterdam, 1944.
——, *Onder de Gouden Zon van het morgenland*, Amsterdam, 1955[?].
Steenkamp, J.C.P., *Heraldich in kunsthistorischen en aesthetischen zin*, Amsterdam, 1948.
Sterck-Proot, J.M., *De historische schoonheid van Haarlem*, Amsterdam, 1942, 1946.
Stols, A.A.M., *Het werk van S.H. de Roos*, Amsterdam, 1942.
Streuvels, Stijn, *Reinaert De Vos*, Amsterdam, n.d.
Stuvel, H.J., *Koorbanken in Nederlandsche kerken*, The Hague, 1946.
Swillens, P.T.A, *Nederland in de prentkunst*, Amsterdam, 1944.
——, *Prentkunst in De Nederlanden tot 1800*, Utrecht, n.d.

Tas, S., *Johan Brouwer, outsider en bezieler*, The Hague, 1946.
Teenstra, Anno et al, *Nederlandse volkskunst*, Amsterdam, 1941.
Tergast, Nes, *Hendrik Chabot*, The Hague, 1946.
Terpstra, P., *Grafiek en tekeningen M.C. Escher*, Zwolle, 1960.
Thienen, Fr. van, *Pieter de Hoogh*, Amsterdam, n.d.
Tierlinck, Herman, *Henry van de Velde*, Brussel, n.d.
Tralbant, M.E.,*Vincent van Gogh, Antwerpsche periode*, Amsterdam, 1948.
Tschichold, Jan, *Wat iedereen van drukwerk behoort te weten*, Amsterdam, 1951.

Valsecchi, Marco,*De metafysische schilderkunst*, Amsterdam, 1960.
Valkenburg, C.T. van, *J. Huizinga, zijn leven en zijn persoonlijkheid*, Amsterdam, 1946.
Various authors, *Paul van Ostaijen*, Amsterdam, 1952.
——, *Uit de werkplaats der Beeldhouwers*, Amsterdam, n.d.
Vaudayer, Jean-Louis, *De Franse impressionisten*, Amsterdam, 1955.
Vemeylen, A., *Hieronymus Bosch*, Amsterdam, n.d.

Velde, Henry van der, *Formules van een moderne esthetiek*, Antwerp, 1928.
Veth, Jan, *Rembrandts leven en kunst*, Amsterdam, 1906.
——, *Rembrandts leven + kunst*, Amsterdam, 1941.
Viollet-le-Duc, E.E., *Geschiedenis van een teekenaar*, Amsterdam, n.d.
Vollgraff, C.W., *Herdenking van Johan Huizinga*, Haarlem, 1945.
Vondel, J. van den, *Gijsbreght van Aemstel*, Amsterdam, 1950.
Vonhoff, H.J.L., *Bewegend verleden*, Alphen aan den Rijn, 1969.
Voorde, Urbain v.d., *Het Raadsel van den Meester van Flemale*, Brussel, 1931.
Vries, A.B. de, *Jan Vermeer van Delft*, Amsterdam, 1939.
Vrijman, Jan, *De werkelijkheid van Karel Appel*, Amsterdam, 1962.
Vroom, N.R.A., *De Schilders van het monochrome banketje*, Amsterdam, 1945.

Waal, H. v.d., *Jan van Goyen*, Amsterdam, n.d.
Waasdijk, Albert van, *Harlekijns*, Rotterdam, 1929.
Wallagh, Bob, *De echte Van Meegeren*, Amsterdam, 1947.
Wasch, Karel, *Glas en kristal*, Rotterdam, 1924.
Wenkebach, L. Oswald, *Een droom*, n.l., n.d.
——, *De Versiering en het handwerk, oratie Delft*, Amsterdam/Leiden, 1935.
Wentinck, Charles, *De moderne beeldhouwkunst in Europa*, Zeist, 1958.
——, *Geschiedenis van moderne schilderkunst*, Utrecht, 1962.
——, *Moderne Kunst*, Zeist, 1962.
Werner, Alfred, *Henri Rousseau*, Amsterdam, 1956.
Wijdeveld, H.Th., *Académie Européenne "Méditerranée"*, Amsterdam, 1933.
——, *De Nieuwe Orde*, Lage Vuursche, 1940.
——, *Elckerlyc*, Lage Vuursche, 1934.
——, *Naar een internationale werkgemeenschap*, Santpoort, 1931.
——, *Vita Nova Nata Est Nobis*, Letanie, 1941.
Wijnbak, D., *De Nachtwacht, de historie van een meesterwerk*, Amsterdam, 1944.
Wijngaert, Frank v.den, *Antoon van Dijck*, Antwerp, 1943.
Wijsenbeek, L. and J.J.P. Oud, *Mondriaan*, Zeist, 1962.
Willink, A.C., *De Schilderkunst in een kritiek stadium*, Amsterdam, n.d.

Zahn, A. von, *Ontleedkundig handboekje*, Bussum, 1911.
Zervos, Christian, *27 weken van Pablo Picasso, 1939-1945*, Brussels, 1946.

German
Anbert, Marcel, *Romenische Plastik in Frankreich*, Berlin, 1937[?].
Antworten, Jahrbuch Freie Akademie der Künste in Hamburg, Hamburg, 1963.
Apollonio, Umbro, *Fauves and Cubists*, Bergauw, 1959.
Arata, G.U., *Mittelalterliche Städte der Toskana*, Berlin, 1941.
——, *Mittelalterliche Städte Umbriens*, Berlin, n.d.
Asmodi, Herbert, *Vincent van Gogh, Sonne und Erde*, Feldafing, 1954.

Bachofer, Ludwig, *Die Kunst der Japanischen Holzschnittmeister*, Munich, 1922.
Badt, Kurt, *Modell und Maler von Jan Vermeer*, Cologne, 1961.

Baeumler, Alfred, *Hegels Aesthetik*, Munich, 1922.
Basler, Otto et al, *Der Grosse Duden, Bildwörterbuch*, Leipzig, 1935.
Baumeister, Willi, *Magie der Form*, Baden-Baden, 1954.
Bazin, Germain, *Die Impressionisten in Louvre*, Heidelberg, 1958.
Beach, Sylvia, *Treffpunkt: ein Buchladen in Paris*, Munich, n.d.
Beenken, Hermann, *Der Meister von Naumburg*, Berlin, 1939.
——, *Hubert und Jan van Eyck*, Munich, 1941.
Begegnungen, Jahrbuch Freie Academie der Kunste, Hamburg, 1953.
Bell, Clive, *Kunst*, Dresden, 1922.
Benesch, Otto, *Der Maler Albrecht Dürer*, Vienna, 1939.
Bissier, Julius, *Farbige Miniaturen*, Munich, 1960.
Blümel, C., *Tierplastik, Bildwerke aus funf Jahrtausenden*, Berlin, 1939.
Bode, Wilhelm von, *Rembrandt und seine Zeitgenossen*, Leipzig, 1923.
Boeck, W. and Kohlhammer, *Picasso*, Stuttgart, 1955.
Boehn, Otto, *Von Geheimnisvollen Massen, Zahlen und Zeichen*, Leipzig, 1929.
Bonde, Ewald U., *Aufklärung, Klassik und Romentik*, Braunschweig, 1925
Bondi, Georg, *Erinnerungen an Stefan George*, Berlin, 1934.
Brödner, Erika, *Immanuel Kroeken, Moderne Schule*, Munich, 1951.
Buckheim, L.G., *Wie malt man abstrakt*, n.l., 1958.
Büddemann, Werner, *Welcher stil ist das?*, Stuttgart, 1938.
Burckhardt, Jacob, *Die Kultur der Renaissance in Italien*, Leipzig, 1908.
——, *Erinnerungen ans Rubens*, Leipzig, 1950[?].
——, *Kulturgeschichte Griechenlands*, Berlin., n.d.
——, *Kulturgeschichtliche Vorträge*, Leipzig, n.d.
——, *Rubens*, Vienna, 1938.
——, *Weltgeschichtliche Betrachtungen*, Leipzig, 1933.
——, *Briefe an einen Architekten*, Munich, 1913.
Burger, Fritz, *Cézanne und Hodler*, Munich, 1918.
Buschor, Ernst, *Griechische Vasen*, Munich, 1940.

Carli, Enzo, *Ambrogio Lorenzetti*, Baden-Baden, 1956.
Ch'i Po-shih, *Farbige Pinselzeichnungen*, n.l., n.d.
Christoffel, Ulrich, *Landschaften Deutschen Romentiker*, Baden-Baden, 1957.
——, *Meisterwerke der Französische Kunst*, Leipzig, 1939.
Cogniat, Raymond, *Bonnard*, Cologne, 1953[?].
——, *Seurat*, Cologne, 1953[?].
Courthion, Pierre, *Raoul Dufy 1877-1953*, Berlin, ca. 1954[?].

Degenhart, Bernhard, *Antonio Diganello*, Vienna, 1940.
Delogu, Guiseppe, *Italienische Bildhauerei*, Zurich, 1942.
Deri, Max, *Die neue Malerei*, Leipzig, 1921.
Deschner, Karlheinz, *Kitsch Konvention und Kunst*, Munich, 1948.
Dessauer, Friedrich et al, *Merssinger, Befeurung der Technik*, Stuttgart/Berlin, 1931.
Die Spur des Menschen, Jahrbuch Freie Academie der Kunste, Hamburg, 1954.
Dülberg, Franz, *Frans Hals, ein leben und ein Werk*, Stuttgart, 1930.

Dussler, Luitpolt, *Italienische Meisterzeichnungen*, Frankfurt am Main, 1938.
Dresler, Adolf, *Deutsche Kunst und entartete Kunst*, Munich, 1938.
Duret, Th., *Die Impressionisten*, Berlin, 1920.
Dvorak, Jan, *Pieter Brueghel, Flämisches Volksleben*, Berlin, 1935.
Dvorak, Max, *Die Gemalde Peter Bruegels des älteren*, Vienna, 1944.

Edschmid, Kasimir, *Lebendiger Expressionismus*, Munich, 1964.
Engels, Matthias T., *August Mache*, Recklinghausen, 1958.
Evens, Hans Gerhard, *Peter Paul Rubens*, Munich, 1942.

Fechter, Paul, *Der Expressionismus*, Munich, 1920.
Fiocco, Guiseppe, *Giorgione*, Hamburg, 1941.
Fraenger, Wilhelm, *Matthias Grünewald*, Berlin, 1936.
Francois-Poncet, André, *Als Botschaften in "Dritter Reich"*, Mainz, 1980.
Friedlaender, Ludwig, *Sittengeschichte Roms*, Vienna, 1934.
Friedländer, Max J., *Die Altniederländische Malerei*, Berlin, 1927.
——, *Pieter Bruegel*, Berken, 1921.

Geist, Hans Friedrich, *Paul Klee*, Hamburg, 1948.
Gerstenberg, Kurt, *Albrecht Dürer*, Berlin, 1936.
——, *Tilman Riemenschneider*, Vienna, 1941.
Gertz, Ulrich, *Plastiek der Gegenwart*, Berlin, 1953.
Giedion, Siegfried, *Spätbarocher und Romentischer Klassizismus*, Munich, 1922.
Giedion-Welcker, Carola, *Paul Klee*, Teufen/St Gallen, 1954.
Gluck, Heinrich and Duz, *Die Kunst des Islam*, Berlin, 1925.
Goethe, Johann von, *Kunstphilosophie*, Leipzig, 1905.
——, *Kunstschriften*, vol 2, Leipzig, 1920.
Gradmann, Erwin, *Indische Miniaturen*, Bern, 1949.
Graeffe, Julius Meier, *Eduard Manet*, Munich, 1912.
Grassi, Daniele, *Emilio Greco, Plastiken und Zeichnungen*, Munich, 1959.
Graul, Richard, *Rembrandt Handzeichnungen*, Leipzig, n.d.
Griesmaier, Viktor, *Impressionismus*, Vienna, 1956.
Grothe, Heinz, *Junge Bildhauer unserer Zeit*, Berlin/Königsberg/Leipzig, 1940.
Grimm, Herman, *Leben Michelangelos*, Vienna, n.d.
——, *Raphael*, Vienna, n.d.
Gröbner, Karl, *Die Bildwerke des Bamberger Domo*, Leipzig, n.d.
Grohmann, Will, *Deutsche Abstrakte Malerei*, Baden-Baden, 1954.
——, *Henry Moore*, Berlin, 1960.
——, *Josef Hegenbarth Zeichnungen*, Berlin, 1959.
——, *Max Ackermann*, Stuttgart, 1955.
——, *Wassily Kandinsky*, Cologne, 1958.
Gröning, Karl, *Die Bühnenbilder*, Hamburg, 1962.
Grosse, Ralph, *Die Holländische Landschaftskunst 1600-1650*, Berlin/ Leipzig, 1925.
Guyer, S., *Siena und die Hügelstädte der Toskana*, Augsburg, n.d.

Haeckel, Ernst, *Die Natur als Künstlerin*, Berlin, 1913.

Haftmann, Werner, *Deutsche abstrakte Maler*, n.l., n.d.
——, *Malerei in 20. Jahrhunderts*, Munich, 1935.
——, *Malerei in 20. Jahrhundert*, Munich, 1954.
——, *Paul Klee*, Munich, 1950.
Hamann, Richard, *Die Früh Renaissance der Italienischen Malerei*, Jena, 1909.
——, *Geschichte der Kunst*, Berlin, 1933.
——, *Tierplastik in Wandel der Zeiten*, Maxburg, 1949.
Händler, Gerhard, *Deutsche Maler der Gegenwart*, Berlin, 1956.
Hausenstein, Wilhelm, *Was bedeutet die moderne Kunst*, Stuttgart, 1949.
——, *Das Bild, Atlanten zur Kunst*, Munich, 1922.
——, *Das Werk des Vittore Carpaccio*, Stuttgart/Berlin/Leipzig, 1925.
——, *Giotto*, Berlin, 1923.
Hauser, Heinrich, *Notre Dame von der Wogen*, Jena, 1937.
Hegemann, Hans W., *Giovanni Battista Tiepolo*, Berlin, 1940.
Heidrich, Ernst, *Alt-Niederländische Malerei*, Jena, 1924.
——, *Vlaemische Malerei*, Jena, 1924.
Hentzen, Alfred, *Lyonel Feininger, Aquarelle*, Munich, 1958.
Hermann Unde-Bernays, *Künstlerbriefe Uber Kunst*, Dresden, 1926.
Henze, Anton, *Fibel der Modernen Malerei*, Baden-Baden, n.d
Hess, Hans, *Dank in Farben*, Munich, 1957.
Heyck, Ed, *Luckas Cranach*, Bielefeld/Leipzig, 1927.
Hildebrand, Adolf, *Das Problem der Form in der bildende Kunst*, Strassburg, 1910.
Hoff, August, *Wilhelm Lehmbruck*, Berlin, 1936.
Hofmann, Werner, *Henry Moore, Schriften und Skulpturen*, Frankfurt, 1959.
——, *Klee*, Frankfurt, 1961.
——, *Zeichnen und Gestalt*, Frankfurt, 1957.
Holbein, Hans, *Bildnisse*, Leipzig, n.d.
Holzhausen, Walter, *August Mache*, Munich, 1956.
Houttmann, Max, *Die Kunst des Frühen Mittelalters*, Berlin, 1929.
Huck, Ricarda, *Michael Unger*, Leipzig, 1940.
Huebner, Friedrich M., *Hieronymus Bosch*, Berlin, 1939.
——, *Niederländische Plastik*, Dresden, n.d.
Hüth, Erich, *Gabriël Riesser 1806-1863*, Hamburg, 1963.

Jedding, Hermann, *Raoul Duffy*, Berken, n.d.
Jedlincka, Gotthard, *Französische Malerei*, Zürich/Berlin, 1938.
——, *Pieter Bruegel*, Erlenbach, 1938.
Jodl, Friedrich, *Asthetisch der Bildenden Künste*, Stuttgart/Berlin, 1920.
Justi, Carl, *Velazquez und sein Jahrhundert*, Zurich 1933.

Kahnweiler, D-H., *Picasso, Keramik*, Hannover, 1957.
Kandinsky, Wassily, *Farben und Klänge*, Baden-Baden, 1956.
Katz, Richard, *Drei Gesichter Luzifers; Vorm, Maschine, Geschaft*, Leipzig, 1934.
Klee, Paul, *Engel bringt das gewunschte*, Basel, 1953.

——, *Handzeichnungen*, Wiesbaden, 1951.
——, *Im hande Edelstein*, Baden-Baden, 1952.
——, *Optische Regionen*, Feldafing, 1955.
——, *Tagebücher 1898-1918*, Cologne, 1957.
——, *Vogel-Begegnung*, Munich, 1960.
Knapp, Fritz, *Grünewald*, Leipzig, 1935.
Kolbe, Georg, *Bildwerke; vom Künstler ausgewählt*, Leipzig, 1900.
——, *Vom Leben der Plastik*, Berlin, n.d.
Kontrapunkte, Jahrbuch Freie Akademie der Künste in Hamburg, Hamburg, 1956.
Kreis, Friedrich, *Die Autonomie des Asthetischen in der neueren Philosophie*, Tübingen, 1922.
Kriegbaum, Friedrich, *Michelangelo Buonarroti, die Bildwerke*, Berlin, 1940.
Kroll, Bruno, *Deutsche Mahler der Gegenwart*, Berlin, 1937
Kühnel, Ernst, *Indische Miniaturen*, Berlin, 1937.
Kurth, Julius, *Die Prunieven des Japan holz schnitts*, Dresden, 1922.
Kusenberg, Kurt, *Mit Bildern Leben*, Munich, 1955.
——, *Picasso*, Munich, 1953.

Lange, Kurt, *Egyptische Kunst*, Berlin, 1939.
Langyet, I. Schneider, *Griechische Terrakotten*, Munich, 1936.
Lankhiet, Klaus, *Franz Marc*, Berlin, 1950.
Lants, Jan, *Antonello da Messina*, Vienna, 1940.
——, *Das Stundenbuch der Duc de Berry*, Baden-Baden, 1953.
——, *Domenico Ghirlandaio*, Vienna, 1943.
Larck, Carl van, *Tilman Riemerschneider*, Berlin/Königsberg/Leipzig, 1939.
Léger, Fernand, *Menschen und Objekte, Zeichnungen*, Feldafing, 1955.
Lönnest, Elias, *Kalevala*, Stuttgart, 1978.
Leporini, Heinrich, *Hans Holbein der jungere*, Berlin, 1926.
Loewenstein, Fritz E., *Die Handzeichnungen der Japanischen Holzschnittmuster*, Planen im Vogtland, 1922.
Ludwig, Emil, *Michelangelo*, Berlin, 1930.
——, *Kunst und Schicksal*, Berlin, 1928.

Mache, August, *Aquarelle*, Munich, 1958.
Manteuffel, K.Z. von, *Die Künstlerfamilie Van de Velde*, Leipzig, 1927.
——, *Pieter Brueghel, Landschaften*, Berlin, 1934.
Martin, W., *Altholländische Bilder*, Berlin, 1921.
Matisse, Henri, *Farbe und Gleidmis, Gesammelte Schriften*, Hamburg, 1960.
Mauclair, Camille, *Brügge im Bild*, Berlin, 1936[?].
Meier-Graefe, Julius, *Paul Cézanne*, Munich, 1913.
——, *Vincent*, Munich, 1910.
Melchers, Bernd, *China, Der Tempelbau, die Lochan van king-yän-sï*, Hagen, 1921.
Meursen, Theodor, *Geestige Landerkunde Holland*, Nuremburg, 1956
Meumann, E., *Asthetik der Gegenwart*, Leipzig, 1912.

Meyer, Alfred G., *Donatello*, Leipzig, 1926.
Mondrian, Piet, *Neue Gestaltung, Neoplastizismus, Nieuwe beelding*, Munich, 1925.
Moore, Henry, *Katakomben*, Munich, 1956.
Müseler, Wilhelm, *Deutsche Kunst*, Berlin, 1941.

Nebbia, Ugo, *Michelangelo, Bildhauer, Maler, Architekt, Dichter*, Leipzig, 1940.
Nemitz, Fritz, *Die Kunst Russlands*, Berlin, 1940.
Neumayer, Heinrich, *Expressionismus*, Vienna, 1956.
——, *Fauvism*, Vienna, 1956.
Neutra, Richard, *Auftrag für Morgen*, Hamburg, 1962.
Neuwirth, Arnulf, *Abstraktion*, Vienna, 1956.
Nicodemi, Giorgo, *Leonardo da Vinci, Gemälde Zeichnungen*, Leipzig, 1940.

Olivier, Fernande, *Neues Jahre mit Picasso*, Munich, 1959.
Ostwald, Wilhelm, *Die Farbenfibel*, Leipzig, 1921.
——, *Die Harmonie der Farben*, Leipzig, 1921.
——, *Grosse Mönner, Studien zur Biologie des Genies*, Leipzig, 1927.

Penrose, R., *Picasso, Leben und Werk*, Munich, 1961.
Pfister, Kurt, *Herkules Segers*, Munich, 1921.
——, *Hieronymus Bosch*, Potsdam, 1922.
Picasso, Pablo, *Ballettzeichnungen*, Feldafing, 1956.
——, *Lithographien*, Feldafing, 1955.
——, *Wort und Bekenntnis*, Zurich, 1954; Berlin, 1957.
Pisanello, Antonio, *Die Vision des Reikgen Eustachius*, Berlin, 1948.
Planiscig, Leo, *Andrea del Verocchio*, Vienna, 1941.
——, *Bernardo und Antonio Rosselino*, Vienna, 1942.
——, *Desiderio da Settignano*, Vienna, 1942.
——, *Donatello*, Vienna, 1939.
——, *Lorenzo Ghiberti*, Vienna, 1940.
——, *Luca della Robbia*, Vienna, 1940.
Platschek, Hans, *Dichtung moderner Maler*, Wiesbaden, 1956.
Platte, Hans, *Malerei*, Munich, 1957.
——, *Plastik*, Munich, 1957.
Plietzsch, Eduard, *Vermeer van Delft*, Munich, 1939.
Popp, Joseph, *Die Figurale Wandmalerei*, Leipzig, 1921.
——, *Die Technik als Kulturproblem*, Munich, 1929.
Posse, Hans, *Lucas Cranach d.A.*, Vienna, 1942.
Pretorius, Emil, *Persische Miniaturen*, Munich, 1958.

Quesne-van Gogh, E. du, *Persönliche Erinnerungen an Vincent van Gogh*, Munich, 1913.

Rank, Otto, *Der Künstler*, Leipzig, 1925.
Raphael, Max, *Von Monet zu Picasso*, Munich, 1913.
Raynal, Maurice, *Picasso*, Munich, 1921.

Regamey, P., *Kirche und Kunst im XX. Jahrhundert*, Graz, 1954.
Richardson, John, *Pablo Picasso, Aquarelle und Gonachen*, Basel, 1956.
Richter, Horst, *El Lissitzky, Sieg Uber die Sonne, zur Kunst des Konstruktivismus*, Cologne, 1958.
Riegl, A., *Das Holländische Gruppenportrait*, Vienna, 1931.
Révész-Alexander, M., *Die Alten Lagerhäuser*, Amsterdam/The Hague, 1928.
Rilke, Rainier Maria, *Auguste Rodin*, Leipzig, 1913.
——, *Die Aufzeichnungen des Malte Laurids Brigge*, Leipzig, 1926.
Roditz, Eduard, *Dialoge über Kunst*, Wiesbaden, 1960.
Roh, Franz, *Nach-Expressionismus*, Leipzig, 1925.
——, *Hollandische Landschaftsmalerei des XVII Jahrhunderts*, Leipzig, 1923.
——, *Holländische Malerei*, Jena, 1921.
Rothkirch, Wolf von, *Deutsche Kunst*, Berlin, 1934.
Rosenberg, Adolf, *Terborch und Jan Steen*, Leipzig, 1897.
Rosenberg, Alfred, *Der Mythus der XX Jahrhunderts*, Munich, 1933.
Rosenblum, Robert, *Der Kubismus*, Teufen, 1960.
Rothes, Walter, *Hans Memling und die Renaissance in der Niederlanden*, Munich, 1926.
Ruskin, John, *Vorlesungen Uber Kunst*, Leipzig, n.d.

Sammer, Johannes, *Werner Peiner*, Königsberg, 1940.
Sandberg, Willem, *Experimenta typographical*, Cologne, 1955.
Sauerlandt, Max, *Die Kunst der letzten 30 Jahre*, Berlin, 1935.
——, *Michelangelo*, Düsseldorf/Leipzig, 1911.
Scheffler, Karl, *Form als Schicksal*, Leipzig, 1939.
Scheidegger, Ernst et al, *Sophie Tauber Arp, Hans Arp*, Zurich, 1960.
Schmidt, Georg, *Die Malerei in Deutschland, 1918-1955*, Königstein, 1960.
Schmidt, Paul F., *Die Kunst der Gegenwart*, Berlin, n.d.
——, *Geschichte des Modernen Malerei*, Stuttgart, 1952.
Schmittkenner, Paul, *Das sanfte Gesetz in der Kunst*, Stuttgart, 1954.
Schneider, Alfonds Maria, *Die Hagia Sophia zie Konstantin*, Berlin, 1939.
Schneller, Alfred, *Kubismus*, Vienna, 1956.
——, *Surrealismus*, Vienna, 1956.
Schubring, Paul, *Fra Angelico, der Maler und Mönth*, Munich, n.d.
Schudt, Ludwig, *Caravaggio*, Vienna, 1942.
Schuette, Marie, *Perzer-Teppiche*, Leipzig, 1935.
Schürer, Oscar, *Pablo Picasso*, Berlin, 1927.
Schweicher, Curt, *Vuillard*, Berne, 1955.
Schweinfurth, Philipp, *Geschichte der russischen Malerei im Mittelalter*, The Hague, 1930.
Sedlmayr, Hans, *Die Revolution der modernen Kunst*, Hamburg, 1955.
Seidlitz, W. von, *Leonardo da Vinci*, Vienna, n.d.
Seifert-Wattenberg, R., *Rembrandt Harmenz. van Rijn*, Munich, n.d.
——, *Van Eyck und Bruegel*, Munich, n.d.
Seilen, Herald, *Franz Marc*, Munich, 1956.

Springer, Jaro (ed), *Fuftfzig Biltniszeichnungen von Albrecht Dürer*, n.l., n.d.
Stein, Erwin et al, *Monographien Deutscher Städte, Altona*, Berlin, 1928.
Steindorff, Georg, *Die Kunst der Agypter*, Leipzig, 1928.
Stockmeyer, Ernst, *Gedanken Uber eine neue Aesthetik*, n.l., n.d.
Sydow, Eckart von, *Die Kunst der Naturvölker und der Vorzeit*, Berlin, 1932.

Tessenow, Heinrich, *Handwerk und Kleinstadt*, Berlin, 1919.
Thwaites, John A., *Ich hasse die moderne Kunst!* Frankfurt, 1960.
Tierzeichnüngen aus acht Jahr hunderten, Frankfurt am Main, n.d.
Trier, Eduard, *Marino Marini*, Cologne, 1954.
———, *Moderne Plastik*, Berlin, 1954.
———, *Zudiner des XX Jahrhunderts*, Berlin, 1956.
Tschichold, Jan, *Meister Buch der Schrift*, Ravensburg, 1952.
Tschuang-Tse, *Reden und Gleichnisse*, Leipzig, 1922.
Tucholsky, Kurt, *Das Lächeln der Mona Lisa*, Berlin, 1929.

Uhde, Wilhelm, *Henri Rousseau*, Dresden, 1921.
———, *Vincent van Gogh*, Vienna, 1936.
Umwege, Jahrbuch Freie Academie der Kunste, Hamburg, 1955.
Usinger, Fritz, *Ernst Wilhelm Nay*, Munich, 1956.

Valker, Dora, *Georges Braque, vom Geheimnis in der Kunst*, Zurich, 1958.
Various authors, *Abstrakte Kunst, Theorien und Tendenzen*, Baden-Baden, n.d.
Vasari, Giorgio, *Lebensbeschreibungen der ausgezeichnetsten Maler, Bildhauer und Architekten der Renaissance*, Berlin, 1911.
Velde, Henry van der, *Die drei Sünden wider die Schönheit*, Zurich, 1918.
———, *Geschichte meines Lebens*, Munich, 1962.
Verdet, André, *Fernand Léger*, Zurich, 1957.
Verrier, Bruno E., *Deutsche Plastik der Gegenwart*, Berlin, 1940.
Vollard, Ambroise, *Erinnerungen eines Kunsthändlers*, Berlin, 1957.
Vosgt, Georg, *Die Renaissance*, Berlin, 1932.
Vriesen, G., *August Mache*, Stuttgart, 1953.

Waetzoldt, Wilhelm, *Bildnisse deutscher Kunsthistoriker*, Leipzig, 1921.
———, *Dürer und seine zeit*, Vienna, 1935.
———, *Jacob Burckhardt als Kunsthistoriker*, Leipzig, 1940.
Warringer, Wilhelm, *Egyptische Kunst*, Munich, 1927.
Weiler, Clemens, *Aknej Jawlensky*, Cologne, 1959.
Weinberger, Martin, *Ruisdael, der Maler der Landschaft*, Munich, n.d.
Westheim, Paul, *Künstler Bekentnisse*, Berlin, n.d.
——— et al, *Europa almanach*, Potsdam, 1925.
Wichenhagen, Ernst, *Geschichte der Kunst*, Berlin, 1932.
Wild, Doris, *Moderne Malerei*, Zurich, 1950.
———, *Modern French Painters*, London, 1947.
Willrich, Wolfgang, *Säuberung des Kunsttempels*, Munich/Berlin, 1938.
Wilm, Hubert, *Die Gothische Holzfigur*, Stuttgart, 1940.
Winckelmann, J., *Geschichte der Kunst des Altertums*, Vienna, 1934.

Wingler, Hans M., *Das Bauhaus*, Berlin, 1962.
Winkler, Friedrich, *Du Altniederländische Malerei*, Berlin, 1924.
Winzinger, Franz, *Kitagawa Utamaro*, Baden-Baden, 1955.
——, *Suzuh Harunobu Mädchen und Frauen*, Baden-Baden, 1956.
Wölfflin, Heinrich, *Albrecht Dürer, Handzeichnungen*, Munich[?], 1919.
——, *Das Erklären von Kunstwerken*, Leipzig, 1940.
——, *De Klassische Kunst*, Munich, 1924.
——, *Gedanken zur Kunstgeschichte*, Basel, 1941.
——, *Italiën und das Deutsche Famgefühl*, Munich, 1931.
——, *Kunstgeschichte Grundbegriffe*, Munich, 1921.
——, *Renaissance und Baroch*, Munich, 1926.
Wolfradt, Willie, *Lyonel Feininger*, Leipzig, 1924.
Wolzogen, A.F. von, *Ans Schinkels Nachlass*, Berlin, 1862.
Worringer, Wilhelm, *Abstraktion und Einfühlung*, Munich, 1919.

Zahn, Leopold, *Einführung in die Französische Malerei der Gegenwart*, Baden-Baden, n.d.
——, *Kleine Geschichte der modernen Kunst*, Berlin, 1956.
——, *Vincent van Gogh, Landschaftszeichnungen*, Baden-Baden, 1955.

English
Barr, Alfred H. Jr., *Masters of modern art*, New York, 1954.
——, *Picasso, Fifty years of historical art*, New York, 1946.
——, *Vincent van Gogh*, New York, 1936.
——, et al, *Georges Hugnet, fantastic art, Dada, Surrealism*, New York, 1936.
Benesch, Otto, *Rembrandt as a draughtsman*, London, 1960.
Bell, Clive, *The French Impressionists in full colour*, London, 1952.
Ben Sussan, René, *Marcel Brion, Raoul Dufy*, London, 1958.

Catton, Daniël, *Henri Rousseau*, New York, 1946.
Cooper, Douglas, *Nicolas de Stliel*, London, 1961.
——, *Paul Klee*, Middlesex, 1950.
Cowles, Fleur, *The case of Salvador Dali*, London, 1954.

Deighton, Harold, *The art of lettering*, London, 1947.
Duncan, D.D., *Picasso's Picassos*, London, 1961.
Dvorâk, F., *Twentieth-century painters, the Paris School*, London, n.d.

Elgar, Frank, *Van Gogh*, London, 1958.

Flenner, James Thomas, *American painting*, New York, 1950.
Friedländer, Max J., *On art and connoisseurship*, Oxford, 1946.

Gabo, Naum, *Of divers arts*, Washington, 1962.
Ghiselin, Brewster, *The creative process*, New York, 1955.
Grigson, Geoffrey, *Henry Moore*, Harmondsworth, 1944.

Hill, G.F., *Pisanello*, London/New York, 1911.

Hobson, R.L., *British Museum, handbook of the pottery and porcelain of the far east*, Oxford, 1937.
Holme, C.G. and Wainwright, *Decorative art 1930*, London, 1930.
Hope, Henry R.,*Georges Braque*, New York, 1949.
Howard, Edmund, *Genoa, history and art in an old seaport*, Genoa, 1971.
Hunter, Sam, *Modern French Painting*, New York, 1956.
——, *Dufy*, New York, 1954.

Kuh, Katharine, *Léger*, Chicago, 1953.

Lambert, R.S., *Art in England*, Harmondsworth, 1938.
Lazzaro, G. di San, *Klee*, London, 1957.
——, *Painting in France 1895-1949*, London, 1949.
Lewis, David, *Mondrian*, London, n.d.
Longhi, Roberto, *Piero della Francesca*, New York, 1949.

Mautain, Jacques, *Georges Rouault*, New York, 1954.
Muensterberger, W., *Vincent van Gogh, drawings, pastels, studies*, Bussum, 1949.

Newton, Eric, *Stanley Spencer*, Middlesex, 1947.
——, *European painting and sculpture*, Harmondsworth, 1945.
Novotny, F., *Cézanne*, London, 1961.

Powys, John Cowper, *The meaning of culture*, London, 1932.

Ramsden, E.H., *Twentieth century sculpture*, London, 1949.
Read, Herbert, *A concise history of modern painting*, London, 1959.
——, *Art Now*, London, 1948.
——, *Contemporary British art*, Harmondsworth, 1951.
——, *The meaning of art*, London, 1950.
——, *The philosophy of modern art*, London, 1952.
Rewald, John, *Post-impressionism: from Van Gogh to Gauguin*, New York, 1956.
——, *The History of Impressionism*, New York, 1946.
Rice, David Talbot, *Russian icons*, London/New York, 1947.
Robertson, Bryan, *Jackson Pollock*, London, 1960.
Rodin, Auguste, *Art*, London, 1912.
Roos, Frank J. Jr., *An illustrated handbook of art history*, New York, 1937.
Russell, John, *G. Braque*, London, 1959.

Seuphor, Michel, *Piet Mondrian, life and work*, Amsterdam, 1956.
Soby, James Thrall, *Joan Miró*, New York, 1959.
Sonchére, Dor de la, *Picasso in Antibes*, London, 1960.
Summerson, John, *Ben Nicolson*, Middlesex, 1948.
Sutton, Denys, *André Derain*, London, 1959.

Taylor, Basil, *The Impressionists and their world*, London, 1953.
Thoene, Peter, *Modern German art*, Harmondsworth, 1938.

Thwaites, J.A., *The Bauhaus painters and the new-style epoch* [reprint from *Art Quarterly*], n.l., 1951.
Tomkinson, R.R., *Children as artists*, London/New York, 1947.

Various authors, *Naum Gabo, Antoine Peisher*, New York, 1948.
——, *The romance of Chinese art*, New York, 1936.

Werner, Alfred, *Maurice Utrillo*, London, 1953.
Wilenski, R.H., *An introduction to Dutch art*, London, 1929.
——, *Modern French painters*, London, 1947.
Wright, W.H., *Modern painting*, London, 1916.

French
Adhémar, Jean, *Goya*, Paris, 1941.
Argan, Giulio Carlo, *Fra Angelico*, Geneva, 1955.

Babelon, Joan, *Pisanello*, Paris, 1931.
Barr, Alfred H. jr., *The Museum of Modern Art, New York*, Paris, 1950.
Basler, Adolphe, *Maurice Utrillo,* Paris, 1931.
Bataille, Georges, *Manet*, Geneva, 1955.
Bayard, Emile, *Le Style Louis XIV*, Paris, n.d.
Bazin, Germain, *Fra Angelico*, Paris, 1941.
——, *Memking*, Paris, 1939.
Berenson, B., *Les peintres Italiens de la renaissance*; Paris, 1926.
Bergson, Henri, *L'Evolution Créatrice*, Paris, 1948.
Besson, George, *Claude Monet*, Paris, n.d.
——, *Johan-Barthold Jongkind*, Paris, 1940.
——, *La Peinture Francaise au XXme siecle*, Paris, 1949.
——, *Sisley*, Paris, 1946.
——, *Paul Signac*, Paris, 1950.
——, *Signac*, Paris, 1935.
Bonnet, Philippe, *Peintures*, Paris, 1956.
Boudor-Lamotte, E., *Paris*, Paris, 1939.
Bouret, Jean, *Picasso*, Paris, 1950.
Brion, Marcel, *Art abstrait*, Paris, 1956
——, *Bosch*, Paris, 1938.
——, *Domela*, Paris, 1961.
——, *Georges Rouault*, Paris, 1950.
——, *Klee*, Paris, 1957.

Cassau, Jean, *Picasso*, Paris, 1940.
——, *Picasso*, Paris, 1949.
——, *Matisse*, Paris, 1939.
——, *Raoul Dufy, poète et artisan*, Geneva, n.d.
Catanne, Berre, *Van Gogh*, Paris, n.d.
Cathelin, Jean, *Arp,* Paris, 1959.
Catlin, Stanton L., *Art moderne Mexicain*, Paris, 1951.

Cayrol, Jean, *Manessier*, Paris, 1955.
Chastel, André, *Vuillard, Gemälde 1890-1930*, Paris, 1950.
Cladel, Judith, *Maillol*, n.l., n.d.
Cocteau, Jean, *Modigliani*, Paris, 1950.
Cogniat, Raymond, *Gauguin*, Paris, 1930.
——, *Raoul Dufy*, Paris, 1950.
——, *Cézanne*, Paris, 1939.
——, *Georges Rouault*, Paris, 1930.
Colombier, Pierre du, *Poussin*, Paris, 1931.
Cooper, Douglas, *William Turner*, Paris, 1949.
Coquiot, Gustave, *Paul Cézanne*, Paris, 1920[?].
Courthion, Pierre, *Le romantisme*, Geneva, 1961.

Dauval, Bernard, *De Parise School*, Paris, 1961.
——, *Les peintres du Vinqtième siecle*, Paris, 1957.
Degand, Leon and Rouart, *Claude Monet*, Geneva, 1958.
Delacroix, Eugene, *Oevres littéraires*, Paris, 1923.
Delevoy, Robert L., *Léger*, Geneva, 1962.
Des Carques, Pierre, *Amedeo Modigliani*, Paris, 1951.
Deshie, Jules, *Van der Weijden*, Brussel, 1926.
Dowal, Bernard, *Les peintres du XXe siecle*, Paris, 1957.
Dumont-Wilden, L., *Estephens, en Belgique*, Paris, 1939.
Duret, Theodore, *Van Gogh*, Paris, 1916.

Elgar, Frank, *Leger, peintures, 1911-1948*, Paris, 1948.
——, *Picasso et Léger, deux hommes, deux mondes*, Paris, 1954.
——, *Robert Mallard, Picasso*, Paris, n.d.
Escholier, Raymond, *La peinture Francaise XXe siecle*, Paris, 1937.
Estienne, Charles, *Chagall*, Paris, ca. 1951.
——, *Gauguin*, Geneva, 1953.
——, *Van Gogh*, Geneva, 1953.

Faille, J.B. de la, *Vincent van Gogh*, Paris, 1939.
Fels, Florent, *Claude Monet*, Paris, 1925.
Fierens, Paul, *Jean van Eyck*, Paris, 1931.
——, *Marcel Baugniet*, Paris, 1942.
——, *Memkric*, Paris, 1934.
——, *Marc Chagall*, Paris, 1929.
——, *Pemeke*, Paris, 1930.
Fouchet, Man Pal, *Bissiére*, Paris, 1955.
Fosca, Francois, *Degas*, Geneva, 1954.
Fraigneau, André, *Paul Facchetti, Venice*, Paris, n.d.
Fumet, Stanilas, *Braque*, Paris, 1946.

Genaille, Robert, *La Peinture Hollandaise*, Paris, 1956.
Genevoix, Maurice, *Vlaminck I l'homme*, Paris.
Gieure, Maurice, *G. Braque*, Paris, 1956.

Gindertael, Roger van, *Entretien avec César Domela*, Paris, 1970.
Giono, Jean, *Bernard Buffet*, Paris, 1956.
Gleizes, Albert, *Et le Cubisme*, Basel, 1962.
Graber, Hans, *Pierodella Francesca*, Basel, 1920.
Gros, Gabriël-Joseph, *Maurice Utrillo*, Paris, 1927.

Habasque, Gruy, *Le Cubisme*, Geneva, 1959.
Hauert, Roger and Verdet, *Pablo Picasso*, Genève, 1956.
Hourticq, Louis, *La peinture Francaise XVIIIe siècle*, Paris, 1939.
Huyghe, René, *Cézanne*, Paris, 1959.
——, *Du dessin francais*, n.l., 1959.
——, *Hommage a Frits Lugt*, Paris, 1971.

Ilyin, Maximilian, *Utrillo*, Paris, 1953.
Ingres, Jean August, *Penseés*, Paris, 1922.

Jadlicka, Gotthard, *Pissarro*, Berne, 1950.
Jamot, Paul, *Corot*, Paris, 1936.
Jandot, Maurice, *Legér*, Paris, 1956.
——, *Le Corbusier*, Paris, 1955.
Jewell, Edward Alden, *Georges Rouault*, Paris, 1947.
Jourdain, Francis, *Margnet*, Paris, 1959.
——, *Utrillo*, Paris, 1948.

Kahnweiler, D-H., *Klee*, Paris, 1950.
Kunstler, Charles, *Camille Pissarro*, Paris, 1930.
——, *Gauguin*, Paris, 1937.

Laprade, Jacques de, *Georges Seurat*, Monaco, 1945.
——, *Soutine*, Paris, 1954.
Lefebre, Henri, *Pignon*, Paris, 1956.
Lassaiane, Jacques, *Rouault*, Geneva, n.d.
——, *Lautrec*, Geneva, 1953.
Legendre, M. and Harris, *La peinture Espagnole*, Paris, 1937.
Lejard, André, *Braque*, Paris, 1949.
——, *Matisse, peintures, 1939-1946*, Paris, 1950, 1952.
——, *Mausse*, Paris, 1952.
Leymarie, Jean, *Braque*, Geneva, 1961.
——, *L'Impressionisme*, Geneva, 1953.
——, *Le Fauvisme*, Geneva, 1959.
Lion-Goldschmidt, D., *Les arts de Chine*, Paris, 1937.

Maritain, Jacques, *Réponser a Jean Cocteau*, Paris, 1926.
Martinie, A.H., *Pisanello*, Paris, 1930.
Marx, Claude Roger, *Bonnard*, Paris, 1950.
——, *Seurat*, Paris, 1931.
Mathey, Francois, *L'Impressionnisme*, Paris, 1956.
Meier-Graefe, Julius, *Auguste Renoir*, Paris, 1912.

Mermillon, Marius, *Maurice Utrillo*, Paris, n.d.
Muller, Joseph-Emile, *Le Fauvisme*, Paris, 1956.

Pichard, Joseph, *L'Art sacré Moderne*, Paris, 1953.
Pierrefun, François de, *Le Corbusier, La Maison des Hommes*, Paris, 1942.
Ponente, Nello, *Peinture moderne, tendances contemporaines*, Paris, 1960.

Ragon, Michel, *Fauthier*, Paris, 1957.
——, *Poliakoff*, Paris, 1956.
Raynal, Maurice, *Campigli*, Paris, 1949.
——, *Cézanne,* Geneva, 1954.
——, *Picasso*, Geneva, 1953.
——, *Peinture moderne*, Geneva, 1958.
Reinhardt, Hans, *Holbein*, Paris, 1938.
René-Jean, *Gauguin*, Paris, 1948.
Rewald, John, *Aristide Maillol*, Paris, 1950.
——, *Cézanne*, Paris, 1939.
——, *Seurat*, Paris , 1940[?].
——, *Gauguin*, Paris, 1938.
——, *Maillol*, Paris, 1939.
——, *Pissaro*, Paris, n.d.
Rey, Robert, *Daumier*, Paris, n.d.
——, *Gauguin*, Paris, 1923.
——, *Maurice de Vlaminck*, Paris, 1955.
Ridder, André de, *J.B.S. Chardin*, Paris, 1932.
Roger-Marse, Claude, *La Graulere originale en France de Manet à nos jours*, Paris, 1939.
Rouart, Denis, *Renoir,* Geneva, 1954.
Roy, Claude, *Modigliani*, Geneva, 1958.

Sabartes, Jaimie, *Picasso*, Paris, 1946.
Salmon, André, *Cezanne*, Paris, 1923.
Saustelle, J. and Verger, *Aux Menique*, Paris, 1938.
Sauvage, Marcel, *Vlaminck sa vie et son message*, Geneva, 1956.
Schmidt, Georg, *Chagall*, Paris, 1952.
Schneider, Edouard, *Fra Angelico*, Paris, 1938.
Scupha, Michiel, *La sculpture de siécle*, Neuchatel, 1959.
Seintlaz, Maurice,*Corot*, Paris, 1951.
Soulié de Maank, G., *Historie de l'art Chinois*, Paris, 1928.
Sterking, Charles, *La nature morte de l'antiquité à nos jours*, Paris, 1952.
——, *Les Primitifs*, Paris, 1938.

Taine, H., *Philosophie de l'art*, Paris, 1909.
Tapie, Michel, *Un art autre*, Paris, 1952.
Taure, Elie, *Corot*, Paris, 1950.
Tierlinck, Herman, *Henry van de Velde*, Brussels, n.d.

Unde, Wilhelm, *Cinq maitres primitifs*, Paris, 1949.

Vandayer, Jean-Louis, *Italie des Alpen à Sienne*, Paris, 1936.
Vanderwal, F.J., *Impressions artistiques d'outre mer*, Angers, 1951.
Various authors, *Histoire de la peinture moderne de Picasso au Surréalisme*, Geneva, 1950.
——, *Histoire de la peinture moderne, De Baudelaire à Bonnard*, Geneva, 1949.
——, *Histoire de la peinture moderne, Matisse, Munch, Roault*, Geneva, 1950.
Velde, Henry van der, *La voie sacrée*, Brussels, 1933.
Venturi, Lionello, *Chagall*, Geneva, 1956.
——, *La Peinture Irakenie du Savage à Modigliani*, Geneva, 1952.
——, *Piero della Francesca*, Geneva, 1954.
——, *Rouault*, Geneva, 1959.
Verdet, André, *Atlan*, Paris, 1956.
Vollard, Ambroise, *Paul Cézanne*, Paris, 1919.

Weelen, Guy, *Miró*, 1925-1940, Paris, 1960.
Wild, Doris, *Les Icones, Art religieuse de l'Orient*, Lausanne, 1947.

Zervos, Christian, *Picasso*, Paris, 1949.

Italian

d'Ancona, Paolo, *Leonardo da Vinci*, Milan, 1952.

Barrati, Cesare, *La Simmetria dinamica*, Milan, 1952.
Bucarelli, Palma et al., *Piet Mondrian*, Rome, 1956.

Carrieri, Raffaele, *Marino Marini*, Milano, 1948.
——, *Campigli*, Venice, 1945.
Cogniat, Raymond, *Raoul Dufy*, Milan, n.d.

Faldi, Italo, *Il Primo de Chirico*, Venezia, 1949.

Russilo, Franco, *Pablo Picasso*, Milan, 1953.

Serna, R. Gómez de la, *Picasso*, Turin, 1945.
Sinagra, —, *Marino seitavde a colari*, Milan, 1954.

Trincanato, Egle R., *Venezia Minore*, Milan, 1948.

Vagnetti, Luigi, *Il disegno del vero*, Genoa, 1955.
——, *Il secondo corso di "disegno dal vero,"* Rome, 1955.
——, *L'insegnamento del disegno del vero nelle facolta*, Rome, 1957.
——, *Un esperimento didattico*, Rome, 1959.
Valsecchi, Marco, *A. Snago*, Milan, 1952.
——, *Sirani*, Milan, 1950.

Venturi, Adolfo, *Architetti dal XV al XVIII secolo, . . . Alberti*, Rome, 1923.

Zervos, Christian, *Picasso a colai*, Milan, 1951.

C. ITEMS BEARING AN INSCRIPTION

Berlage, H.P., *Over Stijl in bouw- en meubelkunst*, Rotterdam, 1908. Signed and stamped Berlage.
Biezen, Jan, *Rode Reus, blauwe Poseidon, gele Hades*, The Hague, 1971. Inscribed by author.
Blysha, R., *Hoogtevrees*, Amsterdam, 1954.
Boenin, J., *De Zaak Kornet Jelaqin*, Amsterdam, n.d.
Boer, Julius de, *Jan Toorop*, Amsterdam, 1911. Inscribed by Annie Dinaux.
Brion, Marcel, *Domela*, Paris, 1961. Inscribed by César Domela.

Carpanelli, Franco, *Come si costruisce oggi nel mondo*, Milan, 1955..

Das Kunsthaus in Zurich, Zurich, 1911. Inscribed by Karl Moser.
Das Werk, February 1925. Inscribed by Hannes Meyer.
Doesburg, Theo van, *Classique—baroque—moderne*, Paris, n.d. Inscribed by author, Weimar 4 September 1921.

Eras, Vincent J.M., *Sloten + Sleutels door de eeuwen heen,*, n.l., n.d. Inscribed, with 3 letters from author.

Forbat, Fred, *Wohnungsbauten, 1930-1931* (reprinted from *Bauwelt*, no 47, 1931). Inscribed by author.

Gypsumist, October, 1925. Inscribed by Barry Dwyer.

Haftmann, Werner, *Schilderkunst in de 20e eeuw*, Rotterdam, 1956. Inscribed for Annie Oud from Karel Wiekart.
Hawranck, Alfred, *Zur Asthetik des Ingenieurbauwesens* (reprint from *Zeitschrift des Deutschen Vereines für die Geschichte Mährens und Schlesiens*, no 4, 1924). Inscribed by author.
Hermans, Toon, *Kladboek van Toon Hermans*, Amsterdam, n.d. Inscribed by author.
Hillenius, D., *Tegen het vegetarisme*, Amsterdam, 1961. Inscribed Karel Wiekart.
Hitchcock, Henry-Russell and Drexler, *Built in USA: Post-war Architecture*, New York, n.d. Inscribed by Philip Johnson.
Hofmann, Hans, *Baugesinnung*, Zurich, 1942. Inscribed by author.

Kallan, Aino, *Doodende Liefde*, 1929, n.l. Inscribed by the translator.
Kallenbach-Greller, Lotte, *Grundias einer Musikphilosophie*, n.l., n.d. Inscribed by author.

Lönnest, Elias, *Kalevala*, Stuttgart, 1978.
Lurcat, André, *Formes composition et lois d'harmonie*, Paris, 1933. Inscribed by author.

Mayer, H.K.F., *Der Baumeister Otto Bartnung und die Wiederentdeckung des Raumes*, Heidelberg, 1951. Inscribed by Bartnung.
Melchers, Bernd, *China, Der Tempelbau, die Lochan van king-yän-sï*, Hagen, 1921. Anonymous inscription.

Michel-Lurcat, Renée, *Divers et variés*, La Bastide, 1963. Inscribed by author.
Morris, Desmond, *The human zoo*, London, 1969. Inscribed for Mrs Oud.

Popp, Joseph, *Die Figurale Wandmalerei*, Leipzig, 1921. Inscribed by author.
——, *Die Technik als Kulturproblem*, Munich, 1929. Inscribed by author.

Retera Wzn., W., *Nederlandsche bouwmeesters, P. Kramer*, Amsterdam, n.d. Inscribed by Piet Kramer.
Rohlfs, Christian et al, *Wenn Maler dichten*, Wuppertal, 1951.
Rost, Nico, *Het nieuwe tooneel in het nieuwe Rusland*, Arnhem, 1927. Inscribed by author.

Spinoza, Benedictus de, *Ethica*, Amsterdam, n.d. Inscribed C.J.E.Dinaux.
Städtebau, no 3-4, 1925. Inscribed by W. Hegemann.
Stockmeyer, Ernst, *Gedanken Uber eine neue Aesthetik*, n.l., n.d. Inscribed by author, with letter to Oud 10 May 1932.

Tapie, Michel, *Un Art Autre*, Paris, 1952. Inscribed by author.
Teister, Alain, *De huisgod spreekt*, Amsterdam, 1964.
Tusschenbroek, Otto van, *Achter blinkende vensters*, Leiden, 1950. Inscribed by van de S—— [?].

Vagnetti, Luigi, *Disegno e architettura*, Genoa, 1958. Inscribed by author.
Vanderwal, F.J., *Impressions artistiques d'outre mer*, Angers, 1951.
Various authors, *De schoonheid van ons land. Het landschap*, Amsterdam, 1941. Inscribed by "Leerlingen J and E [?]."
Vriend, J.J., *De bouwkunst van ons land, de steden*, Amsterdam, 1949. Inscribed by author.
——, *De bouwkunst van ons land, het interieur*, Amsterdam, 1950. Inscribed by author.
——, *De bouwkunst van ons land, het platteland*, Amsterdam, 1949. nscribed by author.
——, *Nieuwere architectuur*, Bussum, 1957. Inscribed by author.

Wasmuths Monatshefte für Baukunst, no 3, 1925. Inscribed by W. Hegemann.
West, G.H., *Gothic architecture in England and France*, London, 1911. Inscribed to Kas (Oud)

Index of Personal Names

Numbers in italics refer to pages of the text of the essay "The Rise and Fall of a Hero"; other numbers refer to entry numbers in the bibliography.

Aalto, Alvar, 867
Ache, Jean, 604
Adam, Hubertus, 1150
Adler, Leo, 138, 139, 223, 224
Agate, Gustave, 326
Albarda, Jan H., 622, 979
Allan, John, 1044
Alley, Ronald, 859
Alma, Peter, 369
Anderson, M.L, 274
Andritzky, Michael, 872
Anzivino, Gina, 859
Appel, Karel, 434, 530
Arets, Wiel, 980
Argan, Giulio Carlo, 443, 448, 540, 591
Arnason, H.H., 697
Asselbergs, Fons, 752, 944

Baaij, Hans, 1079
Badovici, Jean, 073, 074, 095, 113, 174
Bakema, Jan Berend, 453, 464, 465, 470, 475, 476, 516, 545, 566, 622, 770
Bakker, Bert, 941
Baljeu, Joost, 575, 683, 746
Banham, Reyner, 487, 569, 603, 698
Barbieri, Sergio Umberto, 117, 806, 834, 845, 856, 883, 885, 935, 937, 946, 980,
981, 1025, 1045, 1046, 1072, 1080
Barkema, M., 831
Baroni, Daniele, 766, 768
Barr, Alfred H., *17*, *22*, 248, 311, 462
Bauer, Catherine K., 275
Baumgart, Fritz, 699
Bazel, K.P.C de, 067, 455
Beckett, Jane, 025, 103, 797, 799, 807, 817, 827, 846, 859, 898, 951
Beek, Johan van de, 692, 755
Beeren, Wim, 857
Beerends, A., 703
Begeer, Carel J.A., 131
Behne, Adolf, *12*, 045, 050, 059, 092, 096, 119, 775
Behrendt, Walter Curt, *12*, 097, 175, 327
Behrens, Peter, 130, 159, 603
Bell, Keith, 900
Benevolo, Leonardo, 570, 591
Benton, Timothy, 026, 753, 754, 799
Berendsen, Anne, 502
Bergeijk, Herman van, 1097, 1120
Bergh, Wim van den, 980
Berghoef, J.P., 510
Bergvelt, Ellinoor, 947, 1139
Berkovich, Elmer, 266, 278
Berlage, Corrie, *2*

Berlage, Hendrik Petrus, *2, 6, 10, 22*, 015, 033, 043, 049, 088, 209, 249, 283, 305, 342, 372, 488, 567, 586, 752, 798, 862, 1146
Berlage, Miep van R., 296
Bernini, Beatrice, 1033
Besnyö, Eva, 341
Bijhouwer, Roy, 966
Bijl, Rob van der, 902
Bijvoet, Bernard, 718
Blake, Peter, 571
Bless, Frits, 550, 858
Bliek, Nicole, 1073
Blijstra, Rein, 488, 503, 521, 526, 528, 582, 635, 642, 653
Block, Fritz, 202
Blok, Cor, 733
Blotkamp, Carel, 859, 873, 969, 1034, 1109, 1140
Blotkamp, Hoost, 774
Blumberger, Susanne, 1099
Boasson, Dorien, 815
Bock, Manfred, 863, 884
Boddaert, Joris, 1081
Boeken, Albert, 141, 312, 449
Boekraad, Cees, 031, 726, 806, 847, 885, 952, 1132
Boer, J.B. de, 533
Boerhave Beekman, W., 348
Boersma, J.M., 606
Boersma, Tjeerd, 1110
Bois, Yve-Alain, 859, 863, 874, 885, 900, 982, 1022
Bollery, Franziska, 948, 983
Bonaventura, Paul, 859, 951
Bonset, I.K. (Theo van Doesburg), *4*
Bonta, Juan Pablo, 798
Boogh, K.A., 436
Bool, Flip, 816, 885
Boom, A.van de, 402
Boom, G.H. van, 707
Booven, H. van, 007
Borsi, Franco, 949
Bos, Lillian, 956
Bosch, W.Th.H. ten, 356
Bosma, Koos, 1121
Bosman, Jos., 931, 1153
Bosshard, Hans Rudolf, 1135
Botman, A., 903
Bourgeois, Victor, *13*

Bowness, Alan, 730
Brandes, Gustav, 137
Brederoo, Nico J., 860
Brehm, Burckhard, 861
Bremer, G.C., 411, 468
Breuer, Marcel, *20*
Brevet, F.J., 436
Brinkman, Johannes, 210, 273
Brinkman, Michiel, 845
Brion, Marcel, 588
Broek, Johannes Hendrik van den, *20*, 370, 464, 465, 470, 475, 503, 545, 553, 623
Broekhuizen, Dolf, 1102, 1106, 1133, 1140
Broos, Kees, 816, 863
Brouwer, Willem C., 011, 012, 047, 215, 826
Brouwers, Ruud, 796, 922, 962, 966, 1094
Brown, Theodore M., 536, 678
Brugman, Til, 369
Brunelleschi, Filippo, 793
Brunius, A., 060
Brusse, M.J., 291
Bucarelli, Palma, 501, 511
Buch, Joseph, 1110
Buchanan, Peter, 1047
Buffinga, A., 436, 622
Bulhof, Francis, 762
Bullhorst, Rainer, 794, 848, 941
Burckhardt, Lucius, 769
Buys, H., 314

Camini, Aldo (Theo van Doesburg), *4*
Camp, D.L., 1062
Campbell, Joan, 786
Campbell-Cole, Barbie, 799
Campo, Marc à, 808
Caprarola, Cola di, 793
Carandente, Giovanni, 501
Carasso, Dedalo, 439, 984
Casciato, Maristella, 800, 1022, 1048, 1146
Caspers, Paulien, 956
Casteels, Maurice, 209
Celant, Germano, 1034
Cerruti, Marisa, 609
Champigneulle, Bernard, 589, 604
Cheney, Sheldon, 210
Clairet, Alain, 787

Colenbrander, Bernard, 295, 834, 869, 918, 970, 1055, 1095, 1097, 1118
Colijn, A.W., 504
Collins, Christine, 605
Collins, George, 605
Collins, Peter, 654
Compton, Michael, 817
Conrads, Ulrich, 605, 617, 636
Copplestone, Trewen, 618
Cornelis, A., 904
Cramer, Max, 818
Crouwel, Wim H., 732
Curl, James Steven, 736
Curtis, William J.R., 862
Cusveller, Sjoerd, 1035
Cuypers, Joseph Th. J., *2*
Cuypers, P.J.H., 305

Dal Co, Francesco, *17*, 765
Daldrop, Norbert W., 795
Dam, Herman van, 542
Dearstyne, Howard, 950
Derwig, Jan, 1130
Dethmers, H., 528, 909, 1074
Dettingmeijer, Rob, 809, 1120
Dibbets, Jan, 1152
Dijk, Hans van, 828, 1104
Dinaux, Carel, 575
Dingemans, C.F.J., 338
Dobbelaar, de Kovel and de Vroom [architectural firm], 962, 966, 1078
Dobbelsteen, Hans van den, 915
Docker, Richard, 921
Doelman, Cees, 587
Doesburg, Nelly van, 447
Doesburg, Theo van, *3*, *5*, *7-11*, 016, 017, 018, 023, 027, 030, 031, 036, 037, 051, 098, 099, 120, 250, 255, 297, 309, 495, 524, 536, 608, 633, 636, 649, 659, 679, 683, 695, 708, 733, 746, 762, 798, 807, 822, 837, 847, 852, 873, 875, 881, 885, 887, 890, 899, 901, 932, 942, 951, 967, 969, 990, 998, 1007, 1010, 1017, 1038, 1054, 1055, 1069, 1070, 1118, 1139, 1155
Doesburg, Theodorus, *3*
Doig, Allan, 875, 951, 1038
Domela, César, *3*, 574, 588, 673, 787, 816, 1014
Dongen, F. van, 683
Dop, G., 014
Dorgelo, A., 572
Duchateau, P.G., 946
Dudok, Willem Marinus, *3*, 011, 012, 043, 136, 147, 200, 209, 210, 269, 273, 365, 376, 388, 411, 423, 429, 464, 470, 475, 543, 604, 633, 736, 798, 802, 818, 839, 974, 1029, 1120, 1144
Duiker, Johannes, 718,
Dunster, David, 916, 973
Dupuits, Petra, 1008
Duyvis, Paul Donker, 857

Eaton, Leonard K., 752, 1146
Ebbinge, E., 826
Eckardt, Wolf von, 573
Eckstein, Hans, 769
Eesteren, Cornelis van, *3*, 150, 225, 369, 395, 447, 636, 679, 852, 1044
Eibink, Adolf, 328
Eigen, Edward, 1100
Ekstant, S., 624
Elno, K.N., 624
Elte, Hans, 427
Elzas, A., 297
Emanuel, Muriel, 986
Emden, S.J. van, 371
Emery, Marc, 887
Emmen, J., 003
Engel, Henk, 834, 847, 849, 952
Engelman, Jan, 454
Es, A. van, 876
Es, Rob van, 1122
Essen-Vinckers, Mrs van, *3*, 014, 021
Esser, Cateau, *3*
Ettinger, J. van, 472
Everts, F.E.C., 537
Eyck, Charles, 454

Fagiolo, Marcello, 690
Fanelli, Giovanni, 116, 473, 685, 788, 887
Fawcett, Trevor, 763
Fernandez-Galiano, Luis, 1136
Filler, Martin, 863
Fischer, Wend, 527, 655
Fischer, Theodor, *2*, *9*
Fisher, Thomas R., 1009, 1026
Flagge, Ingeborg, 1088
Fleming, John, 665
Flon, Christine, 758

254 Index

Flouquet, P.-L., 267
Frampton, Kenneth, 704, 819, 840, 863, 888, 1087
Francastel, Pierre, 554
Frank, Dimitri Frenkel, 587
Frank, Josef, 921
Frank, Suzanne Shulof, 015, 153, 155, 767
Frank, Werner, 801
Franks, H.G., 552
Franssen, Bert, 985
Fraser, Murray, 1044
Freud, Sigmund, *18*
Friedhoff, Gijsbert, *18*, 350
Friedman, Martin, 863
Friedman, Mildred, 863
Fries, H. de, 089
Fuchs, Hans, 1089, 1151
Furse, John, 986
Futagawa, Yukio, 888, 1003

Galfetti, Gustau Gili, 1123
Gallotti, Alicia, 997
Garner, Philippe, 820
Garrel, B. van, 905
Geary, David, 859
Geest, Jan van, 755, 810, 821
Gelder, H.G. van, 350
Gelderen, W. van, 279, 666
Gerretsen, W.J., 328
Gerwen, J.L.J.M. van, 1124
Geurst, Jeroen, 889
Geurtsen, Rein, 705, 739
Geus, W. de, *5*
Geuskens, Jan, 966
Giedion, Siegfried, 142, 174, 198, 225, 228, 229, 358, 390, 404, 455
Gispen, Willem Hendrik, 090, 755, 799, 821, 947, 989, 1001, 1016, 1040, 1148
Godoli, Ezio, *8*
Goethals, Guy, 1113
Gorter, Sadi de, 574
Gössel, Peter, 1064
Gouwe, W.J., 250
Govan, Michael, 1034
Graeff, Werner, *3*
Granpré Molière, Marinus Jan, *5*, 374, 382, 567, 740
Grassi, Giorgio, 850
Gratama, Jan, 023, 037, 051, 634

Grautauff, Otto, 034
Grieken, Hans van, 818
Grinberg, Donald I., 770, 829
Groenendijk, Paul, 971, 1027, 1082, 1096
Groot, A. de, 869
Gropius, Walter, *1, 9, 12, 13, 17, 19, 22*, 054, 091, 099, 177, 251, 372, 425, 443, 461, 462, 512, 515, 610, 633, 695, &83, 793, 921
Gruyter, W. Jos. de, *10-11*, 201, 230, 291, 298, 331, 444, 644
Guarneri, Libero, 484
Gubler, Jacques, 756
Günther, Roland, 938, 941, 1049, 1119
Gustmann, Kurt, 998

Haagsma, F., 796
Haagsma, Ids, 490, 835, 999
Haan, Hilde de, 155, 490, 835, 999
Haar, Gert ter, 1125
Haas, C. de, 764
Haas, H.J. de, 381, 543
Haesaerts, Luc, 121
Haesaerts, Paul, 121
Hägele, Rainer, 855
Hahn, Peter, 091
Halliday, F.L., 326
Hamlin, Talbot Faulkner, *21*, 380, 354, 459
Hammacher, A.M., 454, 637
Hannema, D., *18*, 299, 314, 506
Harfield, Stephen, 1010
Harmsen, Ger, 863
Hartmann, Kristiana, 948, 983, 1050
Hartsuyker, Hendrick, 458, 622
Hartveld, Cita, 1111
Haskell, Douglas, *18-19*
Hatje, Gerd, 620, 891
Hausbrand, Frans, 319
Havelaar, Just, 122
Hecke, Gust. van, 253
Hedrick, Hannah, 822
Heer, Jan de, 885, 952, 967
Hefting, Paul, 752
Heijbroek, J.F., 830
Heissenbüttel, Helmut, 801
Hellman, Louis, 749
Helmond, Toke van, 1048, 1112
Hendricks, J.P.L., 328, 339
Henkels, Herbert, 885

Henkes, Peter, 1105
Henket, H.J., 1066
Henning, Michael, 1142
Hensbergen, Gijs van, 901
Henvaux, E., 268
Herbert, Gilbert, 757
Herk, C. van, 334, 344
Herst, Sonja, 1131
Hertog-Oud, A., *2*
Heuvel, Wim van, 1028, 1051, 1058, 1086, 1097
Highton, John E., 294
Hilberseimer, Ludwig, *12*, 054, 061, 062, 075, 133, 134, 205, 638, 921, 1104
Hilding, Ekelund, 231
Hill, Oliver, 420
Hitchcock, Henry-Russell Jr., *14-17, 19, 22*, 176, 177, 199, 226, 248, 251, 254, 357, 538, 633, 803, 897, 1064, 1150, 1157
Hoek, Els, 939
Hoeven, Ernst-Philip van der, 1097
Hoff, Rob van 't, *3, 4, 7-9*, 683, 1052, 1106, 1140
Hoffmann, Gretl, 725
Hoffmann, Josef, 741
Hofhuizen, Herman, 592
Hofmann, Werner, 724
Hofstede, Annigje C.H., 1016
Hollingsworth, Mary, 1000
Holt, G.H., 395
Honour, Hugh, 665
Hooff, Dorothee van, 1113
Hoogenberk, Egbert J., 049
Hoogendonk, Mabel, 312
Hoogewoud, Guido, 341
Hoogveld, Carine, 1017
Hoost Blotkamp, 774
Hoste, Huib, 017, 023, 024, 280, 281, 315, 455, 728
Hougichi, Sutemi, 078
Housden, Brian, 693
Hoyer, Th.B.F., 334
Huber, Dorothee, 142
Hubers, H. Wouter, 838
Hulsman, Bernard, 1029
Hulzen, G. van, 008
Huszár, Vilmos, *3*, 659
Huygens, W., 561
Huyghe, René, 589, 711

Hylckama Vlieg, van, 013

Ibelings, Hans, 956, 1094, 1126, 1141
Irace, Fulvio, 922

Jacobsen, Wouter A., 577
Jacobus, John M. Jr., 618, 667
Jaeger, Falk, 927
Jaffé, Hans Ludwig Charles, 020, 028, 031, 117, 447, 489, 513, 625, 639, 656, 659, 679, 694, 712, 864, 890, 953, 1038
Jager, Ida, 956, 1012
Jager, J. de, 429, 970, 1041
Jakstein, Werner, 063
Jans, Jan, 285
Jansens, Johan, 1083
Joedicke, Jürgen, 555, 559, 622, 686, 687, 771, 1018, 1036
Johnson, Donald Leslie, 802, 1037, 1154
Johnson, Philip, *14-17, 18-20, 22*, 227, 248, 251, 257, 291, 462, 590, 803, 933, 1064, 1116
Jones, Cranston, 590
Jonge van Ellemeet, M.J.I. de, *17*, 232
Jonge, D. de, 715
Jonge, Harmen de, 772
Jongert, Jac[ob], 004, 870
Jongh, Ankie de, 737
Jonker, Gert, 578
Joosten, Joop, 863, 865
Jordy, William H, 626, 731
Jung, Carl, *18*

Kähler, Gert, 1063
Kallenbach, H., *12,* 054, 058, 063, 074, 092, 854, 1132,
Kalthegener, Hildegarde, 1056
Kamerlingh Onnes, Harm Hendrick , 022, 250, 743, 844, 905, 1017
Kamerlingh Onnes, Menso, *5*, 024, 086, 305
Karsten, Charles F.J., 700, 732, 733
Karstkarel, Peter, 834, 923, 940
Kaufmann, Edgar jr, 421
Kazemier, G., 528
Keppler, Arnie, 043
Kief, Heidemarie, 789
Kirsch, Karin, 1019
Kleijn, Koen, 1127
Klein, Alexander, 144

Klerk, Michel de, 015
Kloos, Jan Piet, *20*, 394, 834, 918, 928
Kloot Meijburg, Herman van der, 044
Klotz, Heinrich, 1020
Knobel, Lance, 929
Knorre, Alexander, 1142
Knuttel, G. Wzn., 131, 522
Kobold, H.W. Muller, 707
Koch, André, 969, 1001
Koekebakker, Olof, 1137
Kok, Anthony, *3*
Kok, Janny, 956
Koldewey, B.J., 239, 316
Kolling-Dandrieú, Francis Bach, 895
Komter, Auke, 383
Koolhaas, Rem, 1026
Korevaar, A., 500
Kostof, Spiro, 930
Kraayvanger, H.M., 359
Kramer, Ferdinand, 145, 804
Krayl, Carl, 055
Kremerskothen, Josef, 954, 998
Kroes, Jan Jaap de, 1074
Kromhout, H., 707
Kromhout, Johan Cornelis, 365
Kromhout, Willem, 024, 043, 082
Kropholler, A.J., *18*, 302, 317, 350, 360,
Kruger, J., 522
Kühne, Günther, 582
Kuipers, Marieke, 858, 972
Kultermann, Udo, 539, 724, 773, 1098
Küper, Marijke, 1084, 1128, 1139,
Kurrent, Friedrich, 1143

Laan, Barbara, 1148
Ladenius, Jan, 962
Lagas, Teun, 906
Lampmann, Gustav, 145
Lampugnani, Vittorio Magnago, 823, 866, 891
Lange, Eric de, 892, 1129, 1152
Langmead, Donald, 955, 987, 1010, 1052, 1144, 1145, 1154
Laprade, Albert, 645
Lauweriks, Johannes L.M., *9*, 135, 682
Le Corbusier, *1*, *13*, *17*, *22*, 081, 139, 177, 200, 207, 252, 277, 340, 366, 425, 462, 548, 606, 660, 741, 793, 921, 923, 931
Leck, Bart van der, *3*, *4*, 298, 659, 863
Leering, Jean, 726, 1053

Leeuwenburgh, A., 680
Lehning, Arthur Muller, 059, 150, 153, 155
Leidelmeijer, Frans, 896
Leitner, Bernhard, 738
Leliman, J.H.W., 048, 071
Lemoine, Serge, 1038
Leuthäuser, Gabriele, 1064
Lewin, Elysa, 764
Lewis, David, 517
Lewis, Hilary, 1116
Ley, Paul de, 962, 966, 1047
Liefrinck, Ida, 146, 147
Liesbrock, Heinz, 1099
Lieshout, Marcel van, 906
Linge, E. van, 478
Lionni, Leo, 282
Lissitzky, El, *11*, 649, 676
Lissitzky-Küppers, Sophie, 676
Locatelli, Vittorio, 1054
Loghem, Johannes Bernardus van, 212, 252, 340, 634
Lohuizen, Th. K. van, 194
Lønberg-Holm, Knud, 064, 213, 233, 752
Loos, Adolf, 741
Lootsma, Bart, 931
Lotzeler, Heinrich, 523
Lubinski, P.M., 214
Lugt, Reyn van der, 834, 988
Lupfer, Gilbert, 1071
Lynton, Norbert, 863

Maaskant, Huig Aart, 477, 646
Mácel, Otakar, 755, 1085
Magdelijns, Hans, 854, 908
Maillart, Robert, 407
Major, Máté, 917
Maler, Wilhelm, 532
Malespine, Emile, 234
Man, Paul, 582
Mang, Karl, 804
Mansell, George, 805
Mansum, C.J. van, 444
Manzoni, Pietro Scurati, 668
Mariani, Leonardo, 518, 529
Martinius, Warna Oosterbaan, 1039
Mattie, Erik, 1130
Mayer, Hans F.K., 450
McGrath, Raymond, 276
McKinsey, Kristan H., 1011

Meijer, J., 750
Meijer, Jan de, 281
Meindersma, Heero, 838, 909
Melis, Liesbeth, 1047
Meller, P., 123
Mendelsohn, Erich, 9, *11*, *19*, 200, 205, 487, 515, 573
Mens, Robert, 931
Merkelbach, Benjamin, 317, 318, 537, 545
Mesel, Alfred, *2*
Mesnil, Jacques, 235, 254
Metz, Tracy, 963, 964, 965, 970
Meulen Smith, Peter van der, 204
Meurs, Paul, 1090, 1138
Meuwissen, Joost, 803, 851, 1002
Meyer, Adolf, *9*, 054
Meyer, Erna, 114, 148
Meyer, Hannes, 124
Meyer, P., 076
Mieras, J.P., 017, 115, 328, 430, 444, 485
Mies van der Rohe, Ludwig, *1*, *11*, *16*, *17*, *19*, 321, 425, 462, 610, 695, 793, 921, 933
Migeonnes, Pierre, 298
Mik, Edzard, 1029
Miller, J.N., 132
Millon, Henry A, 640
Milner, John, 695
Minnucci, Gaetano, 116
Moholy-Nagy, Laszlo, *12*, 031, 099
Molema, Jan, 752, 1146
Molenaar, Joris, 889
Möller, Werner, 1085
Mondrian, Piet, *3*, *4*, *7*, *10*, 034, 352, 369, 392, 501, 511, 514, 607, 637, 659, 694, 712, 741, 873, 939, 969, 982, 1034, 1054, 1109, 1132
Moody, Ella, 669
Mook, Jan Willem van, 956
Moorsel, C.M. van, 317
Morgan, Ann Lee, 986
Morgan, Giulio, 627
Moscoviter, Herman, 924, 1012, 1041, 1055, 1114
Moser, Karl, 756
Mual, M., 1040
Mulhern, Elvira, 367
Mumford, Lewis, *20*, 248, 335, 404, 544
Muratore, Giorgio, 841

Mus, Cor, 463
Musgrove, John, 759, 973
Muthesius, Hermann, *2*, 006

Nägele, Hermann, 1086
Naylor, Colin, 986
Naylor, Gillian, 760, 932
Neefs, A. Raymond, 121
Nerdinger, Winfried, 1147
Neret, Gilles, 957
Nettinga, Willem, 940
Neumann, Eckhard, 713, 716
Neumann, Guido E., 149
Niegemann, J., 405
Niesten, Joop, 831
Nooteboom, Cees, 824
Norberg-Schulz, Christian, 747, 1003
Norwich, John Julius, 758
Nycolaas, Jacques, 739

O'Connor, John, 1116
Ockman, Jane, 1100
Okada, Takoa, 078
Olbrich, Joseph, *2*
Oorthuys, Cees, 755
Oosterman, Arjen, 1089, 1094
Orwell, George, *1*
Otten, Albert, 203, 215
Otto, Christian F., 1067
Oud, Gerrit, *2*, *12*, 010, 021, 576
Oud, Hendrik Emile (Hans), *6*, *14*, *15*, 451, 497, 556, 706, 709, 781, 856, 879, 909, 918, 978, 1074, 1107, 1152
Oud, Pieter Jacobus, 576
Oud-Dinaux, J.M.A. (Annie), *2*, 444, 575, 675, 709, 940, 990, 992, 1002, 1013
Oudenaarden, Jan, 1079
Oudin, Bernard, 714
Overmeire, Katrien, 1066
Overy, Paul, 513, 701, 859, 864, 877, 951, 1065, 1075, 1103
Oxenaar, Rudolf Willem Daan, 528, 863

Padovan, Richard, 768, 852, 857, 863, 869, 878, 885, 900, 901, 1065
Pallottino, Massimo, 540, 591
Palmes, J.C., 759
Passmore, Edward, 399
Patijn, Wytze, 966, 1012, 1035, 1044, 1058, 1066, 1089

Pehnt, Wolfgang, 620, 891, 893
Peltz, Gudrun, 1142
Penaat, Willem, 292, 298, 323
Penn, Colin, 349
Perogalli, Carlo, 641
Perrée, Rob, 1131
Perret, Auguste, 741
Peter, John, 803, 1115
Petersen, Ad, 688
Pétrasch, Charles, 271
Peutz, F.P.J., 980
Pevsner, Nikolaus, *21*, 313, 352, 366, 598, 665, 689
Pfankuch, Peter, 775
Pfeiffer, Bruce Brooks, 460, 919
Phillpot, Clive, 763
Pica, Agnoldomenico, 304, 359, 622, 696
Piret, Jean, 705
Pischel [-Fraschini], Gina, 670
Plantenga, J.H., 402
Plath, Christian, 687, 771
Platz, Gustav Adolf, *10*, 136
Plaut, James S., 493
Plazcek, Adolf, 880
Ploeg, Hella van der, 1045
Pluym, Willem van der, 486
Poelzig, Hans, *13*, 921
Polak, Henri, 256
Polano, Sergio, 020, 025, 026, 028, 779, 834, 841, 863, 952, 967, 1034
Polasek, J., 183
Pommer, Richard, 1004, 1067
Pontier, J.H., 778
Pontrémolly, -----, 105
Porphyrios, Demetri, 867
Portoghesi, Paolo, 690
Posener, Julius, 811, 836
Postma, Frans, 1132
Postmaa, Casper, 879, 1013, 1109, 1133
Praag, M.M. van, 671
Prak, Niels Luning, *11*, 920, 1068
Prins, Henrico, 966
Pronk, Heleen, 818

Rädecker, "Nouki", 1105
Rädecker, John, *21*, 439, 467, 519, 526, 643, 935, 984, 1105
Rading, Adolf, 921
Radovic, Ranko, 925
Ragon, Michel, 541, 628, 720, 734, 863

Rand, Ayn, 385
Rasch, Bodo, 780
Rasch, Horst, 998
Rathke, Ewald, 716
Ratsma, P., 868
Rau, Uwe, 1032
Ravesteyn, Sybold van, 229, 252, 258, 316, 599, 774
Ravesteyn, L.J.C.J. van, 391
Raynal, Maurice, 422
Rebel, Bernhard (Ben), *16*, 781, 894, 1117
Reedijk, Hein, 796
Reinhartz-Tergau, Elisabeth, 989, 1001, 1014, 1041
Reitsma, Meine, 727
Retera, W., 237, 329
Révèsz-Alexander, Magda, 288
Reygers, Leonie, 639
Richards, James Maude, 355, 758, 776
Richardson, Sara, 1021
Rietveld, Gerrit Thomas, *3*, *22*, 036, 040, 258, 298, 303, 332, 353, 390, 447, 455, 536, 537, 545, 550, 611, 649, 695, 768, 796, 798, 820, 839, 858, 863, 1028, 1075, 1084, 1103
Riga, Adina, 832
Rijk, Timo de, 1033
Riley, Terence, 1087
Rinsema, Evert, *3*
Riphagen, Gert, 966
Ritzen, Jos., 211
Robertson, Howard, 399, 472, 1023
Robie, Fred C., 025, 028, 779, 797
Roer, Robert van de, 941
Roggeveen, Dirk, 018
Ronchi, Lisa, 552
Röntgen, F.E., 707
Rood, A.H. van, 159
Roos, Frank John jr, 330
Roosenburg, Dirk, *18*, 350, 429
Rooy, Max van, 821, 834, 918, 989
Rooy, A.J.J. van, 624
Rosa, Giancarlo, 1076
Rosdorff, Flip, 995
Rosenberg, Léonce, 679
Rosenburg, H.P.R., 1005
Rossi, Vittorio, 479
Roth, Alfred, 741
Rothschild, Richard, 259

Rotzler, Willy, 777
Rouw, J.F.H., 782
Rowe, Peter G., 1101
Rowland, Kurt, 742
Rubinger, Krystyna, 837
Rudel, Jean, 711
Rutgers van der Loeff, M., 533
Ruys, B., 024

Saenredam, Pieter, 340
Saint, Andrew, 973
Saliga, Pauline, 1006
Salomons, Izak, 833, 834, 918
Sanderson, Warren, 838
Sant'Elia, Antonio, 038
Sartoris, Alberto, 403, 524
Schaal, Rolf, 1042
Scharoun, Hans, 159, 921
Schelling, H.G.J., 460, 481, 494
Schmidt, Bertus, 956
Schmitz, Marcel, 388
Schmuck, Friedrich, 1056
Schneck, Adolf, 178
Schneider, Jos., 990
Schnitker, M., 869
Schoonen, Rob, 941
Schouten, Martin, 941
Schröder, Truus, *4*
Schrofer, Jurriaan, 059, 150, 153
Schulze, Franz, 863, 933, 1116
Schwitters, Kurt, 153, 767
Scrivano, Paolo, 1157
Scully, Vincent Jr., 551, 897
Searing, Helen, 752, 803, 880, 897, 910
Segal, Walter, 751
Seip, Dick, 584
Selier, Herman, 1030
Selz, Peter Howard, 839
Serenyi, Peter, 660
Sers, Philippe, 720
Seuphor, Michel, 369, 501, 514
Sevenhuijsen, Augustus M.J., 137
Shand, P. Morton, 305
Sharp, Dennis, 352, 661, 672, 677, 735, 758
Sheppard, Richard, 807
Sherwood, Roger, 790
Sijmons, K.L., 306
Singel, Daan van der, 896
Slebos, J.C., 497

Sluijs, F. van der, 974
Sluyterman, K., 048
Smets, Marcel, 728
Smit, Frank, 911
Smit, Jos., 1127
Smithson, Peter, 495, 632, 662, 681, 729
Smithson, Alison, 662, 681, 729
Someren, W. van, 429
Sörgel, Herman, 106
Sperlich, Hans G., 605
Spörhase, Rolf, 126, 160
Sprenkels-ten Hoorn, Jet, 895
Staal, Arthur, 360
Staal, Gert, 975
Staal, Jan Frederik, 203, 273, 308
Stam, Mart, *13*, 068, 119, 307, 341, 608 921, 1028, 1067
Stamm, Brigitte, 791
Stamm, Günther, 783, 791, 812, 1049
Stangos, Nikos, 840
Stankard, Mark, 859, 951
Starý, Oldrich, 056
Stenchlak, Marian, 899
Stepmann, Eckhard, 872
Stern, Walter, 185
Steur, A.J. van der, 071, 215, 218, 472, 480
Stigter, Bianca, 1152
Stimson, Miriam, 976
Stock, Wolfgang Jean, 1057
Stockmeyer, Ernst, 057
Stoffels, A., 125
Stolk, H., 707
Straaten, Evert van, 898, 1007, 1017, 1069
Strasser, Emil E., 118
Strasser, George, 1022
Stuijt, Jan, 2
Sullivan, Louis, 426
Summerson, John, 392, 793
Sutterland, H., 778
Swieten, Peter van, 1058
Szénássy, István L., 702

Tafel, Cornelius, 1147
Tafuri, Manfredo, *17*, 691, 765, 841
Taut, Bruno, *12*, 055, 201, 617, 672, 921, 1097
Taut, Max, *13*, 921
Taverne, Ed R.M., 059, 117, 853, 912,

Index 259

1102, 1106, 1133, 1140
Teige, Karel, 084
Thienen, F.W.S. van, 423
Thunnissen, Claudia, 1127
Tijen, Willem van, 455, 477, 599, 646, 717, 740
Tillema, J.A.C., 317
Timmer, Petra, 1008, 1134
Timon, Kalman, 991
Toorop, Charley, 860
Torry, Euphemia, 260
Trebbi, Giorgio, 1031
Trotsky, Leon, *1*
Troy, Nancy Joslin, 863, 881, 900
Tummers, Nico H.M., 682, 683, 692, 726, 956
Tusschenbroek, Otto van, 289, 361, 362, 435, 506
Twijnstra Gudde [architectural firm], 1074

Uytdehaage, A., 680

Vaillat, Léandre, 085
Valk, H., 882
Valstar, Arta, 942
Vantongerloo, Georges, *3, 4*
Veenstra, R.W., 707
Veersema, M.J., 906
Veissière, Gabriel, 069
Velde, Henry van de, 741
Veldhoen, Lex, 992, 1012
Ven, Cornelis J.M. van de, 784, 792
Verbaan, Danny, 1107
Verbeek, N.H.W., 1124
Verhagen, Hans, 1077
Verhorst, J.H.G., 707
Vermeer, Gerrit, 1117
Vermeijden, M., 813, 834
Vermeulen, Frans A.J., 224, 496
Vernon, Christopher, 1146
Veronesi, Guilia, 473, 540, 647
Vickery, Robert, 718
Vischer, J., 205
Vlugt, Leendert Cornelis van der, 108, 210, 273, 320, 889
Vöge, Peter, 960, 1103
Vollaard, Piet, 971, 1035, 1082, 1096
Vordemberge-Gildewart, Friedrich, *3*, 458
Vorrink, Koos, 092

Votteler, Arno, 855
Vriend, Jacobus Johannes, 337, 379, 412, 438, 439, 444, 447, 503, 516, 525, 545, 557, 558, 560, 567, 575, 582, 585, 587, 595, 606, 621, 622, 634, 642, 706, 709, 748, 891
Vries, Jan de, 1155
Vries-Hermansader, D. de, 1062
Vroegh, Hanny, 1013

Wagenaar, Cor, 1121, 1156
Wagt, George van der, 1105
Wagt, Wim de, 1041, 1153
Wal, Oege van der, 854
Walden, Russell, 785
Walenkamp, H.J.M., *9*
Warnaars, F.H., 481
Warncke, Carsten-Peter, 1070
Watkin, David, 961
Wattjes, Jannes Gerhardus, 058, 115, 231, 356
Weaver, Mike, 684
Wedepohl, Edgar, 161, 1156
Weeber, Carel, 845
Wegerif, A.H., 516
Welsh, Robert P., 762, 863
Wenckebach, L. Oswald, 564, 606, 613
Werfe, Jouke van der, 1113
Werner, Frank R., 1059
Wesiecker, Wilhelm, 413
Westerveld, Bab, 960
Westheim, Paul, 162, 186
Weston, Richard, 1149
Wevers, M.H., 464
Whittick, Arnold, 424, 515
Wick, Rainer, 869, 885, 894, 901
Wiekart, Karel, 020, 028, 047, 102, 103, 157, 377, 396, 409, 431, 452, 453, 454, 461, 465, 530, 531, 547, 548, 566, 575, 582, 596, 600, 606, 615, 629, 630, 642, 648, 657, 692, 709
Wiersma, A., 774
Wiese, Stephan von, 842
Wiessing, H.P.L., 332, 342, 643
Wijdeveld, H. Th., *10, 19*, 102, 752
Wijk, Kees van, 155
Wijsenbeek, L.J.F., 607
Willinge, Mariet, 869

Wils, Jan, *3, 4, 5, 7-8*, 043, 052, 071, 118, 209, 1017, 1140
Wilson, Colin St John, 649
Wilson, Vicky, 1023
Wilson, Wim, 813
Wingler, Hans Maria, 031, 091, 608, 842
Wit, C.P.A. de, 414
Witt, Dennis de, 977
Witt, Elizabeth de, 977
Wolf, N.H., 187
Wolfe, Tom, 843
Wolff, Lina, 163
Wolterbeek, C., 429
Woodham, Jonathan M., 1043
Wörner, Martin, 1071
Woud, Auke van der, 742, 901
Woudhuysen, James, 859
Wright, Frank Lloyd, *5, 6, 7-11, 19, 22*, 025, 027, 032, 036, 102, 117, 209, 327, 342, 352, 357, 372, 426, 448, 460, 538, 551, 560, 604, 606, 655, 683, 689, 698, 718, 752, 779, 789, 792, 862, 875, 919, 958, 1003, 1037, 1052

Yamaguchi, Hiroshi, 943
Yashiro, Masaki, 1091, 1104
Yerbury, Francis Rowland, 115, 1023
Yorke, Francis, 277, 290, 349

Zadkine, Ossip, 434
Zantman, Erwin, 966
Zervos, Christian, 673
Zevi, Bruno Benedetto, *20*, 425, 426, 474, 552, 579, 631, 708, 793, 811, 836
Zijl, Ida van, 1084
Zijlmans, Canis, 966, 1089
Zuithoff, J., 415
Zwiers, H.T., 203, 429

About the Author

DONALD LANGMEAD is Professor of Architectural History at the University of South Australia. His previous books include *Willem Marinus Dudok, A Dutch Modernist: A Bio-Bibliography* (Greenwood, 1996), *Makers of 20th Century Modern Architecture: A Bio-Critical Sourcebook* (Greenwood, 1996), and *Dutch Modernism: Architectural Resources in the English Language* (Greenwood, 1996).

Recent Titles in
Bio-Bibliographies in Art and Architecture

Paul Gauguin: A Bio-Bibliography
Russell T. Clement

Henri Matisse: A Bio-Bibliography
Russell T. Clement

Georges Braque: A Bio-Bibliography
Russell T. Clement

Willem Marinus Dudok, A Dutch Modernist: A Bio-Bibliography
Donald Langmead